SpringBoard®

Level 6

English Textual Power™

CollegeBoard
inspiring minds™

THE COLLEGE BOARD
inspiring minds™

About the College Board
The College Board is a mission-driven not-for-profit organization that connects students to college success and opportunity. Founded in 1900, the College Board was created to expand access to higher education. Today, the membership association is made up of more than 5,900 of the nation's leading educational institutions and is dedicated to promoting excellence and equity in education. Each year, the College Board helps more than seven million students prepare for a successful transition to college through programs and services in college readiness and college success — including the SAT® and the Advanced Placement Program®. The organization also serves the education community through research and advocacy on behalf of students, educators and schools.

For further information, visit www.collegeboard.com.

ISBN: 0-87447-917-7
· ISBN: 978-0-87447-917-1

2 3 4 5 6 7 8   11 12 13 14
Printed in the United States of America

Acknowledgments

The College Board gratefully acknowledges the outstanding work of the classroom teachers and writers who have been integral to the development of this revised program. The end product is testimony to their expertise, understanding of student learning needs, and dedication to rigorous but accessible language arts education.

Susie Challancin
English Teacher
Bellevue School District 405
Bellevue, Washington

Paul De Maret
English Teacher
Poudre School District
Fort Collins, Colorado

Suzie Doss
District English/ Language Arts
  Coordinator
Hobbs Municipal Schools
Hobbs, New Mexico

John Golden
English Teacher
Grant High School
Portland, Oregon

Nancy Gray
English Teacher
West Shore Junior/Senior High School
Melbourne, Florida

Ellen Greig
English Teacher, Consultant
Charlotte, North Carolina

Karen Hanson
Exceptional Student Teacher
Volusia Public Schools
DeLand, Florida

Cheryl Harris
English Teacher Consultant
Bedford, Texas

Susie Lowry
English Teacher
Volusia Public Schools
DeLand, Florida

Julie Manley
Middle School Language Arts
  Tech-Curriculum Coach and
  Humanities Teacher
Bellevue School District 405
Bellevue, Washington

Joely Negedly
Secondary Reading and
  Language Arts Specialists
Volusia Public Schools
DeLand, Florida

JoEllen Victoreen
Instructional Specialist,
  SpringBoard
San Jose, California

Douglas Waugh
Administrative Coach,
  SpringBoard
Bellevue, Washington

Nina Wooldridge
Instructional Specialist,
  SpringBoard
Los Angeles, California

Advisors, Reviewers, Special Feature Writers

The following teachers and writers provided invaluable assistance in creating special features and reviewing manuscript. We gratefully acknowledge their contributions to this revised edition.

Gary Cowan
English/Language Arts Coordinator
Metro Nashville Public Schools
Nashville, Tennessee

Nicki Junkins
Administrative Coach,
  SpringBoard
DeLand, Florida

Jeanneine Jones
Professor, Departments of Middle,
  Secondary, and K-12 Education
University of North Carolina
Charlotte, North Carolina

William McBride
Emeritus Professor of English
Colorado State University
Fort Collins, Colorado

Daniel Millet
English Teacher
Weld county School District
  Re-8
Fort Lupton, Colorado

Melanie Sangalli
English Teacher
Irving Public Schools
Irving, Texas

Special Acknowledgments

The College Board wishes especially to acknowledge the writers of the original *Pacesetter* program. Much of their work continues in use today. The result of their efforts was a program that helped both teachers and students succeed. With its roots in Pacesetter, the current program had an excellent foundation on which to build.

Willie Mae Crews
Educator
Birmingham, Alabama

R. Steven Green, Ed.D.
Educator
Kansas City, Missouri

Ellen Greenblatt
University High School
San Francisco, California

Alice Kawazoe
Educational Consultant, California Academic
   Partnership Program
San Carlos, California

Jenny Oren Krugman
Vice President, Southern Region
College Board
Miami, Florida

William McBride, Ph.D.
Emeritus Professor of English
Colorado State University
Fort Collins, Colorado

Robert Scholes, Ph.D.
Research Professor, Brown University
Providence, Rhode Island

In addition, we wish to acknowledge the educators and writers whose work on prior editions helped to continue the *Pacesetter* excellence and to establish the high expectations for which the College Board's SpringBoard program is known.

Lance Balla
Bellevue, Washington

Bryant Crisp
Charlotte, North Carolina

Nancy Elrod
Atlanta, Georgia

Ann Foster
Melbourne, Florida

Ana Gandara
Edinburg, Texas

Alex Gordin
Portland, Oregon

Kenyatta Graves
Washington, DC

Don Keagy
Poultney, Vermont

Don Kirk
Poultney, Vermont

Dana Mebane
Baltimore, Maryland

Bob Messinger
Providence, Rhode Island

Debi Miller
Miami, Florida

Melanie Ross Mitchell
Atlanta, Georgia

Lisa Rehm
DeLand, Florida

Penny Riffe
Palm Bay, Florida

Rick Robb
Clarksville, Maryland

Sue Rodriguez
Miami, Florida

Research and Planning Advisors

We also wish to thank the members of our SpringBoard Advisory Council, the SpringBoard Language Arts Trainers, and the many educators who gave generously of their time and their ideas as we conducted research for the program. Their suggestions and reactions to ideas helped immeasurably as we planned the revisions. We gratefully acknowledge the teachers and administrators in the following districts:

Broward County Public Schools
Fort Lauderdale, Florida

Cherry Creek School District
Cherry Creek, Colorado

Chicago Public Schools
Chicago, Illinois

DeKalb County School System
DeKalb County, Georgia

Duval County Public Schools
Jacksonville, Florida

Guilford County Schools
Greensboro, North Carolina

Hillsborough County Public Schools
Tampa, Florida

Hobbs Municipal Schools
Hobbs, New Mexico

Indianapolis Public Schools
Indianapolis, Indiana

Miami-Dade County Public Schools
Miami, Florida

Metropolitan Nashville Public Schools
Nashville, Tennessee

The City School District of New Rochelle
New Rochelle, New York

Orange County Public Schools
Orlando, Florida

School District of Palm Beach County
Palm Beach, Florida

Peninsula School District
Gig Harbor, Washington

Pinellas County Schools
Largo, Florida

San Antonio Independent School District
San Antonio, Texas

Spokane Public Schools
Spokane, Washington

Volusia County Schools
DeLand, Florida

Editorial Leadership

The College Board gratefully acknowledges the expertise, time, and commitment of the language arts editorial manager.

Betty Barnett
Educational Publishing Consultant

Level 6 Contents

To the Student viii

Instructional Units

Unit 1 The American Dream 1

Unit 2 American Forums: The Marketplace of Ideas 97

Unit 3 The Power of Persuasion 209

To the Student

Welcome to the SpringBoard program. We hope you will discover how SpringBoard can help you achieve high academic standards, reach your learning goals, and prepare for success in your study of literature and language arts. The program has been created with you in mind: the content you need to learn, the tools to help you learn, and the critical-thinking skills that help you build confidence in your own knowledge and skills.

The College Board publishes the SpringBoard program as a complete language arts curriculum that prepares you for Advanced Placement and college-level study. SpringBoard maps out what successful students should know and be able to do at each grade level to develop the language, reading, writing, and communication skills needed for success. College Board also publishes the SAT and Advanced Placement exams—exams that you are likely to encounter in your high school years.

Connection to Advanced Placement

The College Board's Advanced Placement program provides the opportunity to complete college-level courses while in high school. In addition to receiving college credits, participation in AP courses helps you develop the skills and knowledge that add to your confidence and ease the transition from high school to college.

The SpringBoard program assists you in preparing for AP-level courses in several ways:

- ▶ Exposing you to the same types of tasks as on the AP Language and Literature exams; for example, close reading of fiction and nonfiction texts, responding to writing prompts, writing under timed conditions, and writing for multiple purposes (persuasion, argumentation, literary analysis, and synthesis).
- ▶ Introducing you to AP strategies, such as TP-CASTT and SOAPSTone, that help you analyze literary and other texts, giving you the tools you need to independently analyze any text.
- ▶ Preparing you for higher-order skills and behaviors required for college-level work through ongoing practice in key skills such as generating and organizing ideas, analysis of different types of texts, synthesis and explanation of concepts, and original writing in a variety of modes.

What Is the Foundation for SpringBoard?

The foundation of SpringBoard is the College Board Standards for College Success, which set out the knowledge and critical-thinking skills you should acquire to succeed in high school and in future college-level work.

The English Language Arts College Board Standards are divided into five categories: reading, writing, speaking, listening, and media literacy.

Your success as a **reader** depends on many factors, including your interest and motivation to read, the amount of time you spend reading, understanding the purpose for reading, knowledge about a topic, and knowledge about how to read different kinds of text.

Your success as a **writer** depends on learning many words and how to use those words effectively to communicate a story or information for others to read and understand. Successful writers determine their purpose for writing, such as to explore, inform, express an opinion, persuade, entertain, or to share an experience or emotion. As they write, they also consider their audiences and choose the language that will help them communicate with that audience. Writing is a process that involves several steps, and you will have many opportunities in this program to learn the process and to improve your own writing.

Your success as a **speaker** is based on how well you communicate orally. What is your message, what words will best communicate it, how do you prepare, or rehearse, for a speech? Good speakers also consider the audience and what they know about a specific topic. They can then deliver a message that uses a shared understanding, or develops one based on common knowledge, with their listeners.

Being a good **listener** is the other part of effective communication. Communication includes the speaker, listener, message, feedback, and noise (the conditions surrounding the communication). You'll have opportunities throughout the program to practice both your speaking and listening skills.

Finally, being **media literate** means that you can interpret, analyze, and evaluate the messages you receive daily from various types of media. Being media literate also means that you can use the information you gain to express or support a point of view and influence others.

As you complete the activities in this text, you will develop your skills and knowledge in all of these areas.

How Is SpringBoard Unique?

SpringBoard is unique because it provides instruction with hands-on participation that involves you and your classmates in daily discussions and analysis of what you're reading and learning. The book is organized into multiple activities that invite participation by providing adequate space for taking notes and writing your own thoughts and analyses about texts you're reading or questions you're answering. Among the key features that make SpringBoard a unique learning experience are:

▶ Activities that thoroughly develop topics, leading to deep understanding of the concepts and enabling you to apply learning in multiple situations.

▶ Extensive opportunities to explore a variety of texts—both fiction and nonfiction—that introduce you to many different ways of thinking, writing, and communicating.

▶ Questions that help you examine writing from the perspective of a reader and a writer and the techniques that good writers use to communicate their messages effectively.

▶ Built-in class discussions and collaborative work that help you explore and express your own ideas while integrating the ideas of others into your base of knowledge.

▶ Integrated performance-based assessments that give you practice in showing what you know and can do, not just repeating what you've read.

▶ Assessments that help you decipher tasks and plan how to accomplish those tasks in timed situations like those for standardized tests.

Strategies for Learning

As you complete the activities in this text, you will work on many reading, writing, and oral presentation assignments. You will often work in groups and pairs. To help you do your best, you and your teacher will use a variety of reading, writing, and collaborative learning strategies.

Reading strategies give you specific tools to help you improve your skills in reading and making meaning from text. These strategies will help you improve your ability to analyze text by developing skills in using context clues, finding meaning for unfamiliar words, or organizing your responses to what you read. As you learn to use different reading strategies, it's important to think about which ones work best for you and why.

Writing strategies help you focus on your purpose for writing and the message you want to communicate to your readers. Using writing strategies will help you analyze your own writing for specific purposes and identify how to improve that writing using better word choices or punctuating differently or using sentence structure in different ways.

You and your classmates will use *collaborative strategies* to explore concepts and answer text-related questions as you work in pairs or in groups to discuss the work you're doing and to learn from each other.

Performance Portfolio

You will learn to use language in both written and spoken forms in this course. You are encouraged to keep your work in a Working Folder from which you can choose examples to show where you started and how you are growing in your skills and knowledge during the year. Presenting your best work in a Portfolio not only helps you evaluate your own work and improvement, but also helps you explore your unique style and analyze how your work can best represent you.

Presenting your portfolio provides direction as you revisit, revise, and reflect on your work throughout the year. Your teacher will guide you as you include items in your portfolio that illustrate a wide range of work, including examples of reading, writing, oral literacy, and collaborative activities. As you progress through the course, you will have opportunities to revisit prior work, revise it based on new learning, and reflect on the learning strategies and activities that help you be successful. The portfolio:

- ▶ Gives you a specific place to feature your work and a way to share it with others.
- ▶ Provides an organized, focused way to view your progress throughout the year.
- ▶ Allows you to reflect on the new skills and strategies you are learning.
- ▶ Enables you to measure your growth as a reader, writer, speaker, and performer.
- ▶ Encourages you to revise pieces of work to incorporate new skills.

As you move through each unit, your teacher will instruct you to include certain items in your portfolio. Strong portfolios will include a variety of work from each unit, such as first drafts, final drafts, quickwrites, notes, reading logs, audio and video examples, and graphics that represent a wide variety of genre, forms, and media created for a variety of purposes.

We hope you enjoy using the SpringBoard program. It will give you many opportunities to explore your own and others' ideas about becoming effective readers, writers, and communicators.

How to Use This Book

English Textual Power, Level 6, introduces the concept of the American Dream and how pursuit of individual dreams has formed the people and the country. This year you will look at what it means to pursue the American Dream through the eyes of many different writers whose experiences and voices have helped shape our notion of the American Dream. You will also look at how writers and speakers persuade others to support their ideas and learn to present yourself through public speaking.

Preview the Unit

Essential Questions pose questions to help you think about the "big ideas" and make connections between what you learn and how you apply that learning.

Unit Overview sets the stage by:

▶ Providing a bridge from what you know to what you'll be learning in the unit.

▶ Outlining the big ideas in the unit and how the book's theme is connected from unit to unit.

Unit Contents give a snapshot of the unit activities and identify the texts and genres you'll explore in the unit.

▶ **Goals**–skills and knowledge you'll learn in the unit.

▶ **Academic Vocabulary**–key terms to use in the unit and to help you gain the vocabulary needed for AP courses and college.

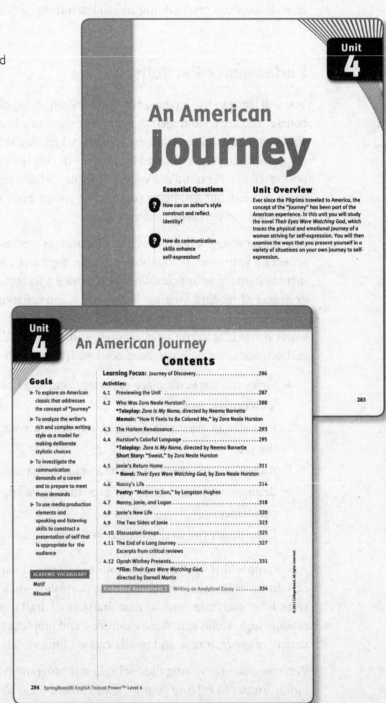

Unit 4

An American Journey

Essential Questions

? How can an author's style construct and reflect identity?

? How do communication skills enhance self-expression?

Unit Overview

Ever since the Pilgrims traveled to America, the concept of the "journey" has been part of the American experience. In this unit you will study the novel *Their Eyes Were Watching God*, which traces the physical and emotional journey of a woman striving for self-expression. You will then examine the ways that you present yourself in a variety of situations on your own journey to self-expression.

283

Unit 4

An American Journey
Contents

Goals

▶ To explore an American classic that addresses the concept of "journey"

▶ To analyze the writer's rich and complex writing style as a model for making deliberate stylistic choices

▶ To investigate the communication demands of a career and to prepare to meet those demands

▶ To use media production elements and speaking and listening skills to construct a presentation of self that is appropriate for the audience

ACADEMIC VOCABULARY

Motif

Résumé

284 SpringBoard® English Textual Power™ Level 6

Preparing for Learning

Learning Focus connects what you already know with what you'll learn in the unit and why it's important.

▶ Highlights key terms.

▶ Connects learning from unit to unit.

▶ Introduces concepts for the unit.

Previewing the Unit helps you identify the expectations for knowledge and skills you'll need to learn in the unit by asking you to read and respond to:

▶ **Essential Questions**

▶ **Unit Overview–Learning Focus**

▶ **Embedded Assessment and Scoring Guide**

Starting with the End in Mind

Graphic organizer helps you:

▶ Map out the skills and knowledge you'll need for the Embedded Assessments.

▶ Read the assignment and the Scoring Guide (see page xvi) and outline what you'll need to do.

▶ Identify skills and knowledge to be assessed.

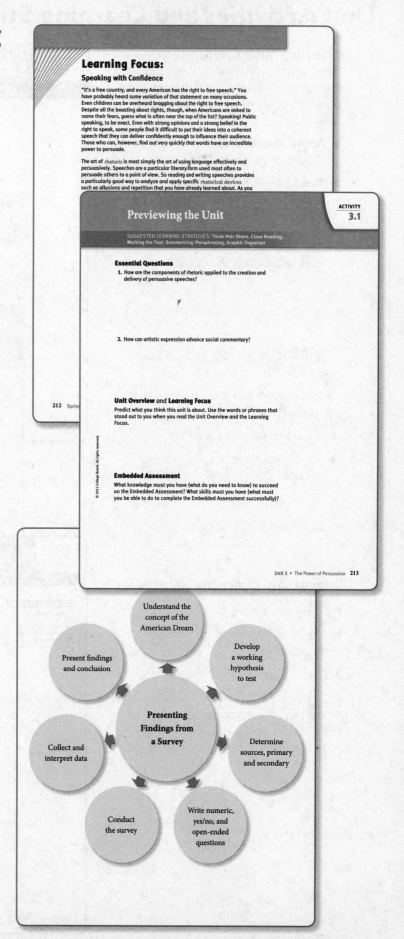

Learning Focus:
Speaking with Confidence

"It's a free country, and every American has the right to free speech." You have probably heard some variation of that statement on many occasions. Even children can be overheard bragging about the right to free speech. Despite all the boasting about rights, though, when Americans are asked to name their fears, guess what is often near the top of the list? Speaking! Public speaking, to be exact. Even with strong opinions and a strong belief in the right to speak, some people find it difficult to put their ideas into a coherent speech that they can deliver confidently enough to influence their audience. Those who can, however, find out very quickly that words have an incredible power to persuade.

The art of rhetoric is most simply the art of using language effectively and persuasively. Speeches are a particular literary form used most often to persuade others to a point of view. So reading and writing speeches provides a particularly good way to analyze and apply specific rhetorical devices such as allusions and repetition that you have already learned about. As you

212 Spring

Previewing the Unit

ACTIVITY 3.1

SUGGESTED LEARNING STRATEGIES: Think-Pair-Share, Close Reading, Marking the Text, Summarizing/Paraphrasing, Graphic Organizer

Essential Questions

1. How are the components of rhetoric applied to the creation and delivery of persuasive speeches?

2. How can artistic expression advance social commentary?

Unit Overview and **Learning Focus**

Predict what you think this unit is about. Use the words or phrases that stood out to you when you read the Unit Overview and the Learning Focus.

Embedded Assessment

What knowledge must you have (what do you need to know) to succeed on the Embedded Assessment? What skills must you have (what must you be able to do to complete the Embedded Assessment successfully)?

Unit 3 • The Power of Persuasion **213**

Graphic organizer:

- Understand the concept of the American Dream
- Develop a working hypothesis to test
- Determine sources, primary and secondary
- Write numeric, yes/no, and open-ended questions
- Conduct the survey
- Collect and interpret data
- Present findings and conclusion

Presenting Findings from a Survey

Unit Activities and Learning Strategies

Literary and Other Texts

from classic to contemporary introduce you to a variety of writers, stories, themes, and perspectives to help you interact with all types of writing.

▶ **About the Author** provides author's background and insights about the text.

▶ **Texts** include examples from a variety of genres, including poetry, film, autobiography, essay, print and online articles, folk tales, myths, fables, memoir, short stories, novel excerpts, interviews, Informational text, and drama.

My Notes provides space for you to interact with the text by:

▶ Jotting down your thoughts and ideas as you read.

▶ Using the space to analyze text.

▶ Writing notes about literary elements in texts.

Suggested Learning Strategies

▶ Clearly listed at the top of the page.

▶ Suggest strategies that are most appropriate for the activity.

▶ Over the course of the year, you'll learn which strategies work best for you.

▶ You'll find these strategies consistent with those used in AP courses.

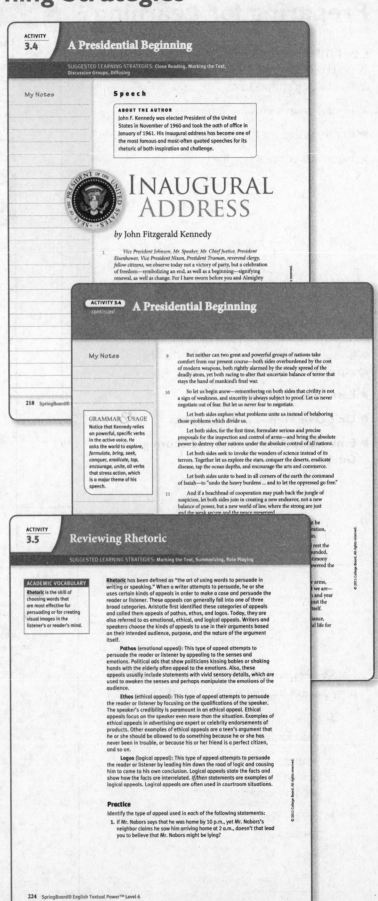

Integrated Language Skills

Vocabulary and Word Study

▶ **Academic Vocabulary** highlights key words you'll need to know for the unit and to expand your vocabulary for AP and college.

▶ **Literary Terms** define key words as you encounter them in your reading and analysis of text.

▶ **Word Connections** help you use context clues from Latin and other roots, understand analogies, and identify words with multiple meanings.

Grammar & Usage

▶ Offers tips about points of grammar and how to avoid common errors.

▶ Shows how writers use various grammatical constructions to clarify their text and to convey meaning for readers.

▶ Helps both speakers <u>and</u> writers use grammar to make their text or message more effective.

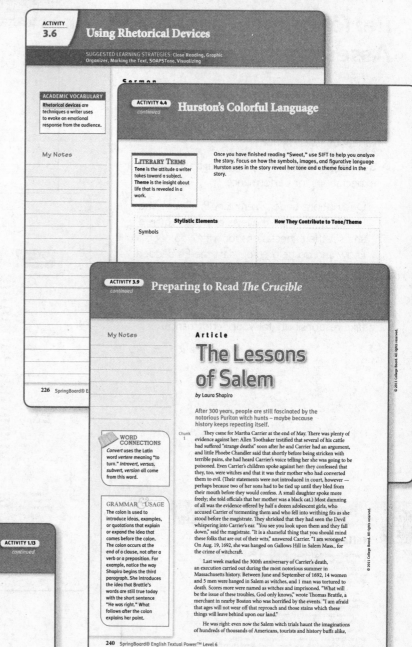

The Structure of an Argument

You have been introduced to the structure of an argument. As a review, read through the five key elements that are usually found in a good argument.

1. **The Hook** (Setting readers up to agree with you)
   • The hook grabs the readers' attention and catches their interest.
   • It often establishes a connection between readers and writers and provides background information.
   • It can be, but is not limited to, an anecdote, an image, a definition, or a quotation.

2. **The Claim** (Your thesis, what you are arguing)
   • Usually comes in the opening section of your paper.
   • States your belief and what it is that you wish to argue.
   • Can be straightforward and clear, i.e. "I believe that..."

3. **Concessions and Refutations** (Build the other side up...then knock them down)
   • You recognize the arguments made by the other side.
   • You build credibility by being able to discuss the other side with (apparent) objectivity.
   • You grant that the other side has some validity, then...
   • Argue at length against the opposing viewpoint by proving your side has MORE validity.

4. **Support** (Start stacking your facts to convince them)
   • You set out the reasoning behind your argument.
   • Provide supporting evidence of your claim (data, quotes, anecdotes).
   • Blend together logical and emotional appeals.

5. **Call to Action** (The final word)
   • Draw your argument to a close and restate your claim.
   • Make a final new appeal to values.
   • Voice a final plea.
   • Try not to repeat information, but sum up your argument with a few final facts and appeals.

Writing Prompt: On a separate piece of paper, use the five elements of an argument to draft a response to one of the following prompts:

• Compose a letter to the maid service company stating problems the maids face. Provide suggestions for what the company can do to improve conditions.

• Compose a letter to a local newspaper citing a need for a change in the attitudes of people toward those in service occupations, particularly those who are maids and wear uniforms.

Writing

▶**Writing Process** is defined and practiced through opportunities to draft, revise, edit, and prepare publishable writing.

▶ **Writing Prompts & Timed Writings** provide practice in identifying specific writing tasks and writing under timed conditions.

▶ **Portfolios** are encouraged to collect your writing throughout the year to show your progress.

Performance-Based Assessment

▶ **Embedded Assessments** provide opportunities to demonstrate your knowledge and your skills in applying that knowledge in a variety of assessments.

▶ **Scoring Guide** walks you through the expectations for performance.

- Descriptions under Exemplary, Proficient, and Emerging describe the level of work required and set the expectations for what you need to know and do <u>before</u> you start the Embedded Assessment.

- Using the descriptions for Exemplary, Proficient, and Emerging, you decide what you'll do and take responsibility for your performance.

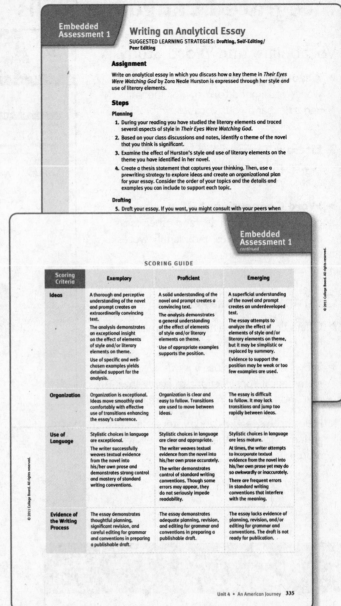

Embedded Assessment 1

Writing an Analytical Essay
SUGGESTED LEARNING STRATEGIES: Drafting, Self-Editing/Peer Editing

Assignment
Write an analytical essay in which you discuss how a key theme in *Their Eyes Were Watching God* by Zora Neale Hurston is expressed through her style and use of literary elements.

Steps

Planning

1. During your reading you have studied the literary elements and traced several aspects of style in *Their Eyes Were Watching God*.
2. Based on your class discussions and notes, identify a theme of the novel that you think is significant.
3. Examine the effect of Hurston's style and use of literary elements on the theme you have identified in her novel.
4. Create a thesis statement that captures your thinking. Then, use a prewriting strategy to explore ideas and create an organizational plan for your essay. Consider the order of your topics and the details and examples you can include to support each topic.

Drafting

5. Draft your essay. If you want, you might consult with your peers when

Embedded Assessment 1 *continued*

SCORING GUIDE

Scoring Criteria	Exemplary	Proficient	Emerging
Ideas	A thorough and perceptive understanding of the novel and prompt creates an extraordinarily convincing text. The analysis demonstrates an exceptional insight on the effect of elements of style and/or literary elements on theme. Use of specific and well-chosen examples yields detailed support for the analysis.	A solid understanding of the novel and prompt creates a convincing text. The analysis demonstrates a general understanding of the effect of elements of style and/or literary elements on theme. Use of appropriate examples supports the position.	A superficial understanding of the novel and prompt creates an underdeveloped text. The essay attempts to analyze the effect of elements of style and/or literary elements on theme, but it may be simplistic or replaced by summary. Evidence to support the position may be weak or too few examples are used.
Organization	Organization is exceptional. Ideas move smoothly and comfortably with effective use of transitions enhancing the essay's coherence.	Organization is clear and easy to follow. Transitions are used to move between ideas.	The essay is difficult to follow. It may lack transitions and jump too rapidly between ideas.
Use of Language	Stylistic choices in language are exceptional. The writer successfully weaves textual evidence from the novel into his/her own prose and demonstrates strong control and mastery of standard writing conventions.	Stylistic choices in language are clear and appropriate. The writer weaves textual evidence from the novel into his/her own prose accurately. The writer demonstrates control of standard writing conventions. Though some errors may appear, they do not seriously impede readability.	Stylistic choices in language are less mature. At times, the writer attempts to incorporate textual evidence from the novel into his/her own prose yet may do so awkwardly or inaccurately. There are frequent errors in standard writing conventions that interfere with the meaning.
Evidence of the Writing Process	The essay demonstrates thoughtful planning, significant revision, and careful editing for grammar and conventions in preparing a publishable draft.	The essay demonstrates adequate planning, revision, and editing for grammar and conventions in preparing a publishable draft.	The essay lacks evidence of planning, revision, and/or editing for grammar and conventions. The draft is not ready for publication.

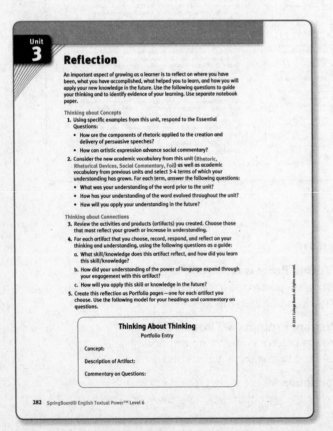

Unit 3

Reflection

An important aspect of growing as a learner is to reflect on where you have been, what you have accomplished, what helped you to learn, and how you will apply your new knowledge in the future. Use the following questions to guide your thinking and to identify evidence of your learning. Use separate notebook paper.

Thinking about Concepts

1. Using specific examples from this unit, respond to the Essential Questions:
   - How are the components of rhetoric applied to the creation and delivery of persuasive speeches?
   - How can artistic expression advance social commentary?

2. Consider the new academic vocabulary from this unit (Rhetoric, Rhetorical Devices, Social Commentary, Foil) as well as academic vocabulary from previous units and select 3-4 terms of which your understanding has grown. For each term, answer the following questions:
   - What was your understanding of the word prior to the unit?
   - How has your understanding of the word evolved throughout the unit?
   - How will you apply your understanding in the future?

Thinking about Connections

3. Review the activities and products (artifacts) you created. Choose those that most reflect your growth or increase in understanding.

4. For each artifact that you choose, record, respond, and reflect on your thinking and understanding, using the following questions as a guide:
   a. What skill/knowledge does this artifact reflect, and how did you learn this skill/knowledge?
   b. How did your understanding of the power of language expand through your engagement with this artifact?
   c. How will you apply this skill or knowledge in the future?

5. Create this reflection as Portfolio pages—one for each artifact you choose. Use the following model for your headings and commentary on questions.

Thinking About Thinking
Portfolio Entry

Concept:

Description of Artifact:

Commentary on Questions:
---

282 SpringBoard® English Textual Power™ Level 6

Unit Reflection helps you to take ownership of your learning by stopping at regular points to think about:

▶ What you've learned.

▶ What strategies and tools helped you learn.

▶ What you still need to work on in the future.

The American
Dream

Essential Questions

? In what ways does the American Dream manifest itself in American life?

? How does one create a personal definition of the American Dream?

Unit Overview

If asked to describe the essence and spirit of America, you would probably refer to "the American Dream." First coined as a phrase in 1931, the phrase "the American Dream" characterizes the unique promise that America has offered immigrants and residents for nearly 400 years. People have come to this country for adventure, opportunity, freedom, and the chance to experience the particular qualities of the American landscape. Consequently, different groups of people have left their imprint on the philosophical foundations of this country and contributed to what has become a modern American Dream. In this unit you will explore the foundations of the American Dream through literary movements and a variety of American voices. You will also investigate how this Dream might be realized in your own life and in the lives of those around you through a survey investigating assumptions about the American Dream. The unit will prepare you for a wide body of literature that continues to incorporate this idea and help you to synthesize this information into your own understanding of the concept.

The American Dream

Contents

Goals

▶ To understand and define the concept of the American Dream

▶ To identify and synthesize a variety of perspectives that exist about the American Dream

▶ To conduct a survey and use primary sources as a functional text to prove or disprove an assumption

ACADEMIC VOCABULARY

Survey

Primary Source

Secondary Source

Learning Focus:

Making Text Come to Life

Whether you have seen it in a movie, read about it in a book, watched it on a popular sitcom, heard it from your parents, or viewed it being played out in a presidential campaign, "the American Dream" has become a part of our culture and a term used in our everyday lives. But what does it mean? Is there one kind of American Dream, or is it unique to each and every one of us? More importantly, do we all have the same access to that dream?

Reading **primary** and **secondary sources** exposes you to different viewpoints concerning the American Dream. Much has been written about the American Dream, and many secondary sources provide a more objective look at various points of view that have been developed about the American Dream. Encountering a wide variety of points of view allows you to deepen and broaden your understanding of how this idea came into being and how it has changed throughout our history.

Reading original or primary texts allows you to access the thinking of writers in a certain time period without the filter of another's analysis. You get a writer's subjective view of ideas of success, money, work, failure, and access—all aspects of the American Dream as it has been articulated through the ages.

Having the opportunity to conduct your own primary source survey puts you in the position of a researcher testing and validating your own ideas of what makes up the American Dream.

Independent Reading: In this unit, you will read a variety of texts that explore different perspectives on the American Dream. For independent reading, look for nonfiction essays, biographies, or memoirs whose authors focus on pursuing or acquiring aspects of the American Dream.

Previewing the Unit

SUGGESTED LEARNING STRATEGIES: Think-Pair-Share, Skimming/ Scanning, Marking the Text, Close Reading, KWL Chart

Essential Questions

1. In what ways does the American Dream manifest itself in American life?

2. How does one create a personal definition of the American Dream?

Unit Overview and Learning Focus

Predict what you think this unit is about. Use the words or phrases that stood out to you when you read the Unit Overview and the Learning Focus.

Embedded Assessment 1

What knowledge must you have (what do you need to know) to succeed on Embedded Assessment 1? What skills must you have (what must you be able to do)?

What Is the American Dream?

Anticipation Guide

As you read each statement below, use a scale from 1 – 10 to rate the extent to which these ideas are prevalent today. If the idea presented in the statement is something you are exposed to on a regular basis, rate it a 10. If you do not see evidence of the statement at all, rate it a 1 (and remember there are plenty of numbers in between).

_____ 1. Education is important primarily to increase one's self-knowledge.

_____ 2. Individuals' rights are superior to the needs of society.

_____ 3. Belief in God has been characteristic of the American experience.

_____ 4. Mankind is basically evil.

_____ 5. Education is important primarily to get a job.

_____ 6. Truth is found in faith.

_____ 7. Human beings are basically good and getting better.

_____ 8. Individual liberties must always be controlled by government authority.

_____ 9. A free press is important to equal rights for everyone.

_____ 10. Truth can be found in science.

_____ 11. The American Dream means making lots of money.

_____ 12. Hard work equals success.

_____ 13. Everyone can achieve the American Dream.

_____ 14. The American Dream includes getting married and having children.

Quickwrite: Reflect on your rankings. Share your responses with a partner or a small group. You might choose to share your responses with the whole class. Consider the class discussion and select one or two statements above. Describe your position in reaction to the statement(s) and explain the rationale for your thinking.

What Is Your Source?

You have been exposed to a variety of sources throughout your high school experience. Some of these sources have been **primary sources** and some have been **secondary sources**.

1. Brainstorm examples of primary and secondary sources, and then define primary and secondary sources in the space below. Consider the similarities and differences and even examples of sources you have used in the past.

Primary Source:

Secondary Source:

2. Your teacher will provide dictionary definitions of these terms. Copy them below. How close were you? What did you already know and what is new?

Primary Source:

Secondary Source:

3. Apply your knowledge to the following list. Next to each example, write either "primary" or "secondary" to identify the type of source.

Interview

Biography

Book Analyzing the Civil War

Original Photograph

Original Work of Art

Article Critiquing a Work of Art

Works of Literature

History Book

Letters

Video of a Musical Performance

Coming to America

1. Brainstorm a list of characteristics or traits you believe are part of the American Dream. Write your list in the space at the left.

2. **Quickwrite:** Select one trait from your list and write about that trait.

"Ellis Island"

3. Read the poem "Ellis Island" silently. Volunteer to read the poem aloud to the class or listen while others read. Underline the dreams and disappointments of the people as they are expressed in the poem. Discuss the underlined passages with the class.

4. Brainstorm about the dreams, hopes, and backgrounds of your ancestors. Share your thoughts in a small group.

Biographical Sketch

5. Before reading the poem "Europe and America" complete a brief biography for yourself. On separate paper, write the following information regarding you and your family (past and present). Then share your answers with another student.

   - Place of birth for you, for your parents and/or grandparents
   - Places lived – you, your parents, and/or grandparents
   - Schools attended – you, your parents, grandparents
   - Significant adults or people in your life
   - Dreams of your parents and/or dreams for yourself
   - Challenges of your parents and/or challenges for yourself

"Europe and America"

6. Read the poem to yourself or listen while your teacher reads the poem aloud to the class. Highlight **images** in the poem that show the contrast between the experiences of the father and son.

> **LITERARY TERMS**
> An **image** is a mental picture or sensation created by vivid language.

by Joseph Bruchac

> **ABOUT THE AUTHOR**
> Part Native American, Joseph Bruchac began telling Native American stories for his own children and published his first book of stories in 1975. An award-winning writer and professional storyteller, Bruchac has since written dozens of books for children and adults that seek to promote and preserve Native American stories and culture.

Beyond the red brick of Ellis Island
where the two Slovak children
who became my grandparents
waited the long days of quarantine,
after leaving the sickness,   5
the old Empires of Europe,
a Circle Line ship slips easily
on its way to the island
of the tall woman, green
as dreams of forests and meadows   10
waiting for those who'd worked
a thousand years
yet never owned their own.

Like millions of others,
I too come to this island,   15
nine decades the answerer
of dreams.

Yet only part of my blood loves that memory.
Another voice speaks
of native lands   20
within this nation.
Lands invaded
when the earth became owned.
Lands of those who followed
the changing Moon,   25
knowledge of the seasons
in their veins.

My Notes

Poetry

> **ABOUT THE AUTHOR**
> David Ignatow was born in Brooklyn, New York, in 1914 to Russian immigrants. His early jobs included working in a family butcher shop and a bindery. His poetry, which is written in straightforward language, often portrays urban life and the lives of the working poor. Ignatow won many prestigious awards for his poetry before he died in 1997.

Europe *and* America

by David Ignatow

My father brought the emigrant bundle
of desperation and worn threads,
that in anxiety as he stumbles
tumble out distractedly;
5 while I am bedded upon soft green money
that grows like grass.
Thus, between my father
who lives on a bed of anguish for his daily bread,
and I who tear money at leisure by the roots,
10 where I lie in sun or shade,
a vast continent of breezes, storms to him,
shadows, darkness to him, small lakes, rough channels
to him, and hills, mountains to him, lie between us.
My father comes of a small hell
15 where bread and man have been kneaded and baked
together.
You have heard the scream as the knife fell;
while I have slept
as guns pounded offshore

Denotation and Connotation in "Europe and America"

Denotation refers to the dictionary definition of a word. Connotation refers to the associations connected to a word. A word's connotation usually has a more powerful effect on the reader. It may be a visual image or an idea to ponder.

7. Look at the examples listed. Then state the denotation and connotation of key phrases from the poem "Europe and America." Discuss the effect that those particular words have on the reader. Choose some words or phrases of your own to analyze (use separate paper).

Word or Phrase	Denotation	Connotation	Effect on the Reader
emigrant bundle of desperation	**emigrant:** one who leaves the country of his or her birth **bundle:** a group of objects held together by tying or wrapping **desperation:** recklessness arising from losing all hope	The father is associated with that which is negative, bringing all his hopelessness to the new world.	The words set up the reader to contrast the father's experience with the son's.
bedded on soft green money			
bed of anguish			
vast continent of breezes, storms to him			

8. Create a graphic organizer that compares and contrasts the ideas and dreams of past and present generations.

Sentence Synthesis

Consider how the effect on the reader might change if you change any of the key phrases in "Europe and America."

9. Imagine that instead of "bedded on soft green money," the poet were to have written "funded by filthy bills." How does that change affect the reader? Write your answer in the space below.

10. Now look again at the phrases you examined on your own paper. Exchange the key word(s) in those phrases with different word(s) that have a similar meaning but different connotation. Reflect on how the change might affect the reader's interpretation.

Word or Phrase	New Word or Phrase	Effect on Reader

Historic Pathways to the American Dream

SUGGESTED LEARNING STRATEGIES: Double-Entry Journal, Graphic Organizer, Discussion Groups

After reflecting on the idea of the American Dream and those who came from distant lands to find their own pathways to the dream, you will next look at some historical groups and the imprint they have left on the American Dream through their philosophical underpinnings.

You will research a particular historical group and its philosophy in order to teach fellow students about your findings. You will then, in turn, learn from your peers regarding other philosophies that have permeated America's diverse belief systems so that you can make connections to the texts and ideas in this unit.

1. Read your assigned pieces (which are primary sources) in order to research the philosophy that has been assigned to you. For each source you analyze, record two to three quotations that grab your attention. Using a three-column journal, document the source and the quote in the left column of the paper. In the middle column, write your response to the quote in connection to the philosophy your group is studying. In the right column, note any modern connections.

2. Locate an additional primary source (or excerpt) that adequately reflects the philosophy's identified characteristics. You might have already done this in your initial research. While this is the individual portion of the assignment, check in with your group members to make sure you have a diverse set of primary sources so when you return to your groups, you will have a blend of voices and experiences to discuss. You will want to include quotes and responses from this source in your journal.

3. Use your research and journal entries to answer the questions listed on the following pages for your assigned historical group. Through this process, you should have a firm understanding of the core tenets associated with your philosophy.

4. Using your research, your understanding of the assigned texts, your responses to the questions, and your individual primary sources, create a concept map on chart paper or poster board. Use pictures, symbols, and words to represent the information learned regarding the specific philosophy. It might also be wise to include a copy or a created image of the additional primary source you located. Include characteristics of the philosophy, major writings, historical and modern connections, and key people. Present the map to the entire class. Each group is responsible for giving the class a comprehensive overview of its assigned philosophy.

Group 1: Puritans

1. Research to answer the following questions regarding the Puritans:

   What is their view of God?

   What are their values?

   How do they define truth?

   Do they have an optimistic or pessimistic view of life? Cite evidence.

   What are their views of work and worldly success?

   What is their view of society?

   Who is their authority?

   What is their view of education?

   Do they view man as inherently good, evil, or somewhere in between?
   Cite evidence.

2. Read the excerpt from *The New England Primer*. Discuss with your group the purpose of reading according to this book. How widespread was reading meant to be? What is the image of God and religion presented by the primer?

3. Read "The Trial of Martha Carrier." What are the charges against Martha Carrier? What is the evidence against her? Discuss how the Puritan sense of justice and evidence is on trial in this presentation of the Salem witch trials of 1692.

4. Research Puritans and find at least one primary source which gives further insight into and specific examples of their philosophy and how it translated into how they lived.

5. Look back at the anticipation guide you completed in Activity 1.2. Identify any Puritan philosophy embedded in the questions.

6. How would the Puritans have defined the American Dream?

Group 2: Revolutionaries

Research to answer the following questions regarding the Revolutionaries:

What is their view of God?

What are their values?

How do they define truth?

Do they have an optimistic or pessimistic view of life? Cite evidence.

What are their views of work and worldly success?

What is their view of society?

Who is their authority?

What is their view of education?

Do they view man as inherently good, evil, or somewhere in between? Cite evidence.

On your own paper define the term *perfection*. Define *moral*. Find both terms in a dictionary and compare the definitions. Do you believe it is possible for a person to achieve moral perfection? Write a paragraph in which you take a pro or con position. Support your thesis with examples from personal observation, reading, or experience. Share your paragraph with your group and discuss.

Read "Moral Perfection" from *The Autobiography of Benjamin Franklin*. Discuss the qualities that Franklin chose in his autobiography and compare them to the details you included in your paragraph and to details in the paragraphs of your group members. Do you think trying to arrive at moral perfection is a worthwhile goal? If it is, what does it show about a person who would try to do this?

Create your own list of virtues for yourself. State how you will try to achieve each virtue.

Read the "Sayings of Poor Richard," from Poor *Richard' s Almanack* by Benjamin Franklin. Discuss these sayings in your group. Choose at least five and rewrite them for a modern audience.

Research the Revolutionaries and find at least one primary source that provides additional insight into and specific examples of their philosophy. How did that philosophy translate into how they lived?

Look back on the anticipation guide you completed in Activity 1.2. Identify Revolutionary ideas embedded in the questions.

How would you define the American Dream according to the Revolutionaries? Explain.

Group 3: Transcendentalists

Research to answer the following questions regarding the Transcendentalists:

> What is their view of God?
>
> What are their values?
>
> How do they define truth?
>
> Do they have an optimistic or pessimistic view of life? Cite evidence.
>
> What are their views of work and worldly success?
>
> What is their view of society?
>
> Who is their authority?
>
> What is their view of education?
>
> Do they view man as inherently good, evil, or somewhere in between? Cite evidence.

Read the excerpt from "Self-Reliance." Pick two or three passages from the selection that state a strong opinion. Write a personal response to the passages.

Read the excerpt from *Walden*. As you read, underline or highlight specific examples of Transcendentalist philosophy. Write the connection in the margin. In your group, summarize Thoreau's criticisms of society. Identify a facet of modern society that Thoreau would object to and explain why he would find it objectionable.

Research Transcendentalists and find at least one primary source that provides additional insight into and specific examples of their philosophy. How did that philosophy translate into how they lived?

Look back on the anticipation guide you completed in Activity 1.2. Identify Transcendentalist ideas embedded in the questions.

The New England Primer

For more than a hundred years, Puritan children received their first schooling from *The New England Primer*. Since the chief purpose of education in Puritan times was to enable people to read the Bible, it was natural that the alphabet rhymes chanted by the children should be based on Bible stories. The *Primer* is believed to have been in existence by 1688. Several versions have been printed, often with different verses for the letters.

T	*Time* cuts down all Both great and small.
U	*Uriah's* beauteous Wife Made *David* seek his Life.
W	*Whales* in the Sea God's Voice obey.
X	*Xerxes* the great did die, And so must you & I.
Y	*Youth* forward slips Death soonest nips.
Z	*Zacheus* he Did climb the Tree His Lord to see,

A	In ADAM'S Fall, We sinned all.
B	Heaven to find; The Bible Mind.
C	Christ crucify'd For sinners dy'd.
D	The Deluge drown'd The Earth around.
E	ELIJAH hid, By Ravens fed.
F	The judgment made *Felix* afraid.

G	As runs the Glass, Our Life doth pass.
H	My Book and Heart Must never part.
J	JOB feels the Rod, Yet blesses GOD.
K	Proud Korah's troop Was swallowed up
L	LOT fled to *Zoar*, Saw fiery Shower On *Sodom* pour.
M	MOSES was he Who *Israel's* Host Led thro' the Sea.

N	NOAH did view The old world & new.
O	Young OBADIAS, DAVID, JOSIAS, All were pious.
P	PETER deny'd His Lord and cry'd.
Q	Queen ESTHER sues And saves the Jews.
R	Young pious RUTH, Left all for Truth.
S	Young SAM'L dear, The Lord did fear.

T	Young TIMOTHY Learnt sin to fly.
V	VASHTI for Pride Was set aside.
W	Whales in the Sea, GOD'S Voice obey.
X	XERXES did die, And so must I.
Y	While youth do chear Death may be near.
Z	ZACCHEUS he Did climb the Tree Our Lord to see.

My Notes

Essay

ABOUT THE AUTHOR

Cotton Mather (1663–1728) entered Harvard University at the age of 12 and became an influential Puritan minister who wrote over 400 works. Some of his works describe the Puritan beliefs in the spiritual world and in the work of the devil in promoting witchcraft. He wrote reports to the judges of the Salem witch trials and then a history of the trials.

The TRIAL of MARTHA CARRIER

by Cotton Mather

I. Martha Carrier was indicted for bewitching certain persons, according to the form usual in such cases, pleading *not guilty* to her indictment[1]. There were first brought in a considerable number of the bewitched persons, who not only made the Court sensible of any horrid witchcraft committed upon them, but also deposed[2] that it was Martha Carrier, or her shape, that grievously tormented them by biting, pricking, pinching, and choking of them. It was further deposed that while this Carrier was on her examination before the Magistrates[3], the poor people were so tortured that every one expected their death upon the very spot, but that upon the binding of Carrier they were eased. Moreover, the look of Carrier then laid the afflicted people for dead, and her touch, if her eye at the same time were off them, raised them again: which things were also now seen upon her trial. And it was testified that upon the mention of some having their necks twisted almost round, by the shape of this Carrier, she replied, *It's no matter though their necks had been twisted quite off.*

II. Before the trial of this prisoner, several of her own children had frankly and fully confessed not only that they were witches themselves, but that this mother had made them so. This confession they made with great shows of repentance, and with much demonstration of truth. They related place,

---

[1] **indictment**: accusation or blame
[2] **deposed**: testified under oath
[3] **magistrate**: a judge

time, occasion; they gave an account of journeys, meetings, and mischiefs by them performed and were very credible in what they said. Nevertheless, this evidence was not produced against the prisoner at the bar, inasmuch as there was other evidence enough to proceed upon.

III. Benjamin Abbot gave his testimony that last March was a twelvemonth, this Carrier was very angry with him, upon laying out some land near her husband's. Her expressions in this anger were *that she would stick as close to Abbot as the bark stuck to the tree, and that he should repent of it afore seven years came to an end, so as Doctor Prescot should never cure him.* These words were heard by others besides Abbot himself, who also heard her say she would hold his nose as close to the grindstone as ever it was held since his name was Abbot. Presently after this he was taken with a swelling in his foot, and then with a pain in his side, and exceedingly tormented. It bred into a sore, which was lanced[4] by Doctor Prescot, and several gallons of corruption ran out of it. For six weeks it continued very bad, and then another sore bred in the groin, which was also lanced by Doctor Prescot. Another sore then bred in his groin, which was likewise cut and put him to very great misery. He was brought until death's door and so remained until Carrier was taken and carried away by the Constable, from which very day he began to mend and so grew better every day and is well ever since.

Sarah Abbot, his wife, also testified that her husband was not only all this while afflicted in his body, but also that strange, extraordinary, and unaccountable calamities[5] befell his cattle, their death being such as they could guess at no natural reason for.

IV. Allin Toothaker testified that Richard, the son of Martha Carrier, having some difference with him, pulled him down by the hair of the head. When he rose again, he was going to strike at Richard Carrier, but fell down flat on his back to the ground and had not power to stir hand or foot until he told Carrier he yielded: and then he saw the shape of Martha Carrier go off his breast.

This Toothaker had received a wound in the wars and now testified that Martha Carrier told him he should never be cured. Just afore the apprehending of Carrier, he could thrust a knitting needle into his wound, four inches deep; but presently, after her being seized, he was thoroughly healed.

He further testified that when Carrier and he sometimes were at variance, she would clap her hands at him, and say he should get nothing by it; whereupon he several times lost his cattle by strange deaths, whereof no natural causes could be given.

---

[4] **lanced**: opened or cut through
[5] **calamity**: great misfortune or disaster

WORD CONNECTIONS

Malicious comes from the Latin root *-mal-* meaning "ill will" or "spite." This root is also in *malign*, *malfunction*, and *malady*.

My Notes

V. John Rogger also testified that upon the threatening words of this malicious Carrier, his cattle would be strangely bewitched, as was more particularly then described.

VI. Samuel Preston testified that about two years ago, having some difference with Martha Carrier, he lost a cow in a strange preternatural[6], unusual matter: and about a month after this, the said Carrier, having again some difference with him, she told him he had lately lost a cow and it should not be long before he lost another, which accordingly came to pass: for he had a thriving and well-kept cow, which without any known cause quickly fell down and died.

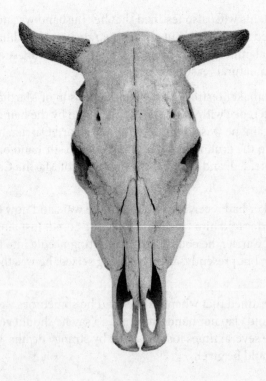

---

[6] **preternatural**: unnatural

by Benjamin Franklin

My Notes

> **ABOUT THE AUTHOR**
> One of seventeen children in a poor family, Benjamin Franklin (1706–1790) represents the classic American success story. Enormously talented and popular, Franklin succeeded as a scientist, statesman, inventor, publisher, and writer.

It was about this time I conceived the bold and arduous[1] project of arriving at moral perfection. I wished to live without committing any fault at any time; I would conquer all that either natural inclination, custom, or company might lead me into. As I knew, or thought I knew, what was right and wrong, I did not see why I might not always do the one and avoid the other. But I soon found I had undertaken a task of more difficulty than I had imagined. While my care was employed in guarding against one fault, I was often surprised by another, habit took the advantage of inattention; inclination was sometimes too strong for reason. I concluded, at length, that the mere speculative[2] conviction that it was our interest to be completely virtuous, was not sufficient to prevent our slipping, and that the contrary habits must be broken, and good ones acquired and established, before we can have any dependence on a steady, uniform rectitude[3] of conduct. For this purpose I therefore contrived the following method.

In the various enumerations[4] of the moral virtues I had met with in my reading, I found the catalog more or less numerous, as different writers included more or fewer ideas under the same name. Temperance, for example, was by some confined to eating and drinking, while by others it was extended to mean the moderating every other pleasure, appetite, inclination, or passion, bodily or mental, even to our avarice and ambition. I proposed to myself, for the sake of clearness, to use rather more names, with fewer ideas annexed to each, than a few names with more ideas; and I included under thirteen names of virtues all that at that time occurred to me as necessary or desirable, and annexed to each a short precept, which fully expressed the extent I gave to its meaning.

---

[1] **arduous**: requiring much energy; difficult
[2] **speculative**: based on conjecture or abstract reasoning
[3] **rectitude**: moral virtue; rightness of principle
[4] **enumerations**: lists, catalogues

Historic Pathways to the American Dream

My Notes

WORD CONNECTIONS

Order is a word that may have different meanings. It can mean a directive to do something or a sequence. Use connotation to determine Franklin's meaning for *order*.

These names of virtues, with their precepts, were:

1. Temperance

Eat not to dullness; drink not to elevation.

2. Silence

Speak not but what may benefit others or yourself; avoid trifling conversation.

3. Order

Let all your things have their places; let each part of your business have its time.

4. Resolution

Resolve to perform what you ought; perform without fail what you resolve.

5. Frugality

Make no expense but to do good to others or yourself; i.e., waste nothing.

6. Industry

Lose no time; be always employed in something useful; cut off all unnecessary actions.

7. Sincerity

Use no hurtful deceit; think innocently and justly, and, if you speak, speak accordingly.

8. Justice

Wrong none by doing injuries, or omitting the benefits that are your duty.

9. Moderation

Avoid extremes; forbear resenting injuries so much as you think they deserve.

10. Cleanliness

Tolerate no uncleanliness in body, clothes, or habitation.

11. Tranquility

Be not disturbed at trifles, or at accidents common or unavoidable.

12. Chastity

Rarely use venery but for health or offspring, never to dullness, weakness, or the injury of your own or another's peace or reputation.

13. Humility

Imitate Jesus and Socrates.[7]

---

[7] **Socrates** (sok′rətēz′): 469 BC–399 BC, Greek philosopher who lived humbly

SAYINGS
of Poor Richard

by Benjamin Franklin

ABOUT THE AUTHOR
Benjamin Franklin published *Poor Richard's Almanack*, which included advice and popular sayings, many of which are still common today. Franklin expanded and adapted sayings from common culture and other writers, but he also composed original sayings.

From Poor Richard's Almanack

Experience keeps a dear school, but a fool will learn in no other.

Hunger is the best pickle.

Love your neighbor; yet don't pull down your hedge.

If a man empties his purse into his head, no man can take it away from him.

Three may keep a secret if two of them are dead.

A small leak will sink a great ship.

Silks and satins, scarlet and velvet, put out the kitchen fire.

If a man could have half his wishes, he would double his troubles.

A lie stands on one leg, truth on two.

He that is of the opinion that money will do everything may well be suspected of doing everything for money.

Early to bed, early to rise, makes a man healthy, wealthy, and wise.

God helps them that help themselves.

A word to the wise is enough.

Fish and visitors smell in three days.

My Notes

LITERARY TERMS
An **aphorism** is a short, clever saying about life.

The used key is always bright.

Lost time is never found again.

The sleeping fox catches no poultry.

He that falls in love with himself has no rivals.

One today is worth two tomorrows.

Little strokes fell great oaks.

Since thou are not sure of a minute, throw not away an hour.

Beware of little expenses; a small leak will sink a great ship.

Fools make feasts and wise men eat them.

When the well's dry, they know the worth of water.

If you would know the worth of money, go and try to borrow some.

Make hay while the sun shines.

He that lieth down with dogs shall rise up with fleas.

'Tis hard for an empty bag to stand upright.

The worst wheel of the cart makes the most noise.

If you would have your business done, go; if not, send.

From

Self-Reliance

Excerpt, by Ralph Waldo Emerson

> **ABOUT THE AUTHOR**
> Educated at Harvard University, Ralph Waldo Emerson
> (1803–1882) founded a new American movement called
> Transcendentalism. Fueled by strong optimism and the
> belief in the importance of the individual, Emerson helped
> to inspire social reforms in education, slavery, and the
> rights of women and Native Americans.

There is a time in every man's education when he arrives at the conviction that envy is ignorance; that imitation is suicide; that he must take himself for better, for worse, as his portion; that though the wide universe is full of good, no kernel of nourishing corn can come to him but through his toil bestowed[1] on that plot of ground which is given him to till. The power which resides in him is new in nature, and none but he knows what he can do, nor does he know until he has tried....

Society everywhere is in conspiracy against the manhood of every one of its members. Society is a joint-stock company, in which the members agree, for the better securing of his bread to each shareholder, to surrender the liberty and culture of the eater. The virtue in most request is conformity. Self-reliance is its aversion.[2] It loves not realities and creators, but names and customs.

Whoso would be a man must be a nonconformist. He who would gather immortal palms must not be hindered by the name of goodness, but must explore if it be goodness. Nothing is at last sacred but the integrity of your own mind....

A foolish consistency is the hobgoblin[3] of little minds, adored by little statesmen and philosophers and divines. With consistency a great soul has simply nothing to do. He may as well concern himself with his shadow on the wall. Speak what you think now in hard words, and tomorrow speak what tomorrow thinks in hard words again, though it contradict everything you said today. "Ah, so you shall be sure to be misunderstood." Is it so bad, then, to be misunderstood? Pythogoras was misunderstood, and Socrates, and Jesus, and Luther, and Copernicus, and Galileo, and Newton, and every pure and wise spirit that ever took flesh. To be great is to be misunderstood....

---

[1] **bestowed**: presented as a gift or an honor
[2] **aversion**: strong feeling of dislike
[3] **hobgoblin**: something causing superstitious fear

My Notes

GRAMMAR & USAGE

Emerson's use of parallel **infinitive phrases** effectively creates a memorable line:

To be great is to be misunderstood.

Infinitive phrases may function as nouns, adjectives, or adverbs. In this sentence, Emerson uses infinitive phrases as the subject and as the predicate nominative in the sentence.

WORD CONNECTIONS

Analogies express relationships between meanings of words. When creating or analyzing analogies, pay attention to consistency in parts of speech. For example, if a set of words is noun : adjective, then the related set of words will be noun : adjective. Determine whether this analogy is correct. Explain why or why not.

appoint : ambassador :: elect : President

My Notes

The civilized man has built a coach, but has lost the use of his feet. He is supported on crutches, but lacks so much support of muscle. He has got a fine Geneva watch, but he has lost the skill to tell the hour by the sun. A Greenwich nautical almanac he has, and so, being sure of the information when he wants it, the man in the street does not know a star in the sky. The solstice he does not observe; the equinox he knows as little; and the whole bright calendar of the year is without a dial in his mind. His notebooks impair his memory; his libraries overload his wit; the insurance office increases the number of accidents; and it may be a question whether machinery does not encumber[4]; whether we have not lost by refinement some energy, by a Christianity entrenched in establishments and forms some vigor of wild virtue. For every Stoic was a Stoic; but in Christendom, where is the Christian?

---

[4] **encumber**: to impede or hinder

Where I Lived and What I Lived For

by Henry David Thoreau

From Walden

My Notes

> ### ABOUT THE AUTHOR
>
> Well-educated and brilliant, Henry David Thoreau (1817–1862) defied expectations to live an uncommon life of reflection and simplicity. As an experiment to reconnect with nature and discover the meaning of life, he lived for two years in a cabin in the woods of Concord, Massachusetts. He wrote about his experiences in *Walden*, one of the most well-known works in American literature.

When first I took up my abode in the woods, that is, began to spend my nights as well as days there, which by accident, was on Independence Day, or the Fourth of July, 1845, my house was not finished for winter, but was merely a defense against the rain, without plastering or chimney, the walls being of rough, weather-stained boards, with wide chinks, which made it cool at night. The upright white hewn studs and freshly planed door and window casings gave it a clean and airy look, especially in the morning, when its timbers were saturated[1] with dew, so that I fancied that by noon some sweet gum would exude[2] from them….

I was seated by the shore of a small pond, about a mile and a half south of the village of Concord and somewhat higher than it, in the midst of an extensive wood between that town and Lincoln,[3] and about two miles south of our only field known to fame, Concord Battle Ground;[4] but I was so low in the woods that the opposite shore, half a mile off, like the rest, covered with wood, was my most distant horizon….

Every morning was a cheerful invitation to make my life of equal simplicity, and I may say innocence, with Nature herself. I have been as sincere a worshiper of Aurora[5] as the Greeks. I got up early and bathed in the pond; that was a religious exercise, and one of the best things which I did. They say that characters were engraven on the bathing tub of King Tching-thang to this effect: "Renew thyself completely each day; do it again, and again, and forever again." I can understand that. Morning brings back the heroic ages. I was as much affected by the faint hum of a mosquito making its invisible and unimaginable tour through my apartment at earliest dawn, when I was sitting

---

[1] **saturated**: soaked, full to capacity
[2] **exude**: to ooze or spread in all directions
[3] **Lincoln**: Small town in Massachusetts between Concord and Sudbury, which is mentioned in the next paragraph.
[4] **Concord Battle Ground**: A reference to Emerson's poem "Concord Hymn."
[5] **Aurora**: Greek goddess of dawn

My Notes

with door and windows open, as I could be by any trumpet that ever sang of fame. It was Homer's requiem[6]; itself an *Iliad* and *Odyssey* in the air, singing its own wrath and wanderings.[7] There was something cosmical about it; a standing advertisement, till forbidden, of the everlasting vigor and fertility of the world. The morning, which is the most memorable season of the day, is the awakening hour. Then there is least somnolence[8] in us; and for an hour, at least, some part of us awakes which slumbers all the rest of the day and night. After a partial cessation of his sensuous life, the soul of man, or its organs rather, are reinvigorated each day, and his Genius tries again what noble life it can make. All memorable events, I should say, transpire in morning time and in a morning atmosphere. The Vedas[9] say, "All intelligences awake with the morning." Poetry and art, and the fairest and most memorable of the actions of men, date from such an hour. All poets and heroes, like Memnon,[10] are the children of Aurora, and emit their music at sunrise. To him whose elastic and vigorous thought keeps pace with the sun, the day is a perpetual morning. It matters not what the clocks say or the attitudes and labors of men. Morning is when I am awake and there is a dawn in me. Moral reform is the effort to throw off sleep. Why is it that men give so poor an account of their day if they have not been slumbering? They are not such poor calculators. If they had not been overcome with drowsiness, they would have performed something. The millions are awake enough for physical labor; but only one in a million is awake enough for effective intellectual exertion, only one in a hundred millions to a poetic or divine life. To be awake is to be alive. I have never yet met a man who was quite awake. How could I have looked him in the face?

We must learn to reawaken and keep ourselves awake, not by mechanical aids, but by an infinite expectation of the dawn, which does not forsake us in our soundest sleep. I know of no more encouraging fact than the unquestionable ability of man to elevate his life by a conscious endeavor. It is something to be able to paint a particular picture, or to carve a statue, and so to make a few objects beautiful; but it is far more glorious to carve and paint the very atmosphere and medium through which we look, which morally we can do. To affect the quality of the day, that is the highest of arts. Every man is tasked to make his life, even in its details, worthy of the contemplation of his most elevated and critical hour. If we refused, or rather used up, such paltry information as we get, the oracles would distinctly inform us how this might be done.

I went to the woods because I wished to live deliberately, to front only the essential facts of life, and see if I could not learn what it had to teach, and not, when I came to die, discover that I had not lived. I did not wish to live what was not life, living is so dear; nor did I wish to practice resignation, unless it was quite necessary. I wanted to live deep and suck out all the marrow of life, to live

WORD CONNECTIONS

Infinite comes from the Latin word meaning "unbounded" or "unlimited." The word is formed from the root *-fini-*, meaning "end" plus *in*, meaning "not." Other words based on *-fini-* include *final, confine, definitive*.

---

[6] **requiem:** a mass or a solemn ceremony for a deceased person

[7] **wrath and wanderings:** Homer's *Iliad* concerns the "wrath" of Achilles, and the *Odyssey* tells of the "wanderings" of Odysseus

[8] **somnolence:** sleepiness, drowsiness

[9] **Vedas:** Collection of sacred Hindu literature

[10] **Memnon:** In Greek mythology, the King of the Ethiopians whom Zeus made immortal. Memnon's statue at Thebes was supposed to emit musical notes at dawn.

so sturdily and Spartanlike[11] as to put to rout all that was not life, to cut a broad swath and shave close, to drive life into a corner, and reduce it to its lowest terms, and, if it proved to be mean, why then to get the whole and genuine meanness of it, and publish its meanness to the world; or if it were sublime,[12] to know it by experience, and be able to give a true account of it in my next excursion. For most men, it appears to me, are in a strange uncertainty about it, whether it is of the devil or of God, and have *somewhat hastily* concluded that it is the chief end of man here to "glorify God and enjoy him forever."[13]

Still we live meanly, like ants; though the fable tells us that we were long ago changed into men; like pygmies we fight with cranes; it is error upon error, and clout upon clout, and our best virtue has for its occasion a superfluous and evitable[14] wretchedness. Our life is frittered away by detail. An honest man has hardly need to count more than his ten fingers or in extreme cases he may add his ten toes, and lump the rest. Simplicity, simplicity, simplicity! I say, let your affairs be as two or three, and not a hundred or a thousand; instead of a million count half a dozen, and keep your accounts on your thumbnail. In the midst of this chopping sea of civilized life such are the clouds and storms and quicksands and thousand-and-one items to be allowed for, that a man has to live, if he would not founder and go to the bottom and not make his port at all, by dead reckoning,[15] and he must be a great calculator indeed who succeeds. Simplify, simplify. Instead of three meals a day, if it be necessary eat but one; instead of a hundred dishes, five; and reduce other things in proportion. Our life is like a German Confederacy,[16] made up of petty states, with its boundary forever fluctuating, so that even a German cannot tell you how it is bounded at any moment. The nation itself, with all its so-called internal improvements, which, by the way are all external and superficial, is just such an unwieldy and overgrown establishment, cluttered with furniture and tripped up by its own traps, ruined by luxury and heedless expense, by want of calculation and a worthy aim, as the million households in the land; and the only cure for it, as for them, is in a rigid economy, a stern and more than Spartan simplicity of life and elevation of purpose. It lives too fast. Men think that it is essential that the Nation have commerce, and export ice, and talk through a telegraph, and ride thirty miles an hour, without a doubt, whether they do or not; but whether we should live like baboons or like men, is a little uncertain. If we do not get out sleepers,[17] and forge rails and devote days and nights to the work, but go to tinkering upon our lives to improve them, who will build railroads? And if railroads are not built, how shall we get to heaven in season? But if we stay at home and mind our business, who will want railroads? We do not ride on the railroad; it rides upon us. Did you ever think what those sleepers are that underlie the railroad? Each

---

[11] **Spartanlike**: like the inhabitants of the ancient Greek city-state of Sparta, who were famed for their courage, discipline, and frugality

[12] **sublime**: elevated or lofty in thought or language

[13] **"glorify…forever"**: from the Presbyterian book of beliefs, *Westminister Shorter Catechism*

[14] **evitable**: avoidable

[15] **dead reckoning**: nautical term for a method of positioning a ship without using the more reliable method of astronomical observation

[16] **German Confederacy**: in 1815, the first ineffective alliance of German territories

[17] **sleepers**: wooden beams to which railway tracks are riveted

My Notes

GRAMMAR & USAGE

Among the rhetorical devices Thoreau uses is **antithesis**—the use of contrasting balanced elements. Look at this example:

We do not ride on the railroad; it rides upon us.

The balanced sentence parts express contrasting ideas. The result is an effective and memorable statement.

My Notes

one is a man, an Irishman, or a Yankee man. The rails are laid on them, and they are covered with sand, and the cars run smoothly over them....

For my part, I could easily do without the post office. I think that there are very few important communications made through it. To speak critically, I never received more than one or two letters in my life — I wrote this some years ago — that were worth the postage. The penny post is, commonly, an institution through which you seriously offer a man that penny for his thoughts which is so often safely offered in jest. And I am sure that I never read any memorable news in the newspaper. If we read of one man robbed, or murdered, or killed by accident, or one house burned, or one vessel wrecked, or one steamboat blown up, or one cow run over on the Western Railroad, or one mad dog killed, or one lot of grasshoppers in the winter — we never need read of another. One is enough. If you are acquainted with the principle, what do you care for myriad instances and applications? To a philosopher all news as it is called, is gossip, and they who edit and read it are old women over their tea. Yet not a few are greedy after this gossip. There was such a rush, as I hear, the other day at one of the offices to learn the foreign news by the last arrival, that several large squares of plate glass belonging to the establishment were broken by the pressure — news which I seriously think a ready wit might write a twelvemonth, or twelve years, beforehand with sufficient accuracy....

Shams and delusions are esteemed for soundest truths, while reality is fabulous. If men would steadily observe realities only, and not allow themselves to be deluded, life, to compare it with such things as we know, would be like a fairy tale and the Arabian Nights' Entertainments. If we respected only what is inevitable and has a right to be, music and poetry would resound along the streets. When we are unhurried and wise, we perceive that only great and worthy things have any permanent and absolute existence, that petty fears and petty pleasures are but the shadow of the reality. This is always exhilarating and sublime. By closing the eyes and slumbering, and consenting to be deceived by shows, men establish and confirm their daily life of routine and habit everywhere, which still is built on purely illusory foundations. Children, who play life, discern its true law and relations more clearly than men, who fail to live it worthily, but who think that they are wiser by experience, that is, by failure....

Time is but the stream I go-a-fishing in. I drink at it; but while I drink I see the sandy bottom and detect how shallow it is. Its thin current slides away, but eternity remains. I would drink deeper; fish in the sky, whose bottom is pebbly with stars. I cannot count one. I know not the first letter of the alphabet. I have always been regretting that I was not as wise as the day I was born. The intellect is a cleaver; it discerns and rifts its way into the secret of things. I do not wish to be any more busy with my hands than is necessary. My head is hands and feet. I feel all my best faculties concentrated in it. My instinct tells me that my head is an organ for burrowing, as some creatures use their snout and forepaws, and with it I would mine and burrow my way through these hills. I think that the richest vein is somewhere hereabouts; so by the divining rod and thin rising vapors I judge; and here I will begin to mine.

America, the Beautiful

Poetry

> **ABOUT THE AUTHOR**
> After witnessing the view from Pike's Peak in Colorado in 1893, Katharine Lee Bates (1859–1929) wrote the words to her most well-known poem, "America the Beautiful." She was an accomplished poet and professor who founded the New England Poetry Club and taught English literature at Wellesley College.

America, the Beautiful

by Katharine Lee Bates

O beautiful for spacious skies,
For amber waves of grain,
For purple mountain majesties
Above the fruited plain.
America! America!   5
God shed His grace on thee,
And crown thy good with brotherhood
From sea to shining sea.

O beautiful for pilgrim feet,
Whose stern impassioned stress   10
A thoroughfare for freedom beat
Across the wilderness.
America! America!
God mend thine ev'ry flaw,
Confirm thy soul in self-control,   15
Thy liberty in law.

My Notes

> **GRAMMAR & USAGE**
> Writers create rhythm and vivid mental pictures by using **parallel structure** and effective verbs and adjectives. Bates uses parallel structure in the first three lines of "America the Beautiful" with a prepositional phrase that begins with *for*. The strong adjectives *spacious*, *amber* and *purple* make a simple phrase vivid, rhythmic, and memorable. Notice how the poem "America" relies on strong verbs: *feeds, sinks, tests, sweeps, gaze.* Use these techniques to develop your writing.

My Notes

O beautiful for heroes proved
In liberating strife,
Who more than self their country loved,
20 And mercy more than life!
America! America!
May God thy gold refine
Till all success be nobleness,
And ev'ry gain divine!

25 O beautiful for patriot dream
That sees beyond the years.
Thine alabaster cities gleam,
Undimmed by human tears.
America! America!
30 God shed his grace on thee,
And crown thy good with brotherhood,
From sea to shining sea!

AMERICA

by Claude McKay

ABOUT THE AUTHOR

Born in 1890 in Jamaica, Claude McKay traveled to America to attend college, where he experienced the harsh realities of racism. He wrote poetry on political and social concerns and became a major writer of the Harlem Renaissance, a movement in the early 1920s.

Although she feeds me bread of bitterness,

And sinks into my throat her tiger's tooth,

Stealing my breath of life, I will confess

I love this cultured hell that tests my youth!

Her vigor flows like tides into my blood,   5

Giving me strength erect against her hate.

Her bigness sweeps my being like a flood.

Yet as a rebel fronts a king in state,

I stand within her walls with not a shred

Of terror, malice, not a word of jeer.   10

Darkly I gaze into the days ahead,

And see her might and granite wonders there,

Beneath the touch of Time's unerring hand,

Like priceless treasures sinking in the sand.

My Notes

America, the Beautiful

Poetry

> **ABOUT THE AUTHOR**
> Born in Pittsburgh, Robinson Jeffers (1887–1962) lived most of his adult life on the coast of California in a stone cottage that he helped to build. His poetry celebrates the divine beauty of nature and contrasts it with the destructive and impermanent nature of civilization and individuals.

Shine, Perishing Republic

by Robinson Jeffers

While this America settles in the mould of its vulgarity, heavily thickening to empire

And protest, only a bubble in the molten mass, pops and sighs out, and the mass hardens,

I sadly smiling remember that the flower fades to make fruit, the fruit rots to make earth.

Out of the mother; and through the spring exultances, ripeness and decadence; and home to the mother.

5 You making haste on decay: not blameworthy; life is good, be it stubbornly long or suddenly

A mortal splendor: meteors are not needed less than mountains: shine, perishing republic.

But for my children, I would have them keep their distance from the thickening center; corruption

Never has been compulsory, when the cities lie at the monster's feet there are left the mountains.

And boys, be in nothing so moderate as in love of man, a clever servant, insufferable master.

10 There is the trap that catches noblest spirits, that caught – they say – God, when he walked on earth.

Writing Prompt: Choose which speaker and tone in the previous poems and song most closely resembles your attitude toward America and discuss why. Describe how personal experiences align you with this attitude and any small differences in your viewpoints.

> **LITERARY TERMS**
> **Tone** is the writer's attitude toward the topic of a work.

America's Voices: Call and Response

SUGGESTED LEARNING STRATEGIES: Graphic Organizer, Oral Reading, Rehearsal, Oral Interpretation, Drafting

Read "I Hear America Singing," "I, Too, Sing America," and "Indian Singing in Twentieth-Century America." Consider how the **diction** communicates the writer's feelings and then complete the chart for the poem(s) assigned to you. Then, as a group, perform your assigned poem for the class. Consider your movements (real and symbolic), voice inflection, and facial expressions in relaying the appropriate *tone* for the piece. While you watch other students perform their poems, fill in the remainder of the chart appropriately.

> **LITERARY TERMS**
> **Diction** is the writer's choice of words.

Title	Feelings About America	Words or Phrases That Reveal Those Feelings
"I Hear America Singing"		
"I, Too, Sing America"		
"Indian Singing in Twentieth-Century America"		

Read the poem "next to of course god america i" and fill in the appropriate chart. On your own paper, write a paragraph that describes the poem's tone.

Title	Feelings About America	Words or Phrases That Reveal Those Feelings
"next to of course god america i"		

My Notes

Poetry

> **ABOUT THE AUTHOR**
> Walt Whitman (1819–1892), who did not attend college, worked as a journalist, carpenter, and building contractor before publishing a collection of his poems, *Leaves of Grass*, in 1855. Calling himself the "people's poet," Whitman wrote poetry in free verse, used common speech patterns, and celebrated the country's working class and cultural diversity.

I Hear America Singing

by Walt Whitman

I hear America singing, the varied carols I hear,

Those of mechanics, each one singing his as it should be blithe and
    strong,

The carpenter singing his as he measures his plank or beam,

The mason singing his as he makes ready for work, or leaves off work,

5   The boatman singing what belongs to him in his boat, the
    deckhand singing on the steamboat deck,

The shoemaker singing as he sits on his bench, the hatter singing as he
    stands,

The woodcutter's song, the plowboy's on his way in the morning, or at
    noon intermission or at sundown.

The delicious singing of the mother, or of the young wife at work, or of
    the girl sewing or washing,

Each singing what belongs to him or her and to none else.

10   The day what belongs to the day — at night the party of young

fellows, robust, friendly,

Singing with open mouths their strong melodious songs.

Poetry

> **ABOUT THE AUTHOR**
> Fascinated with jazz rhythms and the lyrics of blues music, Langston Hughes's first book of poetry, *The Weary Blues,* was published in 1926. A major figure in the Harlem Renaissance, Hughes also wrote novels, short stories, plays, and nonfiction. His works captured and celebrated the colorful culture of black America.

I, Too, Sing America

by Langston Hughes

I, too, sing America.

I am the darker brother.
They send me to eat in the kitchen
When company comes,
But I laugh,   5
And eat well,
And grow strong.

Tomorrow,
I'll be at the table
When company comes.   10
Nobody'll dare
Say to me,
"Eat in the kitchen,"
Then.

Besides,   15
They'll see how beautiful I am
And be ashamed —

I, too, am America.

My Notes

My Notes

Poetry

> **ABOUT THE AUTHOR**
> A Native American poet, visual artist, and professor, Gail Tremblay was born in Buffalo, New York. She received her M.F.A. in Creative Writing from the University of Oregon and teaches at Evergreen State College. She has received many awards for her visual art and poetry, both of which reflect Native American motifs.

Indian Singing *in* TWENTIETH-CENTURY AMERICA

by Gail Tremblay

We wake; we wake the day,
the light rising in us like sun —
our breath a prayer brushing
against the feathers in our hands.
5   We stumble out into streets;
patterns of wires invented by strangers
are strung between eye and sky,
and we dance in two worlds,
inevitable as seasons in one,
10   exotic curiosities in the other
which rushes headlong down highways,
watches us from car windows, explains
us to its children in words

that no one could ever make

sense of. The image obscures   15

the vision, and we wonder

whether anyone will ever hear

our own names for the things

we do. Light dances in the body,

surrounds all living things —   20

even the stones sing

although their songs are infinitely

slower than the ones we learn

from trees. No human voice lasts

long enough to make such music sound.   25

Earth breath eddies between factories

and office buildings, caresses the surface

of our skin; we go to jobs, the boss

always watching the clock to see

that we're on time. He tries to shut

out magic and hopes we'll make   30

mistakes or disappear. We work

fast and steady and remember

each breath alters the composition

of the air. Change moves relentless,

the pattern unfolding despite their planning —   35

we're always there — singing round dance

songs, remembering what supports

our life — impossible to ignore.

WORD CONNECTIONS

Factory has as its root the Latin word *facere* meaning "to do." Other words using the root *-fact-* are *faction*, *benefactor*, *confection*, and *manufacture*.

My Notes

Poetry

> **ABOUT THE AUTHOR**
> After graduating from Harvard University, E.E. Cummings (1894–1962) volunteered to drive an ambulance in France during World War I. He was accused of being a spy and was thrown in jail in France for three months. After the war, he wrote prose, poetry, and plays, but he is best known for experimenting with and breaking rules of traditional poetry, sentence structure, and punctuation.

next to of course god america i

by e. e. cummings

"next to of course god america i
love you land of the pilgrims' and so forth oh
say can you see by the dawn's early my
country 'tis of centuries come and go
5   and are no more what of it we should worry
in every language even deafanddumb
thy sons acclaim your glorious name by gorry
by jingo by gee by gosh by gum
why talk of beauty what could be more beaut-
10   iful than these heroic happy dead
who rushed like lions to the roaring slaughter
they did not stop to think they died instead
then shall the voice of liberty be mute?"

He spoke. And drank rapidly a glass of water.

Essay

THEY LIVE
the Dream

by Dan Rather

It is the phrase we reach for most often to describe this land of ours. It has reflected what is best in us as a country and a people. It is the American Dream, and it has filled me with awe for as long as I can remember.

Growing up in Houston during the Great Depression, it took shape for me around the radio, as I listened spellbound to Edward R. Murrow's World War II dispatches and dreamed of becoming a reporter myself. My neighborhood was not a place that led me to think I should be reaching for such a faraway star. Yet — and this still gives me a thrill today — within 20 years, there I was, a correspondent in New York City, meeting Murrow, my childhood hero.

The American Dream, you see, holds me in its grasp because I have been blessed to live my own version of it. There is no typical American and no typical American Dream. For some, the Dream is one of freedom; for others it is of fortune or family or service to one's fellows. Some place greatest emphasis on the pursuit of happiness or of keeping alive the innovative spirit. But however we define it, it defines us as a people.

The people you'll meet here are the result of my quest to discover The American Dream as your neighbors are creating it today. I think you will find them inspirational. I know I did.

DELORES KESLER

She started her company just to survive and retired a millionaire.

Chunk 1

Delores Kesler's dream began with a $10,000 loan she used to found a temporary staffing agency in Jacksonville, FL, in 1977. When she retired 20 years later, her company, AccuStaff, had projected revenues of $2 billion. Kesler says she didn't plan to become a millionaire: Divorced and with a small child, she began her career at 22 with a series of dead-end jobs, struggling to make ends meet.

My Notes

When she founded her company, there were few women entrepreneurs. But her father had often told Kesler she could do anything she wanted to do, and she was determined to succeed. As time went on, however, Kesler realized it was not just financial gain she was pursuing: She wanted to make a contribution to her community. And, as her business grew, she started requiring her employees to devote time to community service and insisting that her company contribute to local charities. And she didn't stop there. In time, Kesler's company was earning $50 million a year, and a large portion was going back into the community.

When Kesler retired, she set a new course for her life. Today, the Delores Pass Kesler Foundation focuses on changing young lives through education, mentoring and children's programs. In 1997, she gave $1 million to the University of North Florida to provide scholarships to students from Raines High School in Jacksonville. She cried before an audience of thousands when the principal thanked her. She told them that they didn't know how good it felt to be able to give that money away. "An awful lot of people benefited from what started with a $10,000 loan," Kesler says.

Chunk 2

Wayne Ward Ford believes we all have a destiny – not a predetermined fate but a place that a higher power wants us to go – and he's proof of it.

WAYNE WARD FORD

A troubled young man, he had an odd premonition about his future.

Wayne Ford was in eighth grade when a teacher asked the class to write their obituaries. How would they like to be remembered? Ford, who lived in a rough area of Washington, D.C., came up with a curious response: He said he would make his mark in the Midwest. He would be active in politics and in charge of a community center.

Wayne Ford would go on to get in trouble in high school. "I was doing drugs, robbing, breaking into apartments," he recalls. To get away, he accepted a football scholarship to a small, nearly all-white Minnesota college. Once there, however, racism threatened to throw him off course. Instead, he turned his anger to activism and founded the school's black student union.

"Then," he says, "it all started to come together. The worst things in my life were the things that had the potential to make me great." Ford devoted himself to academics. History especially gave him a new perspective." When I started reading it," he says, "I thought, 'My God, the world has gone through hell, not just Wayne Ford.'"

After graduation, Ford turned to politics. Today, he's living the dream he had as a boy: He's the only black member of the Iowa State Legislature and the founder and executive director of Urban Dreams, a nonprofit community program for at-risk youth. Last year, he spoke before the Democratic National Convention. It was one of the biggest achievements of his life, but he says, "It wasn't the cherry on the ice cream. The best is yet to come."

SHAWN CARLSON

His grandfather's struggle to be accepted inspired him to encourage others.

Chunk 3

Shawn Carlson says his dream and his passion — the Society of Amateur Scientists, which he founded — was inspired by his grandfather. "I've been privileged to know some of the greatest scientists alive today," says Carlson, who has a Ph.D. in nuclear physics. "And no one had a greater raw scientific talent than my grandfather." But, he adds, his grandfather's work was consistently rejected "because he didn't have the letters 'Ph.D.' next to his name."

"Amateur scientists," he says, "are overflowing with passion," and his aim is to teach them standards and procedures so the larger scientific world will take them seriously. He and his wife, Michelle, sank their life savings of $10,000 into starting the Society for Amateur Scientists in 1994 and endured several tough years. Then Carlson was awarded a MacArthur "genius" fellowship, which allowed him to keep the Society afloat.

Although he has been criticized by some in the scientific community, Carlson continues to pursue his dream of opening scientific innovation to everyone. "The ability to come up with something original and be respected because you are a maverick — that's very much part of the American tradition," he says.

OSCAR CARLOS ACOSTA

Everything he wanted was within his grasp. Then, it seemed, it was gone.

Chunk 4

As a boy in tiny Elida, NM, Oscar Acosta had a talent for throwing a baseball that brought him a college scholarship and a chance at athletic glory. Getting to the Majors was his dream, and he neglected everything else — his schoolwork, and his wife and children — to get there. "I became consumed," he says. He made it to the minor leagues, but when a torn rotator cuff ended his pitching career, his life spiraled out of control. His wife took the kids and left. He was broke. He lost any belief in himself. "I'd just given up," he says." I thought I was destined to go back and be a cow-puncher the rest of my life."

My Notes

WORD CONNECTIONS

Amateur comes from the Latin root *am-* meaning "love." This root is also found in *amorous, enamored, amicable.*

My Notes

When he got a second chance — an offer to coach in the Texas Rangers' minor league system — Acosta says, he realized it was time to change. His identity, he swore, would never be tied exclusively to baseball. He reconciled with his wife and for the next 11 years built back what he'd lost, taking his blessings as they came. "I told my daughter, if God wants me to be a minor league instructor, that's what I'm going to do," he says.

Acosta did make it to the Majors — as a pitching coach for the Chicago Cubs. Now 44, he lives not far from where he grew up. Recently, Acosta watched his son play in the Little League game on the same field where he'd learned to pitch. "This was a big deal," Acosta says. "It was like watching myself — like my life had started all over."

EILEEN COLLINS

Chunk 5

She found what she wanted to do in life, but how in the world would she get there?

The first woman to pilot the Space Shuttle and to command a Shuttle mission grew up in public housing in Elmira, NY. There wasn't much money for family outings when she was a child. "One thing my father liked to do," recalls Eileen Collins, "was take us to the airport to watch the planes take off." She knew she wanted to fly, so Collins saved up for lessons, and she had enough by the time she attended community college. Once in the pilot's seat, her future seemed clear: "You know how you find the thing that you like to do in life?" she says. "I found it."

Collins pursued her dream, joining Air Force ROTC at Syracuse University and being among the first women allowed into the pilot-training program. But she didn't stop there. Eventually, she set her sights even higher — on NASA.

She recalls an early look out the window of the Shuttle: "Looking back at Earth is just beautiful. It's blue, it's white, it's tan. The jungles are a dark green. There's so much water. It's just amazing." And when Collins got the opportunity to land the Shuttle — the first woman to do so — she says, "I knew all those women pilots out there were watching me and thinking, 'Eileen, you better make a good landing.'" She did.

"I'm an explorer," says Collins, now 44. "I want to go places that are new and different, learn new things. I think that's what being human is all about. It's what life is all about — exploring and learning."

CURTIS G. AIKENS SR.

His dream — and his future — were on hold until he finally decided to ask for help.

Curtis Aikens, who grew up in rural Conyers, GA, puts a face to one of those literacy statistics we hear but sometimes cannot believe: He went through high school and five semesters of college without learning how to read. One of the millions who fall through the cracks and keep falling, Aikens believes that he would have disappeared completely if he hadn't, at 26, finally asked for help. Of his literacy tutors, Aikens says, "They didn't change my life. They saved my life."

Aikens put his new skills to good use. A lifelong lover of cooking and food, he started his own produce company in his hometown, became a food columnist and began to focus on his version of The American Dream: "I said to myself, 'I'm going to become a celebrity.'" But it wasn't fame alone he was pursuing, he explains. "It was so, when I talk about the fact that I couldn't read, other nonreading adults will say, 'If he can do it, I can too!'" Today, Aiken has three cookbooks to his name and appears on Calling All Cooks on the Food Network. But, he says, he hasn't reached his goal. "I'm still trying to obtain The American Dream, because I want to give everybody the ability to read. I know that sounds hokey, but there it is."

YOU MAY SENSE A COMMON THREAD running through many of these stories. The American Dream affords us opportunity and the freedom to seize it. It has also created, in my experience, some of the most generous people in the world. Americans who find their own dream make the dreams of their fellow citizens possible as well. For them, and for the rest of us the Dream remains both a hope and a promise, even as we add to its meaning with each new chapter of our lives.

Chunk 6

My Notes

My Notes

Article

LIFELONG DREAMER
— Vietnam Boat Person

by Mary-Beth McLaughlin

Nancy Pham says that she had been a dreamer most of her life.

Her dreams have taken her from a crowded refugee boat in the choppy seas off war-torn South Vietnam to the quiet confines of a former church in suburban Toledo where she'd opened her own beauty salon.

She's still navigating choppy seas — any entrepreneur trying to launch a new business in tough economic times knows the going isn't easy. But she exudes a quiet confidence.

"I'm already a success, because I've already done what I wanted to do," said the owner of the Fifth Avenue beauty salon, which opened three months ago at the corner of Sylvania and McCord Roads.

Such confidence is born from a lifetime of beating the odds, starting at age 13, when the Vietnam War came to the city of Saigon where she lived with her family.

Confidence also comes from having survived a 15-day boat trip with her husband and two small children, one of whom was so sick, she feared she would have to bury the child by tossing her into the sea.

And still more confidence comes from having survived ending up in Oak Harbor, OH, with no job or money, not speaking English, and not even being sure of the size of the United States.

Speaking in soft, accented English, Mrs. Pham retold her story quietly. Only the long pauses and heavy sighs gave away the pain of surviving during wartime. From 1963 on, there were sandbags in the living room where the family ran during bombings that occurred every night.

"I was not afraid of it. Sometimes, I would just sleep in my bed and you could feel the whole house shake. It was really, really noisy," she said. "And then I would get up in the morning and I was not scared. I would feel wonderful I'm alive. And I would walk around the neighborhood and check and see who is alive and who is dead."

My Notes

But life went on and Mrs. Pham did the "normal" things: graduated from high school; learning shorthand, typing, and English, and getting a job as a secretary at Macvee II, a company associated with the U.S. Army.

She met and married Chinh, a man 11 years her elder, who was in the Navy. They had two children, Huy (renamed William) and Trang (renamed Jenny). After Jenny was born in 1973, Mrs. Pham quit Macvee to become a full-time mother.

Although it was nerve-wracking to ride on buses or go to hotels where Americans stayed — both were prime targets for bombs — the South Vietnamese people love the Americans and Saigon thrived with their presence, she said.

But in 1972, the Americans started their withdrawal, and things began to change. By 1975, with Saigon on the verge of falling, all former and current Macvee employees were promised safe passage to the U.S. if they wanted.

Mrs. Pham's sister, still a Macvee employee, typed up the forms for the whole family to leave.

Their mother, who did not speak English, but already had moved once to escape Communism, was determined to leave. But Mrs. Pham hesitated.

"I worry, what will I do over [in the U.S.]? We have money, and a business and a house, and I thought, I never did anything to the Communists, they won't do anything to me. So I don't go," she said.

So while her sister, mother, and remaining family members headed for the ship in the harbor, Mrs. Pham stayed with her two small children — until her husband arrived the next day and demanded to know why they hadn't left.

Brushing aside her arguments, he loaded the kids in the car with clothes and borrowed milk, told neighbors they would return the next day after a visit to her aunt, and set off for the harbor.

Mr. Pham ignored the restrictions on service personnel leaving the country and boarded the boat with his family.

On April 29, 1975, the ship pulled out of the harbor as the radio blared news that Ho Chi Minh was now in charge of Saigon.

Pausing while lost deep in memories, Mrs. Pham whispered, "It seems like yesterday."

They had no idea where they were going or how long it would take to get there, she said.

There was no roof, no room to move, and canned Army rations included raw fish with a worm inside. And there was no milk for 10-month-old Jenny, so they fed her sugar and water. But as days went by, Jenny became weak until she all but stopped moving, and her mother thought she had died.

> ### GRAMMAR & USAGE
> Direct quotes in an essay make the writing and the person being quoted seem more real. Quotations can be part of a longer sentence that describes how the words were said: for example, *Pausing while lost deep in memories, Mrs. Pham whispered, "It seems like yesterday."*

Getting to Know the American Dream

"I don't know where I'm at. Even if there had been a coconut floating by, I would have had some idea. My husband was crying and I was running from one room to another but there was no medicine," she said. "We were just hoping they would stop somewhere."

"I kept thinking, 'If she dies in the ship, we'd have to throw her in the ocean,'" Mrs. Pham said.

But in the first of what she called "miracles," the ship carrying the Phams stopped at Subic Bay, The Philippines, after 15 days at sea.

The family boarded another ship to Guam, and eventually was sent to a camp in Pennsylvania, where they waited for a family or church to sponsor them.

Many families requested sponsors located in sunnier climates like Florida or California, but Mr. Pham couldn't wait.

"I did not know how big the U.S. is and I was worrying about everything. I wanted to get out and see what outside world is, and so I tell my husband we have to get out and make a living," she said.

Her mother moved to New Jersey, her sister to California, and the Pham family was sponsored by St. John Lutheran Church, in Rocky Ridge, near Oak Harbor. On July 16, 1975, the Pham family boarded a plane for Ohio.

Nancy said she was anxious, having been told Ohio was full of snow and ice and cold.

"I'm such a worrier, that I looked down, picturing snow and ice and no living thing," she said. "I look down and everything was so green and there were mountains and rivers. I feel so happy. I feel like I'm a bird, like I'm a fish. Everything is so beautiful and I think, 'I can make a living.'"

The Phams stayed with an Oak Harbor family for two weeks, then moved when the church found a house for them to rent.

Chinh found a job at Glasstech, Inc., within two weeks, while Nancy took English lessons. But Nancy said she quickly knew that life in a rural community wasn't for her, and started urging her husband to move the family closer to Toledo.

Eventually, Mrs. Pham borrowed money from her brother and the family bought a small house in east Toledo.

She sewed clothes for a next door neighbor, made and sold egg rolls, cleaned people's houses, and worked as a lunchtime waitress. Along the way, she had Thomas, now 10.

But always, always she was dreaming.

"There was a lot of things I want to do, but I have no money and I can't stand it," she said.

"I've always had my dreams. I dream all the time and I think I can do anything," she says. While working as a waitress she said she dreamed of someday having her own business.

She became a student at Ma Chere Hair Style Academy, and later a manicurist, renting space at Paul & Co.

Louise Hedge, owner of Ma Chere, said she never had any doubt that Nancy Pham would someday have her own shop.

"I'm not surprised because that was her goal. She really wanted it and kept telling me that," Miss Hedge said. "She was an excellent student because she had a lot of personality. I don't mind having them when they really want it." Mrs. Pham remembers having difficulty with the language, and over-compensating by taping lectures and memorizing them while she made egg rolls.

She spent most of the 1980s working at Paul & Co., but always dreaming of her own shop.

"I like to be my own boss and I want to treat employees fair and equal. I like to take and give. I don't want people who only take and don't give," she said.

This year, Mrs. Pham got to be her own boss when her husband noticed that the church at the corner of McCord and Sylvania roads was up for sale.

He wanted to open a restaurant in the old church, but after Mrs. Pham convinced him that would be too much work, she broached the idea of a beauty salon.

Donna Pollex, an agent with Loss Realty Co. who handled the deal, had nothing but praise for the Phams.

"They are fantastic people. They're very dedicated and very honest and try to please people and I wish them lots of success," she said. "They just brought themselves up from nothing and I know they will be successful. The hours she puts in are incredible and it's really a family affair. The husband does the yard and the daughter handles appointments and both sons also help out."

"They are very, very hard working people," she said.

With the help of workers, the church was remodeled into a beauty salon which opened about three months ago.

Mrs. Pham said she doesn't worry about whether her business will be a success.

My Notes

"What you want to do, you should do. You may lose money, but you do not lose what you want to do," she said. "I don't worry about being famous or about being rich. I ... want to have a beauty salon for everyone."

It is an attitude that sits well with her eight employees.

Madonna Fong, a hair stylist at Fifth Avenue, said she has been in the beauty business for 16 years and has worked at a lot of salons that have been "temples of egos."

"[Nancy] is very kind, very caring," she said. "And she has such a great sense of peace in herself."

Mrs. Pham said if she seems peaceful, it's only because she still has dreams.

"If I stopped dreaming, that means I already died," she said.

Mary-Beth McLaughlin is a newspaper journalist for the Toledo Blade.

Sentence Analysis

Analyzing sentence structure can help you improve your writing. Analyze the excerpt you read from Dan Rather's "They Live the Dream" by completing the following chart as your teacher directs. Afterward, reflect on what the chart tells you about this particular text. What might using this sentence opening sheet (SOS) chart tell you about your own writing?

Sentence Number	First Four Words	Special Features: Figurative Language	Verbs	Number of Words per Sentence
1	She started her company		started	

Writing Prompt: What generalizations can you make about the text you are analyzing using the information you have gathered?

Next revisit your one-page response from Activity 1.6 and analyze your sentence structure.

Money and the American Dream

Money Quotes

The love of money is the root of all evil. (from *The Bible*)

Remember that time is money. (*Benjamin Franklin*)

Put not your trust in money, but your money in trust. (*Oliver Wendell Holmes*)

A good reputation is more valuable than money. (*Publilius Syrus*)

If money be not thy servant, it will be thy master. (*Sir Francis Bacon*)

The safest way to double your money is to fold it over twice and put it in your pocket. (*Frank McKinney Hubbard*)

Those who believe money can do everything are frequently prepared to do everything for money. (*George Savile*)

There's no money in poetry, but then there's no poetry in money, either. (*Robert Graves*)

Mammon, *n.*: The god of the world's leading religion. (*Ambrose Bierce*)

Money cannot buy happiness. (*Anonymous*)

A fool and his money are soon parted. (*Benjamin Franklin*)

A penny saved is a penny earned. (*Benjamin Franklin*)

Money is like manure. If you spread it around, it does a lot of good, but if you pile it up in one place, it stinks like hell. (*Thornton Wilder*)

MONEY

by Dana Gioia

My Notes

> **ABOUT THE AUTHOR**
>
> After fifteen years in a business career, Dana Gioia became a full-time writer in 1992. He is a literary and music critic, poet, and radio commentator who has also served as the Chairman for the National Endowment of the Arts. His essay "Can Poetry Matter?" is considered one of the most influential literary criticisms in the last quarter century.

Money, the long green,
cash, stash, rhino, jack
or just plain dough.

Chock it up, fork it over,
shell it out. Watch it
burn holes through pockets.   5

To be made of it! To have it
to burn! Greenbacks, double eagles,
megabucks and Ginnie Maes.

It greases the palm, feathers a nest,   10
holds heads above water,
makes both ends meet.

Money breeds money.
Gathering interest, compounding daily.
Always in circulation.   15

Money. You don't know where it's been,
but you put it where your mouth is.
And it talks.

Money Personified

1. After reading and discussing this poem, look at the definition of *personification*. Then, skim the poem and find examples of how money is personified. Underline your examples.

2. If money could talk, what would it say? Draft a monologue assuming the voice of money.

> **LITERARY TERMS**
> **Personification** is a figure of speech that describes an object as having human qualities.

Drama

ABOUT THE AUTHOR

Lorraine Hansberry (1930–1965) grew up in Chicago in an educated, successful and activist family. Her father moved the family into a white neighborhood to challenge discriminatory housing practices. Her play, a huge literary and commercial success that won significant awards, was developed out of that experience.

From A RAISIN IN THE SUN

by Lorraine Hansberry

Walter: No — there ain't no woman! Why do women always think there's a woman somewhere when a man gets restless. *(coming to her)* Mama — Mama — I want so many things…

Mama: Yes, son —

Walter: I want so many things that they are driving me kind of crazy… Mama — look at me.

Mama: I'm looking at you. You a good-looking boy. You got a job, a nice wife, a fine boy and —

Walter: A job. *(looks at her)* Mama, a job? I open and close car doors all day long. I drive a man around in his limousine and I say, "Yes sir; no, sir; very good, sir; shall I take the Drive, sir?" Mama, that ain't no kind of job… that ain't nothing at all. *(very quietly)* Mama, I don't know if I can make you understand.

Mama: Understand what, baby?

Walter: *(quietly)* Sometimes it's like I can see the future stretched out in front of me — just plain as day. The future, Mama. Hanging over there at the edge of my days. Just waiting for me — a big, looming blank space — full of nothing. Just waiting for me. *(pause)* Mama — sometimes when I'm downtown and I pass them cool, quiet-looking restaurants where them white boys are sitting back and talking 'bout things… sitting there turning deals worth millions of dollars… sometimes I see guys don't look much older than me —

Mama: Son — how come you talk so much 'bout money?

My Notes

Walter: *(with immense passion)* Because it is life, Mama!

Mama: *(quietly).* Oh — *(very quietly)* So now it's life. Money is life. Once upon a time freedom used to be life — now it's money. I guess the world really do change…

Walter: No — it was always money, Mama. We just didn't know about it.

Mama: No… something has changed. *(She looks at him.)* You something new, boy. In my time we was worried about not being lynched and getting to the North if we could and how to stay alive and still have a pinch of dignity too… Now here come you and Beneatha — talking 'bout things we ain't never even thought about hardly, me and your daddy. You ain't satisfied or proud of nothing we done. I mean that you had a home; that we kept you out of trouble till you was grown; that you don't have to ride to work on the back of nobody's streetcar — You my children — but how different we done become.

Walter: *(a long beat. He pats her hand and gets up.)* You just don't understand, Mama, you just don't understand.

Mama: Son — do you know your wife is expecting another baby? (WALTER *stands, stunned, and absorbs what his mother has said.)* That's what she wanted to talk to you about. (Walter *sinks down into a chair.)* This ain't for me to be telling — but you ought to know. *(She waits.)* I think Ruth is thinking 'bout getting rid of that child.

Walter: *(slowly understanding)* No — no — Ruth wouldn't do that.

Mama: When the world gets ugly enough — a woman will do anything for her family. The part that's already living.

Walter: You don't know Ruth, Mama, if you think she would do that.

(Ruth *opens the bedroom door and stands there a little limp.)*

Ruth: *(beaten)* Yes I would too, Walter. *(pause)* I gave her a five-dollar down payment.

(There is total silence as the man stares at his wife and the mother stares at her son.)

Mama: *(presently)* Well — *(tightly)* Well — son, I'm waiting to hear you say something… I'm waiting to hear how you be your father's son. Be the man he was… *(pause)* You wife say she going to destroy your child. And I'm waiting to hear you talk like him and say we a people who give children life, not who destroys them — *(She rises.)* I'm waiting to see you stand up and look like your daddy and say we done give up one baby to poverty and that we ain't going to give up nary another one… I'm waiting.

Walter: Ruth —

Mama: If you a son of mine, tell her! (Walter *turns, looks at her and can say nothing. She continues, bitterly.)* You… you are a disgrace to your father's memory. Somebody get me my hat.

My Notes

Short Story

> **ABOUT THE AUTHOR**
> Born William Sydney Porter in 1862, O. Henry used a variety of pen names while writing short stories during a prison sentence for embezzlement. Upon release, he chose to become O. Henry and moved to New York City, where he became a prolific writer of popular short stories. His stories are known for their surprise endings.

MAMMON AND THE ARCHER

by O. Henry

Old Anthony Rockwall, retired manufacturer and proprietor of Rockwall's Eureka Soap, looked out the library window of his Fifth Avenue mansion and grinned. His neighbor to the right — the aristocratic clubman, G. Van Schuylight-Suffolk Jones — came out to his waiting motor-car, wrinkling a contumelious[1] nostril, as usual, at the Italian renaissance sculpture of the soap palace's front elevation.

"Stuck-up old statuette of nothing doing!" commented the ex-Soap King. "The Eden Musee'll get that old frozen Nesselrode yet if he don't watch out. I'll have this house painted red, white, and blue next summer and see if that'll make his Dutch nose turn up any higher."

And then Anthony Rockwall, who never cared for bells, went to the door of his library and shouted "Mike!" in the same voice that had once chipped off pieces of the welkin on the Kansas prairies.

"Tell my son," said Anthony to the answering menial,[2] "to come in here before he leaves the house."

When young Rockwall entered the library the old man laid aside his newspaper, looked at him with a kindly grimness on his big, smooth, ruddy countenance,[3] rumpled his mop of white hair with one hand and rattled the keys in his pocket with the other.

---

[1] **contumelious**: like or having to do with a humiliating insult
[2] **menial**: servant
[3] **countenance**: facial expression

"Richard," said Anthony Rockwall, "what do you pay for the soap that you use?"

Richard, only six months home from college, was startled a little. He had not yet taken the measure of this sire of his, who was as full of unexpectednesses as a girl at her first party.

"Six dollars a dozen, I think, dad."

"And your clothes?"

"I suppose about sixty dollars, as a rule."

"You're a gentleman," said Anthony, decidedly. "I've heard of these young bloods spending $24 a dozen for soap, and going over the hundred mark for clothes. You've got as much money to waste as any of 'em, and yet you stick to what's decent and moderate. Now I use the old Eureka — not only for sentiment, but it's the purest soap made. Whenever you pay more than 10 cents a cake for soap you buy bad perfumes and labels. But 50 cents is doing very well for a young man in your generation, position and condition. As I said, you're a gentleman. They say it takes three generations to make one. They're off. Money'll do it as slick as soap grease. It's made you one. By hokey! it's almost made one of me. I'm nearly as impolite and disagreeable and ill-mannered as these two old Knickerbocker gents on each side of me that can't sleep of nights because I bought in between 'em."

"There are some things that money can't accomplish," remarked young Rockwall, rather gloomily.

"Now, don't say that," said old Anthony, shocked. "I bet my money on money every time. I've been through the encyclopedia down to Y looking for something that you can't buy with it; and I expect to have to take up the appendix next week. I'm for money against the field. Tell me something money won't buy."

"For one thing," answered Richard, rankling a little, "it won't buy one into the exclusive circles of society."

"Oho! won't it?" thundered the champion of the root of evil. "You tell me where your exclusive circles would be if the first Astor hadn't had the money to pay for his steerage passage over?"

Richard sighed.

"And that's what I was coming to," said the old man, less boisterously. "That's why I asked you to come in. There's something going wrong with you, boy. I've been noticing it for two weeks. Out with it. I guess I could lay my hands on eleven millions within twenty-four hours, besides the real estate. If it's your liver, there's the *Rambler* down in the bay, coaled, and ready to steam down to the Bahamas in two days."

GRAMMAR & USAGE

O. Henry's syntax includes a variety of **clauses**. Look at these examples of noun and adjective clauses:

...some things *that money can't accomplish.* (adjective clause modifying *things*)

... You tell me *where your exclusive circles would be....* (noun clause as direct object)

And that's *what I was coming to....* (noun clause as predicate nominative)

Anthony Rockwall, *who never cared for bells,...* (adjective clause modifying *Anthony Rockwall*)

An elliptical clause is one in which words are omitted but understood.

Tell me something [that] money won't buy.

The relative pronoun *that* is omitted but clearly understood.

Money and the American Dream

My Notes

"Not a bad guess, dad; you haven't missed it far."

"Ah," said Anthony, keenly; "what's her name?"

Richard began to walk up and down the library floor. There was enough comradeship and sympathy in this crude old father of his to draw his confidence.

"Why don't you ask her?" demanded old Anthony. "She'll jump at you. You've got the money and the looks, and you're a decent boy. Your hands are clean. You've got no Eureka soap on 'em. You've been to college, but she'll overlook that."

"I haven't had a chance," said Richard.

"Make one," said Anthony. "Take her for a walk in the park, or a straw ride or walk home with her from church. Chance! Pshaw!"

"You don't know the social mill, dad. She's part of the stream that turns it. Every hour and minute of her time is arranged for days in advance. I must have that girl, dad, or this town is a blackjack swamp forevermore. And I can't write it. I can't do that."

"Tut!" said the old man. "Do you mean to tell me that with all the money I've got you can't get an hour or two of a girl's time for yourself?"

"I've put it off too late. She's going to sail for Europe at noon day after tomorrow for a two years' stay. I'm to see her alone tomorrow evening for a few minutes. She's at Larchmont now at her aunt's. I can't go there. But I'm allowed to meet her with a cab at the Grand Central Station tomorrow evening at the 8:30 train. We drive down Broadway to Wallack's at a gallop, where her mother and a box party will be waiting for us in the lobby. Do you think she would listen to a declaration from me during that six or eight minutes under those circumstances? No. And what chance would I have in the theatre or afterward? None. No, dad, this is one tangle that your money can't unravel. We can't buy one minute of time with cash; if we could, rich people would live longer. There's no hope of getting a talk with Miss Lantry before she sails."

"All right, Richard, my boy," said old Anthony, cheerfully. "You may run along down to your club now. I'm glad it ain't your liver. But don't forget to burn a few punk sticks in the joss house to the great god Mazuma from time to time. You say money won't buy time? Well, of course, you can't order eternity wrapped up and delivered at your residence for a price, but I've seen Father Time get pretty bad stone bruises on his heels when he walked through the gold diggings."

That night came Aunt Ellen, gentle, sentimental, wrinkled, sighing, oppressed by wealth, in to Brother Anthony at his evening paper, and began discourse on the subject of lovers' woes.

"He told me all about it," said Brother Anthony, yawning. "I told him my bank account was at his service. And then he began to knock money. Said money couldn't help. Said the rules of society couldn't be bucked for a yard by a team of ten-millionaires."

"Oh, Anthony," sighed Aunt Ellen, "I wish you would not think so much of money. Wealth is nothing where a true affection is concerned. Love is all-powerful. If he only had spoken earlier! She could not have refused our Richard. But now I fear it is too late. He will have no opportunity to address her. All your gold cannot bring happiness to your son."

At eight o'clock the next evening Aunt Ellen took a quaint old gold ring from a moth-eaten case and gave it to Richard.

"Wear it tonight, nephew," she begged. "Your mother gave it to me. Good luck in love she said it brought. She asked me to give it to you when you had found the one you loved."

Young Rockwall took the ring reverently[4] and tried it on his smallest finger. It slipped as far as the second joint and stopped. He took it off and stuffed it into his vest pocket, after the manner of man. And then he phoned for his cab.

At the station he captured Miss Lantry out of the gadding mob at eight thirty-two.

"We mustn't keep mamma and the others waiting," said she.

"To Wallack's Theatre as fast as you can drive!" said Richard loyally.

They whirled up Forty-second to Broadway, and then down the white-starred lane that leads from the soft meadows of sunset to the rocky hills of morning.

At Thirty-fourth Street young Richard quickly thrust up the trap and ordered the cabman to stop.

"I've dropped a ring," he apologized, as he climbed out. "It was my mother's and I'd hate to lose it. I won't detain you a minute — I saw where it fell."

In less than a minute he was back in the cab with the ring.

But within that minute a crosstown car had stopped directly in front of the cab. The cab-man tried to pass to the left, but a heavy express wagon cut him off. He tried the right and had to back away from a furniture van that had no business to be there. He tried to back out, but dropped his reins and swore dutifully. He was blockaded in a tangled mess of vehicles and horses.

---

[4] **reverently**: deeply respectful

Money and the American Dream

My Notes

One of those street blockades had occurred that sometimes tie up commerce and movement quite suddenly in the big city.

"Why don't you drive on?" said Miss Lantry impatiently. "We'll be late."

Richard stood up in the cab and looked around. He saw a congested flood of wagons, trucks, cabs, vans, and street cars filling the vast space where Broadway, Sixth Avenue, and Thirty-fourth Street cross one another as a twenty-six inch maiden fills her twenty-two inch girdle. And still from all the cross streets they were hurrying and rattling toward the converging point at full speed, and hurling themselves into the straggling mass, locking wheels and adding their drivers' imprecations to the clamor. The entire traffic of Manhattan seemed to have jammed itself around them. The oldest New Yorker among the thousands of spectators that lined the sidewalks had not witnessed a street blockade of the proportions of this one.

"I'm very sorry," said Richard, as he resumed his seat, "but it looks as if we are stuck. They won't get this jumble loosened up in an hour. It was my fault. If I hadn't dropped the ring we — "

"Let me see the ring," said Miss Lantry. "Now that it can't be helped, I don't care. I think theatres are stupid, anyway."

At 11 o'clock that night somebody tapped lightly on Anthony Rockwall's door.

"Come in," shouted Anthony, who was in a red dressing-gown, reading a book of piratical adventures.

Somebody was Aunt Ellen, looking like a gray-haired angel that had been left on earth by mistake.

"They're engaged, Anthony," she said, softly. "She has promised to marry our Richard. On their way to the theatre there was a street blockade, and it was two hours before their cab could get out of it."

"And oh, brother Anthony, don't ever boast of the power of money again. A little emblem of true love — a little ring that symbolized unending and unmercenary affection — was the cause of our Richard finding his happiness. He dropped it in the street, and got out to recover it. And before they could continue the blockade occurred. He spoke to his love and won her there while the cab was hemmed in. Money is dross compared with true love, Anthony."

"All right," said old Anthony. "I'm glad the boy has got what he wanted. I told him I wouldn't spare any expense in the matter if — "

"But, Brother Anthony, what good could your money have done?"

"Sister," said Anthony Rockwall. "I've got my pirate in a devil of a scrape. His ship has just been scuttled, and he's too good a judge of the value of money to let drown. I wish you would let me go on with this chapter."

The story should end here. I wish it would as heartily as you who read it wish it did. But we must go to the bottom of the well for the truth.

The next day a person with red hands and a blue polka-dot necktie, who called himself Kelly, called at Anthony Rockwall's house, and was at once received in the library.

"Well," said Anthony, reaching for his check-book, "it was a good bilin' of soap. Let's see — you had $5,000 in cash."

"I paid out $300 more of my own," said Kelly. "I had to go a little above the estimate. I got the express wagons and cabs mostly for $5; but the trucks and two-horse teams mostly raised me to $10. The motormen wanted $10, and some of the loaded teams $20. The cops struck me hardest — $50 I paid two, and the rest $20 and $25. But didn't it work beautiful, Mr. Rockwall? I'm glad William A. Brady wasn't onto that little outdoor vehicle mob scene. I wouldn't want William to break his heart with jealousy. And never a rehearsal, either! The boys was on time to the fraction of a second. It was two hours before a snake could get below Greeley's statue."

"Thirteen hundred — there you are, Kelly," said Anthony, tearing off a check. "Your thousand, and the $300 you were out. You don't despise money, do you, Kelly?"

"Me?" said Kelly. "I can lick the man that invented poverty."

Anthony called Kelly when he was at the door.

"You didn't notice," said he, "anywhere in the tie-up, a kind of fat boy without any clothes on shooting arrows around with a bow, did you?"

"Why, no," said Kelly, mystified. "I didn't. If he was like you say, maybe the cops pinched him before I got there."

"I thought the little rascal wouldn't be on hand," chuckled Anthony. "Good-bye, Kelly."

SUGGESTED LEARNING STRATEGIES: Graphic Organizer,
Think-Pair-Share, Marking the Text

My Notes

Song

HARLAN MAN

by Steve Earle

I'm a Harlan Man
Went down in the mine when I was barely grown
It was easy then
'Cause I didn't know what I know now
5   But I'm a family man
And it's the only life that I've ever known
But I'm a Harlan Man
Just as long as my luck and lungs hold out

I'm a mountain man
10   Born in east Kentucky and here I'll stay
And if it's the good Lord's plan
I'll wake up in the mornin' and find
I'm lookin' at the end
Of another long week and I can draw my pay
15   'Cause I'm a Harlan Man
Never catch me whinin' cause I ain't that kind

I'm a union man
Just like my daddy and all my kin
I took a union stand
20   No matter what the company said
I got me two good hands
And just as long as I'm able I won't give in
'Cause I'm a Harlan Man
A coal minin' mother 'til the day I'm dead

Song

The Mountain

by Steve Earle

I was born on this mountain a long time ago
Before they knocked down the timber and strip-mined the coal
When you rose in the mornin' before it was light
To go down in that dark hole and come back up at night

I was born on this mountain, this mountain's my home   5
She holds me and keeps me from worry and woe
Well, they took everything that she gave, now they're gone
But I'll die on this mountain, this mountain's my home

I was young on this mountain but now I am old
And I knew every holler, every cool swimmin' hole   10
'Til one night I lay down and woke up to find
That my childhood was over and I went down in the mine

There's a hole in this mountain and it's dark and it's deep
And God only knows all the secrets it keeps
There's a chill in the air only miners can feel   15
There're ghosts in the tunnels that the company sealed

My Notes

Listen While You Work

As you listen to the songs or read the lyrics, fill in the chart in order to get a sense of the speakers' perspectives on work.

Title	What is the speaker's age? What makes you come to this conclusion?	What are the speaker's feelings about the job? Why?	What is the theme of the song? Support your response.

Song 1: _____   Song 2: _____

Thesis Statement: Compose a thesis statement comparing the two speakers. Support your statement with a paragraph of explanation.

Thesis Statement:

Support Paragraph:

My Notes

Poetry

ABOUT THE AUTHOR

Martín Espada is an award-winning poet who was born in 1957 in Brooklyn, N.Y. One of his books, *The Republic of Poetry,* was a finalist for the Pulitzer Prize in Poetry.

Who Burns *for the* Perfection *of* Paper

by Martín Espada

At sixteen, I worked after high school hours
at a printing plant
that manufactured legal pads:
Yellow paper
5   stacked seven feet high
and leaning
as I slipped cardboard
between the pages,
then brushed red glue
10   up and down the stack.
No gloves: fingertips required
for the perfection of paper,
smoothing the exact rectangle.
Sluggish by 9 PM, the hands
15   would slide along suddenly sharp paper,
and gather slits thinner than the crevices
of the skin, hidden.
Then the glue would sting,
hands oozing
20   till both palms burned
at the punchclock.

Ten years later, in law school,
I knew that every legal pad
was glued with the sting of hidden cuts,
25   that every open lawbook
was a pair of hands
upturned and burning.

As you read the poem, "Who Burns for the Perfection of Paper," complete the following chart:

"Who Burns for the Perfection of Paper"

Choose a statement that reflects what the speaker learned from his work.	
Write a description, and then create a visual of the last image of the poem.	
What do you think the title means?	
Write an interpretive statement about the speaker's realization.	

Working Toward the Dream

Complete the following SOAPSTone to analyze the interview "Roberto Acuna Talks About Farm Workers," recorded by Studs Terkel.

Speaker What can you say about the speaker based on references in the text? Is race, gender, class, or age important?	
Occasion What issues may have motivated the speaker to think about the incident or occasion?	
Audience Who is being addressed? Identify some characteristics of the audience.	
Purpose What is the message and how does the author want the audience to respond?	
Subject What is the focus? The subject can be stated by using a few words.	
Tone Using textual support, how would you describe the overall tone of the passage?	

Roberto Acuna Talks
About Farm Workers

from Working

by Studs Terkel

> **ABOUT THE AUTHOR**
> Studs Terkel (1912–2008), famous Chicago radio broadcaster, interviewer, and writer, was born Louis Terkel in New York. A Pulitzer Prize winner, Terkel wrote more than two dozen books, but he is probably most famous for his oral histories.

I walked out of the fields two years ago. I saw the need to change the California feudal system, to change the lives of farm workers, to make these huge corporations feel they're not above anybody. I am thirty-four years old and I try to organize for the United Farm Workers of America....

If you're picking lettuce, the thumbnails fall off 'cause they're banged on the box. Your hands get swollen. You can't slow down because the foreman sees you're so many boxes behind and you'd better get on. But people would help each other. If you're feeling bad that day, somebody who's feeling pretty good would help. Any people that are suffering have to stick together, whether they like it or not, whether they be black, brown, or pink....

I began to see how everything was so wrong. When growers can have an intricate watering system to irrigate their crops but they can't have running water inside the houses of workers. Veterinarians tend to the needs of domestic animals but they can't have medical care for the workers. They can have land subsidies[1] for the growers but they can't have adequate unemployment compensation for the workers. They treat him like a farm implement. In fact, they treat their implements better and their domestic animals better. They have heat and insulated[2] barns for the animals but the workers live in beat-up shacks with no heat at all.

Illness in the fields is 120 percent higher than the average rate for industry. It's mostly back trouble, rheumatism, and arthritis, because of the damp weather and the cold. Stoop labor is very hard on a person. Tuberculosis is high. And now because of the pesticides, we have many respiratory diseases.

The University of California at Davis had government experiments with pesticides and chemicals. They get a bigger crop each year. They haven't any

---

[1] **subsidy**: a grant or contribution of money
[2] **insulate**: to surround or fill with material that prevents the passage of heat or cold

My Notes

GRAMMAR & USAGE

Repeating a grammatical structure, even one as simple as an infinitive phrase, creates rhythm and emphasis through parallel structure. Notice that Roberto Acuna emphasizes his commitment with parallel infinitive phrases modifying *need*: "I saw the need to change the California feudal system, to change the lives of farm workers, to make these huge corporations feel they're not above anybody."

WORD
CONNECTIONS

Pesticide is a hybrid word from the English word *pest* and *–cide*, which comes from the Latin word *cidium* meaning "a killing." Other words based on *cidium* include *homicide* and *suicide*.

My Notes

regard as to what safety precautions are needed. In 1964 and '65, an airplane was spraying these chemicals on the fields. Spraying rigs they're called. Flying low, the wheels got tangled in the fence wire. The pilot got up, dusted himself off, and got a drink of water. He died of convulsions. The ambulance attendants got violently sick because of the pesticide he had on his person. A little girl was playing around a sprayer. She stuck her tongue on it. She died instantly.

These pesticides affect the farm worker through the lungs. He breathes it in. He gets no compensation. All they do is say he's sick. They don't investigate the cause.

There were times when I felt I couldn't take it anymore. It was 105 in the shade and I'd see endless rows of lettuce and I felt my back hurting…. I felt the frustration of not being able to get out of the fields. I was getting ready to jump any foreman who looked at me cross-eyed. But until two years ago, my world was still very small.

I would read all these things in the papers about Cesar Chavez and I would denounce[3] him because I still had that thing about becoming a first class patriotic citizen. In Mexicali[4] they would pass out leaflets and I would throw 'em away. I never participated. The grape boycott didn't affect me much because I was in lettuce. It wasn't until Chavez came to Salinas[5] where I was working in the fields, that I saw what a beautiful man he was. I went to this rally, I still intended to stay with the company. But something — I don't know — I was close to the workers. They couldn't speak English and wanted me to be their spokesman in favor of going on strike. I don't know — I just got caught up with it all, the beautiful feeling of solidarity.

You'd see the people on the picket lines at four in the morning, at the camp fires, heating up beans and coffee and tortillas. It gave me a sense of belonging. These were my own people and they wanted change. I knew this is what I was looking for. I just didn't know it before.

My mom had always wanted me to better myself. I wanted to better myself because of her. Now when the strikes started, I told her I was going to join the union and the whole movement. I told her I was going to work without pay. She said she was proud of me. (His eyes glisten. A long, long pause.) See, I told her I wanted to be with my people. If I were a company man, no one would like me anymore. I had to belong to somebody and this was it right here. She said, "I pushed you in your early years to try to better yourself and get a social position. But I see that's not the answer. I know I'll be proud of you."

All kinds of people are farm workers, not just Chicanos. Filipinos started the strike. We have Puerto Ricans and Appalachians too, Arabs, some

---

[3] **denounce:** to openly condemn or censure
[4] **Mexicali** (mek′ si kal′ ē): capital of the Mexican state of Baja California Norte
[5] **Salinas** (sə lē′nəs): city in west central California

Japanese, some Chinese. At one time they used us against each other. But now they can't and they're scared, the growers. They can organize conglomerates. Yet when we try organization to better our lives, they are afraid. Suffering people never dreamed it could be different. Cesar Chavez tells them this and they grasp the idea — and this is what scares the growers.

Now the machines are coming in. It takes skill to operate them. But anybody can be taught. We feel migrant workers should be given the chance. They got one for grapes. They got one for lettuce. They have cotton machines that took jobs away from thousands of farm workers. The people wind up in the ghettos of the cities, their culture, their families, their unity destroyed.

We're trying to stipulate[6] it in our contract that the company will not use any machinery without the consent of the farm workers. So we can make sure the people being replaced by the machines will know how to operate the machines.

Working in the fields is not in itself a degrading job. It's hard, but if you're given regular hours, better pay, decent housing, unemployment, and medical compensation, pension plans — we have a very relaxed way of living. But growers don't recognize us as persons. That's the worst thing, the way they treat you. Like we have no brains. Now we see they have no brains. They have only a wallet in their head. The more you squeeze it the more they cry out.

If we had proper compensation we wouldn't have to be working seventeen hours a day and following the crops. We could stay in one area and it would give us roots. Being a migrant, it tears the family apart. You get in debt. You leave the area penniless. The children are the ones hurt the most. They go to school three months in one place and then on to another. No sooner do they make friends, they are uprooted again. Right here, your childhood is taken away. So when they grow up, they're looking for this childhood they have lost.

If people could see — in the winter, ice on the fields. We'd be on our knees all day long. We'd build fires and warm up real fast and go back onto the ice. We'd be picking watermelons in 105 degrees all day long. When people have melons or cucumber or carrots or lettuce, they don't know how they got on their table and the consequences to the people who picked it. If I had enough money, I would take busloads of people out to the fields and into the labor camps. Then they'd know how that fine salad got on their table.

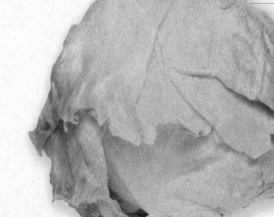

WORD CONNECTIONS

The Latin term *quid pro quo* means an equal exchange or substitution. For example, in a work situation, the employee receives wages, and the employer receives the work done. Whether the two are of equal value is sometimes a point of dispute.

My Notes

---

[6] **stipulate**: to lay down a condition of an agreement

With Liberty and Access to All?

SUGGESTED LEARNING STRATEGIES: Double-Entry Journal,
Discussion Groups

Use information from *Nickel and Dimed: On (Not) Getting By in America* to complete this double-entry journal. Your journal should include at least five quotes from the excerpt that contain something that "grabs" your attention or emotions. On the left side of the journal, copy the text portion, along with the paragraph number. On the right side of the journal, write your response to the quote. Use additional paper if necessary.

Double-Entry Journal

Quoted Material from the Text	Paragraph Number	The Effect of the Quote on You

From
NICKEL AND DIMED:

On (Not) Getting By in America

by Barbara Ehrenreich

ABOUT THE AUTHOR
Barbara Ehrenreich, a social activist, feminist, and political essayist has written for several well-known publications about controversial topics such as health care, war, families, and women's issues. In the excerpt here, she writes about working for a maid service in Maine, part of her experience of working with the nation's "working poor" in entry-level jobs.

My Notes

1 … So here I am on my knees, working my way around the room like some fanatical penitent crawling through the stations of the cross, when I realize that Mrs. W. is staring at me fixedly—so fixedly that I am gripped for a moment by the wild possibility that I may have once given a lecture at her alma mater and she's trying to figure out where she's seen me before. If I were recognized, would I be fired? Would she at least be inspired to offer me a drink of water? Because I have decided that if water is actually offered, I'm taking it, rules or no rules, and if word of this infraction gets back to Ted, I'll just say I thought it would be rude to refuse. Not to worry, though. She's just watching that I don't leave out some stray square inch, and when I rise painfully to my feet again, blinking through the sweat, she says, "Could you just scrub the floor in the entryway while you're at it?"

2 I rush home to the Blue Haven at the end of the day, pull down the blinds for privacy, strip off my uniform in the kitchen—the bathroom being too small for both a person and her discarded clothes—and stand in the shower for a good ten minutes, thinking all this water is *mine*. I have paid for it, in fact, I have earned it. I have gotten through a week at The Maids without mishap, injury, or insurrection. My back feels fine, meaning I'm not feeling it at all; even my wrists, damaged by carpal tunnel syndrome years ago, are issuing no complaints. Coworkers warned me that the first time they donned the backpack vacuum they felt faint, but not me. I am strong and I am, more than that, good. Did I toss my bucket of filthy water onto Mrs. W.'s casual white summer outfit? No. Did I take the wand of my vacuum cleaner and smash someone's Chinese porcelain statues or Hummel figurines? Not once. I was at all times cheerful, energetic, helpful, and as competent as a new hire can be

My Notes

expected to be. If I can do one week, I can do another, and might as well, since there's never been a moment for job-hunting. The 3:30 quitting time turns out to be a myth; often we don't return to the office until 4:30 or 5:00. And what did I think? That I was going to go out to interviews in my soaked and stinky postwork condition? I decide to reward myself with a sunset walk on Old Orchard Beach.

3   On account of the heat, there are still a few actual bathers on the beach, but I am content to sit in shorts and T-shirt and watch the ocean pummel the sand. When the sun goes down I walk back into the town to find my car and am amazed to hear a sound I associate with cities like New York and Berlin. There's a couple of Peruvian musicians playing in the little grassy island in the street near the pier, and maybe fifty people—locals and vacationers—have gathered around, offering their bland end-of-summer faces to the sound. I edge my way through the crowd and find a seat where I can see the musicians up close—the beautiful young guitarist and the taller man playing the flute. What are they doing in this rinky-dink blue-collar resort, and what does the audience make of this surprise visit from the dark-skinned South? The melody the flute lays out over the percussion is both utterly strange and completely familiar, as if it had been imprinted in the minds of my own peasant ancestors centuries ago and forgotten until this very moment. Everyone else seems to be as transfixed as I am. The musicians wink and smile at each other as they play, and I see then that they are the secret emissaries of a worldwide lower-class conspiracy to snatch joy out of degradation and filth. When the song ends, I give them a dollar, the equivalent of about ten minutes of sweat.

4   The superwoman mood does not last. For one thing, while the muscles and joints are doing just fine, the skin has decided to rebel. At first I think the itchy pink bumps on my arms and legs must be poison ivy picked up at a lockout. Sometimes an owner forgets we are coming or forgets to leave a key under the mat or changes his or her mind about the service without thinking to notify Ted. This is not, for us, an occasion for joy like a snow day for the grade-school crowd, because Ted blames us for his customers' fecklessness. When owners forget we are coming, he explains at one of our morning send-off meetings, it "means something," like that they're dissatisfied and too passive-aggressive to tell us. Once, when I am with Pauline as my team leader, she calls Ted to report a lockout and his response, she reports ruefully, is, "Don't do this to me." So before we give up and declare a place a lockout, we search like cat burglars for alternative points of entry, which can mean trampling through overgrowth to peer into windows and test all the doors. I haven't seen any poison ivy, but who knows what other members of the poison family (oak, sumac, etc.) lurk in the flora of Maine?

Or maybe the cleaning fluids are at fault, except that then the rash should have begun on my hands. After two days of minor irritation, a full-scale epidermal breakdown is under way. I cover myself with anti-itch cream from Rite Aid but can manage to sleep only for an hour and a half at a time before the torment resumes. I wake up realizing I can work but probably shouldn't, if only because I look like a leper. Ted doesn't have much sympathy for illness, though; one of our morning meetings was on the subject of "working through it." Somebody, and he wasn't going to name names, he told us, was out with a migraine. "Now if I get a migraine I just pop two Excedrins and get on with my life. That's what you have to do—work through it." So it's in the spirit of a scientific experiment that I present myself at the office, wondering if my speckled and inflamed appearance will be enough to get me sent home. Certainly I wouldn't want anyone who looks like me handling my children's toys or bars of bathroom soap. But no problem. Must be latex allergy, is Ted's diagnosis. Just stay out of the latex gloves we use for particularly nasty work; he'll give me another kind to wear.

I should, if I were going to stay in character, find an emergency room after work and try to cop a little charitable care. But it's too much. The itching gets so bad at night that I have mini-tantrums, waving my arms and stamping my feet to keep from scratching or bawling. So I fall back on the support networks of my real-life social class, call the dermatologist I know in Key West, and bludgeon him into prescribing something sight unseen. The whole episode—including anti-itch cream, prednisone, prednisone cream, and Benadryl to get through the nights—eats up $30. It's still unseasonably hot, and I often get to look out on someone's azure pool while I vacuum or scrub, frantic with suppressed itching. Even the rash-free are affected by the juxtaposition of terrible heat and cool, inaccessible water. In the car on one of the hottest days, after cleaning a place with pool, pool house, and gazebo, Rosalie and Maddy and I obsess about immersion in all imaginable forms—salt water versus fresh, lakes versus pools, surf versus smooth, glasslike surfaces. We can't even wash our hands in the houses, at least not after the sinks have been dried and buffed, and when I do manage to get a wash in before the sinks are off-limits, there's always some filthy last-minute job like squeezing out the rags used on floors once we get out of a house. Maybe I picked up some bug at a house or maybe it's the disinfectant I squirt on my hands, straight from the bottle, in an attempt at cleanliness. Three days into the rash, I make another trip to Old Orchard Beach and wade into the water with my clothes on (I didn't think to bring a bathing suit from Key West to Maine), trying to pretend it's an accident when a wave washes over me and that I'm not just some pathetic street person using the beach as a bathtub.

5

6

With Liberty and Access to All?

7   There's something else working against my mood of muscular elation. I had been gloating internally about my ability to keep up with, and sometimes outwork, women twenty or thirty years younger than myself, but it turns out this comparative advantage says less about me than it does about them. Ours is a physical bond, to the extent that we bond at all. One person's infirmity can be a teammate's extra burden; there's a constant traffic in herbal and over-the-counter solutions to pain. If I don't know how my coworkers survive on their wages or what they make of our hellish condition, I do know about their back pains and cramps and arthritic attacks. Lori and Pauline are excused from vacuuming on account of their backs, which means you dread being assigned to a team with them. Helen has a bum foot, which Ted, in explaining her absence one day, blames on the cheap, ill-fitting shoes that, he implies, she perversely chooses to wear. Marge's arthritis makes scrubbing a torture; another woman has to see a physical therapist for her rotator cuff. When Rosalie tells me that she got her shoulder problem picking blueberries as a "kid"—she still is one in my eyes, of course—I flash on a scene from my own childhood, of wandering through fields on an intense July day, grabbing berries by the handful as I go. But when Rosalie was a kid she worked in the blueberry fields of northern Maine, and the damage to her shoulder is an occupational injury.

8   So ours is a world of pain—managed by Excedrin and Advil, compensated for with cigarettes and, in one or two cases and then only on weekends, booze. Do the owners have any idea of the misery that goes into rendering their homes motel-perfect? Would they be bothered if they did know, or would they take a sadistic pride in what they have purchased—boasting to dinner guests, for example that their floors are cleaned only with the purest of fresh human tears? In one of my few exchanges with an owner, a pert muscular woman whose desk reveals that she works part-time as a personal trainer, I am vacuuming and she notices the sweat. "That's a real workout, isn't it?" she observes, not unkindly, and actually offers me a glass of water, the only such offer I ever encounter. Flouting the rule against the ingestion of anything while inside a house, I take it, leaving an inch undrunk to avoid the awkwardness of a possible refill offer. "I tell all my clients, "the trainer informs me, "'If you want to be fit, just fire your cleaning lady and do it yourself.'" "Ho ho," is all I say, since we're not just chatting in the gym together and I can't explain that this form of exercise is totally asymmetrical, brutally repetitive, and as likely to destroy the musculoskeletal structure as to strengthen it.

The Structure of an Argument

You have been introduced to the structure of an argument. As a review, read through the five key elements that are usually found in a good argument.

1. **The Hook** (Setting readers up to agree with you)
   - The hook grabs the readers' attention and catches their interest.
   - It often establishes a connection between readers and writers and provides background information.
   - It can be, but is not limited to, an anecdote, an image, a definition, or a quotation.

2. **The Claim** (Your thesis, what you are arguing)
   - Usually comes in the opening section of your paper.
   - States your belief and what it is that you wish to argue.
   - Can be straightforward and clear, i.e. "I believe that…"

3. **Concessions and Refutations** (Build the other side up…then knock them down)
   - You recognize the arguments made by the other side.
   - You build credibility by being able to discuss the other side with (apparent) objectivity.
   - You grant that the other side has some validity, then…
   - Argue at length against the opposing viewpoint by proving your side has MORE validity.

4. **Support** (Start stacking your facts to convince them)
   - You set out the reasoning behind your argument.
   - Provide supporting evidence of your claim (data, quotes, anecdotes).
   - Blend together logical and emotional appeals.

5. **Call to Action** (The final word)
   - Draw your argument to a close and restate your claim.
   - Make a final new appeal to values.
   - Voice a final plea.
   - Try not to repeat information, but sum up your argument with a few final facts and appeals.

Writing Prompt: On a separate piece of paper, use the five elements of an argument to draft a response to one of the following prompts:

- Compose a letter to the maid service company stating problems the maids face. Provide suggestions for what the company can do to improve conditions.

- Compose a letter to a local newspaper citing a need for a change in the attitudes of people toward those in service occupations, particularly those who are maids and wear uniforms.

Creating a Survey About the American Dream

SUGGESTED LEARNING STRATEGIES: Brainstorming, Discussion Groups, Graphic Organizer

ACADEMIC VOCABULARY

A **survey** is a method of collecting data from a group of people. It can be written, such as a print or online questionnaire, or oral, such as an in-person interview.

Start with this assumption about Americans and money:

American teenagers are more obsessed with money than American adults.

Your job will be to prove or disprove this assumption by creating, conducting, and interpreting a **survey**. Individually, consider the following questions.

1. What groups of people will you need to survey?

2. What information will you need to gather about your respondents?

In small groups, brainstorm different types of questions that could appear on your survey. When you create a question that you think will be effective, write it on separate paper. When writing questions, remember to:

- Create a question that can be answered with a "yes" or "no" response.
- Write a question that can be answered numerically. For instance, you could ask respondents to rate something on a scale from 1 to 10.
- Write a question that asks respondents to categorize themselves. For instance, a political candidate might ask a respondent to state whether they are likely to vote, not likely to vote, or undecided.
- Write two questions that have open-ended responses — questions that need to be answered with words or phrases of the respondent's own choosing.

As a class, share your sample questions and with your teacher's help, come to consensus on the five questions that will give you the best information to prove or disprove the assumption. Be sure that you have asked for the respondent's age on your survey.

Your teacher will give you copies of your completed survey to distribute. Each student in your small group should plan on getting responses from at least ten people, being sure that half are teenagers and half are adults.

Gathering Data

1. Total number of respondents: _____

   Total number of adults: _____

   Total number of teenagers: _____

2. Calculate the percentage of your "yes" and "no" responses.

Adults:	Yes: _____	No: _____
Teenagers:	Yes: _____	No: _____
Overall:	Yes: _____	No: _____

3. Calculate the average of your numeric responses:

   Adults: _____

   Teenagers: _____

   Overall: _____

4. Calculate the percentages of respondents who identified themselves in particular categories:

	Adults	Teenagers	Overall
Category 1: _____	_____	_____	_____
Category 2: _____	_____	_____	_____
Category 3: _____	_____	_____	_____
Category 4: _____	_____	_____	_____

5. Look through the open-ended responses. Write down words and phrases that seem to be repeated by each group.

   Adults:

   Teenagers:

   Both groups:

Creating a Survey About the American Dream

Interpreting the Data

1. Summarize your findings in the space below. Did you prove or disprove the assumption about American teenagers and adults and money? Are the results inconclusive? Explain your answer, referring to the specific percentages you calculated on the previous page.

Presenting the Data

2. The circle below represents 100 percent of the respondents to the survey. Write one of your numeric questions above the circle and shade in different colors the percentage of teenagers who responded one way and the percentage of adults who responded the same way.

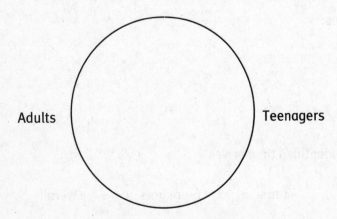

Adults   Teenagers

3. What other methods of presenting data visually might work for your survey?

4. Select an idea from the mock survey, and create a visual representation (such as a graph, chart, table, map, or diagram) to convey supporting data. Be prepared to explain how this visual supports the survey data, anticipates reader's questions, and aids comprehension of the information.

Reflecting on the Survey

5. You and your classmates conducted the exact same survey. Compare your results with those of the rest of the class. Which questions seemed to work well for your survey and which questions would you change if you could? Why?

Assignment

Working in pairs, your assignment is to develop, conduct, interpret, and present the findings of a survey that is designed to prove or disprove an assumption about the American Dream.

Steps

1. As a class, brainstorm ideas, hypotheses, or assumptions you have about people's attitudes regarding America or the American Dream.

2. Determine a target group for your survey and develop a working hypothesis like the one in the previous activity: "American teenagers are more obsessed with money than American adults." You may wish to consider race, culture, age, and gender among other variables. Look to texts and ideas from the unit to help you develop your questions.

3. Consider who the targets of your survey will be to prove or disprove your thesis. What are some general questions you might ask?

4. Create survey questions that will provide both numeric and open-ended responses. Write the most effective questions on separate paper as a rough draft of your survey.

5. Exchange drafts with another pair of students and take each other's survey. Share thoughts about any questions that might be confusing or ineffective, and revise your draft accordingly.

6. Edit your survey for correct grammar, punctuation, and spelling to produce a technically sound document for distribution. Type your survey using a word processing program. Double-check that your survey asks for all of the information about the respondent that you will need: age, gender, race, among others.

7. Hand out your survey to at least 30 people. Be sure that your surveys are widely distributed to a variety of people.

8. Collect your data and categorize it as you did for the previous activity.

9. Interpret your data by asking whether you were able to prove or disprove your assumption. Consider ways to present your findings visually.

10. You will present your findings in the manner described by your teacher, but you should include the following:

    a. An introduction that identifies the assumption you made, why you think that this assumption is important to prove or disprove, and what your findings revealed.

    b. Body paragraphs that explain your findings using both numerical responses and words and phrases. Be sure to include your own interpretation of the findings.

    c. At least two visual representations of your findings.

    d. A conclusion that summarizes the implications of your findings (how you want people to respond, what you learned from the project).

SCORING GUIDE

Scoring Criteria	Exemplary	Proficient	Emerging
Survey	Questions are focused and effective for the stated assumption; they elicit both open-ended and numeric responses. Questions lead to the underlying attitudes of the respondents.	Questions are appropriate for the stated assumption; they elicit both open-ended and numeric responses.	Questions do not appear to be directly related to the stated assumption and/or may not elicit both open-ended and numeric responses.
Explanatory Text	The analysis of the survey demonstrates a perceptive look at the topic. The text is organized in a way that presents a clear thesis supported by thoughtful connections and insightful conclusions. The text demonstrates excellent understanding of standard writing conventions.	The analysis of the survey demonstrates a clear understanding of what the students learned about perceptions of the topic. The text is organized in a way that presents a clear thesis and support, but the reader may have to infer important details. The text demonstrates an overall understanding of basic writing conventions with some deviation.	The analysis of the survey lacks reflection on learning and/or understanding of the topic. Organization is insufficient. The thesis may be unclear and/or there may be limited evidence to support it. There are frequent errors in standard conventions that seriously interfere with the meaning.
Presentation	Students craft an engaging, well-organized presentation of their survey and analysis. Visuals effectively enhance findings and engage the audience. Both members contribute.	Students craft a well-organized presentation of their survey and analysis. Visuals support presentation of findings. Both members contribute.	Students' presentation may be disorganized. While an attempt to incorporate visuals is made, they may distract or be under-utilized. The two members do not contribute equally.
Additional Criteria			

Comments:

Learning Focus:

Defining Your American Dream

How will you pursue happiness? What is success? What is the American Dream?

An important task of every critical thinker is to be able to read and understand the thinking of others. But the task doesn't end there. More importantly, your work is to reflect on the ideas you encounter, to weigh and evaluate the thinking of others, to mull over in your mind the multitude of ideas presented. This hard work sets you on the path to understanding and articulating your own thinking.

You may find yourself having mental conversations with writers whose ideas you respect or admire or disagree with as you struggle to formulate your own ideas. This is important creative work. It is not enough to simply read and agree or disagree, but as a critical thinker you must gather many ideas and sort through them to find what you can use and what you can discard in formulating your own thinking. This act of synthesis or combining is the creative act of constructing your own definitions of what is important to you.

Synthesizing your own thoughts, your reading, and your research will lead to your own personal understanding of the American Dream. Articulating your own thinking as well as taking ideas from texts and authors and sythesizing them into a thoughtful, personal, and **persuasive argument** puts you in the role of author of your own American Dream.

> ### LITERARY TERMS
> A **persuasive argument** convinces readers to accept or believe a writer's perspective on a topic.

LEARNING STRATEGIES: **Marking the Text, Graphic Organizer, Discussion Groups, SOAPSTone**

ABOUT THE AUTHOR

As a senator from Illinois, Barack Obama rose to national prominence after giving a speech at the 2004 Democratic Convention. In 2008, he was elected the first African American president of the United States.

My Notes

Speech

Keynote Address
from the **2004**
Democratic National Convention
(Excerpt)

by Barack Obama

On behalf of the great state of Illinois, crossroads of a nation, land of Lincoln, let me express my deep gratitude for the privilege of addressing this convention. Tonight is a particular honor for me because, let's face it, my presence on this stage is pretty unlikely. My father was a foreign student, born and raised in a small village in Kenya. He grew up herding goats, went to school in a tin-roof shack. His father, my grandfather, was a cook, a domestic servant to the Brtish.

But my grandfather had larger dreams for his son. Through hard work and perseverance my father got a scholarship to study in a magical place, America, that's shone as a beacon of freedom and opportunity to so many who had come before him. While studying here, my father met my mother. She was born in a town on the other side of the world, in Kansas. Her father worked on oil rigs and farms through most of the Depression. The day after Pearl Harbor he signed up for duty, joined Patton's army and marched across Europe. Back home, my grandmother raised a baby and went to work on a bomber assembly line. After the war, they studied on the G.I. Bill, bought a house through FHA, and moved west, all the way to Hawaii, in search of opportunity.

And they, too, had big dreams for their daughter, a common dream, born of two continents. My parents shared not only an improbable love; they shared an abiding faith in the possibilities of this nation. They would give me an African name, Barack, or "blessed," believing that in a tolerant America your name is no barrier to success. They imagined me going to the best schools in the land, even though they weren't rich, because in a generous America you don't have to be rich to achieve your potential. They are both passed away now. Yet, I know that, on this night, they look down on me with pride.

I stand here today, grateful for the diversity of my heritage, aware that my parents' dreams live on in my two precious daughters. I stand here knowing that my story is part of the larger American story, that I owe a debt to all of those who came before me, and that, in no other country on earth, is my story even possible. Tonight, we gather to affirm the greatness of our nation, not because of the height of our skyscrapers, or the power of our military, or the size of our economy. Our pride is based on a very simple premise, summed up in a declaration made over two hundred years ago, "We hold these truths be self-evident, that all men are created equal, that they are endowed by their Creator with certain inalienable rights, that among these are life, liberty and the pursuit of happiness."

That is the true genius of America, a faith in the simple dreams, the insistence on small miracles; that we can tuck in our children at night and know they are fed and clothed and safe from harm; that we can say what we think, write what we think, without hearing a sudden knock on the door; that we can have an idea and start our own business without paying a bribe; that we can participate in the political process without fear of retribution, and that our votes will be counted — or at least, most of the time.

This year, in this election, we are called to reaffirm our values and our commitments, to hold them against a hard reality and see how we are measuring up, to the legacy of our forbearers, and the promise of future generations. And fellow Americans — Democrats, Republicans, Independents — I say to you tonight: we have more work to do. More to do for the workers I met in Galesburg, Illinois, who are losing their union jobs at the Maytag plant that's moving to Mexico, and now they're having to compete with their own children for jobs that pay seven bucks an hour; more to do for the father I met who was losing his job and choking back tears, wondering how he would pay $4,500 a month for the drugs his son needs without the health benefits he counted on; more to do for the young woman in East St. Louis, and thousands more like her, who has the grades, has the drive, has the will, but doesn't have the money to go to college.

Now, don't get me wrong. The people I meet—in small towns and big cities, in diners and office parks—they don't expect government to solve all their problems. They know they have to work hard to get ahead and they want to. Go into the collar counties around Chicago, and people will tell you: They don't want their tax money wasted by a welfare agency or the Pentagon. Go into any inner city neighborhood, and folks will tell you that government alone can't teach kids to learn. They know that parents have to teach, that children can't achieve unless we raise their expectations and turn off the television sets and eradicate the slander that says a black youth with a book is acting white. They know those things. People don't expect government to solve all their problems. But they sense, deep in their bones, that with just a slight change in priorities, we can make sure that every child in America has a decent shot at life, and that the doors of opportunity remain open to all. They know we can do better. And they want that choice….John Kerry believes in America. And he knows it's not enough for just some of us to prosper. For alongside our famous individualism, there's another ingredient in the American Dream saga, a belief that we are connected as one people. If there's a child on the south side of Chicago who can't read, that matters to me, even if it's not my child. If there's a senior citizen somewhere who can't pay for their prescription and having

My Notes

My Notes

to choose between medicine and the rent, that makes my life poorer, even if it's not my grandmother. If there's an Arab American family being rounded up without benefit of an attorney or due process, that threatens my civil liberties. It is that fundamental belief — it is that fundamental belief — I am my brother's keeper, I am my sisters' keeper — that makes this country work. It's what allows us to pursue our individual dreams, yet still come together as a single American family. "E pluribus unum," out of many, one.

Now even as we speak, there are those who are preparing to divide us, the spin masters and negative ad peddlers who embrace the politics of anything goes. Well, I say to them tonight, there's not a liberal America and a conservative America — there's the United States of America. There's not a black America and white America and Latino America and Asian America; there's the United States of America. The pundits like to slice-and-dice our country into Red States and Blue States; Red States for Republicans, Blue States for Democrats. But I've got news for them, too. We worship an awesome God in the Blue States, and we don't like federal agents poking around our libraries in the Red States. We coach Little League in the Blue States and, yes, we've got some gay friends in the Red States. There are patriots who opposed the war in Iraq and patriots who supported the war in Iraq. We are one people, all of us pledging allegiance to the stars and stripes, all of us defending the United States of America.

In the end, that's what this election is about. Do we participate in a politics of cynicism or a politics of hope? John Kerry calls on us to hope. John Edwards calls on us to hope. I'm not talking about blind optimism here — the almost willful ignorance that thinks unemployment will go away if we just don't talk about it, or the health care crisis will solve itself if we just ignore it. That's not what I'm talking about. I'm talking about something more substantial. It's the hope of slaves sitting around a fire singing freedom songs; the hope of immigrants setting out for distant shores; the hope of a young naval lieutenant bravely patrolling the Mekong Delta; the hope of a mill worker's son who dares to defy the odds; the hope of a skinny kid with a funny name who believes that America has a place for him, too. Hope in the face of difficulty, hope in the face of uncertainty, the audacity of hope!

In the end, that is God's greatest gift to us, the bedrock of this nation; the belief in things not seen; the belief that there are better days ahead. I believe we can give our middle class relief and provide working families with a road to opportunity. I believe we can provide jobs to the jobless, homes to the homeless, and reclaim young people in cities across America from violence and despair. I believe that we have a righteous wind at our backs, and that as we stand on the crossroads of history, we can make the right choices, and meet the challenges that face us....

THE RIGHT TO FAIL

by William Zinsser

ABOUT THE AUTHOR

William K. Zinsser (b. 1922), American critic and writer, was born in New York and educated at Princeton. He has written articles for many leading magazines and newspapers and authored 17 books. He has taught writing at Yale University, the New School, and Columbia University Graduate School.

I like "dropout" as an addition to the American Dream language because it's brief and it's clear. What I don't like is that we use it almost entirely as a dirty word.

We only apply it to people under twenty-one. Yet an adult who spends his days and nights watching mindless TV programs is more of a dropout than an eighteen-year-old who quits college, with its frequently mindless courses, to become, say, a VISTA volunteer. For the young, dropping out is often a way of dropping in.

To hold this opinion, however, is little short of treason in America. A boy or girl who leaves college is branded a failure—and the right to fail is one of the few freedoms that this country does not grant its citizens. The American Dream is a dream of "getting ahead," painted in strokes of gold wherever we look. Our advertisements and TV commercials are a hymn to material success, our magazine articles a toast to people who made it to the top. Smoke the right cigarette or drive the right car—so the ads imply—and girls will be swooning into your deodorized arms or caressing your expensive lapels. Happiness goes to the man who has the sweet smell of achievement. He is our national idol, and everybody else is our national fink.

I want to put in a word for the fink, especially the teen-age fink, because if we give him time to get through his finkdom—if we release him from the pressure of attaining certain goals by a certain age—he has a good chance of becoming our national idol, a Jefferson or a Thoreau, a Buckminster Fuller or an Adlai Stevenson, a man with a mind of his own. We need mavericks and dissenters and dreamers far more than we need junior vice presidents, but we paralyze them by insisting that every step be a step up to the next rung of the ladder. Yet in the fluid years of youth, the only way for boys and girls to find their proper road is often to take a hundred side trips, poking out in different directions, faltering, drawing back, and starting again.

My Notes

GRAMMAR & USAGE

A short sentence often adds punch to an idea, especially if it comes between longer, more complicated sentences. Notice how Zinsser uses a three-word sentence to reinforce the main point of his essay: "Failure isn't fatal." The sentence is direct, simple, and short, which gives it extra attention. Try working short sentences strategically into your own writing.

My Notes

"But what if we fail?" they ask, whispering the dreadful word across the Generation Gap to their parents, who are back home at the Establishment nursing their "middle-class values" and cultivating their "goal oriented society." The parents whisper back: "Don't!"

What they should say is "Don't be afraid to fail!" Failure isn't fatal. Countless people have had a bout with it and come out stronger as a result. Many have even come out famous. History is strewn with eminent dropouts, "loners" who followed their own trail, not worrying about its odd twists and turns because they had faith in their own sense of direction. To read their biographies is always exhilarating, not only because they beat the system, but because their system was better than the one that they beat. Luckily, such rebels still turn up often enough to prove that individualism, though badly threatened, is not extinct. Much has been written, for instance, about the fitful scholastic career of Thomas P. F. Hoving, New York's former Parks Commissioner and now director of the Metropolitan Museum of Art. Hoving was a dropout's dropout, entering and leaving schools as if they were motels, often at the request of the management. Still, he must have learned something during those unorthodox years, for he dropped in again at the top of his profession.

His case reminds me of another boyhood—that of Holden Caulfield in J. D. Salinger's *The Catcher in the Rye*, the most popular literary hero of the postwar period. There is nothing accidental about the grip that this dropout continues to hold on the affections of an entire American generation. Nobody else, real or invented, has made such an engaging shambles of our "goal-oriented society," so gratified our secret belief that the "phonies" are in power and the good guys up the creek. Whether Holden has also reached the top of his chosen field today is one of those speculations that delight fanciers of good fiction. I speculate that he has. Holden Caulfield, incidentally, is now thirty-six.

I'm not urging everyone to go out and fail just for the sheer therapy of it, or to quit college just to coddle some vague discontent. Obviously it's better to succeed than to flop, and in general a long education is more helpful than a short one. (Thanks to my own education, for example, I can tell George Eliot from T. S. Eliot, I can handle the pluperfect tense in French, and I know that Caesar beat the Helvetii because he had enough frumentum.) I only mean that failure isn't bad in itself, or success automatically good.

Fred Zinnemann, who has directed some of Hollywood's most honored movies, was asked by a reporter, when *A Man for All Seasons* won every prize, about his previous film, *Behold a Pale Horse*, which was a box-office disaster. "I don't feel any obligation to be successful," Zimmerman replied. "Success can be dangerous—you feel you know it all. I've learned a great deal from my failures." A similar point was made by Richard Brooks about his ambitious money loser, *Lord Jim*. Recalling the three years of his life that went into it, talking almost with elation about the troubles that befell his unit in Cambodia, Brooks told me that he learned more about his craft from this considerable failure than from his many earlier hits.

It's a point, of course, that applies throughout the arts. Writers, playwrights, painters and composers work in the expectation of periodic defeat, but they wouldn't keep going back into the arena if they thought it was the end of the world. It isn't the end of the world. For an artist—and perhaps for anybody—it is the only way to grow.

Today's younger generation seems to know that this is true, seems willing to take the risks in life that artists take in art. "Society," needless to say, still has the upper hand—it sets the goals and condemns as a failure everybody who won't play. But the dropouts and the hippies are not as afraid of failure as their parents and grandparents. This could mean, as their elders might say, that they are just plumb lazy, secure in the comforts of an affluent state. It could also mean, however, that they just don't buy the old standards of success and are rapidly writing new ones.

Recently it was announced, for instance, that more than two hundred thousand Americans have inquired about service in VISTA (the domestic Peace Corps) and that, according to a Gallup survey, "more than 3 million American college students would serve VISTA in some capacity if given the opportunity." This is hardly the road to riches or to an executive suite. Yet I have met many of these young volunteers, and they are not pining for traditional success. On the contrary, they appear more fulfilled than the average vice-president with a swimming pool.

Who is to say, then, if there is any right path to the top, or even to say what the top consists of? Obviously the colleges don't have more than a partial answer—otherwise the young would not be so disaffected with an education that they consider vapid. Obviously business does not have the answer—otherwise the young would not be so scornful of its call to be an organization man.

The fact is, nobody has the answer, and the dawning awareness of this fact seems to me one of the best things happening in America today. Success and failure are again becoming individual visions, as they were when the country was younger, not rigid categories. Maybe we are learning again to cherish this right of every person to succeed on his own terms and to fail as often as necessary along the way.

My Notes

The Road to Success

Complete the following SOAPSTone to analyze the essay "The Right to Fail," by William Zinsser.

Speaker What can you say about the speaker based on references in the text? Is race, gender, class, or age important?	
Occasion What issues may have motivated the speaker to think about the incident or occasion?	
Audience Who is being addressed? Identify some characteristics of the audience.	
Purpose What is the message and how does the author want the audience to respond?	
Subject What is the focus? The subject can be stated by using a few words.	
Tone Using textual support, how would you describe the overall tone of the passage?	

Defining the Dream

SUGGESTED LEARNING STRATEGIES: Rereading, Notetaking, Discussion Groups

Defining the "American Dream"

In a synthesis essay, it is paramount to define important terms at the beginning of your text. In the case of this prompt, the definition you create becomes a vehicle for establishing your thesis. Consider defining important terms using the following ideas.

Define by Function (What does the "American Dream" do?):

Define by Classification (What groups belong to or have access to the "American Dream"?):

Define by Example (What are some examples of the "American Dream"?):

Define by Negation (What the "American Dream" is not):

Return to the readings and work you have done in this unit. Review them to determine whether and how you can use these readings or writings as sources to support your thinking.

Synthesizing the American Dream

SUGGESTED LEARNING STRATEGIES: Rereading, Notetaking, Prewriting, Drafting, Self-Editing/Peer Editing, Sharing and Responding

Assignment

Your assignment is to synthesize at least three to five sources and your own observations to defend, challenge, or qualify the statement that America still provides access to the American Dream, to the "tired, the poor, and the huddled masses." This question requires you to integrate a variety of sources (3–5) into a coherent, well-written argumentative essay. Be sure to refer to the sources and employ your own observations to support your position. Your argument should be central; the sources and your observations should support this argument.

Steps

Planning

1. As a class or in small groups, review the elements of a strong synthesis paper.
2. Revisit and carefully consider the various texts (sources) from the unit to identify three to five sources that might be relevant to your position.

Drafting

3. Draft your own position on the issue. Consider two or three possible positions you could take and then decide which of those positions you really want to take. Be careful not to generalize, but instead consider the nuances and complexities of the topic.

4. Imagine presenting your position on the issue to each of the authors of your sources. Create an imaginary conversation between you and the author of the source discussing the following questions, and record your findings.

   ▶ Would the author/creator agree with your position? Disagree? Why?

   ▶ Would the author/creator want to qualify your position? Why and how?

   ▶ Does the author make a specific claim about your issue?

   ▶ What assumptions or beliefs are either spoken or unspoken (implicit or explicit)?

5. On the basis of this imagined conversation, revise and refine the point that you would like to make about the issue so it can serve as your central thesis. Draft your opening paragraph in which you introduce this thesis relatively soon after a sentence or two that contextualizes the topic for the reader.

6. Compose your essay considering the elements of argumentation. Be sure to develop the case for your position by incorporating within your thinking the conversations you had with the authors of the primary

r™ Level 6

▶ You should feel free to say things like "Source A would disagree with my viewpoint, but here is why I still maintain my position" or "Source B would agree with the majority of my position but would offer a slightly different perspective in this area."

▶ Don't forget to cite your sources appropriately in the text itself.

Revising

7. Share your draft and solicit peer response for the following areas:

   ▶ Organizational structure: Is your argument structured to provide clarity to the reader?

   ▶ Elements of argumentation: Is each element effective (hook, claim, support, concessions/refutations, and call to action)?

   ▶ Style: Does your draft have sentence variety, coherence, and appropriate diction and tone for your audience?

   Ask for specific suggestions for improvement in each of these areas to help you revise your draft.

Editing

8. Review your draft and correct errors in grammar, punctuation, and spelling to produce a technically sound document.

9. Select an appropriate title and use available technology to create a final draft.

Presenting

10. Present your argument to your peers. Consider the various viewpoints and reflect on your own thinking about your claim. Has your view changed? Did other members of your group have similar views? Different? Record your reflections.

....

⚲**TECHNOLOGY TIP** Use a word processing program to help you create a professional looking product. You may want to incorporate side headings to help guide readers. Take advantage of the program's spell-check feature to check your document.

Synthesizing the American Dream

SCORING GUIDE

Scoring Criteria	Exemplary	Proficient	Emerging
Ideas	The essay effectively synthesizes the sources and the writer's position to defend, challenge, or qualify the central claim of the prompt. The cohesive, sustained argument includes: • a thesis that contextualizes the issue and captures its complexity; • support that convincingly goes beyond the citation of a variety of source material to analyzing the sources' significance to the writer's position; • a conclusion that goes beyond a summary of the thesis by illuminating how the writer's position will continue to influence the reader.	The essay adequately synthesizes the sources and the writer's position to defend, challenge, or qualify the central claim of the prompt. The sound argument includes: • a straightforward thesis that briefly contextualizes the issue; • support that clearly connects and comments on the various source material to the the writer's position; • a conclusion that is logical yet may be somewhat repetitive of the thesis.	The essay tries to synthesize the sources and the writer's position yet inadequately defends, challenges, or qualifies the central claim of the prompt. The attempted argument includes: • a weak thesis or one that is lost in a summary of sources; • support that paraphrases source material with no commentary or analysis of the writer's position; sources may be misunderstood; • a conclusion that returns directly to the attempted thesis or that is missing.
Organization	The essay's effective organization aptly reinforces the ideas of the argument. Ideas move smoothly and comfortably with successful use of transitions enhancing the essay's coherence.	The essay's clear organization supports the ideas of the argument. Ideas are easy to follow. Transitions are used to move between ideas.	The essay's lack of organization detracts from the argument, making the ideas difficult to follow. It may jump too rapidly between ideas and lack transitions.
Use of Language	The essay demonstrates a mature style that advances the writer's ideas. Precise diction and skillful use of syntax, with keen attention to varied sentence openings, help to create a convincing voice. Standard writing conventions (including accurate citation of sources) are followed.	The essay demonstrates a style that adequately supports the writer's ideas. Logical diction and syntax, with some attention to varied sentence openings, help to create a suitable voice. Standard writing conventions (including accurate citation of sources) are followed; errors do not seriously impede readability.	The essay demonstrates a limited style that ineffectively supports the writer's ideas. Lapses in diction or syntax may not sustain a suitable voice throughout the essay. Sentence openings may be repetitive. Errors in standard writing conventions impede readability and sources may be inaccurately cited.

SCORING GUIDE

Scoring Criteria	Exemplary	Proficient	Emerging
Reflection	The reflection perceptively analyzes how the writer has considered various viewpoints and thoroughly reveals the writer's thinking about his/her claim.	The reflection explains how the writer has considered various viewpoints and addresses the writer's thinking about his/her claim.	The reflection does little to analyze how the writer has considered various viewpoints or to show the writer's thinking about his/her claim.
Additional Criteria			

Comments:

Reflection

An important aspect of growing as a learner is to reflect on where you have been, what you have accomplished, what helped you to learn, and how you will apply your new knowledge in the future. Use the following questions to guide your thinking and to identify evidence of your learning. Use separate notebook paper.

Thinking about Concepts

1. Using specific examples from this unit, respond to the Essential Questions:

   • In what ways does the American Dream manifest itself in American life?

   • How does one create a personal definition of the American Dream?

2. Consider the new academic vocabulary from this unit (**Survey, Primary Source, Secondary Source**) and select 3–4 terms of which your understanding has grown. For each term, answer the following questions:

   • What was your understanding of the word prior to the unit?

   • How has your understanding of the word evolved throughout the unit?

   • How will you apply your understanding in the future?

Thinking about Connections

3. Review the activities and products (artifacts) you created. Choose those that most reflect your growth or increase in understanding.

4. For each artifact that you choose, record, respond, and reflect on your thinking and understanding, using the following questions as a guide:

   a. What skill/knowledge does this artifact reflect, and how did you learn this skill/knowledge?

   b. How did your understanding of the power of language expand through your engagement with this artifact?

   c. How will you apply this skill or knowledge in the future?

5. Create this reflection as Portfolio pages—one for each artifact you choose. Use the following model for your headings and commentary on questions.

Thinking About Thinking
Portfolio Entry

Concept:

Description of Artifact:

Commentary on Questions:

American Forums: The Marketplace of Ideas

Essential Questions

? How do newspapers impact public opinion or public perception?

? How does a writer use tone to advance an opinion?

TV news, news magazines, newspapers, radio, and the Internet give us sometimes vital, sometimes trivial, facts and opinions, creating a swirling array of often conflicting information. The resulting chaos of information and perspectives can create an overwhelming presence in our lives, yet this information is also crucial to our ability to make informed decisions about everything from personal beliefs to public policy. Indeed, the ways in which these ideas and voices interact with each other create a marketplace of ideas—a forum through which we can shape, test, and revise our own perspectives on our society and the issues that dominate the day. One place in particular where opinions can be shared, heard, and responded to is the newspaper op-ed page. In this context, and in many others, satire is often used by social critics to challenge or comment upon prevailing attitudes. In this unit you will learn to discern a news story from an opinion piece and a satirical text, and you will be better prepared to know where to go when you want to find out what America is thinking—and to create texts that may influence that thinking.

American Forums:
The Marketplace of Ideas

Contents

Goals

▶ To identify the main components and role of a newspaper's op-ed page

▶ To analyze how writers use logic, evidence, and rhetoric to advance their opinions

▶ To write persuasive pieces and refute the positions of others

▶ To recognize the symbols and references that editorial cartoonists use

▶ To analyze and apply satirical techniques

ACADEMIC VOCABULARY

Bias

Fallacy

Editorial

Parody

*Texts not included in these materials.

Learning Focus:

Browsing in the Marketplace

While the American Dream is central to our shared sense of identity, another of our defining beliefs is in the importance of free speech. As Supreme Court Justice Oliver Wendell Holmes famously observed in 1919, "the best test of truth is the power of the thought to get itself accepted in the competition of the market." Viewed in this way, the expression of contrasting and even conflicting ideas and opinions provides information that is crucial to our ability to make informed decisions about everything from personal beliefs to public policy. Indeed, the ways in which these ideas and voices interact with each other help us to shape, test, and revise our own perspectives on the issues that dominate our lives.

Of course, if you have ever listened to talk radio, watched cable "news" shows, or browsed the Web for blogs, you know what happens when the marketplace becomes a monopoly. Some news is presented with a biased point of view, and when it comes to the expression of **editorial** opinions, sources often rely heavily on language and evidence that attempt to persuade by manipulating. As a result, you should question the information you receive, where it comes from, and the perspective through which the information is filtered. In this unit, you will learn more about how to identify **bias** and how language can be used as a surrogate for logic. You'll analyze how writers use evidence and reasoning in support of their claims—and how failing to do so can result in **fallacies**.

Finally, you'll collaborate with your peers to produce your own contribution to the marketplace of ideas by creating a newspaper op-ed page for Embedded Assessment 1. Can you be a persuasive yet ethical advocate for your positions?

Independent Reading: In this unit, you will read both print and nonprint texts that explore the relationship between news media and a free exchange of ideas in a democracy. For independent reading, choose a topic of interest and explore its coverage in the media across a variety of genres (for example, articles, news stories, editorials, political cartoons, satirical commentary, and so on).

SUGGESTED LEARNING STRATEGIES: Close Reading, Graphic Organizer, KWL Chart, Marking the Text, Summarizing/Paraphrasing, Think-Pair-Share

Essential Questions

1. How do newspapers impact public opinion or public perception?

2. How does a writer use tone to advance an opinion?

Unit Overview and Learning Focus

Predict what you think this unit is about. Use the words or phrases that stood out to you when you read the Unit Overview and the Learning Focus.

Embedded Assessment 1

What knowledge must you have (what do you need to know) to succeed on Embedded Assessment 1? What skills must you have (what must you be able to do)?

Introducing the Media

News Media Survey

1. Rank the following media channels in the order you would turn to them for information on a major news story. (Choose 1 to indicate the outlet you would turn to most often. Write N/A to indicate you would not use that outlet.)

   _____ Newspaper   _____ TV Network News

   _____ Websites/Internet   _____ News Magazines

   _____ Cable News Station   _____ Radio News

2. Rank the following media channels for accuracy and trustworthiness in how they present information. (Rank the most trustworthy outlet 1.)

   _____ Newspaper   _____ TV Network News

   _____ Websites/Internet   _____ News Magazines

   _____ Cable News Station   _____ Radio News

3. Think back on the past month. About how much time (in hours) did you spend receiving news (not entertainment) from the following media channels?

   _____ Newspaper   _____ TV Network News

   _____ Websites/Internet   _____ News Magazines

   _____ Cable News Station   _____ Radio News

4. Rank each of the following reasons that you might give for not reading newspapers. (Write 1 next to the reason most appropriate for you. Write N/A if you disagree with the statement.)

   _____ They are boring.

   _____ They take too long to read.

   _____ They don't have information that applies to me and my life.

   _____ They usually focus on scandals, politics, and gossip.

   _____ They are often filled with mistakes and lies.

   _____ Other:

5. Do you feel that it is important to be knowledgeable about news? Explain.

ACTIVITY 2.2
continued

OH MY!
THE FUTURE OF NEWS

My Notes

by Jeremy Wagstaff

I was asked the other day to address a room full of media types about changes in consumer behavior; where, they wanted to know, are people looking for news in this new digital world?

It's always a bad idea to get me to talk in public, especially on this subject, since I think it's the wrong one. Or at least, the wrong way of looking at the subject. I gave them two reasons:

First, there are no consumers of news anymore. In fact, you've probably heard this said a lot, here and elsewhere that, in the era of MySpace, Wikipedia, OhmyNews and citizen journalism, everyone is a journalist, and therefore a producer, of news. No one is just a consumer.

Second, there is no news. Or at least there is no longer a traditional, established and establishment definition of what is news. Instead we have information. Some of it moving very fast, so it looks like news. But still information.

A commuter taking a photo of a policeman extracting bribes from drivers and then posting the picture on his blog? It's not news, but it's not just information either. It could be news to the policeman, and if he's busted because of it, it could be good news to drivers in that town.

We journalists have been schooled in a kind of journalism that goes back to the days when a German called Paul Julius Reuter[1] was delivering it by pigeon. His problem was a simple one: getting new information quickly from A to B. It could be stock prices; it could be the assassination of Abraham Lincoln.

That definition of news has remained with us until today.

---

[1] British journalist and founder of Reuter's news agency

A lot of the time it remains a good one. When terrorists hit, we'd rather know sooner than later. If stocks in our portfolio are losing their value in a crash, we'd prefer to get that information now.

When Buddhist monks hit the streets of towns in Myanmar we look to AFP, Reuters and AP to get the news out.

But the Internet has changed a lot of this. First off, everyone is connected. By connected I mean they can look up anything they like so long as they're near an Internet-connected computer. Which for a lot of people now means a 3G phone.

Even if you don't have one, the chances are you'll be in spitting range of a computer that is connected to the Internet. Or you could get your information by SMS — from news sites, from colleagues, from family members. It's not that we're not far from a gadget. We're not far from information. This has a critical impact on the idea of news.

Because we're informed, news doesn't hit us in the same way it used to when we weren't.

True, if someone hits a tall building with an airliner, that's news to all of us. The U.S. invades or leaves Iraq; that's news.

But the rest of the time, news is a slippery beast that means different things to different people.

That's because there's another kind of news we're all interested in.

It's hyperlocal news. It's what is around us. In our neighborhood. Since moving house, I'm much less interested in gubernatorial[2] elections and much more in anything that anybody says about en bloc sales and house prices. That is hyperlocal news, and it's where most people spend their day. No nuclear weapons being fired? No terrorist attacks? No meltdown in the financial markets? OK, so tell me more about en bloc sales. Actually, this is just part of hyperlocal news.

If you've used Facebook, you'll know there's another kind of addictive local news: your friends' status updates. A status update, for those of you who haven't tried Facebook, is basically a short message that accompanies your profile indicating what you're up to at that point.

I think of it as a wire feed by real people. Of course it's not news as we'd think of it, but news as in an answer to the questions "What's up?" "What's new?" "What's happening?" "What's new with you?"

---

[2] **gubernatorial:** pertaining to a state governor

In that sense it's news. I call it hyper-hyperlocal news. Even though those people are spread all over the world, they're all part of my friends network, and that means for me they're local.

So news isn't always what we think of as news. News has always meant something slightly different to the nonmedia person; our obsession with prioritizing stories in a summary, the most important item first (How many dead? What color was their skin? Any Americans involved?) has been exposed as something only we tend to obsess over.

Don't believe me? Look at the BBC website. While the editors were putting up stories about Musharraf, North Korea and Japan, the users were swapping stories about Britney Spears splitting with her manager, the dangers of spotty face, and the admittedly important news that the Sex Pistols might be getting back together.

Of course, I'm not saying journalists are from Mars and readers are from Venus. It just looks that way.

What we're really seeing is that now that people have access to information, they are showing us what they're interested in. Unsurprisingly, they're interested in different stuff. What we call audience fragmentation — niche[3] audiences for specialized interests — is actually what things have always been about.

If we're a geek we go for our news to Slashdot. We want gossip? We go to Gawker. We want to change the world? We go to WorldChangingOnline.org. The Internet makes the Long Tail of all those niche audiences and interests possible, and possibly profitable.

What we're seeing with the Internet is not a revolution against the values of old media; a revolution against the notion that it's only us who can dictate what is news.

What we're seeing is that people get their news from whoever can help them answer the question they're asking. We want the headlines, we go to CNN. But the rest of the time, "news" is for us just part of a much bigger search for information, to stay informed.

---

[3] **niche:** a specialized market segment

Introducing the Media

In what different ways does Wagstaff define "news"? Cite several lines in which he characterizes the different meanings the term has in today's media-saturated world.

Write your own answers to the following questions in the space below. Then discuss your responses with your classmates.

How do you respond to Wagstaff's article? How have his purpose and tone influenced your response?

Does Wagstaff's description of media consumers apply to you? In what ways?

Are you a producer and not just a consumer of news? How so?

Is audience fragmentation a good thing? Why or why not?

Do we need to know more than hyperlocal news to be informed? Why or why not?

Writing Prompt: Write a letter to Wagstaff in which you explain how your own experience confirms or challenges his claims about the changing meaning of "news" in our lives.

Consumer's Report

SUGGESTED LEARNING STRATEGIES: Graphic Organizer, Summarizing, Discussion Groups

Informational Text

A Day in the Life of the Media: *Intro*

by The Project for Excellence in Journalism

…To study a day in the life in the media, we picked a universe to be representative of a broad swath of what Americans can choose from. It included three national newspapers, the three primary cable news channels, the three major commercial broadcast networks, PBS, seven news Web sites, seven prominent blogs, and a wide cross-section of TV, radio, newspapers, and ethnic and alternative media in three American cities, Houston, Milwaukee, and Bend, Ore. The result was a study that included 2,125 stories in 57 outlets and 48 hours of programming on radio and television, all offered in a single day, May 11, 2005—plus 112 different blog postings.

To what extent did any of what we saw reflect more than this one day? The results, it turns out — about topics covered, sourcing, and more, in each medium — closely mirror what we have found in these media and others for the last two years, when we took randomly constructed months of news for each, analyzed them by topic and broke down the reporting.

THE MEDIA CULTURE: A LOOSE TYPOLOGY

If different media offer distinctly different news agendas, what did we find about each in our study of May 11?

Online : "The Internet," we found, describes a technology, not a style of media or a set of values or even a journalistic approach. The seven news Web sites we monitored varied widely — from Google's emphasis on speed and bulk to Yahoo's focus on navigability to a local TV news station's site, largely a portal for advertising copy. Many of the most popular sites also remain largely a stepchild of print and wire-service content, especially the so-called Internet-only sites that produce no copy of their own. As a result, while the Internet has added more outlets from which to choose, it has not, our study suggests, added new topics to the agenda.

Ultimately, it still seems unclear what online news will come to represent.

My Notes

GRAMMAR & USAGE

Writers sometimes pose **rhetorical questions,** which are questions used for effect and not because an answer is expected. In this report, the rhetorical question acknowledges and anticipates one of the reader's first questions – how can we trust that information gathered on just one day will be accurate? Using a question instead of a statement is a way to connect to the reader by acknowledging that the question is reasonable.

Consumer's Report

My Notes

Will it be constant updating, focusing on being fast and first? Or more depth, as sites are freed from the confines of space and time? Will online journalism come to mean multi-media convergence, including downloading sound and pictures to PDAs and phones? Or a worrisome intermingling of advertising and editorial? Or will online journalism move toward more citizen voices, more communication with the audience, and more opinion? In the seven sites studied we found all of the above, but none of it all in one place. Two of the most innovative sites we encountered, interestingly, were from old media, a TV network (CBS) and a mid-sized metropolitan newspaper (the Milwaukee Journal Sentinel).

Blogs: If the media culture needs navigators, by day's end the seven popular blogs we studied would offer that — to an extent. As the hours went by, the bloggers sifted through the content of the mainstream media and noted what they deemed important, curious, absent, interesting or objectionable. But contrary to the charge that the blogosphere is purely parasitic, we also found new topics here, and new angles on old ones. Indeed, the blogs were generally less concerned than many traditional journalists with the latest breaking news, and more focused on long-term issues. Yet there was little here that a journalist would call reporting or even sourcing. Only 1% of the posts this day involved a blogger doing an interview, and only another 5% involved some other kind of original research, such as examining documents. There is no summary of the news to be had here. The blogs ultimately are idiosyncratic. It is not citizen journalism in any traditional sense, but something closer to a stylized citizen media forum, often with an insider's tone and its own nomenclature.

Cable News: Up close, the striking thing about much of cable news, the first 24-hour medium, is a fixation with whatever is happening at the moment. The result is a good deal of repetition and a good deal that is ephemeral. The reporting, perhaps because of the time to fill rather than despite it, was shallowest by our indicators of any national media studied.

To a degree that we do not find on network TV, the three main cable news channels have also grown distinct from each other. Fox has built its appeal around trying to help its viewers put the news in some order — a conservative order — even if the production values are sometimes ragged. CNN is far more earnest, and tied to the immediate, and seems less sure what the difference is between its different programs. MSNBC, for its part, seems a different channel virtually from program to program — sometimes an extension of NBC News, sometimes something quite alien from its broadcast cousin. If there is a common thread between Don Imus in the morning, Chris Matthews in the evening and Keith Olbermann at night, it might be an effort at being ironic and glib.

Network: The contrast between the network nightly and morning news is so striking that the term network TV news almost seems a misnomer. It makes more sense to talk nightly news versus morning. The three evening newscasts were virtually identical to each other and very different from their network siblings in the morning.

A close look also suggests just how disadvantaged the traditional 30-minute evening newscasts are today. They are still trying to cover traditional hard news, but they are constrained by airing only once a day, by a newshole that is really 18 minutes, and by limited staff, which seems even more apparent when you look closely. People who want a quick, one-shot fill on the major national and international events of the day can still find that here, but within a set viewing times and brevity of a 30 minute program.

In the mornings, the luxury of an hour time slot makes a difference, but the news agenda is lighter and focused on emotion. Morning News and Features would probably be a more fitting title. Much, too, depends on the ability of two or three anchors to be experts in everything, prepared for everything, and charming all at the same time.

Newspapers: If ink on paper has an advantage, the day would suggest it is in the number of boots on the ground. This is the medium that is covering the most topics, has the deepest sourcing, explores the most angles in stories, and for now is supplying most of the content for the Internet. A reader also discovers probably the closest thing to a medium still trying to provide all the news a consumer might want, though perhaps in language and sourcing tilted toward elites. Looming, as readers inevitably shift to acquiring their news online, is the question of what happens to the more complete reporting that additional time affords. And how many boots will be left on the ground if the print editions that pay the bills continue to shrink.

Local TV: Local TV, at least in the three cities studied, focused on what news managers apparently thought people could use, traffic and weather, and what they were worried about, accidents and crime. Take out traffic, weather and sports, indeed, and half of all the newshole — and an even greater percentage of lead stories — was devoted to crime and accidents. But the bulk of what made up local news in print — issues like government, taxes, infrastructure and civic institutions — was relegated here to brief "tell" stories in the middle of the newscast. In style and format, the stations were strikingly similar, even across cities. The stories here were just the facts. There was little opinion, our statistical breakdown shows. But on average local TV news stories had the shallowest sourcing and explored the fewest angles of events covered of any medium studied except local radio.

Radio: Contrary to the notion that radio news is all

My Notes

My Notes

syndicated national material, we found local radio news today to be very local — but also limited in scope. What listeners get is headlines read from wires, adapted from the newspaper, or provided by national networks. The stories are brief — almost always less than a minute and often less than 30 seconds. What depth of coverage we found came largely from talk show hosts offering opinions on issues or taking call-ins from listeners. But we found little in the way of reporters in the field, or what most journalists would consider reporting. Over all, just 14% of stories would involve field reports, and many were from syndicated network feeds. And the eight stations in three cities monitored this day are strikingly alike, in format and style. . . .

CONCLUSION

In the end, one does draw some conclusions about the different media — what they offer and what they do not. None excel at everything. And there are few, if any, news consumers who rely on only one of these outlets anymore.

The Day in the Life of the News offers two warnings, as well. Consuming the news continuously does not mean being better informed. There is too much repetition, and too much confusion. The most efficient diet means finding the right mix depending on the time of the day, the nature of the news that day, and more. The wrong mix may prove to be a waste of time, the one thing consumers can never get back.

VIEWING LOG

News Source: _____   Date: _____

Time (nonprint) or Location (print)	Story Focus or Headline	Target Audience	Perspective on the Issue Covered

As you compare your source's coverage of "news" with that of other students, what key differences do you notice? What might explain those differences?

Writing Prompt: After discussing differences, write a paragraph on a separate sheet of paper explaining how your source's coverage of "news" is tailored to what you think is its target audience.

LITERARY TERMS

A **target audience** is the intended group for which a work is designed to appeal or reach. A **secondary audience** is the group who may also receive the message or may influence the target audience.

Debating the Newspaper: Part I

Look over the following quotations about newspapers. In the space after each quote, summarize what the author is saying and then state whether you agree and why.

"Were it left to me to decide whether we should have a government without newspapers, or newspapers without a government, I should not hesitate a moment to prefer the latter." — Thomas Jefferson, 1787

"Congress shall make no law ... abridging the freedom of speech or of the press...." — Article One, Bill of Rights of the United States Constitution, 1789

WORD CONNECTIONS

Accurate uses the Latin root *-cur-* from the verb *curare*, meaning "to take care of," plus the common Latin prefix *ad* meaning "to." *Curator*, *pedicure*, and *procure* also come from the same root.

"Newspapers ... give us the bald, sordid, disgusting facts of life. They chronicle, with degrading avidity, the sins of the second-rate, and with the conscientiousness of the illiterate give us accurate and prosaic details of the doings of people of absolutely no interest whatsoever." — Oscar Wilde (1854–1900), playwright

"Here is the living disproof of the old adage that nothing is as dead as yesterday's newspaper... This is what really happened, reported by a free press to a free people. It is the raw material of history; it is the story of our own times."— Henry Steel Commager, preface to a history of *The New York Times*, 1951

"The newspapers, especially those in the East, are amazingly superficial and ... a large number of news gatherers are either cynics at heart or are following the orders and the policies of the owners of their papers."
— Franklin D. Roosevelt, May 7, 1934

WORD CONNECTIONS

Superficial combines two Latin words: *super* meaning "above" and *facies* meaning "face." *Supervise, supernatural, superb* and *face* are some of the many English words that originate in these Latin words.

"For my part I entertain a high idea of the utility of periodical publications; insomuch as I could heartily desire, copies of ... magazines, as well as common Gazettes, might be spread through every city, town, and village in the United States. I consider such vehicles of knowledge more happily calculated than any other to preserve the liberty, stimulate the industry, and ameliorate the morals of a free and enlightened people." — George Washington, 1788

"I read the newspapers avidly. It is my one form of continuous fiction."
— Aneurin Bevan (1897–1960), British Labour politician

"What appears in newspapers is often new but seldom true."
— Patrick Kavanagh (1905–1967), Irish poet

Debating the Newspaper: Part I

WORD CONNECTIONS

Subservient comes from the Latin word *servire* meaning "to serve." *Preserve, conserve, serve, deserve, servant* come from the same Latin word.

"As people get their opinions so largely from the newspapers they read, the corruption of the schools would not matter so much if the Press were free. But the Press is not free. As it costs at least a quarter of a million of money to establish a daily newspaper in London, the newspapers are owned by rich men. And they depend on the advertisements of other rich men. Editors and journalists who express opinions in print that are opposed to the interests of the rich are dismissed and replaced by subservient ones."

— George B. Shaw, Irish playwright, 1949

"Most of us probably feel we couldn't be free without newspapers, and that is the real reason we want the newspapers to be free." — Edward R. Murrow, journalist, 1958

"The decline of competing local daily newspaper voices diminishes not only the availability of local and regional news to consumers but also the availability of competing opinions and ideas, not just at local levels but at all levels. Social thinkers, historians, and political analysts have identified such diversity of thought—a marketplace of ideas—as essential to a functioning democracy." — Steven M. Hallock, journalism professor, 2007

Quickwrite: Write a paragraph or two about your own experiences with or observations about newspapers. Analyze the value or purpose of newspapers, among other things.

How the Rise of the Daily Me Threatens Democracy

by Cass Sunstein

ABOUT THE AUTHOR
Cass Sunstein is a noted American legal scholar who has written dozens of books, essays, and newspaper and magazine articles on public policy, economics, law, and psychology. He has taught at the law schools of University of Chicago, Harvard University, and Columbia.

> **LITERARY TERMS**
> **Reasoning** is the thinking or logic used to make a claim in an argument. **Evidence** is the specific facts, examples, and other details used to support the reasoning.

My Notes

Sunstein's article first appeared on an English Web site, so you will see many words with the British spellings. Read Sunstein's article, marking the text to identify support (reasoning and evidence) he uses to justify his claim that the diminished role of the newspaper is a problem for American democracy. Record your findings in the left column of the graphic organizer on page 118.

More than a decade ago the technology specialist, Nicholas Negroponte, prophesied the emergence of the Daily Me – a fully personalised newspaper. It would allow you to include topics that interest you and screen out those that bore or annoy you. If you wanted to focus on Iraq and tennis, or exclude Iran and golf, you could do that.

Many people now use the internet to create something like a Daily Me. This behaviour is reinforced by the rise of social networking forums, collaborative filtering and viral marketing. For politics, the phenomenon is especially important in campaigns. Candidates in the US presidential race can construct information cocoons in which readers are deluged with material that is, in their eyes, politically correct. Supporters of Hillary Clinton construct a Daily Me that includes her campaign's perspective but offers nothing from Barack Obama, let alone Mitt Romney.

What is wrong with the emerging situation? We can find a clue in a small experiment in democracy conducted in Colorado in 2005. About 60 US citizens were put into 10 groups. They deliberated on controversial issues, such as whether the US should sign an inter-national treaty to combat global warming and whether states should allow same-sex couples to enter into civil unions. The groups consisted of predominantly either leftwing or rightwing members, with the former drawn from left-of-centre Boulder and the latter

My Notes

from Colorado Springs, which tends to be right of centre. The groups, not mixed, were screened to ensure members conformed to stereotypes. (If people in Boulder liked Vice-President Dick Cheney, they were cordially excused.) People were asked to state their opinions anonymously before and after the group discussion.

In almost every group, people ended up with more extreme positions. The Boulder groups favoured an inter-national treaty to control global warming before discussion; they favoured it far more strongly afterwards. In Colorado Springs, people were neutral on that treaty before discussion; discussion led them to oppose it strongly. Same-sex unions became much more popular in Boulder and less so in Colorado Springs.

Aside from increasing extremism, discussion had another effect: it squelched diversity. Before members talked, many groups displayed internal disagreement. These were greatly reduced: discussion widened the rift between Boulder and Colorado Springs.

Countless versions of this experiment are carried out online every day. The result is group polarisation, which occurs when like-minded people speak together and end up in a more extreme position in line with their original inclinations.

There are three reasons for this. First is the exchange of information. In Colorado Springs, the members offered many justifications for not signing a climate treaty and a lot fewer for doing so. Since people listened to one another, they became more sceptical. The second reason is that when people find their views corroborated, they become more confident and so are more willing to be extreme. The third reason involves social comparison. People who favour a position think of themselves in a certain way and if they are with people who agree with them, they shift a bit to hold on to their preferred self-conception.

Group polarisation clearly occurs on the internet. For example, 80 per cent of readers of the leftwing blog Daily Kos are Democrats and fewer than 1 per cent are Republicans. Many popular bloggers link frequently to those who agree with them and to contrary views, if at all, only to ridicule them. To a significant extent, people are learning about supposed facts from narrow niches and like-minded others.

This matters for the electoral process. A high degree of self-sorting leads to more confidence, extremism and increased contempt for those with contrary views. We can already see this in the presidential campaign. It will only intensify when the two parties square off. To the extent that Democratic and Republican candidates seem to live in different political universes, group polarisation is playing a large role.

Polarisation, of course, long preceded the internet. Yet given people's new power to create echo chambers, the result will be serious obstacles not merely to civility but also to mutual understanding and constructive problem solving. The Daily Me leads inexorably also to the Daily Them. That is a real problem for democracy.

> **LITERARY TERMS**
> **Inductive reasoning** is a process of looking at individual facts to draw a general conclusion. In contrast, **deductive reasoning** moves from general information to a specific conclusion. Notice that Sunstein provides evidence (individual facts) in his essay that lead to his concluding thesis (inductive reasoning).

Debating the Newspaper: Part I

In the left-hand column, identify support (reasoning and evidence) Sunstein uses to justify his claim that the diminished role of the newspaper is a problem for American democracy. You will complete the right-hand column after the next activity.

Sunstein	Potter

Quickwrite: Explain how Sunstein's *reasoning* and *evidence* convincingly support his claim that the diminished role of the newspaper is a problem for American democracy.

Editorial

Read Potter's article, marking the text to identify the **concessions and refutations** he uses to counter Sunstein's article and justify his claim that the diminished role of the newspaper is not a problem for American democracy. Record your findings in the right-hand column of your graphic organizer on page 118. Also, identify the writer's use of inductive and deductive reasoning to support his positions.

LITERARY TERMS

A **concession** is an admission in an argument that the opposing side has points. A **refutation** is the reasoning used to disprove an opposing point.

The Newspaper Is Dying
Hooray for Democracy

by Andrew Potter

My Notes

The Newspaper Audience Databank (NADbank) released its readership numbers for 2007 a couple of weeks ago, and for those of us in the industry it was grim reading: almost everywhere you look, circulation, ad revenues and page counts are down, which is why you can now fire a cannon through any given newsroom at midday and not have to worry about committing reportercide.

But unless you work in the business, is there any reason to be especially concerned? Each year may put another loop in the newspaper's death spiral, but the overall consumption of news is on the rise, almost entirely thanks to the myriad online sources. The Internet is eating the newspaper's lunch, but there's plenty of food on the buffet table.

In certain quarters, though, there is growing concern that the demise of the newspaper is a threat to democracy itself. The argument goes something like this: the economic logic of mass circulation meant a newspaper had to try to appeal to as many potential readers as possible. To do so, it brought together in one package a diverse set of voices, presenting each reader with ideas and perspectives that he or she might not otherwise have seen or sought out. This fostered the democratic values of curiosity, enlightenment and toleration, and the worry is that if the newspaper declines, so might democracy.

Debating the Newspaper: Part II

My Notes

The sharpest version of this argument comes from Cass Sunstein, a law professor at the University of Chicago. In a recent column in the Financial Times, Sunstein fusses about the rise of what he calls the Daily Me, the highly personalized and customized information feeds that will allow you to "include topics that interest you and screen out those that bore or anger you." As Sunstein sees it, the Daily Me is the potential Achilles heel of democracy because of a phenomenon called group polarization: when like-minded people find themselves speaking only with one another, they get into a cycle of ideological reinforcement where they end up endorsing positions far more extreme than the ones they started with.

Group polarization is everywhere. It helps explain why, for example, humanities departments are so left-wing, why fraternities are so sexist, why journalists drink so much. But, for the most part, it isn't a problem (for democracy anyway), since we routinely come into contact with so many people from so many different groups that the tendency toward polarization in one is at least somewhat tempered by our encounters with others.

Yet Sunstein is worried that group polarization on the Internet will prove far more pernicious. Why? Because of the image of the blogosphere as a series of echo chambers, where every viewpoint is repeated and amplified to a hysterical pitch. As our politics moves online, he thinks we'll end up with a public sphere that is partisan and extreme, and as an example, he points out that 80 per cent of readers of the left-wing blog Daily Kos are Democrats, while fewer than one per cent are Republicans. The result, he claims, "will be serious obstacles not merely to civility but also to mutual understanding."

As upside-down arguments go, this one is ingenious. For decades, progressive critics have complained about the anti-democratic influence of the mass media, and that newspapers present a selective and highly biased picture of the world, promoting pseudo-arguments that give the illusion of debate while preserving the status quo. (Remember that the villain in Manufacturing Consent, the film about Noam Chomsky, was – wait for it – the New York Times.) And now that the Internet is poised to cast these lumbering dinosaurs of black ink and dead trees into the pit of extinction, we're supposed to say hang on, what about democracy?

There's a basic error here, paired with an equally basic misunderstanding of how the marketplace of ideas works. There is no reason at all to be concerned that 80 per cent of Daily Kos readers are Democrats, any more than to worry that 80 per cent of the visitors to McDonald's like hamburgers. Given what each of these outlets is selling, it would be bizarre if it were otherwise. What would be worrisome was if four-fifths of Democrats read only the Daily Kos, but there is absolutely no evidence that is the case.

Earlier this month, the Project for Excellence in Journalism, a think tank sponsored by the Pew foundation, released its fifth annual report (at journalism.org) on the state of the news media. For the most part, its analysis of the newspaper business confirmed the trends of declining circulation, revenues and staff. But with respect to public attitudes, the PEJ found that most readers see their newspaper as increasingly biased, and 68 per cent say they prefer to get their news from sources that don't have a point of view. The PEJ also found a substantial disconnect between the issues and events that dominate the news hole (e.g. the Iraq surge, the massacre at Virginia Tech) and what the public wants to see covered – issues such as education, transportation, religion and health. What this suggests, is, aside from some failings of newspapers, that readers go online in search of less bias, not the self-absorption of the Daily Me.

Nothing about how people consume media online suggests they are looking for confirmation of pre-existing biases. In fact, we have every reason to believe that as people migrate online, it will be to seek out sources of information that they perceive to be unbiased, and which give them news they can't get anywhere else. The newspaper may be dying, but our democracy will be healthier for it.

My Notes

After recording your findings in the graphic organizer located in Activity 2.4, respond to the following:

When refuting an existing argument, writers rely on a variety of strategies. These strategies of refutation often "attack" different elements of an opponent's position. Some of the most common "attacks" include:

- Attack on a <u>claim</u>: A big picture attack focusing on the writer's overall position.
- Attack on <u>reasoning</u>: Does the evidence the writer uses logically support the conclusions?
- Attack on <u>evidence</u>: Is the evidence timely, accurate, and unbiased? Is there counter-evidence?
- Attack on <u>assumption</u>: What does the writer assume to be true and is that assumption accurate? (Writer's assumptions are often unstated.)

In the following graphic organizer, practice refuting elements adapted from Jeremy Wagstaff's article "Oh my! The future of news."

Element	Your Refutation
Claim: The Internet is transforming the meaning of news.	
Reasoning: People's fascination with movie stars shows that celebrity news is more important than traditional news.	
Evidence: People that use MySpace are producers of news.	
Assumption: Everyone has access to a source of news.	

Writing Prompt: Identify which strategies of refutation Potter uses in his response to Sunstein, and evaluate the effectiveness of those "attacks." In your response, provide examples of inductive and deductive reasoning each writer uses to support or refute claims.

Throughout the course of this unit, you will be asked to read at least one newspaper daily. Use this log to keep track of what and when you read, as well as to write down the titles of significant articles that you encounter in each section. Each day cut out or photocopy one article that you enjoyed reading.

Title of Newspaper _____

Date	Time Spent	Interesting Articles in Front Section	Interesting Articles on Op-Ed Page	Interesting Articles in One Other Section

News or Views: A Closer Look

SUGGESTED LEARNING STRATEGIES: Paraphrasing, Quickwrite, Marking the Text, Think-Pair-Share

ACADEMIC VOCABULARY

Bias is an inclination or mental leaning for or against something, which prevents impartial judgment.

We tend to think that news articles are **objective**, which means they are based on factual information. However, all news reports are to some extent **subjective** – or based on feelings or opinions – since they represent the reporter's analysis of the information surrounding the story's topic. Close analysis of the details of the text's content, structure, and publication context can often reveal subtle indications of bias in terms of how the writer frames the issue. Considering the following aspects of a text gives a basis for understanding that many news stories may be far from objective in their coverage of the stories they construct.

1. BIAS THROUGH SELECTION AND OMISSION

   • An editor can express a bias by choosing to use or not to use a specific news item. An editor might believe that advertisers want younger readers—they spend more money. Therefore, news of specific interest to old people will be ignored.

   • Within a given story, details can be ignored or included to give readers or viewers a different opinion about the events reported. If, during a speech, a few people boo, the reaction can be described as "remarks greeted by jeers" or they can be ignored as "a handful of dissidents . . ." or perhaps not even be mentioned.

   • Bias through the omission of stories or details is very difficult to detect. Only by comparing news reports from a wide variety of outlets can this form of bias be observed.

   • Bias in local news coverage can be found by comparing reports of the same event as treated in different papers.

2. BIAS THROUGH PLACEMENT

   • Readers of papers judge first-page stories to be more significant than those buried in the back. Television and radio newscasts run the most important stories first and leave the less significant to later. Where a story is placed, therefore, influences what a reader or viewer thinks about its importance and suggests the editor's evaluation of its importance.

   For example, a local editor might campaign against the owning of hand guns by giving prominent space to every shooting with a hand gun and gun-related accident in his paper.

- Some murders and robberies receive front-page attention while others receive only a mention on page twenty.

- Similarly, where information appears *within* an article may also reveal evidence of bias. Since most readers only read the first few paragraphs of any given article, burying information at the end may work to suppress a particular point of view or piece of information, while placing it at the beginning emphasizes it. The opposite might be true, though; the end could reveal the writer's closing thought (and thus his/her personal bias) on the issue.

3. BIAS BY HEADLINE

- Many people read only the headline of a news item. Most people scan nearly all the headlines in a newspaper. Headlines are the most read part of a paper. They can summarize as well as present carefully hidden bias and prejudices. They can convey excitement where little exists; they can express approval or condemnation; they can steer public opinion.

4. BIAS BY PHOTOS, CAPTIONS, AND CAMERA ANGLES

- Some pictures flatter a person; others make the person look unpleasant. A paper can choose photos to influence opinion about, for example, a candidate for election. Television can show film or videotape that praises or condemns. The choice of which visual images to display is extremely important. Newspapers run captions that are also potential sources of bias and opinion.

5. BIAS THROUGH STATISTICS AND CROWD COUNTS

- To make a disaster seem more spectacular (and therefore worthy of reading), numbers can be inflated. "One hundred injured in train wreck" can be the same as "Passengers injured in train wreck."

- Crowd counts are notoriously inaccurate and often reflect the opinion of the person doing the counting. A reporter, event sponsor, or police officer might estimate a crowd at several thousand if he or she agrees with the purpose of the assembly— or a much smaller number if he/she is critical of the crowd's purposes or beliefs. News magazines use specific numbers to enhance believability.

WORD CONNECTIONS

The perception of bias depends on evidence supporting or not supporting claims made. *Prima facie* is a Latin term meaning "on the face of it," or at first glance. An example of its use is, "*Prima facie* evidence does not support the conclusions drawn."

6. BIAS BY SOURCE CONTROL

- To detect bias, always consider where a news item "comes from." Is the information supplied by a reporter, by an eyewitness, by police or fire officials, by executives, by elected or appointed government officials? Each might have a particular bias that is presented in the story.

- Puff pieces are supplied to newspapers (and TV stations) by companies or public relations directors—and even sometimes by the government (directly or through press conferences). For example, the "Avocado Growers Association" might send a press release in the form of a news story telling of a doctor who claims that avocados are healthy and should be eaten by all. A food company might supply recipes for a newspaper's food section that recommends use of its products in the recipes. A country's tourist bureau will supply a glowing story, complete with pictures of a pleasant vacation. Recently, even government agencies have sometimes issued such releases.

- A pseudo-event is some event (demonstration, sit-in, ribbon cutting, speech, ceremony, ground breaking, etc.) that takes place primarily to gain news coverage.

- Similarly, the choice of who is quoted in an article can point to bias. Be sure to consider who is quoted, what the quote seems to reveal or imply (negatively or positively) about the position, who is merely paraphrased, and what perspectives are unrepresented or remain silent in the article.

Bias Type	Guiding Questions
Bias Through Selection and Omission	
Bias Through Placement	
Bias by Headline	
Bias by Photos, Captions, and Camera Angles	
Bias Through Statistics and Crowd Counts	
Bias by Source Control	

News or Views: A Closer Look

My Notes

While editorials openly present opinions, newspaper articles may appear objective until carefully examined for evidence that reveals a more subjective agenda. Read the following news stories and carefully evaluate them for subtle evidence of bias using the guiding questions your class has generated.

Article

Facebook Photos Sting Minnesota High School Students

The Associated Press

EDEN PRAIRIE, Minn. — For 16-year-old Nick Laurent, walking out of Eden Prairie High School yesterday to protest the school's punishment of students seen partying on Facebook pages was about asking administrators to be fair.

More than a dozen students joined Laurent after learning of the walkout from fliers the junior handed out the day before. The students said school administrators overreacted to the perception that students in the photos were drinking.

"It's the loudest thing we could do," said Laurent, who organized the walkout but said he wasn't one of the students in the photos.

Laurent tried to make his point by passing out red plastic cups that were similar to those seen in some of the photos. He noted that it was impossible to see what was inside the cups, so administrators couldn't prove that students were drinking.

Laurent agreed that athletes and other students who sign a code of conduct to be involved in activities should face consequences if they break the rule against drinking alcohol. But he said the punishments were too harsh.

"They don't have (the) support of the students to hand out arbitrary punishments and punishments that don't fit the crime," he said.

Once the photos on the social-networking Web site came to the attention of administrators, 42 students were interviewed and 13 face some discipline over the pictures, school officials said.

School officials haven't said how the students were disciplined, but Minnesota State High School League penalties start with a two-game suspension for the first violation. Laurent and other students said they knew of classmates who were banned from their sports teams for five weeks.

Principal Conn McCartan did not return a call seeking comment on the walkout, but students said they expected they'd be punished.

In earlier statements, the school's principal said school officials did not seek out the pictures. But he didn't say who gave the school the photos.

"We do not go out looking at student social networking sites. We do however take action when we are given legitimate information about school or Minnesota State High School League violations," McCartan said in an e-mail to families of his students.

McCartan said interviews with students suggested, however, that the pictures might have been posted on such sites, and warned of the dangers.

"These sites are not private places," he wrote. "Their content forms a permanent and public record of conversations and pictures."

In an e-mail to parents and guardians, Superintendent Melissa Krull said, "We are not legally at liberty to discuss further details of this investigation."

Fourteen-year-old Ali Saley said cutting class for the cause was worth it. She held signs such as, "They walk or we do," in solidarity with the students who were punished. A few cars honked in support of the students as they gathered on a footbridge over the road in front of the school.

The Eden Prairie High School students who got into trouble ran afoul of a new reality: digital cameras and social networking sites make the entire world a public space.

It's becoming increasingly common for schools and potential employers to check social networking sites such as Facebook and MySpace, and to penalize kids or other people for what they find, said William McGeveran, a professor at the University of Minnesota Law School and an expert on data privacy.

"Facebook is largely a public space. Users don't always perceive it that way, but that's what it is," McGeveran said.

Even when young people are cautious about what they put on the pages, he said, friends or acquaintances can post pictures of them in questionable situations without their knowing about it.

McGeveran cited research by the Pew Internet & American Life Project that suggested most teens were aware of the risks of posting personal information on the Internet. A report issued last month found that most teens restrict access to their posted photos and videos at least some of the time, and that few consistently share them without any restrictions.

My Notes

My Notes

"But some students are still foolish about what they put on their pages," he said.

Eden Prairie High School has about 3,300 students, and Facebook lists about 2,800 members in its network for the school, including more than 500 from the current senior class. A spot check on Jan. 9 showed that some had posted dozens and even hundreds of pictures of themselves and their friends. However, most members used a privacy setting to limit access to their profiles to friends and other authorized people.

Schools in Minnesota have limited ability to regulate the conduct of students after hours. When students participate in sports or certain fine-arts activities, however, they must agree in writing to abide by the long-standing rules of the Minnesota State High School League, which prohibit the use of alcohol, tobacco and controlled substances, even over the summer.

League spokesman Howard Voigt noted that parents must sign the forms, too, certifying that they understand the rules and penalties. Still, he said, complaints are common.

"We run into that all the time here — parents call and accuse us of being too hard on their kid," he said.

Voigt said there had been several cases of students' running afoul of league rules because of potential violations posted on social-networking sites.

It's not safe for kids to assume what they do in small groups won't be broadcast to the entire world, McGeveran said.

"I don't think most of us would have liked to have lived our teen years in an era of ubiquitous camera phones and social networking," he said. "It really changes the perception of what places are private and which ones aren't."

Federal Way schools restrict Gore film

by Robert McClure and Lisa Stiffler

This week in Federal Way schools, it got a lot more inconvenient to show one of the top-grossing documentaries in U.S. history, the global-warming alert "An Inconvenient Truth."

After a parent who supports the teaching of creationism and opposes sex education complained about the film, the Federal Way School Board on Tuesday placed what it labeled a moratorium on showing the film. The movie consists largely of a computer presentation by former Vice President Al Gore recounting scientists' findings.

"Condoms don't belong in school, and neither does Al Gore. He's not a schoolteacher," said Frosty Hardison, a parent of seven who also said that he believes the Earth is 14,000 years old. "The information that's being presented is a very cockeyed view of what the truth is. ... The Bible says that in the end times everything will burn up, but that perspective isn't in the DVD."

Hardison's e-mail to the School Board prompted board member David Larson to propose the moratorium Tuesday night.

"Somebody could say you're killing free speech, and my retort to them would be we're encouraging free speech," said Larson, a lawyer. "The beauty of our society is we allow debate."

School Board members adopted a three-point policy that says teachers who want to show the movie must ensure that a "credible, legitimate opposing view will be presented," that they must get the OK of the principal and the superintendent, and that any teachers who have shown the film must now present an "opposing view."

The requirement to represent another side follows district policy to represent both sides of a controversial issue, board President Ed Barney said.

"What is purported in this movie is, 'This is what is happening. Period. That is fact,'" Barney said.

Students should hear the perspective of global-warming skeptics and then make up their minds, he said. After they do, "if they think driving around in cars is going to kill us all, that's fine, that's their choice."

Asked whether an alternative explanation for evolution should be presented by teachers, Barney said it would be appropriate to tell students that other beliefs exist. "It's only a theory," he said.

While the question of climate change has provoked intense argument in political circles in recent years, among scientists its basic tenets have become the subject of an increasingly stronger consensus.

My Notes

GRAMMAR & USAGE

News stories often carry many direct quotes. Notice, however, that this story contains a blend of complete quotations of one or more sentences, quotes of short phrases, and indirect quotes, which are paraphrases. The variety keeps the story from being boring or confusing. The same is true for research papers. Use longer quotes when the words are especially significant. Otherwise, rely on paraphrases and short quoted phrases.

My Notes

"In the light of new evidence and taking into account the remaining uncertainties, most of the observed warming over the last 50 years is likely to have been due to the increase in greenhouse gas concentrations," states a 2001 report by the Intergovernmental Panel on Climate Change, which advises policymakers.

"Furthermore, it is very likely that the 20th-century warming has contributed significantly to the observed sea level rise, through thermal expansion of seawater and widespread loss of land ice."

The basics of that position are backed by the American Meteorological Society, the American Geophysical Union, the American Association for the Advancement of Science and the National Academy of Sciences.

Laurie David, a co-producer of the movie, said that this is the first incident of its kind relating to the film.

"I am shocked that a school district would come to this decision," David said in a prepared statement. "There is no opposing view to science, which is fact, and the facts are clear that global warming is here, now."

The Federal Way incident started when Hardison learned that his daughter would see the movie in class. He objected.

Hardison and his wife, Gayla, said they would prefer that the movie not be shown at all in schools.

"From what I've seen (of the movie) and what my husband has expressed to me, if (the movie) is going to take the approach of 'bad America, bad America,' I don't think it should be shown at all," Gayle Hardison said. "If you're going to come in and just say America is creating the rotten ruin of the world, I don't think the video should be shown."

Scientists say that Americans, with about 5 percent of the world's population, emit about 25 percent of the globe-warming gases.

Larson, the School Board member, said a pre-existing policy should have alerted teachers and principals that the movie must be counterbalanced.

The policy, titled "Controversial Issues, Teaching of," says in part, "It is the teacher's responsibility to present controversial issues that are free from prejudice and encourage students to form, hold and express their own opinions without personal prejudice or discrimination."

"The principal reason for that is to make sure that the public schools are not used for indoctrination," Larson said.

Students contacted Wednesday said they favor allowing the movie to be shown.

"I think that a movie like that is a really great way to open people's eyes up about what you can do and what you are doing to the planet and how that's going to affect the human race," said Kenna Patrick, a senior at Jefferson High School.

When it comes to the idea of presenting global warming skeptics, Patrick wasn't sure how necessary that would be. She hadn't seen the movie but had read about it and would like to see it.

"Watching a movie doesn't mean that you have to believe everything you see in it," she said.

Joan Patrick, Kenna's mother, thought it would be a good idea for students to see the movie. They are the ones who will be dealing with the effects of a warmer planet.

"It's their job," she said. "They're the next generation."

Sometimes a writer compensates for a lack of evidence and logical argumentation by using slanted language and emotional appeals to present a prejudiced depiction of a subject. This happens so often that there are actually many names for these various **"slanters"** (rhetorical devices used to present the subject in a **biased** way). As you read through the techniques described below, try to think of examples from the media that fit the descriptions (adapted from Brooke Noel Moore and Richard Parker's *Critical Thinking*, 8th ed, 2007).

1. **Labeling (euphemisms and dysphemisms):** The use of a highly connotative word or phrase to name or describe a subject or action, a technique also called using loaded language. When the connotations are positive (or less negative), the writer is using euphemism. For example, car dealers try to sell "pre-owned vehicles" rather than "used cars." In the opposite case, negative connotations may be assigned to a term. Consider, for example, the differences between these terms: *freedom fighter, guerrilla, rebel,* and *terrorist. Freedom fighter* is a euphemism while *terrorist* is a dysphemism.

2. **Rhetorical analogy:** The use of a figurative comparison (sometimes a simile or a metaphor) to convey a positive or negative feeling towards the subject. For example, in the 2008 presidential race, Sarah Palin suggested (via a joke) that she was like a pit bull with lipstick. In another famous moment of the campaign, a McCain ad compared Barack Obama to Paris Hilton, thus suggesting he was an unqualified celebrity. "The environment needs George W. Bush like farmers need a drought" is another example.

3. **Rhetorical definition:** The use of emotively charged language to express or elicit an attitude about something. A classic example is defining capital punishment as "government-sanctioned murder." A rhetorical definition stacks the deck either for or against the position it implies.

4. **Rhetorical explanation:** Expressing an opinion as if it were fact, and doing so in biased language. For example, you might say someone "didn't have the guts to fight back" when taunted by another person. This paints the person as motivated by cowardice. Or you might say the person "took the high road, instead of taking a swing."

5. **Innuendo:** The use of language to imply that a particular inference is justified, as if saying "go ahead and read between the lines!" In this way, the speaker doesn't have to actually make a claim that can't be supported; instead, the audience is led to make the leap on their own. For example, a presidential candidate might say, "Think carefully about whom you choose; you want a president who will be ready to do the job on day one." The implication is that the opposing candidate is not ready.

6. **Downplayers**: The use of qualifier words or phrases to make someone or something look less important or significant. In *An Inconvenient Truth*, for example, Al Gore refers several times to the "so-called skeptics," in contrast to how he often refers to the experts he cites in his speech as "my friend." Words like "mere" and "only" work this way, as well, as does the use of quotation marks, to suggest a term is ironic or misleading. For example: "She got her 'degree' from a correspondence school." Often these references are linked to concessions with connectors such as *nevertheless, however, still,* or *but*.

7. **Hyperbole**: The use of extravagant overstatement, which can work to move the audience to accept the basic claim even if they reject the extremes of the word choice. Many of the other "slanters" can be hyperbolic in the way they are worded, but the key part is that the statement or claim is extreme. For example, in response to a dress code, a student might say "This school administration is fascist!"

8. **Truth Surrogates**: Hinting that proof exists to support a claim without actually citing that proof. For example, ads often say "studies show," and tabloids often say things like "according to an insider" or "there's every reason to believe that . . ." If the evidence does exist, the writer is doing a poor job of citing it; meanwhile, the writer has not actually identified any source—or made any claim—that can be easily disproven or challenged.

9. **Ridicule/Sarcasm**: The use of language that suggests the subject is worthy of scorn. The language seeks to evoke a laugh or sarcastically mock the subject.

WORD CONNECTIONS

To analyze analogies, you must look at alternative meanings of words. For example, look at this analogy.

murder : crows ::
team : players

You may first think of *murder* as a crime, but that does not describe the relationship between team and players. If you think of a team being composed of players, then you make the connection that a flock of crows may be called a *murder*. Create your own analogy using words that have multiple meanings.

SUGGESTED LEARNING STRATEGIES: Marking the Text, SMELL,
Discussion Groups, Quickwrite

My Notes

Editorial

Abolish high school football!

by Raymond A. Schroth

Are you sure playing high school football is good for your son?

I had doubts long before I read the report in the New York Times (Sept 15) that of the 1.2 million teenagers who play high school football, an estimated 50 percent have suffered at least one concussion, 35 percent two or more. Since 1997, throughout 20 states, 50 boys have died.

A concussion is a blow to the head that smashes the brain against the skull. Because their brain tissues are less developed, adolescents are most vulnerable. The victim feels "weird," has splotchy vision, falls to the ground, vomits, goes into a coma, dies. If he survives he suffers depression, he can't concentrate, drops out, and/or develops symptoms later in life.

Worst of all, the young men overwhelmingly told the reporter that if they thought their heads had been damaged they would never tell the coach, because he might take them out of the game.

I've felt high school football did more harm than good since I taught high school in the 1960s, since I began getting an inkling of the damage done young bodies in both high school and college, where linemen are encouraged to "bulk up" to a grotesque 300 pounds in order to do more damage to the enemy — to say nothing of the damage done to their own late adolescent bodies by getting so fat.

Football, especially in high school, distorts the goals of the so-called educational institution that sponsors it, turns ordinary boys into bedazzled heroes, tells them they're the kings of the corridors, coddled by teachers afraid to flunk them, as their parents try to live out their glamorous dreams over the broken bodies of their children bashing their helmeted heads into one another as thousands cheer.

Buzz Bissinger's 1990 bestselling "Friday Night Lights," a popular book, film, and TV series, was, in the long run, an indictment of the small Texas town with nothing going for it but its high school football team. If the town had a library, churches, a theater, a park – if the school had any classes – we never saw them. They were irrelevant.

The boys went to high school to play, feeding delusions that they would be noticed by a scout who would get them college scholarships and contracts on pro teams.

But, you say, if high schools drop football, that will deprive colleges and the pros of their feeder system. Right. It will also deprive colleges of many who have come for only one reason – to play – while their paid tutors ease them through the motions of an education.

But, you say, some football players are very bright. Absolutely right. I have taught three in recent years who were the best in the class, straight A's, a delight to have in the room. But they are exceptions to the rule, and few and far between.

Without football, how can ambitious athletes thrive? They can play soccer, basketball, baseball, tennis, lacrosse, and squash. They can run, swim, row, sail, wrestle, and bike. They can also read, write for the paper, act, sing, dance, walk, and pray. And when they graduate their brains will be enriched, not bruised.

The Times article quotes Kelby Jasmon, a high school student in Springfield, Ill., walking around today with two concussions, who says there is "no chance" he would tell the coach if he gets hit hard and symptoms return. "It's not dangerous to play with a concussion," he says. "You've got to sacrifice for the team. The only way I come out is on a stretcher."

If the school officials and his parents read that and leave him on the field, something is very, very wrong.

Fair and Balanced: Part II

SMELL is an effective strategy for analyzing a writer's use of language in support of a position. As you read Schroth's essay, look for evidence of biased language; then fill in the SMELL chart below.

Sender-Receiver Relationship – To whom is the writer explicitly addressing his argument? How does he seem to feel about that target audience? What values does the sender assume the reader shares or argue that they should share?

Message – What is a literal summary of the content? What is the article's ultimate thesis regarding the subject?

Emotional Strategies – What emotional appeals does the writer include? What seems to be their desired effect?

Logical Strategies – What logical arguments/appeals does the writer include? What is their effect?

Language – What specific language/slanters are used in the article to support the message or characterize the opposition?

In the boxes below, copy five of the more slanted passages from Schroth's essay and revise them to be less rhetorically manipulative.

Original Passage	Revised Passage

How to Read an Editorial

ACADEMIC VOCABULARY

An **editorial** is an article in a newspaper or magazine expressing the opinion of its editor or publisher.

How to Read an Editorial

The purpose of a news story is to inform you about a particular and noteworthy event.

The purpose of an **editorial** may also be to inform, but its main objective is to persuade.

When you read an editorial, consider the following:

1. Examine the headline, sub-headline and related cartoon (if it exists). What will this editorial be about? What guesses or assumptions can you make about the writer's perspective at this point?

2. Look at the writer's name and affiliation, if given. What do you know about the writer's background and/or potential bias at this point?

3. Read the first two to three paragraphs very carefully. What issue is the writer discussing and what is his or her stance on this issue?

4. Once you have determined the writer's stance on the issue, stop reading for a moment or two. What is the other side of the issue? Who might think differently? What are one or two reasons that you know that might support a side opposite the writer's stance?

5. Continue reading the editorial. What are two of the strongest pieces of evidence that the writer uses to support his or her side of the issue? Why are they effective?

6. Did the writer persuade you? Did the writer address/refute the main objections of the opposition? Give an example. What did he or she not address? Why might the writer have chosen not to address this element? Do you feel that the writer was fair to the other side? Why or why not?

7. Go back through the editorial and circle words and phrases that are "slanted." How do these words affect your feelings about the issue? About the writer?

8. If the writer were standing right next to you now, what would you say to him or her?

Use the questions on the previous page to guide your responses to the editorial on pages 142–143.

Title _____ Writer _____ Issue _____

Question	Response
1	
2	
3	
4	
5	
6	
7	
8	

My Notes

Editorial

FACING CONSEQUENCES AT EDEN PRAIRIE HIGH

from the *Minneapolis/St. Paul Star Tribune*

This just in: Some high school students drink alcohol and, in the Internet age, some underage drinkers are foolish enough to post party photos on popular websites. In the case of Eden Prairie High School vs. the partying Facebook students, we give administrators credit for their judgment and flunk the students on common sense.

Similarly, any parents considering taking legal action because they think the school went too far in disciplining students need a reality check. Teen drinking remains a serious problem in this state and Eden Prairie administrators deserve praise – not legal threats or complaints from parents – for taking decisive action that they knew would be controversial. Face it, parents, the Facebook kids screwed up, and here's a chance to talk about personal responsibility in the context of an underage drinking escapade that, thankfully, did not involve death or injury.

And here's the reality for students: We know high school students drink, and some experiment with drugs. Most of your baby boomer parents certainly did one or both, and some lost driver's licenses, had serious auto accidents and were suspended from the football team. That's how it goes with risks and consequences.

Your parents can probably tell you a few stories about binge drinking, too, either from their high school or college days or both. If not, go to the search field at startribune.com and type in these names: Jenna Foellmi, Rissa Amen-Reif, Amanda Jax and Brian W. Threet. In the past four months, these four young people all died in drinking-related incidents in Minnesota. Brian's funeral was Thursday afternoon in Farmington.

With that backdrop, protests over invasion of privacy are ridiculous. School administrators weren't surfing social networking sites without

My Notes

cause. They received a complaint and had a responsibility to investigate and act according to school policies. Students who think the Web has been used against them unfairly should fast-forward a few years and consider how they'll feel when a potential employer uses Facebook or MySpace in a background check, with a job offer on the line.

Some are viewing the athletes among the students who were caught red-cupped in Eden Prairie through a surprisingly sympathetic lens. That's wrongheaded. The Minnesota High School League requires student-athletes and their parents to pledge that the students will abstain from alcohol and illegal drugs. Break the pledge, lose the privilege.

We were encouraged by the reaction of Eden Prairie High School parent Larry Burke, whose daughter was not involved in the drinking incident. "The posting is very foolish," Burke told the Star Tribune. "But from a perspective of a parent, I'm glad it happened. There are a lot of discussions going on in a lot of households about alcohol and consequences."

Let's hope other parents bring as much common sense to those conversations as Burke.

facebook®

How to Write an Editorial

SUGGESTED LEARNING STRATEGIES: **RAFT**, Graphic Organizer, Drafting, Sharing and Responding, SOAPStone

How to Write an Editorial

Before You Write

- **Brainstorm for topics:** Choose topics in which you have a genuine interest and some prior knowledge. Be sure that they are issues that are debatable. Do not, for example, argue against school violence since no one in his or her right mind would ever be for such a thing. Many editorials are written as responses to news articles or other editorials, so keep your eyes open for interesting ideas while reading the paper each day.

- **Research your topic:** Ask opinions, conduct interviews, and locate facts. While editorials are opinion pieces, those opinions must still be supported with evidence.

- **Get both sides:** In addition to having support for your position, be certain that you have information about the other side of the issue.

- **Consider your audience:** Use a SOAPSTone as a prewriting strategy to consider details of your audience. What does your audience currently believe about this issue? Why? How will they respond to you? Why? What can you do to persuade them to change their minds? How will using slanted language affect your credibility and persuasiveness with them?

- **Write a thesis:** Before writing your draft, you must have a clearly stated position on this issue with a strongly worded reason for your position.

- **Write out your topic sentences and/or main ideas:** This preparation will help you organize your thoughts as you draft your editorial.

Writing a Draft

- **Get to the point:** Your first paragraph should immediately bring the reader's attention to the seriousness of the issue. Use a "hook" that will sell the piece to the reader: a current event or imminent danger, for example. You should then provide a concise summary of what you're going to tell the reader and include your thesis statement.

- **Provide context:** Give your readers important background information about the issue. This background should not be common knowledge (e.g., "drugs are dangerous"), but should frame the issue and define any key terms that your reader will need in order to understand your argument.

- **Make your point:** Give your strongest two or three reasons why the reader should agree with you. Use relevant and appropriate evidence to support your reasons. Be sure to state the source of your information. Be sure that your argument is clear and organized.

- **Address your opposition:** Reasonable people may think differently than you do on the subject. State at least one or two of the most credible reasons why someone might object to your point of view. Then refute their positions by explaining why their assumptions, claims, logic and/or evidence are wrong.

- **Wrap it up:** Briefly summarize the main points of your argument and think of a powerful way to end your piece. Often this means giving your reader one last thought to consider.

Revising Your Draft

- **Check your evidence:** As you look back through your draft, consider whether you have included enough evidence to convince someone who thinks differently than you. Also, is that evidence relevant to your position?

- **Check your rhetoric:** Where is your language slanted? What words or phrases could you modify to "tone" down your voice and appeal to more people?

- **Check your grammar:** Nothing will make it easier for someone to dismiss your ideas than if you misspell or misuse words or phrases. Triple-check your editorial.

How to Write an Editorial

Issue: Raising Graduation Requirements

Should academic graduation requirements be raised for high school students in your district? Complete the following chart after you have read and analyzed the two editorials that address this question.

Writer	Reasons For	Reasons Against	Strongest Statement of Position
Jack O'Connell			
Nick Thomas			
You			
A Person You Know			

Time to raise the bar in high schools

by Jack O'Connell

The most important challenge we face in public education today is to improve high schools so that all California students graduate prepared to succeed in either college or the workplace. Today, far too many of our 1.7 million high school students are prepared for neither the demands of skilled employment nor the rigors of higher education. Employers consistently complain of graduates who lack critical problem-solving and communications skills. More than half of students entering California State University need remediation in reading or math. It is clearly time for us to re-examine high school in California, to raise the level of rigor we expect of all of our students and begin preparing every high school student to reach higher expectations.

How we meet the challenge of improving high school student achievement will determine the futures of our children and their ability to compete and succeed in the decades to come. Moreover, how we respond to this challenge will significantly affect the economic and social future of our state.

Research shows that students who take challenging, college-preparatory courses do better in school, even if they started out with poor test scores and low expectations. Students who take rigorous courses are also less likely to drop out, and they perform better in vocational and technical courses.

Our high schools today struggle with an achievement gap that leaves African-American, Latino and socioeconomically disadvantaged students lagging behind their peers. A failure to provide and expect all students to take demanding academic coursework has also created a high school "reality gap:" While more than 80 percent of high school students say they intend to go to college, only about 40 percent actually take the rigorous coursework required for acceptance at a four-year university. The numbers are even lower for African-American graduates (24 percent) and Latinos (22 percent).

Many students are not aware that the "minimum requirement" courses they are taking aren't providing the rigorous foundation that will prepare them to fulfill their dreams after high school. In some cases, students are steered away from tough courses or find them overenrolled. The result is thousands of students who must spend significant, unnecessary time and money after high school if they are ever to fulfill their dreams.

To reverse this trend, we must make rigorous courses available to all of our students. We must redefine high schools as institutions that provide all students with a strong academic foundation, whether they are bound for college or the workplace after graduation.

My Notes

GRAMMAR & USAGE

Diction plays an important role in establishing the tone and the credibility of a writer. Notice that O'Connell uses a formal and educated diction, which reflects and enhances his position as the school superintendent. He chooses words such as *remediation* instead of *help*, *rigorous* instead of *difficult*, *overenrolled* instead of *full*.

How to Write an Editorial

My Notes

I am proposing a High Performing High Schools Initiative that will raise expectations for our high schools and high school students. It will provide better training and support for high school principals. And it will establish a state "seal of approval" process for high school instructional materials, giving districts guidance in choosing materials that are standards-aligned, and therefore more rigorous than many used in high schools today.

It is simply wrong to decide for students as young as age 15 whether or not they are "college material" and capable of challenging courses in high school. Guiding students to an easier academic pathway, even if they show little early motivation or curiosity about possibilities beyond high school, virtually guarantees they won't be prepared with important foundational skills. It limits their opportunities for years to come. Years ago, this was called "tracking." Students facing childhood challenges such as poverty or the need to learn English — the description of fully well over a quarter of California's students today — would be tracked to less-challenging courses and denied opportunities after high school as a result.

By advocating for tougher curriculum in high schools, I am not in any way suggesting vocational education programs should be eliminated. In fact, legislation I introduced to improve high school achievement would reward schools that collaborate with businesses or labor unions to expand such successful programs as career partnership academies. These academies have been successful where they have provided rigorous academic instruction geared toward a career pathway.

The truth is that we can no longer afford to hold high expectations only for our college-bound students. Today, all of our students need the skills and knowledge contained in the curriculum that was once reserved only for the college-bound. Strong communications skills, knowledge of foreign language and culture, higher-level math and problem-solving skills are needed in technical trades as well as white-collar professions. The job of K-12 education in California must be to ensure that all of our students graduate with the ability to fulfill their potential — whether that takes them to higher education or directly to their career.

Editorial

New Michigan Graduation Requirements Shortchange Many Students

by Nick Thomas

Imagine waking up in the morning to find the electricity is out, or a pipe has burst or your car won't start. As you look though the Yellow Pages for a technician, do you really care if that person has a working knowledge of matrices, oxidation numbers, and Kepler's laws of planetary motion?

Apparently the state of Michigan does. Its new high school graduation requirements will assure that every graduate, regardless of their career choice, will have taken advanced math and science classes.

Among the new requirements are one credit each of algebra I, geometry and algebra II and an additional math class in the senior year. Also required is one credit of biology, one credit of physics or chemistry and one additional year of science.

This new curriculum may be helpful for a student who plans to go on to college, but it seems excessive for vocational students.

Plumbers, mechanics, construction workers, hairdressers and many other positions do not need an advanced math and science background. Math needed for vocational jobs could be learned through an "applied math" class, or on-site learning.

I'm concerned that when students are forced to take classes that are unnecessary for their chosen careers, they'll feel discouraged and put little effort into their classes. And if they can't take the classes they want, I'm afraid that more of them will drop out.

Advanced classes becoming basic classes

One of my biggest concerns with all students taking advanced classes is that the pace of the courses will slow down. Some students will undoubtedly not try to learn the material, and some will be incapable of learning as fast as others, leaving the teacher compelled to dumb down the class. In effect, advanced classes will become basic classes. This will have no additional benefit for vocational students and will hamper college prep students.

There's yet another way college-bound students might suffer from the new requirements. A very gifted English student who lacks ability in math could have their grade point average lowered significantly when required to take advanced math classes. And of course, when applying to college, high school grades are important.

© 2011 College Board. All rights reserved.

My Notes

A well-rounded education is ideal but can be achieved in many ways, not just through academics. Our economy depends on a variety of jobs. We need carpenters as well as engineers. We need hairdressers as well as doctors, and we need heavy equipment operators as well as lawyers.

All jobs are important, and students deserve to pursue their choice of a career without being forced to take unnecessary classes.

Where's Your Proof?

To support the claims they make, writers use a variety of types of evidence. With a partner or small group, revisit one of the editorials you have read in this unit and fill in the chart below.

Type of Evidence: What is it used for? What are its limitations? "They X, but they Y."	Example from an Editorial in this Unit	Evaluation: What kind of appeal does it make: logos, ethos, or pathos? Does the evidence logically support the writer's claim in this case? Why or why not?
Illustrative Examples (Personal Experience/Anecdotal/Media Example). They give a reality to the claim, but may not be generalizable.		
Hypothetical Cases. They challenge the reader to consider possible circumstances or outcomes, but there's no reason they will definitely happen.		
Analogies/Comparison. They make the unfamiliar or abstract more accessible, but they need to be more similar than different in order to be persuasive.		
Expert Testimony. They provide expert support for causal claims, predictions of outcomes, or possible solutions, but they're still just opinions—and the source needs to be checked carefully!		
Statistics/Surveys. They support generalized claims and make strong logical appeals, but they must be reliable and unbiased.		
Causal Relationships. They suggest possible positive or negative outcomes, but there needs to be a clear link between the cause and the effect.		

Reading and Writing a Letter to the Editor

How to Write a Letter to the Editor

Letters that are intended for publication should be drafted carefully. Here are some tips to keep in mind:

- Make one point (or at most two) in your letter. Be sure to identify the topic of your letter. State the point clearly, ideally in the first sentence.

- Make your letter timely. If you are not addressing a specific article, editorial, or letter that recently appeared in the paper you are writing to, tie the issue you are writing about to a recent event.

- Familiarize yourself with the coverage and editorial position of the paper to which you are writing. Refute or support specific statements, address relevant facts that are ignored, offer a completely different perspective on the issue, but avoid blanket attacks on the media in general or the newspaper in particular.

- Consider your audience (the newspaper's editors and readers).

- What does your audience currently believe about the issue? Why?

- How will they respond to you? Why?

- What can you do to persuade them to change their minds?

- How will using slanted language affect your credibility and persuasiveness?

- Check the letter specifications of the newspaper to which you are writing. Length and format requirements vary from paper to paper. Generally, roughly two short paragraphs are ideal. You also must include your name, signature, address, and phone number.

- Look at the letters that appear in your paper. Is a certain type of letter usually printed?

- Support your facts. If the topic you address is controversial, consider sending documentation along with your letter. But don't overload the editors with too much information.

- Keep your letter brief. Type and spell-check it. Have a peer edit it.

- When possible, find others in the community to write letters to show concern about the issue. If your letter doesn't get published, perhaps someone else's on the same topic will.

Fill in the chart below for each of the letters to the editor in response to the editorial your teacher provided. The last box is for your opinions.

Letter Number	Agree or Disagree with Original Editorial?	Reasons
1		
2		
3		
4		
5		
6		
You		

Writing Prompt: Next, craft a letter of your own in response to the editorial. Be sure to follow all of the guidelines for writing a letter to the editor.

My Notes

Editorial

Why I Hate Cell Phones

by Sara Reihani

In this wild, unpredictable world that modern society has thrust upon us, only one gadget anchors us amid the whirl of Wiis, Wikis and Wi-fi: the cellular phone. From its origins as the pineapple-sized "car phone" exclusive to power-suited 80's business executives to its current incarnation as camera/computer/life coach, the cell phone has gone from convenient utility to graven idol of instant gratification. Scores of modern social phenomena are directly attributable to cell phones including textual flirtation, Bluetooth use disguised as schizophrenia and the ringtone as a profound expression of personal identity.

While being constantly reachable has undeniable advantages, cell phones deceive us into thinking that this accessibility is an inalienable right rather than a flawed privilege. By giving people my cell phone number, I give them permission to contact me whenever they want, no matter where I am or what I am doing. I am thus shackled to their whim, subjecting me to their contact when it may not be desired. I could, of course, simply turn off my phone, but this is no longer an acceptable excuse. After all, what is the use of owning a cell phone if you are going to leave it off all the time?

Those who live lives more unpredictable than mine may have good reason to consider their cell phones crucial lifelines, but for most of us, they are more of a luxury than a necessity. Cell phones are currently dirt cheap to manufacture, but their true cost is insidious and pervasive. Besides the perils of hidden fees and the lubricious[1] allure of text-messaging, one must consider the emotional enslavement that comes with allowing the outside world to contact you almost anywhere. Owning a cell phone guarantees that you can and will be interrupted in movie theaters, libraries or scenes of pastoral tranquility, usually for trivial reasons. In a world full of landlines, pay phones, email, instant messages and Facebook messages, few of us need the accessibility to go that extra mile.

---

[1] **lubricious:** shifty or tricky

The most alluring thing about cell phones for the younger generation (i.e. us) is their efficacy as instruments of spontaneity. They ensure that no matter where you are or what you are doing, you can be notified of other entertainment opportunities; namely, where the new party is at. In this way, we are freed from the responsibility of making plans in advance. We can also cancel plans at the last minute without condemning ourselves to evenings of loneliness — instead, we can just use the opportunity to insinuate ourselves upon everyone else in our electronic phone books. This protean[2] convenience breeds selfishness by liberating us from any solid idea of obligation. The primal human fear of isolation also comes into play here; cell phones feed on this anxiety like blood-hungry mosquitoes, promising a solution for the many who live in vague terror of spending time alone with their thoughts.

In a way, cell phones actually decrease effective communication. They allow us to make calls from almost anywhere, meaning that we do not have to interrupt our other activities to sit down and call someone in particular. We can do anything while talking on the phone: distractedly check Facebook, drive irresponsibly. If I can call someone at any time to obtain or verify information, it lessens my incentive to actually listen to them the first time they tell me something, which is inadvertently disrespectful and powerfully habit-forming. The worst side effect of modern conveniences like cell phones is how easy it is to be dependent on them in the most casual situations.

They give you brain cancer, too.

---

[2] **protean**: diverse, varied

My Notes

ACADEMIC VOCABULARY

Fallacies are false or misleading arguments.

Fallacies are ubiquitous in advertising, political discourse, and everyday conversations—and they will continue to be as long as they work as ways to persuade. However, by learning to recognize them when you see them, you can strip away their power. There are many different ways to categorize fallacies, and many different names for the various types. The following eleven fallacies (adapted from Brooke Noel Moore and Richard Parker's *Critical Thinking*, 8th ed, 2007), a rogue's gallery of most frequent offenders, are divided into the different types of offense they represent. Learn these and you'll be ready to see through many of the rhetorical scams that come your way each day.

LOGICAL FALLACIES: ERRORS IN REASONING

1. Hasty Generalization: The leap to a generalized conclusion based on only a few instances. For example, on a trip to Paris you meet several rude Parisians, leading you to conclude that French people are rude.

2. Post Hoc: Literally meaning "after this," it's a causal fallacy in which a person assumes one thing caused another simply because it happened prior to the other. For instance, the high school soccer team loses an important game the day after they start wearing new uniforms. The coach blames the loss on the new uniforms.

EMOTIVE FALLACIES: REPLACING LOGIC WITH EMOTIONAL MANIPULATION

3. Ad Populum: Literally meaning "to the people"; refers to a variety of appeals that play on the association of a person or subject with values that are held by members of a target group (think of images of the flag in ads playing on patriotism), or the suggestion that "everybody knows" that something is true (as with bandwagon).

4. "Argument" from Outrage: Aristotle said that if you understand what makes a man angry, you can use that anger to persuade him to accept a position without critically evaluating it. This fallacy is the backbone of talk radio and of political rhetoric on both extremes of the political spectrum. It often employs loaded language and labels. It also includes scapegoating—blaming a certain group of people, or even a single person.

5. Ad Misericordiam, or Appeal to Pity: If you've ever asked a teacher to give you a better grade or a second chance because things have been tough recently or because you worked SO hard, you're guilty of this one! It refers to an attempt to use compassion or pity to replace a logical argument.

6. Ad Baculum, or Scare Tactics: An appeal to fear in place of logic. If a candidate for office says "electing my opponent will open the door for new terrorist attacks," it represents an attempt to scare people into rejecting the person, despite providing no evidence to justify the claim.

RHETORICAL FALLACIES: SIDESTEPPING LOGIC WITH LANGUAGE

7. Straw Man: Erecting a distorted or exaggerated representation of a position that is easily refuted. For example, Schroth says, "But, you say, if high schools drop football it will deprive colleges and the pros of their feeder system," an argument that is, of course, a ridiculous attempt to justify high school football—and one that is thus easy to refute.

8. Ad Hominem/Genetic Fallacy: Literally meaning "to the man," ad hominem refers to attacks against a person rather than the ideas the person presents. This is a dominant feature in political campaigns, where sound-bite 30-second advertisements attack a candidate's character, often with mere innuendo, instead of his/her policy positions. When this extends to criticizing or rejecting a general type of something simply because it belongs to or was generated by that type, you have the genetic fallacy. For example to say an idea comes from the "media elite" makes it sound as if it should be rejected—but who are the media elite?

9. Red Herring/Smokescreen: Answering the question by changing the subject. For example, when pulled over for speeding, a person might respond to the officer's question, "Why were you speeding?" by saying, "The school no longers offers driver's education classes."

10. Slippery Slope: Half an appeal to fear and half a causal fallacy; people use a slippery slope when they suggest one action will lead to an inevitable and undesirable outcome. To say that passing gun-show background checks will lead to the repeal of the 2nd Amendment represents a slippery slope argument.

11. **Either/Or (or false dilemma):** This is a conclusion that oversimplifies the argument by suggesting there are only two possible sides or choices. This fallacy is commonly used in debates of policy, where issues are always complex but which politicians reduce to simplistic either/or choices for rhetorical purposes.

   Quickwrite: In the space below or on your own paper, write a letter to the editor in which you use one of these fallacies to support your position. You might modify the letter you wrote in the previous activity or use the topic from today's discussion.

After exploring these fallacies in class and using one in a brief letter to the editor, discuss the following questions in a small group.

- Why are fallacies so common in our political discourse? Which ones are most common and why?

- Why are fallacies so powerful—and so dangerous?

- Why might you choose to use a fallacy—or rhetorical slanters—in a letter or speech?

- What would be the pros and cons of doing so?

- How does the use of fallacies affect the ethos of a writer or speaker?

- What is the relationship between considering your audience and deciding whether to use fallacious appeals or slanters?

How to Read and Write an Editorial Cartoon

Informational Text

An Inside Look at Editorial Cartoons

by Bill Brennen

A few weeks ago, Joy Utecht, the journalism teacher at Grand Island Senior High, asked if I could visit with some of her students about editorial cartoons.

The invitation was exciting because editorial cartoons are one of my favorite subjects. Very few items are as unique to a newspaper as editorial cartoons.

A very brief history lesson: Editorial cartoons first appeared in the United States on single-page broadsheets during the colonial times. The first popular cartoon is a snake severed into 13 parts with the names of each colony by each piece. The caption is simple, "Divided we die."

Such a theme helped the colonies, with their diverse locations and interests, unite under a common cause.

Flash forward to the years in New York City after the Civil War, when Tammany Hall became such a powerful political machine that it nearly sucked the life out of its residents. In addition, William Tweed stole millions from the taxpayers.

Eventually, the *New York Times* and eventually law enforcement officials began investigations of the Tweed Ring, but it was the powerful cartoons of Nast that brought the politicians to their knees. At one point, Nast, who worked for *Harper's Weekly*, turned down a bribe of $500,000 to discontinue his cartoons.

Instead, Nast made Tweed the most recognizable face in America. When Tweed tried to flee conviction, he was arrested in Spain, because authorities recognized his face from Nast's cartoons.

By the way, Nast deserves partial credit for another icon, one that has stood the test of time. Along with an artist named Clement Moore, Nast drew the first Santa Claus.

Photography became a part of America newspapers and magazines as early as the Civil War, but the process was difficult and illustrations remained a part of American newspapers until early into the 20th Century.

My Notes

How to Read and Write an Editorial Cartoon

My Notes

But the sketches known as editorial cartoons are as popular today as they ever have been. People love the humor, simplicity and caricatures of politicians of the day. Caricatures, I told the students at Senior High, are exaggerations of one's physical features.

In recent years, there have been the JFK haircut, the LBJ ears, the Nixon eyebrows, the Carter teeth and the Clinton jaw. Of course, each cartoonist has his or her own style, but it is amazing how they reach out to the same features to identify a politician.

A good editorial cartoon must have five basic features.

- It must be simple…

- People must understand it. The cartoon must make sense to those who read the particular paper. A school newspaper might run a cartoon about cafeteria food that includes an inside joke and isn't readily understood by the general public. The cartoon would only make sense in the school newspaper.

- The cartoon must be timely…

- It must evoke emotion. A good cartoon should make people laugh or make them mad.

- Always, the cartoon must give a point of view. The cartoon may be looking at the truth, but it usually is coming from a specific viewpoint. When we look down at an object, the viewpoint is very different from when we look up at the object. Editorial cartoons are the same way.

The Independent doesn't always agree with the viewpoint of each cartoon in the paper. Most certainly the readers don't always agree with them. But we all should agree that political cartoons are thought provoking. Just like a photograph, a well-illustrated editorial cartoon can be worth a thousand words.

There probably are about 100 newspapers, give or take a few, that employ full-time cartoonists. Unfortunately, it is a luxury that only metropolitan-sized newspapers can afford. Smaller newspapers subscribe to syndicated features for the right to reprint some of the better cartoons that have been published.

The next time you look at an editorial cartoon in the newspaper, try to look at it a new way. Instead of thinking about just whether you agree or disagree with the message, see if the cartoon has the five basic components to it. Then you can determine whether the message is getting through.

"Reading" Editorial Cartoons

1. Since there is so little space for an editorial cartoonist to make his or her point, the cartoonist often uses symbols and allusions as shorthand for the meaning of the cartoon. Examine each of the cartoons your teacher supplies and identify the symbols and allusions. Why might the cartoonist have chosen these symbols or allusions?

2. Most editorial cartoons present a specific political perspective. Do the cartoons you are examining have a specific point of view? How does the cartoonist demonstrate these perspectives?

3. Editorial cartoons are designed to evoke emotion: humor, anger, or outrage, for example. What are the feelings created and how do the cartoonists do this?

4. Based on the questions above, what does the message of the cartoon seem to be, and what can you infer about its intended purpose?

How to Read and Write an Editorial Cartoon

Creating Your Own Editorial Cartoons

Now that you have had some experience reading and analyzing political cartoons, create one of your own. Here are some suggestions to get you started.

- Brainstorm topic ideas by thinking about current events in your school, your hometown, or the world. List a few ideas below:

- Choose one of the ideas above and describe a point that you might want to make about that event. Perhaps you agree and want to show your support or perhaps you would like to ridicule those who might feel differently.

- What symbols, sayings, pop culture allusions, or other easily recognizable references might be appropriate for this topic?

- Sketch a very rough draft of what your cartoon might look like.

Creating an Op-Ed Page

SUGGESTED LEARNING STRATEGIES: **Discussion Group,
Brainstorming, Drafting, Mapping, Sketching**

Assignment

Working in groups, your assignment is to plan, develop, write, revise, and present your own op-ed page as if you were writing for an actual newspaper.

Your op-ed page must have at least two unsigned editorials that reflect the same perspective; at least three editorial cartoons that can represent a variety of viewpoints; at least two guest columnist editorials, two of which must be opposing viewpoints; and several letters to the editor written in response to previous news stories, editorials, or current events. Your final layout and design should reflect that of an actual newspaper.

Steps

Planning

1. Assemble your editorial board by selecting the group with which you want to work. Your teacher will decide on the number of members.

2. Begin brainstorming a list of issues in which your group has an interest. Be sure that issues are both debatable and timely. You should look back through your portfolio of work from this unit to remind yourself of issues that have already been raised, whether school or community-related, political, or social in nature.

3. Determine the role of each person in your group and begin identifying what pieces each member will contribute: editorial, cartoons, letters, and so on.

Creating

4. Begin gathering evidence and support for several of your issues. Conduct interviews, do research, and take surveys that will yield information related to your topics. Write drafts on several different issues. Create drafts of editorial cartoons. You might include pieces you have previously created during this unit.

5. Meet again as an editorial board and make a final determination of which pieces will be included on the final op-ed page. These choices should be made by subject matter, space allotment, and perspective.

6. Write another draft of each piece and have it reviewed and revised by a member of your editorial board using SMELL and other strategies to refine writing.

7. Examine the sample op-ed layout provided on page 166 and consider what modifications would create better visual balance in your own document. You might also consult op-ed pages in a local or national newspaper for additional ideas. Lay out your op-ed page using appropriate software or paste-up techniques. Display it or publish it. As you design your layout, consider what pieces are emphasized or de-emphasized by where they are placed on the page.

Presenting

8. Present your op-ed page as a display or as a consumable page of print in a manner prescribed by your teacher.

9. As a group, review the work of another group and comment on how effectively they have constructed their arguments and their page. Comment on the technical correctness, timeliness, relevance, and the persuasiveness of the group's language and reasoning. Each member of your group should evaluate at least one section of the op-ed page using the provided SMELL organizer. These organizers will become part of your grade and their grade.

10. Write a reflection answering the general question, "How do newspapers impact public opinion or public perception?" Discuss specific persuasive techniques you have used in the pieces you have personally contributed for your group's op-ed page. Why did you choose them, and were they effective? Refer to the feedback you received from your peers in step 9 to evaluate how effective your group was in constructing your pieces and the op-ed page as a whole.

As you evaluate your peers' op-ed page, use the SMELL strategy to review their pieces for fallacies, slanters, and unsupported claims. Suggest revisions that may improve each piece's appeal to a broader audience.

Sender-Receiver Relationship – To whom is the writer explicitly addressing his/her argument? How does he/she seem to feel about that target audience? What values does the sender assume the reader shares or argue that they should share?

Message – What is a literal summary of the content? What is the article's ultimate thesis regarding the subject?

Emotional Strategies – What emotional appeals does the writer include? What seems to be their desired effect? Do they cross the line into becoming fallacies? If so, suggest revisions.

Logical Strategies – What logical arguments/appeals does the writer include? Are these supported with persuasive evidence? Identify any fallacies or unsupported claims in the essay and suggest revisions.

Language – What specific language/slanters are used in the text to support the message or characterize the opposition? How does the language convey the writer's ethos and the text's effectiveness and credibility?

Creating an Op-Ed Page

Masthead
Lists publisher and editorial board

Editorial Cartoon

Guest Columnist

Guest Columnist

Unsigned Editorial 1

_____

_____

_____

_____

_____

_____

Letters to the Editor

Unsigned Editorial 2

_____

_____

_____

_____

_____

_____

_____

_____

Editorial Cartoon

Editorial (Continued)

Letters to the Editor (continued)

SCORING GUIDE

Scoring Criteria	Exemplary	Proficient	Emerging
Ideas	The op-ed page explicitly represents multiple and varied editorial perspectives. Each piece is extremely persuasive and demonstrates a thorough understanding of persuasive techniques.	The op-ed page represents various perspectives that are implied throughout the work as a whole. The majority of the pieces demonstrate a clear intention to persuade and an adequate understanding of persuasive techniques.	The op-ed page represents a limited range of perspectives. A few of the pieces demonstrate an intention to persuade. Some of the pieces may be descriptive or expository rather than persuasive.
Evidence of Research	There is evidence of thorough and original research throughout. Each piece demonstrates appropriate and ample evidence to support the thesis.	Research has obviously been conducted to support the positions. The majority of pieces demonstrate sufficient evidence supporting the thesis.	Adequate research is not demonstrated. The majority of the pieces demonstrate insufficient evidence to adequately support the thesis. Opinions remain unsupported.
Organization	The layout and design of the op-ed page reflect thoughtful planning. Overall organization is enriching to the ideas and purpose and is visually appealing.	The layout and design are appropriate for the project's purpose. Overall organization adequately communicates ideas and purpose.	Layout and design do not enhance the project and reflect little advance thought or planning. The overall organization detracts from ideas and purpose.
Use of Language	The pieces demonstrate purposeful use of rhetoric designed to appeal to the target audience(s). No errors in grammar or conventions are present.	The pieces demonstrate functional use of rhetoric but may not directly appeal to the target audience. Errors in grammar and conventions, if present, are minor and do not interfere with understanding.	The pieces inconsistently demonstrate functional use of rhetoric. Errors in grammar and conventions seriously interfere with the meaning.
Reflection	The text demonstrates thoughtful engagement with peer feedback and offers insightful evaluation of the effectiveness of the various pieces.	The text demonstrates engagement with peer feedback and offers evaluation of the effectiveness of the various pieces.	The text does not demonstrate engagement with peer feedback and/or offers limited evaluation of the the effectiveness of the various pieces.
Additional Criteria			

Comments:

Learning Focus:

The Art of Indirect Persuasion

While the op-ed page is an important forum for the exchange of ideas in our society, not everyone who contributes to the conversation means what they say. **Satire** may be the tool of choice for some writers (and cartoonists) who prefer to use irony and a range of tones to make statements about the issues of the day. If you've ever enjoyed watching late-night comedy shows, you know how effective—and how much fun—this approach can be when it comes to changing perception of the subjects being lampooned.

In the second half of this unit, you'll immerse yourself in the art of satire, exploring how writers use a range of genres and techniques, including **parody**, to present their messages in indirect ways. You'll explore how **diction** and **syntax** can be used to create humor as well as a wide range of satirical **tones**. Finally, you'll explore how satirists manipulate and parody the **conventions** and content of other formats and genres to advance their purposes as writers. In this way, satirists can make powerful contributions to the marketplace of ideas.

Introduction to Satire

Satire

> **ABOUT THE AUTHOR**
> David Bouchier is a British writer who has lived in
> the United States since 1986. He has written fiction,
> nonfiction, commentaries, and humor columns for
> newspapers, literary journals, and magazines. He is also
> an award-winning essayist for National Public Radio.

LET'S HEAR IT FOR THE

Cheerleaders

by David Bouchier

Strange things happen on college campuses in summer. I was nearly
trampled to death the other day by a horde of very young women wearing
very short red skirts and chanting something that sounded like "A fence! A
fence!"

A fence might be a very good idea, perhaps with some razor wire and a
warning sign saying "Danger: Cheerleaders Ahead." Long Island is host to
more than a dozen cheerleader camps. For the educationally gifted, Hofstra
and Adelphi Universities even offer cheerleading scholarships ("Give me an
A! Give me an A!").

But I think there is some intellectual work to be done here. Cheerleading
needs a history, a philosophy and, above all, a more sophisticated theory of
communications.

The cheerleading phenomenon is almost unknown in the rest of the
world. British soccer fans do their own cheerleading, with a medley of
traditional songs, bricks and bottles. In less civilized parts of the world,
fans express their enthusiasm by running onto the field and beating up the
opposing team. Only in America do we have professional partisans to do the
jumping and yelling for us.

Strange as it may seem to foreigners, the cheerleading industry has
many ardent supporters. It is said to build self-confidence, positive attitudes
and a mysterious quality called spirit, which seems to involve smiling a lot.

My Notes

Cheerleading also teaches the value of teamwork, something that women have often despised in the past as a male excuse for mindless violence and idiotic loyalties. "Be 100 percent behind your team 100 percent of the time" is a slogan that would be heartily endorsed by Slobodan Milosevic, the Orange Order and the Irish Republican Army.

Young cheerleaders also acquire valuable practical skills: impossible balancing tricks, back flips and the brass lungs they will need for child raising or being heard at the departmental meeting. Above all, they learn to compete, in hundreds of local and national events. Cheerleaders are clearly the corporate leaders and the political stars of the future.

Cheerleader culture is much broader and shallower that I had imagined. There are glossy magazines and webzines featuring the essential equipment: deodorants, contact lenses, Cheer Gear, makeup, party dresses and miracle diets. Novices can learn how to create a successful cheer routine with hot music, unique moves, fab formations, and multiple levels. They can also learn to make their own pom poms (called just "Poms"). There are international stars out there you've never heard of, and even a few anonymous muscular cheerleading males, whose job it is to support the base of the feminine pyramid.

Despite cheerleaders' obsession with pyramids, my research suggests that cheerleading began in ancient Greece, rather than in Egypt. The first cheerleaders were called Maenads, female attendants of the god Bacchus. Their task was to encourage the crowds to have a good time, with frenzied rites and extravagant gestures. The opposing squad, the Furies, were merciless goddesses of vengeance who would swing into violent action if their team was losing. The ancient Greeks must get the credit for being the first to give young women these important career opportunities.

So many teams were decimated by the Furies or led astray by the Maenads that cheerleading fell into disrepute for 2,000 years, until it was revived in a kinder, gentler form in the United States. But it's still a dangerous activity. In an average year, high school footballers lose 5.6 playing days to injuries, according to the January 1998 Harper's Index, a compilation of statistics. Cheerleaders lose 28.8 days. These accidents are blamed on excessive acrobatics and the passion for building taller and taller pyramids.

But all enthusiasm is dangerous, especially when it takes a physical form. If cheerleading is part of education, let's use it to educate by focusing on the message. Surely we can do better than waving our poms, doing somersaults and chanting:

Champs take it away

Now Play by Play

Move that ball

Win win win.

GRAMMAR & USAGE

Satire gets much of its humor from the writer's diction. Bouchier takes the lighthearted topic of cheerleaders and uses a serious and earnest diction. The mismatch between the topic and the diction contribute to the humor. For example, ancient cheerleaders used "frenzied rites" and "extravagant gestures." Injuries happen because of "excessive acrobatics," and the squads have "brilliant visuals."

Let's face it, this is not exactly a stellar example of the sophisticated use of the English language. To reduce the risk of injury and make the sport more educational and less distracting for the fans, I propose to substitute verbal skills for physical high jinks. Routines should become more static, and chants should become more grammatical, more literary and more conducive to the kinder, gentler society we all hope for in the next century.

Why don't you fellows

Pick up that ball

And move it carefully

To the other end of the field?

If we really want to teach good social values, let's chant this famous verse from Grantland Rice:

For when the one great Scorer comes

To write against your name

He writes not that you won or lost

But how you played the game.

Now there's a catchy message for the millennium!

And why not bring that youthful spirit and those brilliant visuals out of the stadium and into the workplace? Cheerleaders should be in every office, with a chant for every corporate game. In a lawyer's office, for example, a spirited cry of "Rule of Law! Rule of Law! Sue! Sue! Sue!" accompanied by some eyepopping dance steps, would give courage and purpose to desk-bound drones. On Wall Street, a simple chant of "Go Greenspan! Low Interest! Never mind the Asians!" would create a positive environment for investment. And cheerleaders would share their boundless enthusiasm with the rest of us who, in the game of life, so often find ourselves on the losing team.

Introduction to Satire

<table>
<tr><td>

LITERARY TERMS

Satire is a manner of writing that mixes a critical attitude with wit and humor in an effort to improve mankind and human institutions.

</td><td>

As you read Bouchier's essay, highlight anything you find humorous. Once you have finished, fill out the chart below, quoting passages you found funny, explaining why you thought each was funny, and interpreting what each quote is saying. An example has been provided to get you started.

</td></tr>
</table>

Humorous Passage	Why it is funny?	What is the implied message?
"...perhaps with some razor wire and a warning sign saying 'Danger: Cheerleaders Ahead.'"	The writer uses hyperbole and vivid imagery to create a ridiculous picture of cheerleaders as a threat that needs to be contained.	The image seems to suggest that cheerleaders are dangerous.

Humorous Passage	Why it is funny?	What is the implied message?

Now read "Introduction to Satire" on the next page, focusing on terms that seem to fit the examples of humor you have identified in the passages from "Let's Hear It for the Cheerleaders." In the space provided, write a paragraph responding to the following prompt.

Writing Prompt: How does David Bouchier's article fit the definition of satire? Support your answer with specific examples from the text.

Introduction to Satire

Introduction to Satire

Satire is a literary genre that uses irony, wit, and sometimes sarcasm to expose humanity's vices and foibles, giving impetus to change or reform through ridicule. Types of direct satire include Horatian satire, which pokes fun at human foibles with a witty even indulgent tone, and Juvenalian satire, which denounces, sometimes with invective, human vice and error in dignified and solemn tones.

As you read satire, look for these characteristics of satiric writing:

Irony—A mode of expression, through words (verbal irony) or events (irony of situation), conveying a reality different from and usually opposite to appearance or expectation. The surprise recognition by the audience often produces a comic effect, making irony often funny. When a text intended to be ironic is not seen as such, the effect can be disastrous. To be an effective piece of sustained irony, there must be some sort of audience tip-off, through style, tone, use of clear exaggeration, or other device.

Hyperbole—Deliberate exaggeration to achieve an effect; overstatement.

Litotes—A form of understatement that involves making an affirmative point by denying its opposite.

Caricature—An exaggeration or other distortion of an individual's prominent features or characteristics to the point of making that individual appear ridiculous. The term is applied more often to graphic representations than to literary ones.

Wit—Most commonly understood as clever expression, whether aggressive or harmless; that is, with or without derogatory intent toward someone or something in particular. We also tend to think of wit as being characterized by a mocking or paradoxical quality, evoking laughter through apt phrasing.

Sarcasm—Intentional derision, generally directed at another person and intended to hurt. The term comes from a Greek word meaning "to tear flesh like dogs" and signifies a cutting remark. Sarcasm usually involves obvious, verbal irony, achieving its effect by jeeringly stating the opposite of what is meant so as to heighten the insult.

Ridicule—Words intended to belittle a person or idea and arouse contemptuous laughter. The goal is to condemn or criticize by making the thing, idea, or person seem laughable and ridiculous.

Parody—The parodist exploits the peculiarities of an author's expression—the propensity to use too many parentheses, certain favorite words, or other elements of the author's style.

Invective—Speech or writing that abuses, denounces, or attacks. It can be directed against a person, cause, idea, or system. It employs a heavy use of negative emotive language. Example: "I cannot but conclude the bulk of your natives to be the most pernicious race of little odious vermin that nature ever suffered to crawl upon the surface of the earth." (Swift, *Gulliver's Travels*)

> **ACADEMIC VOCABULARY**
>
> **Parody** is an imitation of an author or his/her work with the idea of ridiculing the author, his/her ideas, or the work itself.

The Satirical Spectrum

Use the following questions to discuss the **tone** of the piece you are evaluating. The goal is to identify the impact the tone has on how the audience is encouraged to view the subject.

1. **Choose one tone word that characterizes the entire piece.** In other words, what do you think the writer's attitude or moral view is towards the subject? In 2–3 sentences justify your choice.

2. **Identify and explain one element of irony in the text.**

3. **Where is the tone of the piece most obvious?** Give examples, and justify your response.

4. Your teacher will share some examples of cartoons with you. "Read" each cartoon using the types of evidence you learned in Activity 2.11. How does the visual content contribute to its overall tone?

5. Based on your observations, place your text on the continuum below. Be prepared to justify your answer.

1-------2-------3------4------5-------6-------7------8--------9--------10

Horatian   Juvenalian

SUGGESTED LEARNING STRATEGIES: Marking the Text, Quickwrite

My Notes

GRAMMAR & USAGE

This writer's syntax includes a number of **verbal phrases**. Notice in particular these gerund and participial phrases:

A **gerund** is a verbal that ends in *-ing* and functions as a noun.

Poisoning the earth can be difficult... (gerund phrase as subject)

...many different ways of *putting the waste from*... (gerund phrase as object of preposition *of*)

A **participle** (the present or past participle form of a verb) is a verbal that can function as an adjective.

Keeping this in mind, we should generate.... (participial phrase modifying *we*)

The toxins ... seep into the earth, *guaranteeing that contamination will last*.... (participial phrase modifying *toxins*)

Satire

HOW TO POISON THE EARTH

by Linnea Saukko

Poisoning the earth can be difficult because the earth is always trying to cleanse and renew itself. Keeping this in mind, we should generate as much waste as possible from substances such as uranium-238, which has a half-life (the time it takes for half of the substance to decay) of one million years, or plutonium, which has a half-life of only 0.5 million years but is so toxic that if distributed evenly, ten pounds of it could kill every person on the earth. Because the United States generates about eighteen tons of plutonium per year, it is about the best substance for long-term poisoning of the earth. It would help if we would build more nuclear power plants because each one generates only 500 pounds of plutonium each year. Of course, we must include persistent toxic chemicals such as polychlorinated biphenyl (PCB) and dichlorodiphenyl trichloroethane (DDT) to make sure we have enough toxins to poison the earth from the core to the outer atmosphere. First, we must develop many different ways of putting the waste from these nuclear and chemical substances in, on, and around the earth.

Putting these substances in the earth is a most important step in the poisoning process. With deep-well injection we can ensure that the earth is poisoned all the way to the core. Deep-well injection involves drilling a hole that is a few thousand feet deep and injecting toxic substances at extremely high pressures so they will penetrate deep into the earth. According to the Environmental Protection Agency (EPA), there are about 360 such deep injection wells in the United States. We cannot forget the groundwater aquifers that are closer to the surface. These must also be contaminated. This is easily done by shallow-well injection, which operates on the same principle as deep-well injection, only closer to the surface. The groundwater that has been injected with toxins will spread contamination beneath the earth. The EPA estimates that there are approximately 500,000 shallow injection wells in the United States.

Burying the toxins in the earth is the next best method. The toxins from landfills, dumps, and lagoons slowly seep into the earth, guaranteeing that contamination will last a long time. Because the EPA estimates there are only about 50,000 of these dumps in the United States, they should be located in areas where they will leak to the surrounding ground and surface water.

Applying pesticides and other poisons on the earth is another part of the poisoning process. This is good for coating the earth's surface so that the poisons will be absorbed by plants, will seep into the ground, and will run off into surface water.

Surface water is very important to contaminate because it will transport the poisons to places that cannot be contaminated directly. Lakes are good for long-term storage of pollutants while they release some of their contamination to rivers. The only trouble with rivers is that they act as a natural cleansing system for the earth. No matter how much poison is dumped into them, they will try to transport it away to reach the ocean eventually.

The ocean is very hard to contaminate because it has such a large volume and a natural buffering capacity that tends to neutralize some of the contamination. So in addition to the pollution from rivers, we must use the ocean as a dumping place for as many toxins as possible. The ocean currents will help transport the pollution to places that cannot otherwise be reached.

Now make sure that the air around the earth is very polluted. Combustion and evaporation are major mechanisms for doing this. We must continuously pollute because the wind will disperse the toxins while rain washes them from the air. But this is good because a few lakes are stripped of all living animals each year from acid rain. Because the lower atmosphere can cleanse itself fairly easily, we must explode nuclear test bombs that shoot radioactive particles high into the upper atmosphere where they will circle the earth for years. Gravity must pull some of the particles to earth, so we must continue exploding these bombs.

So it is that easy. Just be sure to generate as many poisonous substances as possible and be sure they are distributed in, on, and around the entire earth at a greater rate than it can cleanse itself. By following these easy steps we can guarantee the poisoning of the earth.

My Notes

 WORD CONNECTIONS

Gravity comes from the Latin word *gravis* meaning "heavy." Other words that use the root *-grav-* are *grave*, *aggravation*, and *grief*.

My Notes

Satire

GAMBLING IN SCHOOLS

by Howard Mohr

[When Minnesota jumped into legalized gambling, it was off the deep end without a lifeguard. First it was Canterbury Downs, a clean, well-lighted horse track that seemed more like a Lutheran church with betting windows. Then came Powerball, Daily Three, Gopher Five (named after the official state rodent), and Scratch-Offs. At the same time Native American casinos were springing up in the land of sky blue waters, raking it in with blackjack and slot machines and high-stakes bingo. What could possibly be next?]

Parents and teachers who have been worried sick about finding enough money just to maintain public schools at a minimal level, worry no more. The Minnesota Legislature last week approved the Education Gambling Bill. The bill allows Video Gaming Devices (VGDS) in K-12 classrooms. Only two machines per classroom will be permitted, unless the class size exceeds thirty, in which case one additional VGD machine will be permitted for each additional ten students. Class size, however, will not be a problem once the gambling revenue begins pouring in.

Students in math classes will be instructed in probability, statistics, and hot streaks. The VGDs in kindergarten classrooms will operate with nickels only. All students will be expected to do their assignments and homework before gambling, unless they're on a roll.

Powerball and Gopher Five tickets will be sold only in the lunchroom during the noon hour. But the attractive neon Minnesota lottery signs will be permitted at the main entrance of the school and near the scoreboard at games.

Pulltabs and Scratch-Offs are specifically outlawed in the bill because they make a big mess, according to the powerful Janitor's Lobby.

Off-track horse betting will be handled in the Principal's office, with a $2 and $5 window initially, but with the option of a $100 window after the first year. Race results will be available in convenient locations. The first half hour of the school day will be a "handicapping homeroom," but students will be encouraged to arrive early if they are psyched up and have the feeling that this is the day.

My Notes

Each school system may publish and sell its own Tip Sheet or it can hire a professional tipster, such as "Gimp" Gordon or "Fast-Forward" Freddy, to be a counselor and role model.

Betting on high school sports will be forbidden, but the morning line for collegiate and professional sports will be broadcast on Channel One and posted in the principal's office near the sports betting window. As a safeguard, students will not be allowed to bet on sporting contests unless they have successfully passed Math II, "Point Spreads and Injuries."

Poker games will be operated as an extracurricular activity from the final bell until four a.m. The School will be the "house" and provide the dealers. There will be a 10 percent rakeoff for each pot up to a maximum of $10 per hand. Only Five-Card Draw, Stud, and Hold-Em will be permitted. Midnight Baseball, Spit in the Ocean, or Mission Impossible will not be permitted because they are silly games of chance and would send the wrong message to students.

Gambling will obviously bring new life and big money to the schools, but there are other advantages:

1: Students will be prepared for jobs in the gambling industry after graduating.

2: Part-time jobs will be created in the schools for change walkers, dealers, security officers, and so on.

3: A wider variety of people will be attracted to the teaching profession.

4: Discipline will be better because the hope of getting something for nothing is one of the oldest drives for excellence.

A bigger gambling issue faces the Legislature soon: Should gaming be permitted in hospitals and medical centers? And if so, how much and what kind? Would patients be able to bet the ponies from their beds? Could nurses deal blackjack in the sunroom? Could you go double or nothing with your physician?

Satire and Society

1. As you read the following statistics, consider their implications. What explains them? What do they say about cultural attitudes in the United States?

   - The United States contains 5% of the world's total population, but 25% of the world's prison population. — "All Things Considered," National Public Radio, 8 May 2008

   - The United States has 2.3 million criminals behind bars, more than any other nation. China, which is four times more populous than the United States, is a distant second, with 1.6 million people in prison. —International Center for Prison Studies at King's College, London

   - The United States has 751 people in prison or jail for every 100,000 in population. (If you count only adults, one in 100 Americans is locked up.) The only other major industrialized nation that even comes close is Russia, with 627 prisoners for every 100,000 people. The other industrialized nations have much lower rates. England's rate is 151; Germany's is 88; and Japan's is 63. —*The New York Times,* 23 April 2008

2. **Quickwrite:** Explain what you think accounts for these statistics. Be prepared to share your responses with your classmates.

3. As you read the following essay out loud as a class, mark the text for lines in which Ehrenreich seems to be making satirical comments regarding our attitudes towards crime and punishment in the United States. You will be responsible for teaching one of the paragraphs to your classmates!

4. Working in a small group, discuss the rhetorical aspects of Ehrenreich's text, using the SOAPSTone strategy. Write your comments or annotations in the My Notes space.

You will be assigned one paragraph of the essay to teach to the rest of the class. Reread and analyze your assigned paragraph, and fill out the chart below noting how Ehrenreich uses language and tone to advance her underlying argument. Paragraph 1 has been done for you as an example.

One sentence summary	Words (diction) contributing to tone	Connotation of word choices	This paragraph's contribution to the argument and the tone
Literally, the author points to the boom in our "Punishment Industry" and wonders what would happen if our nation runs out of criminals.	1. massive, splendid 2. shiny new prisons 3. supply and demand	These words connote that the industry is important, impressive, and larger than life. Usually the word *splendid* is reserved for beautiful or worthy endeavors and so it is odd that it is used to describe the penal system. Usually this system is associated with a failure of our society, but here it is regarded as a successful, powerful business.	This paragraph introduces the satire of the text and the focal question. Already the author is challenging assumptions made about the purpose and focus of our penal system. She "mixes" up word meanings just as she reassigns the purpose of this system. The tone is sarcastic and irreverent.

My Notes

Satire

> **ABOUT THE AUTHOR**
> Barbara Ehrenreich was born in Montana and earned a Ph.D. in cell biology. While working for a nonprofit agency, she discovered a passion for writing. A social activist, feminist, and award-winning author, she has written books, articles, and essays about controversial topics such as health care, war, families, and women's issues.

MAINTAINING THE CRIME SUPPLY

by Barbara Ehrenreich

1   It's impossible to address the problem of crime without beginning to worry about the law of supply and demand. Not that many people go around breaking that particular law, but you can be sure we'd get them if they did. Thanks to tough new legislation, we will soon have the most massive and splendid Punishment Industry on earth today: shiny new prisons for every state, harsh new sentences for every infringement, lethal injections more readily available than measles vaccine! Already the United States has a larger proportion of its population locked up than any other nation, South Africa included, so the only worry is—what if we run out of crime?

2   If punishment actually worked, a crime shortage would develop in no time at all. Would-be criminals would study the available sentences, do a careful cost-benefit analysis, and conclude that armed robbery, or, say, aggravated assault just wasn't their cup of tea. Yes, if deterrence worked, as our leaders seem to think it does, we would soon have a vast oversupply of electric chairs and unattractive, heavily walled, rural real estate.

And if crime frightens you, try to imagine a world without a crime. It would be unthinkable: Nothing on TV except *Sesame Street* and *Jeopardy* reruns. Chuck Norris reduced to panhandling. No execution tailgate parties, no Court Channel or *NYPD Blue*. Because—let us be honest about it—crime is our favorite entertainment spectacle, crime and punishment, that is. Think how many happy hours the average family spends watching the bad guys get perforated by bullets or menaced by Nazi-biker fiends in the pen.

3

This is nothing to be ashamed of. Historically, people have long demanded the pleasure of seeing others punished, and usually in live, nonfiction form. Executions were public as a matter of course, providing a festive occasion for the masses. Participatory punishment, in the form of lynchings and stonings, offered the average citizen a vivid, hands-on experience. In fact, historically speaking, the problem has been not to "stop crime" but to keep the local Punishment Industry supplied with victims. When the Romans ran out of criminals to feed to the lions, they scoured the world for edible prisoners of war. The Athenians used to designate some poor vagrant every year, drive him out of town, and subject him to a ritual stoning-to-death.

4

We think of ourselves as far more enlightened because our victims must be genuine criminals as certified by a court of law. The only exception is in the case of death-row inmates who turn out, at the very last moment, not to be guilty at all. In some cases the courts have ruled that they should fry anyway—because the facilities are ready and waiting and everyone is in the mood.

5

Other than that, we are restricted to criminals, as the word is generally defined, and the supply is by no means unlimited. One line of criminological reasoning, which might be called the "liberal" theory, holds that there is nothing wrong with our present approach to maintaining the crime supply. Just take a quarter of the child population, raise them in desperate poverty (with racial discrimination thrown in where applicable), and subject them to commercials, night and day, advising that life without one-hundred dollar footwear is not worth living. As an added measure, make sure none of the available jobs pay more than about five dollars an hour, and presto—little muggers are born, and in the numbers sufficient to stock the Punishment Industry for years to come!

6

WORD CONNECTIONS

Benefit uses the common Latin word *bene*, meaning "good." *Benefactor*, *benign*, *benediction* all incorporate this word.

My Notes

My Notes

7   Conservatives naturally question the liberal theory. They point to the occasional person who grows up poor and virtuous, or, alternatively, affluent and twisted. Deprivation and temptation are not enough, they say—a good supply of crime requires technology too. Hence the Republicans' understandable reluctance to get behind gun control. Why make it even marginally more difficult for a teenager to get his hands on a gun just as we are about to beef up the Punishment Industry with an ultra-tough new legislation? As even the National Rifle Association is too modest to point out, there is no way we would lead the world in the business of crime and punishment if it were not for our wide-open supply of guns.

8   The other tried-and-true approach is to simply broaden the definition of crime. This is the function of drug prohibition. A few decades ago, a person who smoked marijuana was a degenerate rake or a dashing bohemian, depending on your point of view. Now he or she is a criminal, qualifying for years in the slammer. Some states have gone further, making possession of rolling papers an equally dastardly crime. Similarly the "crime" of graffiti writing could be broadened to include possession of Magic Marker, or crossing state lines with to intent to buy one. The possibilities are endless once you realize that there is no crime, no matter how seemingly minor, that cannot be federalized, subjected to mandatory minimum sentencing, or transformed into a capital offense.

9   But a growing number of experts, including many criminal judges, assure us that there is nothing to worry about. No matter how fiercely Draconian[1] it becomes, the Punishment Industry will never diminish the supply of crime. On the contrary, there is evidence that a few years in the pen serves to season a criminal and make him more productive at his work. So as long as we do nothing to disturb the marvelous synergy[2] of poverty and temptation, guns on the street and gun-fun on the tube, the supply of crime will never fall below the widespread demand for punishment.

10   Or we could decide, all of us law-abiding citizens, to cut off crime at the source, where poverty intersects with weaponry, and to satisfy the public appetite for cruelty with something other than the Punishment Industry. Bearbaiting has been proposed; also cockfighting and the public torment of stray dogs.

---

[1] **Draconian**: severe
[2] **synergy**: mutual advantage

6. Your task is to write a work of satire. Use the following steps to complete the task. As an example, imagine that your school has a large problem with students being late to class (tardiness).

Step 1: Identify the topic.

Students being late to class (tardiness)

Step 2: State the problem in hyperbolic terms.

The staggering lack of students at the beginning of class leaves teachers paralyzed.

(Diction overstates the severity of the problem—"paralyzed" and "staggering.")

Step 3: Propose an ironic solution.

If students are late, they must stand outside the door for 20 minutes.

(Doesn't solve the problem of students not being in class to learn)

1st offense: Students will carry around a 40-pound clock for the remainder of the day.

2nd offense: Students will receive jail time.

(The punishment does not fit the "crime.")

Step 4: Use wit (wordplay, clever language, or rhetorical analogy).

Punishment will be doled out in a *timely* manner. (Word play)

This problem is a *ticking time bomb!* (Rhetorical analogy)

Step 5: Downplay the severity of the punishment using litotes.

Missing class and being ridiculed is a *small price to pay* to promote punctuality.

Sample paragraph using the above process:

It has come to my attention that students have been late to class at an alarming level. The staggering lack of students at the beginning of class leaves teachers paralyzed. To address this problem, we are adopting a new tardy policy. Following the first offense, students will carry around a 40-pound clock for the remainder of the day. Following the second offense, students will receive a night in jail, during which time they will be able to think about what they have done wrong. We promise to dole out this punishment in a timely manner as we have identified this issue as a ticking time bomb!

Writing Prompt: Working with a partner, select one of the topics from the class brainstorm of issues and follow the five steps to draft a satirical paragraph.

Writing a Parody

A **parody** is a specific kind of **satire** that imitates and ridicules an author or a work. The parodist exploits the peculiarities of an author's expression—the propensity to use too many parentheses, certain favorite words, or other elements of the author's style.

1. Based on your discussion of this definition, brainstorm a list of parodies you're familiar with. Think of popular music, television, movies, print sources, etc.

2. As you watch the news excerpt, make a list of things in the show that might be ripe for parody. Think about the people you see, the show's style, the graphics used, the stories reported, etc., that are typical of this show and news broadcasts in general.

3. As you read along with the performance of Barry's "In Depth, but Shallowly," make a list of the different things being parodied by Barry. Then rank them on the scale below. Be prepared to justify your rankings.

1-------2------3------4------5------6------7------8------9------10-----11
Just Plain Silly   Biting Sarcasm/Criticism
(Horatian)   (Juvenalian)

4. Writing Prompt: Based on your analysis of Barry's piece, write a paragraph in the space below analyzing Barry's central thesis/point and how he uses evidence to support it.

My Notes

Parody

> **ABOUT THE AUTHOR**
> Dave Barry is a writer and journalist who wrote a weekly humor column for more than 25 years. He won a Pulitzer Prize for commentary in 1988, the only humor writer to win this prestigious award.

IN DEPTH,
but Shallowly

by Dave Barry

If you want to take your mind off the troubles of the real world, you should watch local TV news shows. I know of no better way to escape reality, except perhaps heavy drinking.

Local TV news programs have given a whole new definition to the word *news*. To most people, *news* means *information* about events that affect a lot of people. On local TV news shows, *news* means *anything that you can take a picture of, especially if a local TV News Personality can stand in front of it*. This is why they are so fond of accidents, burning buildings, and crowds: these are good for standing in front of. On the other hand, local TV news shows tend to avoid stories about things that local TV News Personalities cannot stand in front of, such as budgets and taxes and the economy. If you want to get a local TV news show to do a story on the budget, your best bet is to involve it in a car crash.

I travel around the country a lot, and as far as I can tell, virtually all local TV news shows follow the same format. First you hear some exciting music, the kind you hear in space movies, while the screen shows local TV News Personalities standing in front of various News Events. Then you hear the announcer:

ANNOUNCER: From the On-the-Spot Action Eyewitness News Studios, this is the On-The-Spot Action Eyewitness News, featuring Anchorman Wilson Westbrook, Co-Anchor-person Stella Snape, Minority-Group Member James Edwards, Genial Sports Personality Jim Johnson, Humorous Weatherperson Dr. Reed Stevens, and Norm Perkins on drums. And now, here's Wilson Westbrook.

WESTBROOK: Good evening. Tonight from the On-the-Spot Action Eyewitness News Studios we have actual color film of a burning building, actual color film of two cars after they ran into each other, actual color film of the front of a building in which one person shot another person, actual color film of another burning building, and special reports on roller-skating and child abuse. But for the big story tonight, we go to City Hall, where On-the-Spot Reporter Reese Kernel is standing live.

KERNEL: I am standing here live in front of City Hall being televised by the On-the-Spot Action Eyewitness News minicam with Mayor Bryce Hallbread.

MAYOR: That's "Hallwood."

KERNEL: What?

MAYOR: My name is "Hallwood." You said "Hallbread."

KERNEL: Look, Hallbread, do you want to be on the news or don't you?

MAYOR: Yes, of course, it's just that my name is—

KERNEL: Listen, this is the top-rated news show in the three-county area, and if you think I have time to memorize every stupid detail, you'd better think again.

MAYOR: I'm sorry. "Hallbread" is just fine, really.

KERNEL: Thank you, Mayor Hallbread. And now back to Wilson Westbrook in the On-the-Spot Action Eyewitness News Studios.

WESTBROOK: Thank you, Reese; keep us posted if anything further develops on that important story. And now, as I promised earlier, we have actual color film of various objects that either burned or crashed, which we will project on the screen behind me while I talk about them. Here is a building on fire. Here is another building on fire. Here is a car crash. This film was shot years ago, but you can safely assume that objects just like these crashed or burned in the three-county area today. And now we go to my Co-Anchorperson, Stella Snape, for a Special Report on her exhaustive three-week investigation into the problem of child abuse in the three-county area. Well, Stella, what did you find?

SNAPE: Wilson, I found that child abuse is very sad. What happens is that people abuse children. It's just awful. Here you see some actual color film or me standing in front of a house. Most of your child abuse occurs in houses. Note that I am wearing subdued colors.

WESTBROOK (reading from a script): Are any efforts under way here in the three-county area to combat child abuse?

SNAPE: Yes.

WESTBROOK: Thank you, Stella, for that informative report. On the lighter side, On-the-Spot Action Eyewitness Reporter Terri Tompkins has prepared a three-part series on roller-skating in the three-county area.

My Notes

TOMPKINS: Roller-skating has become a major craze in California and the three-county area, as you can see by this actual color film of me on roller skates outside the On-the-Spot Action Eyewitness News Studio. This certainly is a fun craze. Tomorrow, in Part Two of this series, we'll see actual film color film of me falling down. On Wednesday we'll see me getting up.

WESTBROOK: We'll look forward to those reports. Our next story is from Minority-Group Reporter James Edwards, who, as he has for the last 324 consecutive broadcasts, spent the day in the minority-group sector of the three-county area finding out what minorities think.

EDWARDS: Wilson, I'm standing in front of a crowd of minority-group members, and as you can see, their mood is troubled. (*The crowd smiles and waves at the camera.*)

WESTBROOK: Good report, James. Well, we certainly had a sunny day here in the three-count area, didn't we, Humorous Weatherperson Dr. Reed Stevens?

STEVENS: Ha ha. We sure did, though I'm certainly troubled by that very troubling report Stella did on child abuse. But we should see continued warm weather through Wednesday. Here are a bunch of charts showing the relative humidity and stuff like that. Ha ha.

WESTBROOK: Ha ha. Well, things weren't nearly as bright on the sports scene, were they Genial Sports Personality Jim Johnson?

JOHNSON: No, Wilson, they certainly weren't. The Three-County Community College Cutlasses lost their fourth consecutive game today. Here you see actual color footage of me watching the game from the sidelines. The disgust is evident on my face. I intended to have actual color film of me interviewing the coach after the game, but the team bus crashed and everyone was killed.

WESTBROOK: Thank you, Jim. And now, here is Basil Holp, the General Manager of KUSP-TV, to present an Editorial Viewpoint:

HOLP: The management of KUSP-TV firmly believes that something ought to be done about earthquakes. From time to time we read in the papers that an earthquake has hit some wretched little country and knocked houses down and killed people. This should not be allowed to continue. Maybe we should have a tax or something. What the heck, we can afford it. The management of KUSP-TV is rolling in money.

ANNOUNCER: The preceding was the opinion of the management of KUSP-TV. People with opposing points of view are probably in the vast majority.

WESTBROOK: Well, that wraps up tonight's version of the On-the-Spot Action Eyewitness News. Tune in tonight to see essentially the same stories.

Writing Prompt: Write a TV parody. Choose a partner and choose a subject (a genre such as soap operas, sports broadcasts, children's television programs; or a specific show like *Oprah* or *CSI* or *60 Minutes*, etc.). Next, using the format of a script, write your parody. Use the following questions as a basis for planning your parody:

Details: What images should you include? What images should you avoid? Put your subject in the circle, and then brainstorm a list of conventions and features that might be good parody material. Think about what things in the show are just a *little* annoying. . .

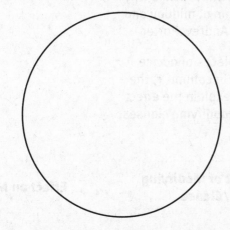

Tone/Purpose: How critical should you be? Is it time for brutal sarcasm or playful wit? Is the show an offense to good taste or just a silly waste of time? Are you out to destroy or merely to tease?

Audience: How familiar is your audience with the show? What is their attitude towards the show? How will these answers affect what you should and should not do in your script? How will the use of irony, overt sarcasm, or ridicule affect your audience's response to your parody? You will present your script to your classmates in a reader's theater, so keep that audience in mind.

Organization: Focusing on the formulas of your subject, how should you start, develop, and end your script?

Diction: What patterns can you identify that would be easy to parody? How stupid or clichéd do you want to make your characters/personalities appear?

Syntax: What about the pacing of the script? Where should it read the most quickly? Where should the reader hang on every word? How is this accomplished?

Need Some Advice?

In "Advice to Youth," Mark Twain uses loose or cumulative sentences
for comedic effect. A **loose sentence** is a string of main clauses
connected with conjunctions, commas, or semicolons, creating a sense
of equality. A loose sentence may have a main clause with a phrase or
subordinate clause, suggesting the first clause is dominant. Consider
this example from a previous selection.

Loose Sentence: "The Newspaper Audience Databank (NADbank)
released its readership numbers for 2007 a couple of weeks ago, and for
those of us in the industry it was grim reading: almost everywhere you
look, circulation, ad revenues and page counts are down, which is why
you can now fire a cannon through any given newsroom at midday and
not have to worry about committing reportercide." —Andrew Potter

In the graphic organizer below, identify at least five pieces of advice
Twain renders to his audience. Write the main clause in column 1, the
main or modifying phrase or clause in column 2, and explain the effect
in column 3. In some cases, Twain may add multiple modifying clauses,
so beware.

Main Clause 1	Main Clause 2 or Modifying Phrase/Clause	Effect on Meaning

Main Clause 1	Main Clause 2 or Modifying Phrase/Clause	Effect on Meaning

Writing Prompt: After completing the organizer, it's your turn to give this technique a try. Use a RAFT to select a Role for you to play and an Audience to whom to impart your great wisdom (your Topic). Finally, use a format of your choice in which to deliver your message to your audience (perhaps an editorial letter . . .). Be sure to use some loose sentence patterns in order to create a humorous effect.

My Notes

Satire

> **ABOUT THE AUTHOR**
> Mark Twain (1835–1910) was born Samuel Clemens in Florida, Missouri. His most famous novel, *The Adventures of Huckleberry Finn*, was revolutionary in American literature. During his life, he was also famous for his humorous lectures, essays, and sayings.

ADVICE TO YOUTH

by Mark Twain

Being told I would be expected to talk here, I inquired what sort of talk I ought to make. They said it should be something suitable to youth—something didactic, instructive, or something in the nature of good advice. Very well. I have a few things in my mind which I have often longed to say for the instruction of the young; for it is in one's tender early years that such things will best take root and be most enduring and most valuable. First, then. I will say to you my young friends—and I say it beseechingly, urgingly—

Always obey your parents, when they are present. This is the best policy in the long run, because if you don't, they will make you. Most parents think they know better than you do, and you can generally make more by humoring that superstition than you can by acting on your own better judgment.

Be respectful to your superiors, if you have any, also to strangers, and sometimes to others. If a person offend you, and you are in doubt as to whether it was intentional or not, do not resort to extreme measures; simply watch your chance and hit him with a brick. That will be sufficient. If you shall find that he had not intended any offense, come out frankly and confess yourself in the wrong when you struck him; acknowledge it like a man and say you didn't mean to. Yes, always avoid violence; in this age of charity and kindliness, the time has gone by for such things. Leave dynamite to the low and unrefined.

Go to bed early, get up early—this is wise. Some authorities say get up with the sun; some say get up with one thing, others with another. But a lark is really the best thing to get up with. It gives you a splendid reputation with everybody to know that you get up with the lark; and if you get the right kind of lark, and work at him right, you can easily train him to get up at half past nine, every time—it's no trick at all.

Now as to the matter of lying. You want to be very careful about lying; otherwise you are nearly sure to get caught. Once caught, you can never again be in the eyes to the good and the pure, what you were before. Many a young person has injured himself permanently through a single clumsy and ill finished lie, the result of carelessness born of incomplete training. Some authorities hold that the young ought not to lie at all. That of course, is putting it rather stronger than necessary; still while I cannot go quite so far as that, I do maintain, and I believe I am right, that the young ought to be temperate in the use of this great art until practice and experience shall give them that confidence, elegance, and precision which alone can make the accomplishment graceful and profitable. Patience, diligence, painstaking attention to detail—these are requirements; these in time, will make the student perfect; upon these, and upon these only, may he rely as the sure foundation for future eminence. Think what tedious years of study, thought, practice, experience, went to the equipment of that peerless old master who was able to impose upon the whole world the lofty and sounding maxim that "Truth is mighty and will prevail"—the most majestic compound fracture of fact which any of woman born has yet achieved. For the history of our race, and each individual's experience, are sewn thick with evidences that a truth is not hard to kill, and that a lie well told is immortal. There in is Boston a monument of the man who discovered anesthesia; many people are aware, in these latter days, that that man didn't discover it at all, but stole the discovery from another man. Is this truth mighty, and will it prevail? Ah no, my hearers, the monument is made of hardy material, but the lie it tells will outlast it a million years. An awkward, feeble, leaky lie is a thing which you ought to make it your unceasing study to avoid; such a lie as that has no more real permanence than an average truth. Why, you might as well tell the truth at once and be done with it. A feeble, stupid, preposterous lie will not live two years—except it be a slander upon somebody. It is indestructible, then, of course, but that is no merit of yours. A final word: begin your practice of this gracious and beautiful art early—begin now. If I had begun earlier, I could have learned how.

Never handle firearms carelessly. The sorrow and suffering that have been caused through the innocent but heedless handling of firearms by the young! Only four days ago, right in the next farm house to the one where I am spending the summer, a grandmother, old and gray and sweet, one of the loveliest spirits in the land, was sitting at her work, when her young grandson crept in and got down an old, battered, rusty gun which had not been

WORD CONNECTIONS

Wide reading in a variety of subject areas will help you analyze the meanings in analogies. For example, knowing about important people and their discoveries or contributions in science, math, history, and literature will help you make connections to relationships expressed in analogies. Complete this analogy.

Twain : humor ::
Aristotle : _____

a. idealism
b. drama
c. logic
d. empiricism

My Notes

_____
_____
_____
_____
_____
_____
_____
_____
_____

touched for many years and was supposed not to be loaded, and pointed it at her, laughing and threatening to shoot. In her fright she ran screaming and pleading toward the door on the other side of the room; but as she passed him he placed the gun almost against her very breast and pulled the trigger! He had supposed it was not loaded. And he was right—it wasn't. So there wasn't any harm done. It is the only case of that kind I ever heard of. Therefore, just the same, don't you meddle with old unloaded firearms; they are the most deadly and unerring things that have ever been created by man. You don't have to take any pains at all with them; you don't have to have a rest, you don't have to have any sights on the gun, you don't have to take aim, even. No, you just pick out a relative and bang away, and you are sure to get him. A youth who can't hit a cathedral at thirty yards with a Gatling gun in three quarters of an hour, can take up an old empty musket and bag his grandmother every time, at a hundred. Think what Waterloo would have been if one of the armies had been boys armed with old muskets supposed not to be loaded, and the other army had been composed of their female relations. The very thought of it makes me shudder.

There are many sorts of books; but good ones are the sort for the young to read. Remember that. They are a great, an inestimable and unspeakable means of improvement. Therefore be careful in your selection, my young friends; be very careful; confine yourselves exclusively to *Robertson's Sermons, Baxter's Saint's Rest, The Innocents Abroad,* and works of that kind.

But I have said enough. I hope you will treasure up the instructions which I have given you, and make them a guide to your feet and a light to your understanding. Build your character thoughtfully and painstakingly upon these precepts, and by and by, when you have got it built, you will be surprised and gratified to see how nicely and sharply it resembles everybody else's.

"Advice to Youth"   **"The War Prayer"**

S

O

A

P

S

Tone

My Notes

Satire

THE WAR PRAYER

by Mark Twain

It was a time of great and exalting excitement. The country was up in arms, the war was on, in every breast burned the holy fire of patriotism; the drums were beating, the bands playing, the toy pistols popping, the bunched firecrackers hissing and spluttering; on every hand and far down the receding and fading spread of roofs and balconies a fluttering wilderness of flags flashed in the sun; daily the young volunteers marched down the wide avenue gay and fine in their new uniforms, the proud fathers and mothers and sisters and sweethearts cheering them with voices choked with happy emotion as they swung by; nightly the packed mass meetings listened, panting, to patriot oratory which stirred the deepest deeps of their hearts, and which they interrupted at briefest intervals with cyclones of applause, the tears running down their cheeks the while; in the churches the pastors preached devotion to flag and country, and invoked the God of Battles beseeching His aid in our good cause in outpourings of fervid eloquence which moved every listener. It was indeed a glad and gracious time, and the half dozen rash spirits that ventured to disapprove of the war and cast a doubt upon its righteousness straightway got such a stern and angry warning that for their personal safety's sake they quickly shrank out of sight and offended no more in that way.

Sunday morning came — next day the battalions would leave for the front; the church was filled; the volunteers were there, their young faces alight with martial dreams — visions of the stern advance, the gathering momentum, the rushing charge, the flashing sabers, the flight of the foe, the tumult, the enveloping smoke, the fierce pursuit, the surrender! Then home from the war, bronzed heroes, welcomed, adored, submerged in golden seas of glory! With the volunteers sat their dear ones, proud, happy, and envied by the neighbors and friends who had no sons and brothers to send forth to the field of honor, there to win for the flag, or, failing, die the noblest of noble deaths. The service proceeded; a war chapter from the Old Testament was read; the first prayer was said; it was followed by an organ burst that shook the building, and with one impulse the house rose, with glowing eyes and beating hearts, and poured out that tremendous invocation

"God the all-terrible! Thou who ordainest! Thunder thy clarion and lightning thy sword!"

Then came the "long" prayer. None could remember the like of it for passionate pleading and moving and beautiful language. The burden of its supplication was, that an ever-merciful and benignant Father of us all would watch over our noble young soldiers, and aid, comfort, and encourage them in their patriotic work; bless them, shield them in the day of battle and the hour of peril, bear them in His mighty hand, make them strong and confident, invincible in the bloody onset; help them to crush the foe, grant to them and to their flag and country imperishable honor and glory.

An aged stranger entered and moved with slow and noiseless step up the main aisle, his eyes fixed upon the minister, his long body clothed in a robe that reached to his feet, his head bare, his white hair descending in a frothy cataract to his shoulders, his seamy face unnaturally pale, pale even to ghastliness. With all eyes following him and wondering, he made his silent way; without pausing, he ascended to the preacher's side and stood there waiting. With shut lids the preacher, unconscious of his presence, continued with his moving prayer, and at last finished it with the words, uttered in fervent appeal, "Bless our arms, grant us the victory, O Lord our God, Father and Protector of our land and flag!"

The stranger touched his arm, motioned him to step aside — which the startled minister did — and took his place. During some moments he surveyed the spellbound audience with solemn eyes, in which burned an uncanny light; then in a deep voice he said:

"I come from the Throne — bearing a message from Almighty God!" The words smote the house with a shock; if the stranger perceived it he gave no attention. "He has heard the prayer of His servant your shepherd, and will grant it if such shall be your desire after I, His messenger, shall have explained to you its import — that is to say, its full import. For it is like unto many of the prayers of men, in that it asks for more than he who utters it is aware of — except he pause and think.

"God's servant and yours has prayed his prayer. Has he paused and taken thought? Is it one prayer? No, it is two — one uttered, the other not. Both have reached the ear of Him Who heareth all supplications, the spoken and the unspoken. Ponder this — keep it in mind. If you would beseech a blessing upon yourself, beware! lest without intent you invoke a curse upon a neighbor at the same time. If you pray for the blessing of rain upon your crop which needs it, by that act you are possibly praying for a curse upon some neighbor's crop which may not need rain and can be injured by it.

"You have heard your servant's prayer — the uttered part of it. I am commissioned of God to put into words the other part of it — that part which the pastor — and also you in your hearts — fervently prayed silently. And ignorantly and unthinkingly? God grant that it was so! You heard these

My Notes

words: 'Grant us the victory, O Lord our God!' That is sufficient. the *whole* of the uttered prayer is compact into those pregnant words. Elaborations were not necessary. When you have prayed for victory you have prayed for many unmentioned results which follow victory—*must* follow it, cannot help but follow it. Upon the listening spirit of God fell also the unspoken part of the prayer. He commandeth me to put it into words. Listen!

"O Lord our Father, our young patriots, idols of our hearts, go forth to battle — be Thou near them! With them — in spirit — we also go forth from the sweet peace of our beloved firesides to smite the foe. O Lord our God, help us to tear their soldiers to bloody shreds with our shells; help us to cover their smiling fields with the pale forms of their patriot dead; help us to drown the thunder of the guns with the shrieks of their wounded, writhing in pain; help us to lay waste their humble homes with a hurricane of fire; help us to wring the hearts of their unoffending widows with unavailing grief; help us to turn them out roofless with little children to wander unfriended the wastes of their desolated land in rags and hunger and thirst, sports of the sun flames of summer and the icy winds of winter, broken in spirit, worn with travail, imploring Thee for the refuge of the grave and denied it — for our sakes who adore Thee, Lord, blast their hopes, blight their lives, protract their bitter pilgrimage, make heavy their steps, water their way with their tears, stain the white snow with the blood of their wounded feet! We ask it, in the spirit of love, of Him Who is the Source of Love, and Who is the ever-faithful refuge and friend of all that are sore beset and seek His aid with humble and contrite hearts. Amen.

After a pause. "Ye have prayed it; if ye still desire it, speak! The messenger of the Most High waits!"

It was believed afterward that the man was a lunatic, because there was no sense in what he said.

Peeling the Skin

SUGGESTED LEARNING STRATEGIES: Marking the Text, Graphic Organizer

Satire

Girl Moved To Tears

by *Of Mice and Men* Cliffs Notes

from *The Onion*

My Notes

CHARLOTTESVILLE, VA—In what she described as "the most emotional moment" of her academic life, University of Virginia sophomore communications major Grace Weaver sobbed openly upon concluding Steinbeck's seminal work of American fiction *Of Mice And Men's* Cliffs Notes early last week.

"This book has changed me in a way that only great literature summaries can," said Weaver, who was so shaken by the experience that she requested an extension on her English 229 essay. "The humanity displayed in the Character Flowchart really stirred something in me. And Lennie's childlike innocence was beautifully captured through the simple, ranch-hand slang words like 'mentally handicapped' and 'retarded.'"

Added Weaver: "I never wanted the synopsis to end."

Weaver, who formed an "instant connection" with Lennie's character-description paragraph, said she began to suspect the novel might end tragically after reading the fourth sentence which suggested the gentle giant's strength and fascination with soft things would "lead to his untimely demise."

"I was amazed at how attached to him I had become just from the critical commentary," said Weaver, still clutching the yellow-and-black-striped study guide. "When I got to the last sentence—'George shoots Lennie in the head,'—it seemed so abrupt. But I found out later that the 'ephemeral nature of life' is a major theme of the novel."

Weaver was assigned *Of Mice And Men*—a novel scholars have called "a masterpiece of austere prose" and "the most skillful example of American naturalism under 110 pages"—as part of her early twentieth-century fiction course, and purchased the Cliffs Notes from a cardboard rack at her local Barnes & Noble. John Whittier-Ferguson, her professor for the class, told reporters this was not the first time one of his students has expressed interest in the novel's plot summary.

"It's one of those universal American stories," said Ferguson after being informed of Weaver's choice to read the Cliffs Notes instead of the pocket-sized novel. "I look forward to skimming her essay on the importance of following your dreams and randomly assigning it a grade."

GRAMMAR & USAGE

Notice that the writer uses dashes effectively to heighten the irony and humor. The student explains that she gets to the last sentence of the novel, and the writer sets the line *George shoots Lennie in the head* between dashes. The presentation of this key point as an interruption or an incidental piece of information creates a dramatic and ironic effect.

My Notes

Though she completed the two-page brief synopsis in one sitting, Weaver said she felt strangely drawn into the plot overview and continued on, exploring the more fleshed-out chapter summaries.

"There's something to be said for putting in that extra time with a good story," Weaver said. "You just get more out of it. I'm also going to try to find that book about rabbits that George was always reading to Lennie, so that I can really understand that important allusion."

Within an hour of completing the Cliffs Notes, Weaver was already telling friends and classmates that Steinbeck was her favorite author, as well as reciting select quotations from the "Important Quotations" section for their benefit.

"When I read those quotes, found out which characters they were attributed to, and inferred their context from the chapter outlines to piece together their significance, I was just blown away," said a teary-eyed Weaver. "And the way Steinbeck wove the theme of hands all the way through the section entitled 'Hands'—he definitely deserved to win that Nobel Prize."

Weaver's roommate, Giulia Crenshaw, has already borrowed the dog-eared, highlighted summary of the classic Depression-era saga, and is expecting to enjoy reading what Weaver described as "a really sad story about two brothers who love to farm."

"I loved this book so much, I'm going to read all of Steinbeck's Cliffs Notes," said Weaver. "But first I'm going to go to the library to check out the original version *Of Mice And Men* starring John Malkovich and Gary Sinise."

Fill in the chart below by citing your favorite quotes in the left column—the ones that most powerfully mock Weaver and Cliffs Notes. In the right-hand column, explain the effect of the quote on your perception of the subject: why is it such a slam?

1.	
2.	
3.	
4.	
5.	
6.	
7.	
8.	
9.	
10.	

Writing a Satirical Piece

SUGGESTED LEARNING STRATEGIES: **Drafting, Self-Editing/
Peer Editing**

Assignment

You have been studying how opinions are expressed and perceived in a democratic society through a variety of rhetorical formats including satire. Your assignment is to write a satirical piece critiquing some aspect of our society.

Planning

1. Choose a topic that is relevant, current, and debatable. Remember that the flaws and foibles of all aspects of society—from government to celebrity to religion, from teenagers to presidents to soccer moms—are grist for the satirist's mill.

2. Review the various samples of satire, and choose one to use as a model. Then make a list of conventions typical for that style of satire.

3. Review the techniques of satire: hyperbole, parody, irony, ridicule, etc. Will your piece be more Horatian or Juvenalian? Why?

4. Understand your audience. To whom will you address your satire and why? What tone will be appropriate for this audience and your purpose?

Drafting

5. Draft your piece, keeping in mind the conventions you identified in step 2.

Sharing, Responding, and Revising

6. Review your draft, and revise it to clarify ideas, refine structure, and enhance coherence before sharing it with peers for their review.

7. Identify loose sentences in your draft, and consult a member of your writing group for feedback on the effectiveness of your use of syntax for rhetorical effect.

8. Ask a reader to complete a SOAPSTone analysis of your piece to gauge your effectiveness at constructing your satire. Revise in response to the feedback you receive.

Editing

9. Review your draft, and use all available resources to correct errors in grammar, punctuation, and spelling. Edit accordingly to prepare a technically sound document.

10. Consider the broad satirical ideas in your text, and brainstorm appropriate titles. Choose one, and create a final draft.

TECHNOLOGY TIP Create your final draft using a word processing program. Use the spell-check and grammar-check features to help you produce a final draft. Remember to review the options for spelling or grammar changes the program presents before accepting them. Most programs do not recognize proper names, and the grammar check may recommend contractions (e.g., it's instead of its) or verb choices that you do not want.

SCORING GUIDE

Scoring Criteria	Exemplary	Proficient	Emerging
Ideas	The piece presents a topic that is relevant, current, and debatable. It skillfully demonstrates techniques of satire ideal for the topic; the writer's position is convincingly persuasive.	The piece presents a topic that is generally relevant, current, and debatable. It demonstrates techniques of satire suitable for the topic; the writer's position is clear.	The piece presents a topic that is not fully relevant, current, or debatable. It demonstrates techniques of satire somewhat suitable for the topic; the writer's position is unclear.
Organization	Ideas are presented in an arrangement most conducive to the writer's position. The piece is aptly organized, utilizing typical conventions of the format.	Ideas are logically arranged to support the writer's position. The piece is organized appropriately using typical conventions of the format.	A weak arrangement of ideas detracts from the writer's position. The organization of the piece does not match the typical conventions of the format.
Use of Language	Language used (e.g., skillfully incorporating loose sentences; irony, hyperbole, and litotes; etc.) is extremely effective in achieving the desired tone and satirical effect for the intended audience and purpose. There are no errors in standard writing conventions.	Language used (e.g. appropriately incorporating loose sentences; satirical techniques) is effective in achieving the desired tone and satirical effect for the intended audience and purpose. Errors in writing conventions, if present, are minor and do not interfere with understanding.	Language used is ineffective in achieving the desired tone and satirical effect for the intended audience and purpose. Errors in writing conventions seriously interfere with the meaning.
Additional Criteria			

Comments:

Reflection

An important aspect of growing as a learner is to reflect on where you have been, what you have accomplished, what helped you to learn, and how you will apply your new knowledge in the future. Use the following questions to guide your thinking and to identify evidence of your learning. Use separate notebook paper.

Thinking about Concepts

1. Using specific examples from this unit, respond to the Essential Questions:

   • How do newspapers impact public opinion or public perception?

   • How does a writer use tone to advance an opinion?

2. Consider the new academic vocabulary from this unit (**Bias, Fallacy, Editorial, Parody**), as well as academic vocabulary from previous units. and select 3–4 terms of which your understanding has grown. For each term, answer the following questions:

   • What was your understanding of the word before you completed this unit?

   • How has your understanding of the word evolved throughout this unit?

   • How will you apply your understanding in the future?

Thinking about Connections

3. Review the activities and products (artifacts) you created. Choose those that most reflect your growth or increase in understanding.

4. For each artifact that you choose, record, respond to, and reflect on your thinking and understanding, using the following questions as a guide:

   a. What skill/knowledge does this artifact reflect, and how did you learn this skill/knowledge?

   b. How did your understanding of the power of language expand through your engagement with this artifact?

   c. How will you apply this skill or knowledge in the future?

5. Create this reflection as Portfolio pages—one for each artifact you choose. Use the model in the box for your headings and commentary on questions.

> ## Thinking About Thinking
> ### Portfolio Entry
>
> Concept:
>
> Description of Artifact:
>
> Commentary on Questions:

The Power of
Persuasion

Essential Questions

? How are the components of rhetoric applied to the creation and delivery of persuasive speeches?

? How can artistic expression advance social commentary?

Unit Overview

America's tradition of open debate and lively free speech was established in the early period of the fight for independence from British rule. Before that, the founding settlers had established the basis for a literate democratic society in its schools and system of justice. You have seen from the previous unit that persuasive, free speech is at the heart of our democracy's vitality. Through a study of historic American speeches, this unit provides an opportunity to analyze models of effective persuasive speech in preparation for writing and delivering original speeches. Continuing the idea of free speech, this unit then delves into Arthur Miller's play *The Crucible* and explores both the play itself as well as its relationship to the time period in which it was written.

Unit
3
The Power of Persuasion

Contents

Goals

▶ To define and apply the appeals and devices of rhetoric

▶ To analyze, create, and present persuasive speeches

▶ To interpret and analyze texts and situate them in their communication contexts

▶ To analyze, create, and present a dramatic scene about a societal issue

ACADEMIC VOCABULARY

Rhetoric

Rhetorical Devices

Social Commentary

Foil

*Texts not included in these materials.

Learning Focus:

Speaking with Confidence

"It's a free country, and every American has the right to free speech." You have probably heard some variation of that statement on many occasions. Even children can be overheard bragging about the right to free speech. Despite all the boasting about rights, though, when Americans are asked to name their fears, guess what is often near the top of the list? Speaking! Public speaking, to be exact. Even with strong opinions and a strong belief in the right to speak, some people find it difficult to put their ideas into a coherent speech that they can deliver confidently enough to influence their audience. Those who can, however, find out very quickly that words have an incredible power to persuade.

The art of **rhetoric** is most simply the art of using language effectively and persuasively. Speeches are a particular literary form used most often to persuade others to a point of view. So reading and writing speeches provides a particularly good way to analyze and apply specific **rhetorical devices** such as allusions and repetition that you have already learned about. As you study and view classic American speeches to create and prepare your own persuasive speech, you will review the rhetorical appeals of ethos, pathos, and logos. In the United States, you **do** have the right to free speech. This unit will help you exercise that right with confidence and maturity.

Independent Reading: In this unit, you will read literary fiction and nonfiction texts that explore America's commitment to freedom of speech. For independent reading, choose a play, novel, or collection of short stories or essays that use literature as a venue to make a statement about American society.

Previewing the Unit

SUGGESTED LEARNING STRATEGIES: Think-Pair-Share, Close Reading,
Marking the Text, Summarizing/Paraphrasing, Graphic Organizer

Essential Questions

1. How are the components of rhetoric applied to the creation and
delivery of persuasive speeches?

2. How can artistic expression advance social commentary?

Unit Overview and Learning Focus

Predict what you think this unit is about. Use the words or phrases that
stood out to you when you read the Unit Overview and the Learning
Focus.

Embedded Assessment

What knowledge must you have (what do you need to know) to succeed
on the Embedded Assessment? What skills must you have (what must
you be able to do to complete the Embedded Assessment successfully)?

Fears and Expectations

Quickwrite: On your own paper, respond to each of the following sentence starters:

a. *When I consider the idea of speaking in front of a group, I usually feel....*

b. *My experiences speaking publicly have been....*

c. *When I am watching a peer give an oral presentation, I usually feel....*

1. In small discussion groups brainstorm ways in which both the speaker and the audience can have a positive influence on an oral presentation. Create a T-chart for your ideas. Come up with three to five suggestions for speakers as well as audience members. You will share these ideas with the class and use them as norms for classroom presentations.

Speaker	Audience

2. Write the Pledge of Allegiance on separate paper. Then mark the text by highlighting words and phrases you think should be emphasized.

3. Next, prepare a plan for presenting the Pledge to your classmates. Prepare for your oral interpretation by marking the text for inflection, deciding where you might include an appropriate gesture, and practicing the delivery style you would like to use as well as an approach and exit. Be sure to determine the tone you would like to use and convey that attitude to the listeners through your manner of delivery.

With your group read and discuss the list of suggestions before you present your oral interpretation.

Do	Do Not
Greet your audience.	Start speaking before you are ready.
Make eye contact.	Stare at your notes.
Speak clearly.	Mumble or put your hands or notes in front of your face.
Smile.	Glare at your audience or look at them with fear and apprehension.
Put a smile in your voice.	Sound bored, disgusted, or afraid.
Use variety in volume and pitch.	Speak in a monotone.
Use appropriate gestures.	Grip the podium tightly, play with your hair, or rustle your notes.
Maintain your focus.	Start daydreaming or focusing on the audience's reaction more than your presentation.
Move around (if it is intentional).	Fidget, rock, or pace.
Thank your audience.	Start walking away before you have finished your last sentence and closing.

One way to enhance a speech is to include relevant quotations. To practice this process, first read each of the following quotations. Then, select three quotations on which you can comment. For each of the quotations you choose, create a statement that incorporates the quotation as well as one or two sentences of your own commentary that adds to the message expressed.

> Example: *In the words of Marcus Tulius Cicero, "nothing is so unbelievable that oratory cannot make it acceptable." In the 21st century, when the words of influential men are broadcast around the world within seconds of their first uttererance, we must be careful to weigh the facts and not be convinced that something is true merely because the speaker uses powerful words and a powerful delivery. If we know something to be untrue, we must not be persuaded by those who would attempt to convince us otherwise.*

After you have shared your statements with a partner, choose one statement to present to the class. When you present your statement, try to deliver the words with emphasis and enthusiasm. Decide which words to emphasize and what tone of voice you will use for your delivery.

"In a republican nation, whose citizens are to be led by reason and persuasion and not by force, the art of reasoning becomes of first importance."

—Thomas Jefferson

"Oral delivery aims at persuasion and making the listener believe they are converted. Few persons are capable of being convinced; the majority allow themselves to be persuaded."

—Johann Wolfgang von Goethe

"Men are not governed by justice, but by law or persuasion. When they refuse to be governed by law or persuasion, they have to be governed by force or fraud, or both."

—George Bernard Shaw

"Nothing is so unbelievable that oratory cannot make it acceptable."

— Marcus Tulius Cicero

"The tongue can paint what the eye can't see."

—Chinese Proverb

"Let one who wants to move and convince others, first be convinced and moved themselves."

—**Thomas Carlyle**

"There is nothing in the world like a persuasive speech to fuddle the mental apparatus and upset the convictions and debauch the emotions of an audience not practiced in the tricks and delusions of oratory."

—**Mark Twain**

"To resort to power one need not be violent, and to speak to conscience one need not be meek."

—**Barbara Deming**

"There is no calamity which a great nation can invite which equals that which follows a supine submission to wrong and injustice."

—**Grover Cleveland**

My Notes

Speech

> **ABOUT THE AUTHOR**
> John F. Kennedy was elected President of the United States in November of 1960 and took the oath of office in January of 1961. His inaugural address has become one of the most famous and most-often quoted speeches for its rhetoric of both inspiration and challenge.

INAUGURAL ADDRESS

by John Fitzgerald Kennedy

1   *Vice President Johnson, Mr. Speaker, Mr. Chief Justice, President Eisenhower, Vice President Nixon, President Truman, reverend clergy, fellow citizens,* we observe today not a victory of party, but a celebration of freedom—symbolizing an end, as well as a beginning—signifying renewal, as well as change. For I have sworn before you and Almighty God the same solemn oath our forebears prescribed nearly a century and three quarters ago.

The world is very different now. For man holds in his mortal hands the power to abolish all forms of human poverty and all forms of human life. And yet the same revolutionary beliefs for which our forebears fought are still at issue around the globe—the belief that the rights of man come not from the generosity of the state, but from the hand of God.

2   We dare not forget today that we are the heirs of that first revolution. Let the word go forth from this time and place, to friend and foe alike, that the torch has been passed to a new generation of Americans—born in this century, tempered by war, disciplined by a hard and bitter peace, proud of our ancient heritage—and unwilling to witness or permit the slow undoing of those human rights to which this Nation has always been committed, and to which we are committed today at home and around the world.

Let every nation know, whether it wishes us well or ill, that we shall pay any price, bear any burden, meet any hardship, support any friend, oppose any foe, in order to assure the survival and the success of liberty.

This much we pledge—and more.

To those old allies whose cultural and spiritual origins we share, we pledge the loyalty of faithful friends. United, there is little we cannot do in a host of cooperative ventures. Divided, there is little we can do—for we dare not meet a powerful challenge at odds and split asunder.   3

To those new States whom we welcome to the ranks of the free, we pledge our word that one form of colonial control shall not have passed away merely to be replaced by a far more iron tyranny. We shall not always expect to find them supporting our view. But we shall always hope to find them strongly supporting their own freedom—and to remember that, in the past, those who foolishly sought power by riding the back of the tiger ended up inside.   4

To those peoples in the huts and villages across the globe struggling to break the bonds of mass misery, we pledge our best efforts to help them help themselves, for whatever period is required—not because the Communists may be doing it, not because we seek their votes, but because it is right. If a free society cannot help the many who are poor, it cannot save the few who are rich.   5

To our sister republics south of our border, we offer a special pledge—to convert our good words into good deeds—in a new alliance for progress—to assist free men and free governments in casting off the chains of poverty. But this peaceful revolution of hope cannot become the prey of hostile powers. Let all our neighbors know that we shall join with them to oppose aggression or subversion anywhere in the Americas. And let every other power know that this Hemisphere intends to remain the master of its own house.   6

To that world assembly of sovereign states, the United Nations, our last best hope in an age where the instruments of war have far outpaced the instruments of peace, we renew our pledge of support—to prevent it from becoming merely a forum for invective—to strengthen its shield of the new and the weak—and to enlarge the area in which its writ may run.   7

Finally, to those nations who would make themselves our adversary, we offer not a pledge but a request: that both sides begin anew the quest for peace, before the dark powers of destruction unleashed by science engulf all humanity in planned or accidental self-destruction.   8

We dare not tempt them with weakness. For only when our arms are sufficient beyond doubt can we be certain beyond doubt that they will never be employed.

My Notes

My Notes

GRAMMAR & USAGE

Notice that Kennedy relies on powerful, specific verbs in the active voice. He asks the world to *explore, formulate, bring, seek, conquer, eradicate, tap, encourage, unite*, all verbs that stress action, which is a major theme of his speech.

9   But neither can two great and powerful groups of nations take comfort from our present course—both sides overburdened by the cost of modern weapons, both rightly alarmed by the steady spread of the deadly atom, yet both racing to alter that uncertain balance of terror that stays the hand of mankind's final war.

10   So let us begin anew—remembering on both sides that civility is not a sign of weakness, and sincerity is always subject to proof. Let us never negotiate out of fear. But let us never fear to negotiate.

Let both sides explore what problems unite us instead of belaboring those problems which divide us.

Let both sides, for the first time, formulate serious and precise proposals for the inspection and control of arms—and bring the absolute power to destroy other nations under the absolute control of all nations.

Let both sides seek to invoke the wonders of science instead of its terrors. Together let us explore the stars, conquer the deserts, eradicate disease, tap the ocean depths, and encourage the arts and commerce.

Let both sides unite to heed in all corners of the earth the command of Isaiah—to "undo the heavy burdens ... and to let the oppressed go free."

11   And if a beachhead of cooperation may push back the jungle of suspicion, let both sides join in creating a new endeavor, not a new balance of power, but a new world of law, where the strong are just and the weak secure and the peace preserved.

12   All this will not be finished in the first 100 days. Nor will it be finished in the first 1,000 days, nor in the life of this Administration, nor even perhaps in our lifetime on this planet. But let us begin.

In your hands, my fellow citizens, more than in mine, will rest the final success or failure of our course. Since this country was founded, each generation of Americans has been summoned to give testimony to its national loyalty. The graves of young Americans who answered the call to service surround the globe.

13   Now the trumpet summons us again—not as a call to bear arms, though arms we need; not as a call to battle, though embattled we are— but a call to bear the burden of a long twilight struggle, year in and year out, "rejoicing in hope, patient in tribulation"—a struggle against the common enemies of man: tyranny, poverty, disease, and war itself.

14   Can we forge against these enemies a grand and global alliance, North and South, East and West, that can assure a more fruitful life for all mankind? Will you join in that historic effort?

In the long history of the world, only a few generations have been granted the role of defending freedom in its hour of maximum danger. I do not shrink from this responsibility—I welcome it. I do not believe that any of us would exchange places with any other people or any other generation. The energy, the faith, the devotion which we bring to this endeavor will light our country and all who serve it—and the glow from that fire can truly light the world.

And so, my fellow Americans: ask not what your country can do for you—ask what you can do for your country. 15

My fellow citizens of the world: ask not what America will do for you, but what together we can do for the freedom of man.

Finally, whether you are citizens of America or citizens of the world, ask of us the same high standards of strength and sacrifice which we ask of you. With a good conscience our only sure reward, with history the final judge of our deeds, let us go forth to lead the land we love, asking His blessing and His help, but knowing that here on earth God's work must truly be our own.

My Notes

A Presidential Beginning

Examining Syntax

Syntax refers to the choices an author makes concerning the types of sentences and combinations of sentences included in a text. Certain types of sentences or their arrangement affects the overall effect of the passage significantly. Sometimes, authors deliberately choose a variety of syntactical constructions for their sentences; other times, authors consciously repeat certain types of sentences in order to achieve the desired effect.

You have been assigned one chunk from the inaugural address of President John F. Kennedy to analyze his syntax. Use the information below to identify syntactical elements of the chunk. Highlight and annotate the text using the My Notes space.

Then discuss the effectiveness of the choices and how the writer's purpose influences choices about syntax. Experiment by changing the type or arrangement of sentences in order to examine how those changes might strengthen or weaken the argument.

Sentence Purpose: Declarative, Interrogative, Exclamatory, and Imperative

Declarative – makes a statement: e.g., "The king is sick."

Interrogative – asks a question: e.g., "Is the king sick?"

Exclamatory – provides emphasis or strong emotion:e.g., "The king is dead! Long live the king!"

Imperative – gives a command: e.g., "Cure the king!"

Sentence Length: Telegraphic, Short, Medium, and Long

Telegraphic – sentences shorter than 5 words in length

Short – sentences approximately 5 words in length

Medium – sentences approximately 18 words in length

Long – sentences 30 words or more in length

Sentence Structure: Simple, Compound, Complex, Compound-Complex, Cumulative, Periodic, and Balanced

Simple – contains one independent clause: e.g., "The goalie waved to his fans."

Compound – contains two independent clauses joined by a coordinating conjunction or by a semicolon: e.g., "The goalie bowed to his fans, but he gave no autographs."

Complex – contains an independent clause and one or more subordinate clauses: e.g., "Because the goalie was tired, he went straight to the locker room."

Compound-Complex – contains two or more independent clauses and one or more subordinate clauses: e.g., "The goalie waved while the fans cheered, but he gave no autographs."

Cumulative (or loose) – makes complete sense if brought to a close before the actual ending: e.g., "We reached New York that morning after a turbulent flight and some exciting experiences, tired but exhilarated, full of stories to tell our friends and neighbors."

Periodic – makes sense fully only when the end of the sentence is reached: e.g., "That morning, after a turbulent flight and some exciting experiences, we reached New York."

Balanced – the phrases or clauses balance each other by virtue of their likeness of structure, meaning or length: e.g., "He maketh me to lie down in green pastures; he leadeth me beside the still waters."

Sentence Order: Natural and Inverted

Natural – involves constructing a sentence so the subject comes before the predicate: e.g., "The group sat beside the swimming pool."

Inverted – involves constructing a sentence so the predicate comes before the subject: e.g., "Beside the swimming pool sat the group." This is a device used to create an emphatic or rhythmic effect.

WORD CONNECTIONS

The relationships in analogies can be expressed using letters; for example, A is to B as C is to D. When reading an analogy, if you do not see a relationship between A and B, look to a different pairing such as A is to C as B is to D. For example, complete this analogy.

millennium : medium ::
millennia : _____

Reviewing Rhetoric

ACADEMIC VOCABULARY

Rhetoric is the skill of choosing words that are most effective for persuading or for creating visual images in the listener's or reader's mind.

Rhetoric has been defined as "the art of using words to persuade in writing or speaking." When a writer attempts to persuade, he or she uses certain kinds of appeals in order to make a case and persuade the reader or listener. These appeals can generally fall into one of three broad categories. Aristotle first identified these categories of appeals and called them appeals of pathos, ethos, and logos. Today, they are also referred to as emotional, ethical, and logical appeals. Writers and speakers choose the kinds of appeals to use in their arguments based on their intended audience, purpose, and the nature of the argument itself.

Pathos (emotional appeal): This type of appeal attempts to persuade the reader or listener by appealing to the senses and emotions. Political ads that show politicians kissing babies or shaking hands with the elderly often appeal to the emotions. Also, these appeals usually include statements with vivid sensory details, which are used to awaken the senses and perhaps manipulate the emotions of the audience.

Ethos (ethical appeal): This type of appeal attempts to persuade the reader or listener by focusing on the qualifications of the speaker. The speaker's credibility is paramount in an ethical appeal. Ethical appeals focus on the speaker even more than the situation. Examples of ethical appeals in advertising are expert or celebrity endorsements of products. Other examples of ethical appeals are a teen's argument that he or she should be allowed to do something because he or she has never been in trouble, or because his or her friend is a perfect citizen, and so on.

Logos (logical appeal): This type of appeal attempts to persuade the reader or listener by leading him down the road of logic and causing him to come to his own conclusion. Logical appeals state the facts and show how the facts are interrelated. *If/then* statements are examples of logical appeals. Logical appeals are often used in courtroom situations.

Practice

Identify the type of appeal used in each of the following statements:

1. If Mr. Nabors says that he was home by 10 p.m., yet Mr. Nabors's neighbor claims he saw him arriving home at 2 a.m., doesn't that lead you to believe that Mr. Nabors might be lying?

2. I deserve the position because I have worked faithfully for the past 30 years. I always try to go above and beyond what is required. I was even selected to be the "Employee of the Month."

3. The animal shelter desperately needs your support. It is overflowing with lonely little kittens who spend their days mewing and whimpering and staring forlornly out of their tiny little crates.

Write your thoughts in response to the following questions:

- Under which circumstances might emotional appeals be most effective?

- What about ethical appeals?

- Logical appeals?

Using Rhetorical Devices

ACADEMIC VOCABULARY

Rhetorical devices are techniques a writer uses to evoke an emotional response from the audience.

My Notes

Sermon

ABOUT THE AUTHOR

Jonathan Edwards (1703–1758) was born in Connecticut as the only son in a family of eleven children. He entered Yale College before age 13. After graduating at 17, he entered into theological studies and began preaching before he was 19. During his ministry, he wrote several books of spiritual philosophy. His writings have endured for more than 200 years and have led to his consideration by many as one of the greatest theologians this country has produced.

From Sinners in the Hands of an Angry God

by Jonathan Edwards

The wrath of God is like great waters that are dammed for the present; they increase more and more, and rise higher and higher, till an outlet is given; and the longer the stream is stopped, the more rapid and mighty is its course, when once it is let loose. It is true, that judgment against your evil work has not been executed hitherto; the floods of God's vengeance have been withheld; but your guilt in the mean time is constantly increasing, and you are every day treasuring up more wrath; the waters are constantly rising, and waxing more and more mighty; and there is nothing but the mere pleasure of God, that holds the waters back, that are unwilling to be stopped, and press hard to go forward. If God should only withdraw his hand from the flood-gate, it would immediately fly open, and the fiery floods of the fierceness and wrath of God, would rush forth with inconceivable fury, and would come upon you with omnipotent power; and if your strength were ten thousand times greater than it is, yea, ten thousand times greater than the strength of the stoutest, sturdiest devil in hell, it would be nothing to withstand or endure it.

The bow of God's wrath is bent, and the arrow made ready on the string, and justice bends the arrow at your heart, and strains the bow, and it is nothing but the mere pleasure of God, and that of an angry God, without any promise or obligation at all, that keeps the arrow one moment from being made drunk with your blood.

Thus are all you that never passed under a great change of heart by the mighty power of the Spirit of God upon your souls; all you that were never born again, and made new creatures, and raised from being dead in sin, to a state of new, and before altogether unexperienced light and life, are in the hands of an angry God. However you may have reformed your life in many things, and may have had religious affections, and may keep up a form of religion in your families and closets, and in the house of God, and may be strict in it, you are thus in the hands of an angry God; it is nothing but his mere pleasure that keeps you from being this moment swallowed up in everlasting destruction.

However unconvinced you may now be of the truth of what you hear, by and by you will be fully convinced of it. Those that are gone from being in the like circumstances with you, see that it was so with them; for destruction came suddenly upon most of them; when they expected nothing of it, and while they were saying, Peace and safety: now they see, that those things on which they depended for peace and safety, were nothing but thin air and empty shadows.

The God that holds you over the pit of hell, much as one holds a spider, or some loathsome insect over the fire, abhors you, and is dreadfully provoked: his wrath towards you burns like fire; he looks upon you as worthy of nothing else, but to be cast into the fire; he is of purer eyes than to bear to have you in his sight; you are ten thousand times more abominable in his eyes, than the most hateful and venomous serpent is in ours. You have offended him infinitely more than ever a stubborn rebel did his prince; and yet it is nothing but his hand that holds you from falling into the fire every moment. It is to be ascribed to nothing else, that you did not go to hell the last night; that you was suffered to awake again in this world after you closed your eyes to sleep. And there is no other reason to be given, why you have not dropped into hell since you arose in the morning, but that God's hand has held you up. There is no other reason to be given why you have not gone to hell, since you have sat here in the house of God, provoking his pure eyes by your sinful wicked manner of attending his solemn worship. Yea, there is nothing else that is to be given as a reason why you do not this very moment drop down into hell.

O sinner! Consider the fearful danger you are in: it is a great furnace of wrath, a wide and bottomless pit, full of the fire of wrath, that you are held over in the hand of that God, whose wrath is provoked and incensed as much against you as against many of the damned in hell. You hang by a slender thread, with the fames of divine wrath flashing about it, and ready every moment to singe it and burn it asunder; and you have no interest in any Mediator, and nothing to lay hold of to save yourself, nothing to keep off the flames of wrath, nothing of your own, nothing that you ever have done, nothing that you can do, to induce God to spare you one moment....

LITERARY TERMS

Argument by analogy is a comparison of two similar situations, implying that the outcome of one will resemble the outcome of the other.

An **extended metaphor** is a comparison that extends over several lines or an entire poem.

Repetition is the use of any element of language — sound, word, phrase — more than once.

My Notes

Using Rhetorical Devices

The following graphic organizer presents the definitions of some common **rhetorical devices** used in speeches (examples are from Kennedy's Inaugural Address). Identify other examples of these devices in the speeches of Jonathan Edwards and Patrick Henry. Explain the effect of the device.

Rhetorical Device and Example	Other Examples	Effect
Repetition (anaphora): Repetition at the beginnings of clauses, lines, or sentences. (In Chunks 3-8, Kennedy repeats "To those…")		
Aphorism: A concise statement of truth. (In Chunk 15, Kennedy requests, "And so, my fellow Americans: ask not what your country can do for you—ask what you can do for your country.")		
Parallelism: The use of repeated grammatical structures. (In Chunk 2 "…we all pay any price, bear any burden, meet any hardship…")		
Allusion: A direct or indirect reference to something from history, the Bible, etc. (In Chunk 10, the direct reference to the Book of Isaiah)		
Rhetorical Question: A question for which the answer is obvious. (In Chunk 14, Kennedy asks, "Can we forge against these enemies a grand and global alliance, North and South, East and West, that can assure a more fruitful life for all mankind?")		
Argument by Analogy: A comparison of two similar situations, implying that the outcome of one will resemble the outcome of the other. (In Chunk 4, "those who foolishly sought power by riding the back of the tiger ended up inside.")		
Metaphor and Simile: Comparisons of two unlike things. (In Chunk 11: "And if a beachhead of cooperation may push back the jungle of suspicion…")		

SUGGESTED LEARNING STRATEGIES: Close Reading, Marking the Text, Discussion Groups, Graphic Organizer, SOAPSTone

Speech

> **ABOUT THE AUTHOR**
> Patrick Henry (1736–1799) was born in Virginia. He tried several occupations before becoming a lawyer and then a politician encouraging separation from Great Britain. He served as a delegate from Virginia to the First Session of the Continental Congress in 1774 and became noted as a powerful speaker whose words helped sweep the Colonists toward their declaration of independence.

Speech to the VIRGINIA CONVENTION *March 23, 1775*

by Patrick Henry

No man thinks more highly than I do of the patriotism, as well as abilities, of the very worthy gentlemen who have just addressed the House. But different men often see the same subject in different lights; and, therefore, I hope it will not be thought disrespectful to those gentlemen if, entertaining, as I do, opinions of a character very opposite to theirs, I shall speak forth my sentiments freely and without reserve. This is no time for ceremony. The question before the House is one of awful moment to this country. For my own part, I consider it as nothing less than a question of freedom or slavery; and in proportion to the magnitude of the subject ought to be the freedom of the debate. It is only in this way that we can hope to arrive at truth, and fulfill the great responsibility which we hold to God and our country. Should I keep back my opinions at such a time, through fear of giving offense, I should consider myself guilty of treason towards my country, and of an act of disloyalty toward the Majesty of Heaven, which I revere above all earthly kings.

Mr. President, it is natural to man to indulge in the illusions of hope. We are apt to shut our eyes against a painful truth, and listen to the song of that siren, till she transforms us into beasts. Is this the part of wise men, engaged in a great and arduous struggle for liberty? Are we disposed to be

"Give me Liberty!"

of the number of those who, having eyes, see not and, having ears, hear not, the things which so nearly concern their temporal salvation? For my part, whatever anguish of spirit it may cost, I am willing to know the whole truth; to know the worst, and to provide for it.

I have but one lamp by which my feet are guided, and that is the lamp of experience. I know of no way of judging the future but by the past. And judging by the past, I wish to know what there has been in the conduct of the British ministry for the last ten years to justify those hopes with which gentlemen have been pleased to solace themselves and the House. Is it that insidious smile with which our petition has been lately received? Trust it not, sir; it will prove a snare to your feet. Suffer not yourselves to be betrayed with a kiss. Ask yourselves how this gracious reception of our petition comports with those warlike preparations which cover our waters and darken our land. Are fleets and armies necessary to a work of love and reconciliation? Have we shown ourselves so unwilling to be reconciled that force must be called in to win back our love? Let us not deceive ourselves, sir. These are the implements of war and subjugation; the last arguments to which kings resort. I ask gentlemen, sir, what means this martial array, if its purpose be not to force us to submission? Can gentlemen assign any other possible motive for it?, Has Great Britain any enemy in this quarter of the world, to call for all this accumulation of navies and armies? No sir, she has none. They are meant for us: they can be meant for no other. They are sent over to bind and rivet upon us those chains which the British ministry have been so long forging. And what have we to oppose to them? Shall we try argument? Sir, we have been trying that for the last ten years. Have we anything new to offer upon the subject? Nothing. We have held the subject up in every light of which it is capable; but it has been all in vain. Shall we resort to entreaty and humble supplication? What terms shall we find which have not been already exhausted? Let us not, I beseech you, sir, deceive ourselves. Sir, we have done everything that could be done, to avert the storm which is now coming on. We have petitioned; we have remonstrated; we have supplicated; we have prostrated ourselves before the throne, and have implored its interposition to arrest the tyrannical hands of the ministry and Parliament. Our petitions have been slighted; our remonstrances have produced additional violence and insult; our supplications have been disregarded; and we have been spurned, with contempt, from the foot of the throne! In vain, after these things, may we indulge the fond hope of peace and reconciliation. *There is no longer any room for hope.* If we wish to be free — if we mean to preserve inviolate those inestimable privileges for which we have been so long contending — if we mean not basely to abandon the noble struggle in which we have been so long engaged, and which we have pledged ourselves never to abandon until the glorious object of our contest shall be obtained — we must fight! — I repeat it, sir, we must fight! An appeal to arms and to the God of hosts, is all that is left us!

GRAMMAR & USAGE

Sometimes a writer will invert the word order so that the verb or a part of the verb occurs before the subject. For example, Henry writes, "In vain, after these things, may we indulge the fond hope of peace and reconciliation." The inverted order calls attention to the sentence and emphasizes the verb (and the futility of the hope).

They tell us, sir, that we are weak; unable to cope with so formidable an adversary. But when shall we be stronger? Will it be the next week, or the next year? Will it be when we are totally disarmed, and when a British guard shall be stationed in every house? Shall we gather strength by irresolution and inaction? Shall we acquire the means of effectual resistance by lying supinely on our backs, and hugging the delusive phantom of hope, until our enemies shall have bound us hand and foot? Sir, we are not weak if we make a proper use of those means which the God of nature hath placed in our power. The millions of people, armed in the holy cause of liberty, and in such a country as that which we possess, are invincible by any force which our enemy can send against us. Besides, sir, we shall not fight our battles alone. There is a just God who presides over the destinies of nations and who will raise up friends to fight our battles for us. The battle, sir, is not to the strong alone; it is to the vigilant, the active, the brave. Besides, sir, we have no election. If we were base enough to desire it, it is now too late to retire from the contest. There is no retreat but in submission and slavery! Our chains are forged! Their clanking may be heard on the plains of Boston! The war in inevitable — and let it come! I repeat it, sir, let it come.

It is in vain, sir, to extenuate the matter. Gentlemen may cry, Peace, Peace — but there is no peace. The war is actually begun! The next gale that sweeps from the north will bring to our ears the clash of resounding arms! Our brethren are already in the field! Why stand we here idle? What is it that gentlemen wish? What would they have? Is life so dear, or peace so sweet, as to be purchased at the price of chains and slavery? Forbid it, Almighty God! I know not what course others may take; but as for me, give me liberty, or give me death!

HENRY

It's All in the Delivery

Viewing and Listening Guide for Speeches

Read the following list of items often found within effective speeches.
As you watch or listen to the speech your teacher has assigned, use the
space below to take notes on the components that you see or hear.

Physical	Rhetorical	
Volume	Repetition; anaphora	Logical Appeals
Smooth Delivery	Aphorism	Emotional Appeals
Gestures	Analogy	Ethical Appeals
Dramatic Pauses	Allusion	Striking Syntax
Movement	Metaphor	Parallelism
	Rhetorical Questions	

Physical	Rhetorical

Creating and Presenting a Persuasive Speech

SUGGESTED LEARNING STRATEGIES: **Graphic Organizer, Drafting**

Assignment

Your assignment is to create and present an original persuasive speech. Throughout this unit, you have examined rhetorical appeals and rhetorical devices. You have looked at syntax and its influence on rhetoric. You have also examined effective delivery of speeches. Now, it is your turn to demonstrate the art of persuasion by writing and delivering a two- to three-minute persuasive speech that addresses a contemporary issue.

Steps

Planning

1. Brainstorm a list of contemporary issues about which you can take a strong stance. You can use your portfolio and much of your work from Unit 2 for ideas.

2. Narrow your list and select an issue. Decide which side of the issue you would like to take.

3. Select a strategy and create a graphic organizer that you can use to plan your speech. On it, compose a thesis statement that effectively presents your stand on the issue. List the purpose you will be attempting to achieve. Then, list the supporting evidence you will provide. Also, consider and include the type or types of rhetorical appeals and devices that will help you achieve your desired purpose.

Drafting

4. Compose your speech. Examine and consider your choices in terms of syntax. Consider changes that might make your argument more effective.

Revising

5. Allow at least two peers to read your speech and make constructive comments. Ask them to be sure to identify your purpose, supporting reasons, and use of rhetorical appeals and devices. Use their comments to make revisions.

Creating and Presenting a Persuasive Speech

Rehearsing

6. Then, consider the delivery style you will use to deliver your speech to your classmates. Mark your text for appropriate inflection and use of gestures.

7. Practice delivering your speech. Ask someone to time you as you practice, and revise your speech or delivery style if necessary to fit within the two- to three- minute time frame. You might want to practice in front of a mirror or record your speech so that you can replay it and make changes as needed.

Presenting

8. Be prepared to give your speech on the day your teacher assigns. Consider how your physical appearance will affect your delivery, and try to dress appropriately for the nature of your speech. Be prepared to give your teacher a final draft of your speech prior to your presentation.

Reflecting

9. As you view your peers' speeches, fill out a Peer Critique Form for each speech. After all speeches have been presented, draft a written reflection about the elements that make a speech effective.

Peer Critique Form

Speaker _____ Reviewer _____

Aspect of Presentation	Rating	Examples from Speech	Comments
Takes a clear stand on the issue	• Exemplary • Proficient • Emerging		
Uses rhetorical appeals and devices	• Exemplary • Proficient • Emerging		
Uses syntax that is varied and reflects the intended purpose	• Exemplary • Proficient • Emerging		
Demonstrates a delivery method that is indicative of advance preparation	• Exemplary • Proficient • Emerging		

Overall strengths:

Suggestions for improvement:

Creating and Presenting a Persuasive Speech

SCORING GUIDE

Scoring Criteria	Exemplary	Proficient	Emerging
Ideas	The speech presents a significant and compelling thesis on a contemporary issue; the thesis is clearly developed and supported. The argument is convincing and adeptly uses a variety of rhetorical appeals.	The speech presents a clear thesis on a contemporary issue; the thesis is sufficiently developed and supported. The argument is plausible and effectively uses rhetorical appeals.	The speech presents a position that is difficult to distinguish or is insufficiently developed and supported. An attempt has been made to make an argument, but it is not plausible and uses persuasive appeals ineffectively.
Use of Language	The speaker deliberately and effectively uses rhetorical devices and varied syntax for the intended purpose.	The speaker clearly attempts to use rhetorical devices and varied syntax for the intended purpose.	If the speaker attempts to use rhetorical devices and varied syntax, the result is ineffective for the intended purpose.
Presentation	The speaker demonstrates well-placed inflection and gestures that create an engaging delivery style indicative of advance preparation and rehearsal for the delivery. The overall organization of the speech and the speaker's obvious commitment to the issue compel audience engagement.	The speaker demonstrates some use of inflection and gestures that create an appropriate delivery style indicative of advance preparation and rehearsal. The overall organization of the speech shows a thoughtful attempt to encourage audience engagement.	The speaker demonstrates minimal use of inflection and gestures to create an appropriate delivery style indicative of advance preparation and rehearsal. The speech is disorganized and shows little attempt to encourage audience engagement.
Reflection	The writer's reflection demonstrates a thorough and detailed analysis of the components of an effective speech.	The writer's reflection demonstrates an adequate analysis of the components of an effective speech.	The writer's reflection demonstrates a minimal analysis of the components of an effective speech.

SCORING GUIDE

Scoring Criteria	Exemplary	Proficient	Emerging
Additional Criteria			

Comments:

Learning Focus:

Speaking Your Conscience

Imagine you are a witness to a situation you perceive as being unjust. What is your response? Do you speak out, or remain silent? Now, imagine you are an author who has witnessed an unjust situation, and you decide to speak out, using the most influential forum you know—your writing. Songwriters, poets, dramatists, bloggers, Webmasters – writers and performers of all ages use **social commentary** to speak out against perceived injustices every day. Using art to advance social commentary has long been a hallmark of artistic expression.

Arthur Miller is a leader among the ranks of writers who use their art to comment on social issues. He created *The Crucible* to speak his conscience; he uncovered a setting, developed compelling characters through masterful characterization, created dialogue rich with metaphor and purpose, and structured a plot that transformed ideas into a drama of such persuasive appeal that it continues to speak to audiences all over the world.

The action of *The Crucible,* like all good stories, is driven by conflict and character. Drama is set apart in that the action must take place in two hours while covering a greater expanse of time. The development of the central ideas occurs in a series of dramatic scenes which illuminate and intensify the conflicts that are embodied in characters. Carefully constructed dialogue and realistic, yet symbolic, characterization are the tools of the dramatist. Dialogue must sound real, but must also be purposeful in a way that daily conversation is not. Thus, writers deliberately construct dialogue using language that is more metaphoric, more condensed, and more laden with meaning. Characterization must be accomplished quickly and deeply, so writers use theatrical elements such as costume, and dramatic elements such as **foils**, and minor characters, or antagonists, to illuminate the characteristics of the major protagonist and his or her conflicts.

The most complete way to appreciate a drama of this caliber is to read it, perform it, view it, and finally to emulate it.

Preparing to Read *The Crucible*

SUGGESTED LEARNING STRATEGIES: Rereading, Summarizing, Marking the Text, Quickwrite, Predicting, KWL Chart, Think-Pair-Share

In the My Notes space, annotate the text by summarizing each of the following passages about the Puritans' feelings about God, sin, the Devil, or humankind.

Excerpts from Sinners *in* the Hands *of* an Angry God

by Jonathan Edwards

1. "[Men] deserve to be cast into hell; so that divine justice never stands in the way; it makes no objection against God's using His power at any moment to destroy them. Yea, on the contrary, justice calls aloud for an infinite punishment of their sins."

2. "The devil stands ready to fall upon them, and seize them as his own, at what moment God shall permit him. They belong to him; he has their souls in his possession, and under his dominion. The Scripture represents them as his goods."

3. "The corruption of the heart of man is immoderate and boundless in its fury; and while wicked men live here, it is like fire pent up by God's restraints, whereas if it were let loose, it would set on fire the course of nature; as the heart is now a sink of sin, so, if sin was not restrained, it would immediately turn the soul into a fiery oven, or furnace of fire and brimstone."

4. "God has laid Himself under no obligation, by any promise to keep any natural man out of hell one moment. God certainly has made no promises either of eternal life, or of any deliverance or preservation from eternal death, but what are contained in the covenant of grace, the promises that are given in Christ, in whom all the promises are yea and amen."

5. "So that, thus it is that natural men are held in the hand of God, over the pit of hell; they have deserved the fiery pit, and are already sentenced to it; and God is dreadfully provoked: His anger is as great towards them as those that are actually suffering the execution of the fierceness of His wrath in hell; and they have done nothing in the least to appease or abate that anger, neither is God in the least bound by any promise to hold them up for one moment. The devil is waiting for them, hell is gaping for them, the flames gather and flash about them, and would fain lay hold on them, and swallow them up; the fire pent up in their own heart is struggling to break out."

Quickwrite: How might the attitudes and feelings reflected in this sermon connect with a belief in witchcraft?

My Notes

My Notes

WORD CONNECTIONS

Convert uses the Latin word *vertere* meaning "to turn." *Introvert, versus, subvert, version* all come from this word.

GRAMMAR & USAGE

The colon is used to introduce ideas, examples, or quotations that explain or expand the idea that comes before the colon. The colon occurs at the end of a clause, not after a verb or a preposition. For example, notice the way Shapiro begins the third paragraph. She introduces the idea that Brattle's words are still true today with the short sentence "He was right." What follows after the colon explains her point.

Article

The Lessons of Salem

by Laura Shapiro

After 300 years, people are still fascinated by the notorious Puritan witch hunts – maybe because history keeps repeating itself.

Chunk 1

They came for Martha Carrier at the end of May. There was plenty of evidence against her: Allen Toothaker testified that several of his cattle had suffered "strange deaths" soon after he and Carrier had an argument, and little Phoebe Chandler said that shortly before being stricken with terrible pains, she had heard Carrier's voice telling her she was going to be poisoned. Even Carrier's children spoke against her: they confessed that they, too, were witches and that it was their mother who had converted them to evil. (Their statements were not introduced in court, however — perhaps because two of her sons had to be tied up until they bled from their mouth before they would confess. A small daughter spoke more freely; she told officials that her mother was a black cat.) Most damning of all was the evidence offered by half a dozen adolescent girls, who accused Carrier of tormenting them and who fell into writhing fits as she stood before the magistrate. They shrieked that they had seen the Devil whispering into Carrier's ear. "You see you look upon them and they fall down," said the magistrate. "It is a shameful thing that you should mind these folks that are out of their wits," answered Carrier. "I am wronged." On Aug. 19, 1692, she was hanged on Gallows Hill in Salem Mass., for the crime of witchcraft.

Last week marked the 300th anniversary of Carrier's death, an execution carried out during the most notorious summer in Massachusetts history. Between June and September of 1692, 14 women and 5 men were hanged in Salem as witches, and 1 man was tortured to death. Scores more were named as witches and imprisoned. "What will be the issue of these troubles, God only knows," wrote Thomas Brattle, a merchant in nearby Boston who was horrified by the events. "I am afraid that ages will not wear off that reproach and those stains which these things will leave behind upon our land."

He was right: even now the Salem witch trials haunt the imaginations of hundreds of thousands of Americans, tourists and history buffs alike, who visit Salem for a glimpse of our Puritan past at its most chilling. This year Salem is getting more attention than ever: the city is sponsoring an array of programs commemorating the Tercentenary, including dramatizations of the trials and symposiums of the legal and medical aspects of identifying witches in the 17th century. With the participation of such organizations as Amnesty International, the Tercentenary has placed a special emphasis on human rights and the role of the individual conscience in times of terror. In 1692, those who "confessed" to witchcraft were spared; only those who insisted on their innocence were hanged. Earlier this month a memorial to the victims was unveiled and on that occasion the first annual Salem Award, created to honor a significant contribution to social justice, was presented to Gregory Allen Williams of Inglewood, Calif. In the midst of the Los Angeles riots last spring, Williams, who is black, risked his life to save an Asian-American attacked by a mob.

At the heart of the Tercentenary is the awareness that the witch trials represent more than just a creepy moment in history: they stand for the terrible victory of prejudice over reason, and fear over courage — a contest that has been replayed with different actors, again and again since 1692. Modern witch hunts include the roundup of Japanese-Americans during World War II, the pursuit of Communists in the '50s and, according to an increasing number of critics, some of today's outbreaks of community hysteria over purported sex abuse in preschools. Experts say that although most child-abuse allegations are valid, the preschool cases are the flimsiest, resting as they do on a mixture of parental terror and children's confusion. Just as in Salem, the evidence in these cases tends to spring from hindsight, fueled by suspicion and revulsion. Whatever the truth may be, it has little chance to surface under such conditions.

Like all witch hunts, the troubles of 1692 began in a community that felt torn and besieged. Salem Village, now the town of Danvers, was about eight miles from the seat of local power in Salem Town. A contentious place, chafing to pull free of Salem Town and its taxes, Salem Village had suffered bitter disputes over its first three ministers before settling on a fourth, the Rev. Samuel Parris. During the winter of 1691–92, a few girls, mostly teenagers, started gathering in Parris's kitchen. There they listened to stories, perhaps voodoo tales, told by his Western Indian slave Tituba; they also tried to discern their future husbands by fortunetelling — dropping an egg white into a glass and seeing what shape it took. For girls raised in Puritanism, which demanded lifelong discipline and self-control, these sessions with Tituba represented a rare and risky bit of indulgence in pure fancy. Too risky, perhaps. Suddenly one after another of the girls was seized with fits. Their families were bewildered: the girls raved and fell into convulsions; one of them ran around on all fours and barked. Dr. William Griggs was called in and made his diagnosis: the "evil hand" was upon them.

Chunk 2

My Notes

Preparing to Read *The Crucible*

Fits identified as satanic possession had broken out among adolescent girls at earlier times in New England. Often their distress was traced to local women who, it was said, had entered into a compact with the Devil and were now recruiting new witches by tormenting the innocent until they succumbed. So the adults in Salem Village began pressing the girls with questions: "Who torments you? Who torments you?" Finally they named three women — Tituba, Sarah Good and Sarah Osborne — all of them easily recognizable as Satan's hand-maidens. Tituba was seen as a shameless pagan, Good was a poor beggar given to muttering angrily as she went from house to house and Osborne was known to have lived with her second husband before they were married. The three were arrested and jailed, but the girls' torments did not cease. On the contrary, fits were spreading like smallpox; dozens more girls and young women went into violent contortions, flailing, kicking and uttering names.

And the names! Rebecca Nurse was 71, the pious and beloved matriarch of a large family; she was hanged in July. George Jacobs, an old man whose servant girl was one of the afflicted, thought the whole lot of them were "bitch witches" and said so; he was hanged in August. Susannah Martin was named, but that surprised nobody; people had been calling her a witch for years. Six or seven years earlier, Barnard Peach testified, he had been lying in bed at night when Martin appeared at his window and jumped into his room; she then lay down upon him and prevented him from moving for nearly two hours. Others had similar tales; Martin was hanged in July. Nor was there much doubt about Dorcas Good, who was arrested soon after her mother, Sarah, was jailed. The afflicted girls cried out that Dorcas was biting and pinching them, and although the attacks were invisible to everyone else, the girls had the bite marks to prove it. Dorcas was jailed with the others, and a special set of chains was made for her. She was only 5, and the regular shackles were too big.

All along, there were townspeople who had misgivings about what was happening. Several came to the defense of some of the accused citizens, and others testified that they had heard an afflicted girl saying she had made at least one accusation "for sport." But the machinery seemed unstoppable. If a prisoner was released or a jury decided to acquit someone, the girls went into such shrieking torments that the court quickly reversed itself.

WORD CONNECTIONS

Symptom uses the Greek prefix *syn-* meaning "together." Many English words rely on this prefix, including *sympathy*, *symbol*, *symphony*.

Spectral evidence: Finally, in October, the governor of Massachusetts stepped in. Too many citizens "of good reputation" had been accused, he wrote, including his own wife. What's more, clergy in both Boston and New York were expressing dismay over the witch trials, especially the reliance on "spectral" evidence, such as the sight of the Devil whispering in Martha Carrier's ear — otherworldly evidence invisible to everyone but the person testifying. The governor ruled out the use of spectral evidence, making it virtually impossible to convict any more of the accused. That fall the witch craze effectively ended, and by spring the last prisoners had been acquitted.

What really happened in Salem? Scholars have been trying to understand the events of 1692 for three centuries. Even while the witch hunt was in progress, Deodat Lawson, a former minister at Salem Village, made a visit to his old parish and published the equivalent of a quickie paperback describing "the Misterious Assaults from Hell" he had witnessed there. Like everyone else in Salem — in fact, like everyone else in colonial New England — he believed in witches, though he was powerless to understand why or whether they were truly on the loose in Salem.

Today many scholars believe it was clinical hysteria that set off the girls in Tituba's kitchen. Fits, convulsions, vocal outbursts, feelings of being pinched and bitten — all of these symptoms have been witnessed and described, most often in young women, for centuries. Sometimes the seizures have been attributed to Satan, other times to God, but ever since Freud weighed in, hysteria has been traced to the unconscious. As Dr. Richard Pohl, of Salem Hospital, told a Tercentenary symposium, hysteria "can mimic all the physical diseases known to man," and occurs when repressed thoughts and emotions burst forth and take over the body. Life could be dreary for girls in 17th century Salem: their place was home and their duty was obedience; many were illiterate, and there were few outlets for youthful imagination except in the grim lessons of Puritan theology. Dabbling in magic in the reverend's own kitchen would have been wonderfully scary, perhaps enough to release psychic demons lurking since childhood.

Despite the fact that young girls made the accusations, it was the adults who lodged formal charges against their neighbors and provided most of the testimony. Historians have long believed that local feuds and property disputes were behind many of the accusations, and in "Salem Possessed" (1974), Paul Boyer and Stephen Nissenbaum uncovered patterns of social and civic antagonism that made the community fertile ground for a witch hunt. . . .

Chunk 3

My Notes

1. To prepare for this drama game, practice delivering one of the following lines assigned by your teacher.

Character: Reverend Parris

Line 1: You will confess yourself or I will take you out and whip you to your death, Tituba!

Line 2: How can it be the Devil? Why would he choose my house to strike? We have all manner of licentious people in the village!

Line 3: Rebecca, Rebecca, go to her, we're lost. She suddenly cannot bear to hear the Lord's—

Character: Tituba

Line 1: And I say, "You lie, Devil, you lie!" And then he come one stormy night to me, and he say, "Look! I have white people belong to me. And I look—and there was Goody Good."

Line 2: Mister Reverend, I do believe somebody else be witchin' these children.

Line 3: No, no, don't hang Tituba! I tell him I don't desire to work for him, sir.

Character: Reverend Hale

Line 1: Now let me instruct you. We cannot look to superstition in this. The Devil is precise; the marks of his presence are definite as stone.

Line 2: We shall need hard study if it comes to tracking down the Old Boy.

Line 3: You must have no fear to tell us who they are, do you understand? We will protect you. The Devil can never overcome a minister. You know that, do you not?

Character: Giles Corey

Line 1: Mr. Hale, I have always wanted to ask a learned man—what signifies the readin' of strange books?

Line 2: A fart on Thomas Putnam, that is what I say to that!

Line 3: I will not give you no name. I mentioned my wife's name once and I'll burn in hell long enough for that. I stand mute.

Character: Rebecca Nurse

Line 1: Goody Ann! You sent a child to conjure up the dead?

Line 2: This will set us all to arguin' again in the society, and we thought to have peace this year.

Line 3: I fear it, I fear it. Let us rather blame ourselves and—

Character: John Proctor

Line 1: Can you speak one minute without we land in Hell again? I am sick of Hell.

Line 2: I come to see what mischief your uncle's brewin' now. Put it out of mind, Abby.

Line 3: Ah, you're wicked yet, aren't y'!

Character: Abigail Williams

Line 1: I never sold myself! I'm a good girl! I'm a proper girl!

Line 2: My name is good in the village! I will not have it said my name is soiled! Goody Proctor is a gossiping liar!

Line 3: I danced for the Devil; I saw him; I wrote in his book.

Character: John Putnam

Line 1: ...Mr. Hale. We look to you to come to our house and save our child.

Line 2: Why, we are surely gone wild this year. What anarchy is this? That tract is in my bounds, it's in my bounds, Mr. Proctor.

Line 3: That is a notorious sign of witchcraft afoot, Goody Nurse, a prodigious sign!

2. After the tea party, meet together with others who were assigned your same character. Compare information, and make inferences about your character based on the quotes you have been given. Then, read the commentary sections in Act One that pertain to your character, and try to find specific details about your character. Use the Character Notetaking Chart on the next page to take notes on your character, writing down words and descriptions from the text that indicate Miller's attitude toward that character.

3. Next, work with your new discussion groups to determine what you know about the relationships among all of the tea party characters. Given what you already know about the Salem Witch Trials, make predictions about what might happen to some of these characters. Add these predictions to the graphic organizer. Return to this chart at various times in your reading to update or change your responses.

Character Notetaking Chart

Reverend Parris Notes: Motivations:	**Predictions:**
Tituba Notes: Motivations:	**Predictions:**
Abigail Notes: Motivations:	**Predictions:**
Mr. Putnam Notes: Motivations:	**Predictions:**

John Proctor:

Notes:

Motivations:

Predictions:

Francis and Rebecca Nurse

Notes:

Motivations:

Predictions:

Reverend Hale

Notes:

Motivations:

Predictions:

Giles Corey: pgs. 40–41, sixth commentary section

Notes:

Motivations:

Predictions:

Beginnings

The Beginnings of the Play: After you read Act 1, revisit "An Overture" (pages 3–8). which Arthur Miller includes at the beginning of the play, and take notes on the details he provides about Salem and the Puritans. In the following space, summarize what you have learned about the community of Salem.

The Beginnings of the Lies: Reread the scene when the four girls are alone just prior to Proctor's first entrance. After reading the scene, consider how each girl might have felt about that night. Then, on a separate piece of paper, write a journal entry in the voice of one of the girls, and share your writing with your group. Think about the reasons the girls are lying, and consider who appears to be in control of the situation.

ACADEMIC VOCABULARY

A foil is a secondary character who is contrasted with the main character to offer insights into facets of the main character.

The Beginnings of Characterization: John Hale and **Giles Corey** can be seen as character foils to **John Proctor,** the main character of this drama. A foil is a character whose actions or thoughts are juxtaposed to those of a major character. This juxtaposition serves to highlight key attributes of the major character. With your class, begin a class poster that lists the similarities and differences in actions and attitudes between Hale and Proctor and Proctor and Corey.

Key Scene 1: Proctor and Abby

SUGGESTED LEARNING STRATEGIES: Marking the Text, Oral Reading,
Graphic Organizer, Discussion Groups

Imagine that you are the director of a stage version of *The Crucible*.
You must decide how you will portray the relationship between Proctor
and Abigail. Below are four possible scenarios that provide different
interpretations of their relationship. After you have read the scene in
which they are alone for the first time, match gestures, movements,
looks, facial expressions, vocal delivery to the different interpretations
suggested. Be sure to identify the specific line where the stage
directions would apply.

Proctor Is in Love with Abigail

Line	Gestures	Movements	Facial Expressions	Vocal Delivery

Proctor Hates Abigail

Line	Gestures	Movements	Facial Expressions	Vocal Delivery

Key Scene 1: Proctor and Abby

Proctor Is Afraid of Abigail

Line	Gestures	Movements	Facial Expressions	Vocal Delivery

Proctor Is Conflicted in His Feelings for Abigail

Line	Gestures	Movements	Facial Expressions	Vocal Delivery

After watching the film version of this scene, discuss in a small group which one of the above characterizations the director seemed to have in mind. Why? Did you see any of your choices in the film version? How might you have filmed the scene differently? Why?

Defining Hysteria

SUGGESTED LEARNING STRATEGIES: Word Map, Rereading, Drafting

Use the Word Map below to take notes during your class discussion of *hysteria*.

Associated Words

Definition

Examples

Hysteria

My Notes

Fable

ABOUT THE AUTHOR

James Thurber (1894–1961) was a popular American writer and artist. He was born in Columbus, Ohio, but moved to New York and became a writer and artist for the *New Yorker* magazine. His stories and cartoons were noted for the way he used humor to portray scenes from everyday life.

The Very Proper Gander

by James Thurber

Not so very long ago there was a very fine gander. He was strong and smooth and beautiful and he spent most of his time singing to his wife and children. One day somebody who saw him strutting up and down in his yard and singing remarked, "There is a very proper gander." An old hen overheard this and told her husband about it that night in the roost. "They said something about propaganda," she said. "I have always suspected that," said the rooster, and he went around the barnyard next day telling everybody that the very fine gander was a dangerous bird, more than likely a hawk in gander's clothing. A small brown hen rememberd a time when at a great distance she had seen the gander talking with some hawks in the forest. "They were up to no good," she said. A duck remembered that the gander had once told him he did not believe in anything. "He said to hell with the flag, too," said the duck. A guinea hen recalled that she had once seen somebody who looked very much like the gander throw something that looked a great deal like a bomb. Finally everybody snatched up sticks and stones and descended on the gander's house. He was strutting in his front yard, singing to his children and his wife. "There he is!" everybody cried. "Hawk-lover! Unbeliever! Flag-hater! Bomb-thrower!" So they set upon him and drove him out of the country.

Moral: Anybody who you or your wife thinks is going to overthrow the government by violence must be driven out of the country.

James Thurber made a career out of poking fun at modern human beings and their complicated society. In the preceding fable he uses a play on words to show how rumors, such as those that the girls spread in *The Crucible,* can distort the truth.

Writing Prompt: In the space below, create a script for a scene in which you use the characters of Thurber's fable to point out how hysteria grows out of ignorance, emotionalism, rumor, and unfounded accusations.

WORD CONNECTIONS

Another way to look at analogies is to look for antonyms or synonyms. Determine whether the following relationship uses synonyms or antonyms, and then complete the analogy.

innuendo : insinuation :: _____ : proof

Conflicts in Salem

Even before the accusations of witchcraft start, the people of Salem seem to be in the middle of many different conflicts. After reading Act One, identify who is fighting with whom as well as the reasons for the conflicts. This will be essential information to know as the community starts tearing itself apart.

Character	vs.	Character	Reasons
	vs.		
	vs.		
	vs.		
	vs.		
	vs.		
	vs.		

Writing Prompt: Write a paragraph or short essay that compares and contrasts the conflicts of Salem to the types of conflicts found in present day communities.

Speaking Like a Puritan

SUGGESTED LEARNING STRATEGIES: Diffusing, Graphic Organizer, Drafting

The following words are among many that Miller chose to use in his quest to create a language that was an "echo" of the language spoken by the Puritans.

With a partner or small group, write the definitions of any words you might already know. Then, as you read Act Two, note where the words occur and how they are used. See if the context helps you determine the meanings, and consult a dictionary or other resource for confirmation.

magistrate –

quail (used as a verb) –

fraud –

lechery –

charity –

abomination –

naught –

blasphemy -

poppet –

vengeance –

theology –

conjure –

Speaking Like a Puritan

Another way that Arthur Miller conveys the Puritan setting and central thematic images of *The Crucible* is through the use of metaphoric language. Read the following lines, and work with your group to determine the meaning behind the metaphors.

Metaphor	Meaning
Proctor: " a funeral marches round your heart"	
Elizabeth: "the magistrate sits in your heart"	
Proctor: "I will curse her hotter than the oldest cinder"	
Hale: "Theology is a fortress"	
Francis Nurse: "My wife is the very brick and mortar of the church."	
Proctor: "Vengeance is walking in Salem"	

After looking at the metaphoric language Miller's characters speak, try your hand at creating a metaphor or simile to describe Mary Warren, Hale, or Abigail in the space below.

Key Scene 2: Proctor and Elizabeth

SUGGESTED LEARNING STRATEGIES: Marking the Text, Graphic
Organizer, Discussion Groups

Imagine that you are the director of a stage version of *The Crucible*. Now
you must decide how you will portray the relationship between Proctor
and Elizabeth. Remember that Elizabeth is aware of his relationship
with Abigail. Below are four possible scenarios that describe their
relationship. After you have read the scene where they are alone for
the first time, describe the gestures, movements, facial expressions,
and vocal delivery actors might use at specific places in this scene
to communicate the different interpretations. Be sure to identify the
specific line where the stage directions might take place.

Proctor Is Cold and Distant

Line	Gestures	Movements	Facial Expressions	Vocal Delivery

Elizabeth Is Cold and Distant

Line	Gestures	Movements	Facial Expressions	Vocal Delivery

Key Scene 2: Proctor and Elizabeth

Proctor and Elizabeth Are in Love

Line	Gestures	Movements	Facial Expressions	Vocal Delivery

Select One for Yourself

Line	Gestures	Movements	Facial Expressions	Vocal Delivery

After watching the film version of this scene, which one of the above characterizations of their relationship does the director seem to have in mind? Why? Did you see any of your choices in the film version? How might you have filmed the scene differently? Why? Write your answers in the space below.

Character Metaphors

SUGGESTED LEARNING STRATEGIES: Think-Pair-Share, Graphic
Organizer, Visualizing, Drafting

In Act Two, Proctor says, "I will fall like an ocean on that court!" How
does this comparison describe his character and intended action? With
a partner, look back at Act Two and complete the following graphic
organizer, creating your own metaphors or similes for each of your
assigned characters.

	Significant Actions	Significant Dialogue	Compare to ...
Proctor			
Abigail			
Hale			
Cheever			
Giles Corey			
Mary Warren			

Writing Prompt: The character of Mary Warren is more fully developed
in Act Two. She represents the position of young girls in Salem village.
Compare her role in the Proctor household to her role in the courtroom.
How is Miller using her as emblematic of the girls' position in Salem
society? Write your response on a separate sheet of paper.

Proof and Confessions

SUGGESTED LEARNING STRATEGIES: Quickwrite, Think-Pair-Share, Rereading, Drafting, Role Playing

LITERARY TERMS

Irony is a literary device that exploits readers' expectations. Irony occurs when what is expected turns out to be quite different from what actually happens. *Dramatic irony* occurs when the audience knows more about circumstances or events in a story than the characters within it. *Verbal irony* occurs when a speaker or narrator says one thing while meaning the opposite. *Situational irony* occurs when an event contradicts the expectations of the characters or the reader.

Quickwrite: Think about a typical courtroom trial. What constitutes evidence in the trial? What role do eyewitness testimonies, confessions, and character witnesses play in determining guilt or innocence? What other kinds of proof are typically required for a conviction? Write your response below.

1. After reading Act Three, think about the type of evidence that was used to prove someone guilty of witchcraft. In the space below, list examples from Acts One, Two, and Three of the evidence that was used.

2. Miller uses different kinds of irony in his play to emphasize the senselessness of the accusations and trials. In **situational irony,** a discrepancy takes place between what is expected or appropriate to happen and what actually does happen. How are the false confessions in Act Three examples of situational irony?

3. Conduct a close reading of the court scene in Act Three to analyze the arguments to identify logical fallacies. Discuss your findings.

Writing Prompt: Your teacher will assign you to a group to develop a short scene and script based on one of the scenarios on the next page. Write a script for your scene and assign roles. Then rehearse the scene and perform it for the class.

Scenario A: Needs three characters

You and a friend steal the answer key to a big test. The two of you use the answer key to study the night before. Your friend, who is in a class period before you, gets away with the cheating, but you get caught with a cheat sheet. The teacher tells you that you will receive a 0 on the test, and you will be sent to the principal for possible expulsion if you do not tell who else cheated with you. What will you do?

Scenario B: Needs at least four characters

You are an accountant for a big corporation. Your boss gives you permission to make some transactions that are possibly illegal. When you are investigated by the police, you are told that they do not care about prosecuting you, but they really want to get your boss. If you say that your boss told you to make these transactions, you will not be prosecuted, but if you do not, you could face up to six months in jail and lose your license as an accountant. When you told your coworker about this, he or she said that if you do tell on your boss, you probably would not be able to find work as an accountant again. What will you do?

Scenario C: Needs at least three characters

You donated money to an environmental group last year. You attended one of its meetings six months ago but did not get actively involved. Last week, you heard that a member of the group blew up logging equipment to protest logging in the area. The FBI arrested that person, but it wants to collect the names of everyone involved in the group so that it can prevent further actions. The FBI agent tells you that you have to give him the names of all of the people at the meeting you attended. If you do not give him the names, you will be held in contempt and you could be put in jail until you give him the names. What will you do?

Scenario D: Needs at least two characters

After 9/11, a number of Arab-Americans and other foreign-born citizens and residents were questioned by the FBI. Imagine that you are one of these people. The FBI told you that you would be deported unless you give the names of other Arab-Americans you know, including some of your own family members. If you give the FBI these names, others will find themselves in the same position in which you find yourself. What will you do?

Fearful Consequences

One of the key elements of characterization revolves around the choices a character makes. After reading the scene with Proctor and Elizabeth in the courtroom, complete the following to analyze their choices.

	Proctor	Elizabeth
Secret he or she has		
Choice he or she makes in this scene		
Quotation that demonstrates choice		
Reasons for making choice		
Quotation that supports the reason		
How do you feel about him or her after this?		
How does this choice affect other characters?		
How does this choice relate to the ideas that the author puts forward here?		

Speaking Out

Read the following excerpt from a speech given to protest the activities of the Committee on Un-American Activities, which was formed by the U.S. Congress to investigate and identify Americans who were suspected of being Communists.

Speech

Declaration
of Conscience

by Margaret Chase Smith

EXCERPT FROM A SPEECH DELIVERED TO THE SENATE OF THE UNITED STATES CONGRESS JUNE 1, 1950.

Mr. President:

I would like to speak briefly and simply about a serious national condition. It is a national feeling of fear and frustration that could result in national suicide and the end of everything that we Americans hold dear…

I speak as briefly as possible because too much harm has already been done with irresponsible words of bitterness and selfish political opportunism. I speak as briefly as possible because the issue is too great to be obscured by eloquence. I speak simply and briefly in the hope that my words will be taken to heart.

I speak as a Republican. I speak as a woman. I speak as a United States Senator. I speak as an American.

The United States Senate has long enjoyed worldwide respect as the greatest deliberative body in the world. But recently that deliberative character has too often been debased to the level of a forum of hate and character assassination sheltered by the shield of congressional immunity….

I think that it is high time for the United States Senate and its members to do some soul-searching—for us to weigh our consciences—on the manner in which we are performing our duty to the people of America—on the manner in which we are using or abusing our individual powers and privileges.

I think that it is high time that we remembered that we have sworn to uphold and defend the Constitution. I think that it is high time that we remembered that the Constitution, as amended, speaks not only of the freedom of speech but also of trial by jury instead of trial by accusation.

My Notes

WORD CONNECTIONS

Obscure derives from two Latin prefixes: *ob-* meaning "over" or "against" and the root *-scurus-* meaning "covered." *Obstinate, obstacle,* and *obfuscate* use the same prefix.

GRAMMAR & USAGE

Simple words and phrases become much more powerful when repeated and used in parallel structures. When the same phrase is used to open successive clauses, the writer is using anaphora. Notice that Smith's use of anaphora makes a powerful impact. "I speak as a Republican. I speak as a woman. I speak as a United States Senator. I speak as an American."

My Notes

Whether it be a criminal prosecution in court or a character prosecution in the Senate, there is little practical distinction when the life of a person has been ruined.

Those of us who shout the loudest about Americanism in making character assassinations are all too frequently those who, by our own words and acts, ignore some of the basic principles of Americanism:

The right to criticize;

The right to hold unpopular beliefs;

The right to protest;

The right of independent thought.

The exercise of these rights should not cost one single American citizen his reputation or his right to a livelihood nor should he be in danger of losing his reputation or livelihood merely because he happens to know someone who holds unpopular beliefs. Who of us doesn't? Otherwise none of us could call our souls our own. Otherwise thought control would have set in....

As an American, I am shocked at the way Republicans and Democrats alike are playing directly into the Communist design of "confuse, divide, and conquer." As an American, I don't want a Democratic Administration "whitewash" or "cover-up" any more than a want a Republican smear or witch hunt.

As an American, I condemn a Republican "Fascist" just as much as I condemn a Democrat "Communist." I condemn a Democrat "Fascist" just as much as I condemn a Republican "Communist." They are equally dangerous to you and me and to our country. As an American, I want to see our nation recapture the strength and unity it once had when we fought the enemy instead of ourselves.

It is with these thoughts that I have drafted what I call a "Declaration of Conscience."

The Crucible premiered in 1953—to critical acclaim and to criticism for its implied social commentary on the activities of the Committee on Un-American Activities. Many years later, Arthur Miller wrote an essay to explain why he wrote the play. The essay appears on the following pages. As you read, keep track of the following topics.

> **ACADEMIC VOCABULARY**
>
> **Social commentary** is an expression of an opinion with the goal of promoting change by appealing to a sense of justice.

What are Miller's feelings about McCarthyism?	**What was Hollywood's and society's response to McCarthyism?**	**Why was Miller fascinated by the witch trials?**
What is the connection between witchcraft and Communism?	**What was critical and public reaction to *The Crucible* and other Miller plays?**	**What is the lasting legacy of *The Crucible*?**

After you read the essay, summarize Miller's answer to the title of his essay: Why did he write *The Crucible?*

Essay

> **ABOUT THE AUTHOR**
> Arthur Miller (1915–2005) is considered one of the best American dramatists. Miller began writing as a student at the University of Michigan, and he produced numerous plays during his lifetime. Many of his plays earned prestigious awards, such as the Pulitzer Prize for *Death of a Salesman*, which first premiered in 1949. Miller's plays were often controversial because of their portrayal of issues at the time, such as the connection between the hysteria of the Salem witch trials (*The Crucible*) and the McCarthy hearings.

Why I Wrote *The Crucible*:
An artist's answer to politics

by Arthur Miller

OCTOBER, 1996

As I watched *The Crucible* taking shape as a movie over much of the past year, the sheer depth of time that it represents for me kept returning to mind. As those powerful actors blossomed on the screen, and the children and the horses, the crowds and the wagons, I thought again about how I came to cook all this up nearly fifty years ago, in an America almost nobody I know seems to remember clearly. In a way, there is a biting irony in this film's having been made by a Hollywood studio, something unimaginable in the fifties. But there they are — Daniel Day-Lewis (John Proctor) scything his sea-bordered field, Joan Allen (Elizabeth) lying pregnant in the frigid jail, Winona Ryder (Abigail) stealing her minister-uncle's money, majestic Paul Scofield (Judge Danforth) and his righteous empathy with the Devil-possessed children, and all of them looking as inevitable as rain.

I remember those years — they formed *The Crucible's* skeleton — but I have lost the dead weight of the fear I had then. Fear doesn't travel well; just as it can warp judgment, its absence can diminish memory's truth. What terrifies one generation is likely to bring only a puzzled smile to the next. I remember how in 1964, only twenty years after the war, Harold Clurman, the director of "Incident at Vichy," showed the cast a film of a Hitler speech, hoping to give them a sense of the Nazi period in which my play took place. They watched as Hitler, facing a vast stadium full of adoring people, went up on his toes in ecstasy, hands clasped under his chin, a sublimely self-gratified grin on his face, his body swiveling rather cutely, and they giggled at his overacting.

Likewise, films of Senator Joseph McCarthy are rather unsettling — if you remember the fear he once spread. Buzzing his truculent sidewalk brawler's snarl through the hairs in his nose, squinting through his cat's eyes and sneering like a villain, he comes across now as nearly comical, a self-aware performer keeping a straight face as he does his juicy threat-shtick.

McCarthy's power to stir fears of creeping Communism was not entirely based on illusion, of course; the paranoid, real or pretended, always secretes its pearl around a grain of fact. From being our wartime ally, the Soviet Union rapidly became an expanding empire. In 1949, Mao Zedong took power in China. Western Europe also seemed ready to become Red — especially Italy, where the Communist Party was the largest outside Russia and was growing. Capitalism, in the opinion of many, myself included, had nothing more to say, its final poisoned bloom having been Italian and German Fascism. McCarthy — brash and ill-mannered but to many authentic and true — boiled it all down to what anyone could understand: we had "lost China" and would soon lose Europe as well, because the State Department — staffed, of course, under Democratic Presidents — was full of treasonous pro-Soviet intellectuals. It was as simple as that.

If our losing China seemed the equivalent of a flea's losing an elephant, it was still a phrase — and a conviction — that one did not dare to question; to do so was to risk drawing suspicion on oneself. Indeed, the State Department proceeded to hound and fire the officers who knew China, its language, and its opaque culture — a move that suggested the practitioners of sympathetic magic who wring the neck of a doll in order to make a distant enemy's head drop off. There was magic all around; the politics of alien conspiracy soon dominated political discourse and bid fair to wipe out any other issue. How could one deal with such enormities in a play?

The Crucible was an act of desperation. Much of my desperation branched out, I suppose, from a typical Depression-era trauma — the blow struck on the mind by the rise of European Fascism and the brutal anti-Semitism it had brought to power. But by 1950, when I began to think of writing about the hunt for Reds in America, I was motivated in some great part by the paralysis

My Notes

WORD CONNECTIONS

Miller uses a French term "J'accuse," which means literally "I accuse." He uses it in this essay to emphasize the era of the McCarthy hearings, during which people were deemed guilty simply by accusation.

My Notes

that had set in among many liberals who, despite their discomfort with the inquisitors' violations of civil rights, were fearful, and with good reason, of being identified as covert Communists if they should protest too strongly.

In any play, however trivial, there has to be a still point of moral reference against which to gauge the action. In our lives, in the late nineteen-forties and early nineteen-fifties, no such point existed anymore. The left could not look straight at the Soviet Union's abrogations of human rights. The anti-Communist liberals could not acknowledge the violations of those rights by congressional committees. The far right, meanwhile, was licking up all the cream. The days of "J'accuse" were gone, for anyone needs to feel right to declare someone else wrong. Gradually, all the old political and moral reality had melted like a Dali watch. Nobody but a fanatic, it seemed, could really say all that he believed.

President Truman was among the first to have to deal with the dilemma, and his way of resolving it — of having to trim his sails before the howling gale on the right — turned out to be momentous. At first, he was outraged at the allegation of widespread Communist infiltration of the government and called the charge of "coddling Communists" a red herring dragged in by the Republicans to bring down the Democrats. But such was the gathering power of raw belief in the great Soviet plot that Truman soon felt it necessary to institute loyalty boards of his own.

The Red hunt, led by the House Committee on Un-American Activities and by McCarthy, was becoming the dominating fixation of the American psyche. It reached Hollywood when the studios, after first resisting, agreed to submit artists' names to the House Committee for "clearing" before employing them. This unleashed a veritable holy terror among actors, directors, and others, from Party members to those who had had the merest brush with a front organization.

The Soviet plot was the hub of a great wheel of causation; the plot justified the crushing of all nuance, all the shadings that a realistic judgment of reality requires. Even worse was the feeling that our sensitivity to this onslaught on our liberties was passing from us — indeed, from me. In *Timebends*, my autobiography, I recalled the time I'd written a screenplay ("The Hook") about union corruption on the Brooklyn waterfront. Harry Cohn, the head of Columbia Pictures, did something that would once have been considered unthinkable: he showed my script to the F.B.I. Cohn then asked me to take the gangsters in my script, who were threatening and murdering their opponents, and simply change them to Communists. When I declined to commit this idiocy (Joe Ryan, the head of the longshoremen's union, was soon to go to Sing Sing for racketeering), I got a wire from Cohn saying, "The minute we try to make the script pro-American you pull out." By then — it was 1951 — I had come to accept this terribly serious insanity as routine, but there was an element of the marvelous in it which I longed to put on the stage.

In those years, our thought processes were becoming so magical, so paranoid, that to imagine writing a play about this environment was like trying to pick one's teeth with a ball of wool: I lacked the tools to illuminate miasma. Yet I kept being drawn back to it.

I had read about the witchcraft trials in college, but it was not until I read a book published in 1867 — a two-volume, thousand-page study by Charles W. Upham, who was then the mayor of Salem — that I knew I had to write about the period. Upham had not only written a broad and thorough investigation of what was even then an almost lost chapter of Salem's past but opened up to me the details of personal relationships among many participants in the tragedy.

I visited Salem for the first time on a dismal spring day in 1952; it was a sidetracked town then, with abandoned factories and vacant stores. In the gloomy courthouse there I read the transcript of the witchcraft trials of 1692, as taken down in a primitive shorthand by ministers who were spelling each other. But there was one entry in Upham in which the thousands of pieces I had come across were jogged into place. It was from a report written by the Reverend Samuel Parris, who was one of the chief instigators of the witch-hunt. "During the examination of Elizabeth Procter, Abigail Williams and Ann Putnam" — the two were "afflicted" teen-age accusers, and Abigail was Parris's niece — "both made offer to strike at said Procter; but when Abigail's hand came near, it opened, whereas it was made up, into a fist before, and came down exceeding lightly as it drew near to said Procter, and at length, with open and extended fingers, touched Procter's hood very lightly. Immediately Abigail cried out her fingers, her fingers, her fingers burned...."

In this remarkably observed gesture of a troubled young girl, I believed, a play became possible. Elizabeth Proctor had been the orphaned Abigail's mistress, and they had lived together in the same small house until Elizabeth fired the girl. By this time, I was sure, John Proctor had bedded Abigail, who had to be dismissed most likely to appease Elizabeth. There was bad blood between the two women now. That Abigail started, in effect, to condemn Elizabeth to death with her touch, then stopped her hand, then went through with it, was quite suddenly the human center of all this turmoil.

All this I understood. I had not approached the witchcraft out of nowhere or from purely social and political considerations. My own marriage of twelve years was teetering and I knew more than I wished to know about where the blame lay. That John Proctor the sinner might overturn his paralyzing personal guilt and become the most forthright voice against the madness around him was a reassurance to me, and, I suppose, an inspiration: it demonstrated that a clear moral outcry could still spring even from an ambiguously unblemished soul. Moving crabwise across the profusion of evidence, I sensed that I had at last found something of myself in it, and a play began to accumulate around this man.

My Notes

WORD CONNECTIONS

Inspiration comes from the Latin word *spirare* meaning "to breathe." From the same word come *perspire*, *expire*, *conspire*, and *spirit*.

My Notes

But as the dramatic form became visible, one problem remained unyielding: so many practices of the Salem trials were similar to those employed by the congressional committees that I could easily be accused of skewing history for a mere partisan purpose. Inevitably, it was no sooner known that my new play was about Salem than I had to confront the charge that such an analogy was specious – that there never were any witches but there certainly are Communists. In the seventeenth century, however, the existence of witches was never questioned by the loftiest minds in Europe and America; and even lawyers of the highest eminence, like Sir Edward Coke, a veritable hero of liberty for defending the common law against the king's arbitrary power, believed that witches had to be prosecuted mercilessly. Of course, there were no Communists in 1692, but it was literally worth your life to deny witches or their powers, given the exhortation in the Bible, "Thou shalt not suffer a witch to live." There had to be witches in the world or the Bible lied. Indeed, the very structure of evil depended on Lucifer's plotting against God. (And the irony is that klatches of Luciferians exist all over the country today; there may even be more of them now than there are Communists.)

As with most humans, panic sleeps in one unlighted corner of my soul. When I walked at night along the empty, wet streets of Salem in the week that I spent there, I could easily work myself into imagining my terror before a gaggle of young girls flying down the road screaming that somebody's "familiar spirit" was chasing them. This anxiety-laden leap backward over nearly three centuries may have been helped along by a particular Upham footnote. At a certain point, the high court of the province made the fatal decision to admit, for the first time, the use of "spectral evidence" as proof of guilt. Spectral evidence, so aptly named, meant that if I swore that you had sent out your "familiar spirit" to choke, tickle, poison me or my cattle, or to control my thoughts and actions, I could get you hanged unless you confessed to having had contact with the Devil. After all, only the Devil could lend such powers of invisible transport to confederates, in his everlasting plot to bring down Christianity.

Naturally, the best proof of the sincerity of your confession was your naming others whom you had seen in the Devil's company — an invitation to private vengeance, but made official by the seal of the theocratic state. It was as though the court had grown tired of thinking and had invited in the instincts: spectral evidence — that poisoned cloud of paranoid fantasy — made a kind of lunatic sense to them, as it did in plot-ridden 1952, when so often the question was not the acts of an accused but the thoughts and intentions in his alienated mind.

The breathtaking circularity of the process had a kind of poetic tightness. Not everybody was accused, after all, so there must be *some reason why you were*. By denying that there is *any* reason whatsoever for you to be accused, you are implying, by virtue of a surprisingly small logical leap, that mere chance picked you out, which in turn implies that the Devil might not really be at work in the village, or, God forbid, even exist. Therefore, the investigation itself is either mistaken or a fraud. You would have to be a crypto-Luciferian to say that — not a great idea if you wanted to go back to your farm.

The more I read into the Salem panic, the more it touched off corresponding images of common experiences in the fifties: the old friend of a blacklisted person crossing the street to avoid being seen talking to him; the overnight conversions of former leftists into born-again patriots; and so on. Apparently, certain processes are universal. When Gentiles in Hitler's Germany, for example, saw their Jewish neighbors being trucked off, or farmers in Soviet Ukraine saw the Kulaks vanishing before their eyes, the common reaction, even among those unsympathetic to Nazism or Communism, was quite naturally to turn away in fear of being identified with the condemned. As I learned from non-Jewish refugees, however, there was often a despairing pity mixed with "Well, they must have done *something*." Few of us can easily surrender our belief that society must somehow make sense. The thought that the state has lost its mind and is punishing so many innocent people is intolerable. And so the evidence has to be internally denied.

I was also drawn into writing *The Crucible* by the chance it gave me to use a new language — that of seventeenth-century New England. The plain, craggy English was liberating in a strangely sensuous way, with its swings from an almost legalistic precision to a wonderful metaphoric richness. "The Lord doth terrible things amongst us, by lengthening the chain of the roaring lion in an extraordinary manner, so that the Devil is come down in great wrath," Deodat Lawson, one of the great witch-hunting preachers, said in a sermon. Lawson rallied his congregation for what was to be nothing less than a religious war against the Evil One — "Arm, arm, arm!" — and his concealed anti-Christian accomplices.

But it was not yet my language, and among other strategies to make it mine I enlisted the help of a former University of Michigan classmate, the Greek-American scholar and poet Kimon Friar (He later translated Kazantzakis.) The problem was not to the archaic speech but to try to create a new echo of it which would flow freely off American actors' tongues. As in the film nearly fifty years later, the actors in the first production grabbed the language and ran with it as happily as if it were their customary speech.

The Crucible took me about a year to write. With its five sets and a cast of twenty-one, it never occurred to me that it would take a brave man to produce it on Broadway, especially given the prevailing climate, but Kermit Bloomgarden never faltered. Well before the play opened, a strange tension had begun to build. Only two years earlier, the *Death of a Salesman* touring company had played to a thin crowd in Peoria, Illinois, having been boycotted nearly to death by the American Legion and the Jaycees. Before that, the Catholic War Veterans had prevailed upon the Army not to allow

My Notes

its theatrical groups to perform, first, *All My Sons,* and then any play of mine, in occupied Europe. The Dramatists Guild refused to protest attacks on a new play by Sean O'Casey, a self-declared Communist, which forced its producer to cancel his option. I knew of two suicides by actors depressed by upcoming investigation, and every day seemed to bring news of people exiling themselves to Europe: Charlie Chaplin, the director Joseph Losey, Jules Dassin, the harmonica virtuoso Larry Adler, Donald Ogden Stewart, one of the most sought-after screenwriters in Hollywood, and Sam Wanamaker, who would lead the successful campaign to rebuild the Old Globe Theater on the Thames.

On opening night, January 22, 1953, I knew that the atmosphere would be pretty hostile. The coldness of the crowd was not a surprise; Broadway audiences were not famous for loving history lessons, which is what they made of the play. It seems to me entirely appropriate that on the day the play opened, a newspaper headline read "ALL 13 REDS GUILTY" — a story about American Communists who faced prison for "conspiring to teach and advocate the duty and necessity of forcible overthrow of government." Meanwhile, the remoteness of the production was guaranteed by the director, Jed Harris, who insisted that this was a classic requiring the actors to face front, never each other. The critics were not swept away. "Arthur Miller is a problem playwright in both senses of the word," wrote Walter Kerr of the *Herald Tribune,* who called the play "a step backward into mechanical parable." The *Times* was not much kinder, saying, "There is too much excitement and not enough emotion in 'The Crucible.'" But the play's future would turn out quite differently.

About a year later, a new production, one with younger, less accomplished actors, working in the Martinique Hotel ballroom, played with the fervor that the script and the times required, and *The Crucible* became a hit. The play stumbled into history, and today, I am told, it is one of the most heavily demanded trade-fiction paperbacks in this country; the Bantam and Penguin editions have sold more than six million copies. I don't think there has been a week in the past forty-odd years when it hasn't been on a stage somewhere in the world. Nor is the new screen version the first. Jean-Paul Sartre, in his Marxist phase, wrote a French film adaptation that blamed the tragedy on the rich landowners conspiring to persecute the poor. (In truth, most of those who were hanged in Salem were people of substance, and two or three were very large landowners.)

It is only a slight exaggeration to say that, especially in Latin America, *The Crucible* starts getting produced wherever a political coup appears imminent, or a dictatorial regime has just been overthrown. From Argentina to Chile to Greece, Czechoslovakia, China, and a dozen other places, the play seems to present the same primeval structure of human sacrifice to the furies of fanaticism and paranoia that goes on repeating itself forever as though imbedded in the brain of social man.

WORD CONNECTIONS

Surprise comes from the French word *surpris* (the past participle of the verb *surprendre*), which derived from the Latin *prehendere*. The root *prehend* appears in *prize, apprehend,* and *comprehend.*

I am not sure what *The Crucible* is telling people now, but I know that its paranoid center is still pumping out the same darkly attractive warning that it did in the fifties. For some, the play seems to be about the dilemma of relying on the testimony of small children accusing adults of sexual abuse, something I'd not have dreamed of forty years ago. For others, it may simply be a fascination with the outbreak of paranoia that suffuses the play — the blind panic that, in our age, often seems to sit at the dim edges of consciousness. Certainly its political implications are the central issue for many people; the Salem interrogations turn out to be eerily exact models of those yet to come in Stalin's Russia, Pinochet's Chile, Mao's China, and other regimes. (Nien Cheng, the author of "Life and Death in Shanghai," has told me that she could hardly believe that a non-Chinese — someone who had not experienced the Cultural Revolution — had written the play.) But below its concerns with justice the play evokes a lethal brew of illicit sexuality, fear of the supernatural, and political manipulation, a combination not unfamiliar these days. The film, by reaching a broad American audience as no play ever can, may well unearth still other connections to those buried public terrors that Salem first announced on this continent.

One thing more — something wonderful in the old sense of that world. I recall the weeks I spent reading testimony by the tome, commentaries, broadsides, confessions, and accusations. And always the crucial damning event was the signing of one's name in "the Devil's book." This Faustian agreement to hand over one's soul to the dreaded Lord of Darkness was the ultimate insult to God. But what were these new inductees supposed to have *done* once they'd signed on? Nobody seems even to have thought to ask. But, of course, actions are as irrelevant during cultural and religious wars as they are in nightmares. The thing at issue is buried intentions — the secret allegiances of the alienated heart, always the main threat to the theocratic mind, as well as its immemorial quarry.

My Notes

Considering all the information and details you have learned about John Hale, Giles Corey and John Proctor, fill in the graphic organizer below with as many adjectives as possible to describe each character.

Hale   **Corey**

Proctor

Final Verdicts

1. At the end of the play, both Elizabeth and Proctor make choices that involve personal integrity, and both change their minds. Use the graphic organizer below to help you to recognize the reasons for their choices and how those choices impact the plot and the theme of the play.

	Elizabeth	**Proctor**
At first	She goes to Proctor to ask if he will confess.	He decides to confess.
Quote and explanation to support why		
Changes mind	She decides not to go to him at the end to ask if he will confess.	He decides not to sign his confession.
Quote and explanation to support why		

2. Explain why you think that Miller had his characters make these choices.

Timed Writing

Look over the following prompts for a timed writing on *The Crucible*. In the space between, you might want to jot notes to help you "unpack" the prompt. Although this will be considered first-draft writing, you will want to reserve some time at the end to review your piece for conventions and clarity.

1. A crucible is a severe challenge or test of one's faith. Another definition is the container used to store metals as they are melted at extremely high heats. In an essay, explain how Arthur Miller uses both of these definitions to support major themes of *The Crucible*.

2. The dying words of Giles Corey are "More weight." In an essay, explain how this character acts as a foil to Proctor's character in that Corey serves to illuminate the strengths and weaknesses of the main character.

3. There are many significant changes between the film and the play that lead to different impressions of character, setting, tone, and theme. In an essay, explain how one change between the film and play leads the reader or viewer to a different interpretation of character, theme, tone, or setting.

4. Miller interrupts Act One with commentary about the characters and the social, historical, and religious context of the play. In an essay, explain why Miller felt it necessary to give this information, though it never appears in a dramatic presentation of the play.

5. The plot of *The Crucible* consists of many battles between many opposites. In an essay, identify one such opposite and explain why Arthur Miller included it.

Creating and Performing
a Dramatic Scene

SUGGESTED LEARNING STRATEGIES: **Discussion Groups,
Brainstorming, Self-Editing/Peer Editing, Sharing and Responding,
Rereading**

Assignment

Your assignment is to work with a group to write and perform an original
dramatic script in which you make a statement about a conflict that faces
society.

Steps

Planning

1. Review how Miller was able to create scenes and characters that
   paralleled and illuminated a conflict between the individual and society.
   Note especially the final scene between Proctor and Danforth for its
   connection to the McCarthy hearings (see page 279).

2. Next, brainstorm issues facing contemporary American society that are
   of particular relevance and concern to you and your peers. Consider
   the topics explored in the Op-Ed pages in Unit 2 and presented in the
   persuasive speeches in this unit. Choose one or two issues that you think
   would lend themselves to a dramatic presentation.

3. Share your selected issue and your thoughts about it with your group,
   and listen to the issues your group members share with you. Come to
   a consensus about one or two issues or conflicts that you agree are of
   particular importance.

4. Now that you have narrowed your list to one or two societal issues,
   brainstorm ideas for possible settings that would lend themselves to a
   dramatic scene that would serve as a social commentary on your issue,
   much as Miller couched his criticism of the McCarthy trials in a play about
   the Salem witch trials.

5. Work collaboratively to plan the writing for your scene. You will need to
   create the characters and imagine them in the setting you have agreed
   upon.

6. Choose assignments.

   ▶ The *director* will guide the acting company, will be responsible for
   props, costume pieces, and background music, and will introduce your
   scene on performance day.

   ▶ The *dramaturge* will conduct research in order to provide needed
   background material about the issue and/or the setting you have
   chosen and will explain these connections on performance day.

   ▶ The *actors*, of course, will present the scene for your audience.

Creating and Performing a Dramatic Scene

Drafting

7. After selecting your characters and setting, write your scene. Use *The Crucible* as a model text as you insert stage directions, dialogue, and commentary.

Revising

8. Share the scene you have written collaboratively with another acting company and ask for feedback in order to revise for clarity. The other acting company should be able to identify the statement you are making about society within the context of your scene.

Editing and Publishing

9. Use available resources to edit and publish the written copy of your scene.

Rehearsing

10. As you prepare to present your scene, consider the costumes, movement, props, and set design that will best convey the meaning of your scene. You might find that you need to make a few revisions to the written scene as you make your plans for performance.

11. Rehearse your scene several times. The director's feedback and the dramaturge's research should enhance the acting company's performance.

12. If possible, videotape one of your rehearsals to help you improve the quality of the overall performance. Pay attention to your distance from one another, your position on stage, the pace of your speech, and the volume of your voice. If videotaping is not practical, ask another acting company to watch your dress rehearsal and provide feedback on how you might improve your performance.

Presenting and Viewing

13. Using the props, costumes, music, and movement that you decided on together, present your scene to your class. The director will introduce the scene, and after the performance, the dramaturge will explain how the performance was about the societal issue and/or the setting.

14. As you watch the other performances, take notes regarding the societal issue reflected, the group's stance on that issue, and the group's effective use of dramatic elements to convey the issue.

Reflecting

15. After all groups have presented their scenes, discuss the various issues that were presented as well as the variety of dramatic elements that were used. Finally, write a reflection in which you evaluate the overall effectiveness of your own group's performance.

Reread this passage from "Why I Wrote *The Crucible*" by Arthur Miller, as you begin to consider your assignment for Embedded Assessment 2:

"I am not sure what *The Crucible* is telling people now, but I know that its paranoid center is still pumping out the same darkly attractive warning that it did in the fifties. For some, the play seems to be about the dilemma of relying on the testimony of small children accusing adults of sexual abuse, something I'd not have dreamed of forty years ago. For others, it may simply be a fascination with the outbreak of paranoia that suffuses the play — the blind panic that, in our age, often seems to sit at the dim edges of consciousness. Certainly its political implications are the central issue for many people; the Salem interrogations turn out to be eerily exact models of those yet to come in Stalin's Russia, Pinochet's Chile, Mao's China, and other regimes. (Nien Cheng, the author of *Life and Death in Shanghai*, has told me that she could hardly believe that a non-Chinese — someone who had not experienced the Cultural Revolution — had written the play.) But below its concerns with justice the play evokes a lethal brew of illicit sexuality, fear of the supernatural, and political manipulation, a combination not unfamiliar these days. The film, by reaching a broad American audience as no play ever can, may well unearth still other connections to those buried public terrors that Salem first announced on this continent."

Use the graphic organizer to help you organize your thoughts about the scene you will write.

Contemporary Societal Concern	Underlying, Universal Issues	Parallel Setting
Some examples: The fastest-growing homeless group is families.	People have the attitude "It's their own fault"; there is a large stigma attached to receiving charitable help.	The Great Depression
Environmental issues surrounding fuel	Global economic issues; global environmental issues	At the time of the invention of the automobile

Creating and Performing
a Dramatic Scene

SCORING GUIDE

Scoring Criteria	Exemplary	Proficient	Emerging
Script	The dramatic scene is scripted in a way that demonstrates a sophisticated understanding of Miller's approach to speaking his conscience about a current event through a drama set in an analogous time period. It employs purposeful dialogue and stage directions that effectively serve to provide social commentary on the chosen issue.	The dramatic scene is scripted in a way that demonstrates a clear understanding of Miller's approach to speaking his conscience about a current event through a drama set in an analogous time period. It employs dialogue and stage directions to serve as social commentary on the chosen issue.	The dramatic scene is scripted in a way that demonstrates an unclear understanding of Miller's approach to speaking his conscience about a current event through a drama set in an analogous time period. It may attempt to use dialogue and stage directions, but the social commentary on the chosen issue may be confusing.
Performance	The group's scene is insightful, and the intended effect is clearly communicated to the audience. Participants demonstrate a polished performance by: • skillfully using various theatrical elements • strategically using all elements of vocal delivery • effectively using elements of visual delivery to create focus and maintain energy for the scene.	The group's scene is plausible, and the intended effect is communicated to the audience. Participants demonstrate an organized performance by: • adequately using various theatrical elements • knowledgably using all elements of vocal delivery • using elements of visual delivery to create focus and maintain energy for the scene.	The group's scene may be unclear, and/or the intended effect is not successfully communicated to the audience. Participants demonstrate a disorganized performance and may: • not use various theatrical elements • not use all elements of vocal delivery • not use elements of visual delivery to create focus and maintain energy for the scene.

SCORING GUIDE

Scoring Criteria	Exemplary	Proficient	Emerging
Evidence of Collaboration	Throughout the entire process of planning and presenting, the group cooperates and works successfully to maintain purpose and to achieve goals. The equal sharing of responsibility is evident.	Throughout the process of planning and presenting, the group works together adequately to maintain purpose and achieve goals. The sharing of responsibility is mostly balanced.	Throughout the process of planning and presenting, the group's cooperation is lacking which impedes their ability to maintain a purpose or achieve goals. Responsibilities may not be equally divided.
Reflection	The writer's metacognition demonstrates a thorough and detailed analysis of the entire process including analyzing, rehearsing, and performing the scene. It includes insightful commentary on challenges faced, how they were overcome, and an evaluation of the final performance.	The writer's metacognition demonstrates adequate analysis of the process of analyzing, rehearsing, and performing the scene. It includes commentary on challenges faced, how they were overcome, and an evaluation of the final performance.	The writer's metacognition demonstrates inadequate analysis of the process of analyzing, rehearsing, and performing the scene. Commentary on the challenges faced, how they were overcome, and an evaluation of the final performance may be weak or missing. Analysis and evaluation may be replaced by summary.
Additional Criteria			

Comments:

Reflection

An important aspect of growing as a learner is to reflect on where you have been, what you have accomplished, what helped you to learn, and how you will apply your new knowledge in the future. Use the following questions to guide your thinking and to identify evidence of your learning. Use separate notebook paper.

Thinking about Concepts

1. Using specific examples from this unit, respond to the Essential Questions:

   • How are the components of rhetoric applied to the creation and delivery of persuasive speeches?

   • How can artistic expression advance social commentary?

2. Consider the new academic vocabulary from this unit (**Rhetoric, Rhetorical Devices, Social Commentary, Foil**) as well as academic vocabulary from previous units and select 3-4 terms of which your understanding has grown. For each term, answer the following questions:

   • What was your understanding of the word prior to the unit?

   • How has your understanding of the word evolved throughout the unit?

   • How will you apply your understanding in the future?

Thinking about Connections

3. Review the activities and products (artifacts) you created. Choose those that most reflect your growth or increase in understanding.

4. For each artifact that you choose, record, respond, and reflect on your thinking and understanding, using the following questions as a guide:

   a. What skill/knowledge does this artifact reflect, and how did you learn this skill/knowledge?

   b. How did your understanding of the power of language expand through your engagement with this artifact?

   c. How will you apply this skill or knowledge in the future?

5. Create this reflection as Portfolio pages—one for each artifact you choose. Use the following model for your headings and commentary on questions.

> ## Thinking About Thinking
> ### Portfolio Entry
>
> Concept:
>
> Description of Artifact:
>
> Commentary on Questions:

An American
Journey

Essential Questions

? How can an author's style construct and reflect identity?

? How do communication skills enhance self-expression?

Unit Overview

Ever since the Pilgrims traveled to America, the concept of the "journey" has been part of the American experience. In this unit you will study the novel *Their Eyes Were Watching God*, which traces the physical and emotional journey of a woman striving for self-expression. You will then examine the ways that you present yourself in a variety of situations on your own journey to self-expression.

Unit 4

An American Journey

Contents

Goals

▶ To explore an American classic that addresses the concept of "journey"

▶ To analyze the writer's rich and complex writing style as a model for making deliberate stylistic choices

▶ To investigate the communication demands of a career and to prepare to meet those demands

▶ To use media production elements and speaking and listening skills to construct a presentation of self that is appropriate for the audience

ACADEMIC VOCABULARY

Motif

Résumé

Texts not included in these materials.

285

Learning Focus:

Journey of Discovery

"Ah been a delegate to de big 'ssociation of life. Yessuh! De Grand Lodge, de big convention of livin' is just where Ah been dis year and a half y'all ain't seen me."

Zora Neale Hurston, Their Eyes Were Watching God

One of the great literary discoveries in recent years has been Zora Neale Hurston's novel *Their Eyes Were Watching God*. Unappreciated by some of Hurston's male contemporaries upon its first publication in 1937, the novel slipped out of print until Alice Walker (*The Color Purple*) brought it back to the public eye in the 1970s. Since then, Hurston's story of Janie Crawford, a woman on a journey of self-discovery, has received wide acclaim by diverse readers and has made its own journey into the canon of American literature.

As with any great book, you will read *Their Eyes Were Watching God* with many purposes. Among your purposes will be reading to analyze Hurston's innovative use of literary and stylistic elements. You will also analyze Hurston's distinctive style, as she expertly integrates a variety of voices into one novel. Hurston is noted for her gifted storytelling and honoring **oral tradition**, including **dialect**, which can be both biting and humorous. An author's use of dialect validates the oral traditions of a people, a time, and a place. Through their choice of dialect, authors create a representation of the spoken language, which helps record the history of language as it evolves over generations. Some of the literary elements to look at in Hurston's writing include:

▶ characterization

▶ setting

▶ plot

▶ motifs

Hurston's distinctive use of stylistic elements includes:

▶ figurative language, including metaphors, similes, and personification

▶ diction

▶ imagery

▶ syntax

▶ structure/organization

▶ point of view

▶ tone

Independent Reading: In this unit, you will read a novel exploring the concept of a "journey" as an essential characteristic of achieving one's American Dream. For independent reading, select a novel, nonfiction book, or a collection of essays or short stories about the American experience and a journey of discovery that is of interest to you.

Previewing the Unit

SUGGESTED LEARNING STRATEGIES: **Marking the Text, Think-Pair-Share, Close Reading, Skimming/Scanning, Summarizing/ Paraphrasing, Graphic Organizer**

Essential Questions

1. How can an author's style construct and reflect identity?

2. How do communication skills enhance self-expression?

Unit Overview and Learning Focus

Predict what you think this unit is about. Use the words or phrases that stood out to you when you read the Unit Overview and the Learning Focus.

Embedded Assessment 1

What knowledge must you have (what do you need to know) to succeed on Embedded Assessment 1? What skills must you have (what must you be able to do)?

Who Was Zora Neale Hurston?

"Hurston became an orphan at nine, a runaway at fourteen, maid and manicurist before she was twenty, and with one dress and a dream managed to become Zora Neale Hurston, author and anthropologist."

—*Alice Walker*

1. Based on this statement, what can you infer about Zora Neale Hurston's character?

2. Take notes as you watch the production *Zora Is My Name*.

Observation Notes	Comments and Questions

3. Review your notes and craft a general perception about Zora Neale Hurston.

4. If Zora Neale Hurston were present, what questions would you like to ask her?

5. As you read Zora Neale Hurston's memoir, "How It Feels to Be Colored Me," follow your teacher's instructions for annotating the text in a guided reading.

How It Feels to Be COLORED ME

by Zora Neale Hurston

My Notes</p>

> **ABOUT THE AUTHOR**
> Born in 1891, Zora Neale Hurston was an American anthropologist and writer who wrote her best-known works during the Harlem Renaissance. Hurston grew up in the small town of Eatonville, Florida, the first incorporated black township. Hurston's idyllic childhood was interrupted by the death of her mother when Hurston was only 13. She struggled to finish high school, which she still had not accomplished by age 26. Despite her early struggles, Hurston went on to graduate from Barnard College. *Their Eyes Were Watching God* is considered her master work. She died in 1960.

1   I am colored but I offer nothing in the way of extenuating[1] circumstances except the fact that I am the only Negro in the United States whose grandfather on the mother's side was *not* an Indian chief.

2   I remember the very day that I became colored. Up to my thirteenth year I lived in the little Negro town of Eatonville, Florida. It is exclusively a colored town. The only white people I knew passed through the town going to or coming from Orlando. The native whites rode dusty horses; the Northern tourists chugged down the sandy village road in automobiles. The town knew the Southerners and never stopped cane chewing when they passed. But the Northerners were something else again. They were peered at cautiously from behind curtains by the timid. The more venturesome would come out on the porch to watch them go past and got just as much pleasure out of the tourists as the tourists got out of the village.

3   The front porch might seem a daring place for the rest of the town, but it was a gallery seat for me. My favorite place was atop the gatepost. Proscenium box for a born first-nighter.[2] Not only did I enjoy the show, but I didn't mind the actors knowing that I liked it. I usually spoke to them in passing. I'd wave at them and when they returned my salute, I would say something like this: "Howdy-do-well-I-thank-you-where-you-goin'?" Usually the automobile or the horse paused at this, and after a

---

[1] **extenuating**: lessening or seeming to lessen the seriousness of by giving excuses
[2] **first-nighter**: a person who attends the opening performance of a play, opera, or similar production

My Notes

queer exchange of compliments, I would probably "go a piece of the way" with them, as we say in farthest Florida. If one of my family happened to come to the front in time to see me, of course, negotiations would be rudely broken off. But even so, it is clear that I was the first "welcome-to-our-state" Floridian, and I hope the Miami Chamber of Commerce will please take notice.

4   During this period, white people differed from colored to me only in that they rode through town and never lived there. They liked to hear me "speak pieces" and sing and wanted to see me dance the parse-me-la, and gave me generously of their small silver for doing these things, which seemed strange to me, for I wanted to do them so much that I needed bribing to stop. Only they didn't know it. The colored people gave no dimes. They deplored any joyful tendencies in me, but I was their Zora nevertheless. I belonged to them, to the nearby hotels, to the county — everybody's Zora.

5   But changes came in the family when I was thirteen, and I was sent to school in Jacksonville. I left Eatonville, the town of the oleanders,[3] as Zora. When I disembarked from the riverboat at Jacksonville, she was no more. It seemed that I had suffered a sea change. I was not Zora of Orange County any more, I was now a little colored girl. I found it out in certain ways. In my heart as well as in the mirror, I became a fast brown — warranted not to rub nor run.

6   But I am not tragically colored. There is no great sorrow dammed up in my soul, nor lurking behind my eyes. I do not mind at all. I do not belong to the sobbing school of Negrohood who hold that nature somehow has given them a lowdown dirty deal and whose feelings are all hurt about it. Even in the helter-skelter skirmish that is my life, I have seen that the world is to the strong regardless of a little pigmentation[4] more or less. No, I do not weep at the world — I am too busy sharpening my oyster knife.[5]

7   Someone is always at my elbow reminding me that I am the granddaughter of slaves. It fails to register depression with me. Slavery is sixty years in the past. The operation was successful and the patient is doing well, thank you. The terrible struggle that made me an American out of a potential slave said, "On the line!" The Reconstruction said, "Get set!" and the generation before said, "Go!" I am off to a flying start and I must not halt in the stretch to look behind and weep. Slavery is the price I paid for civilization, and the choice was not with me. It is a bully adventure and worth all that I have paid through my ancestors for it. No one on earth ever had a greater chance for glory. The world to be won and

WORD CONNECTIONS

Ancestor uses the Latin prefix *ante* meaning "before." *Anterior*, *antecedent*, and *antebellum* also rely on this prefix.

---

[3] **oleanders:** evergreen shrubs with fragrant flowers of white, pink, or red
[4] **pigmentation:** coloration due to the presence of pigments in the tissue
[5] **oyster knife:** a reference to the saying "The world is my oyster."

nothing to be lost. It is thrilling to think — to know that for any act of mine, I shall get twice as much praise or twice as much blame. It is quite exciting to hold the center of the national stage, with the spectators not knowing whether to laugh or to weep.

The position of my white neighbor is much more difficult. No brown specter pulls up a chair beside me when I sit down to eat. No dark ghost thrusts its leg against mine in bed. The game of keeping what one has is never so exciting as the game of getting.

I do not always feel colored. Even now I often achieve the unconscious Zora of Eatonville before the Hegira.[6] I feel most colored when I am thrown against a sharp white background.

For instance at Barnard.[7] "Beside the waters of the Hudson" I feel my race. Among the thousand white persons, I am a dark rock surged upon, overswept by a creamy sea. I am surged upon and overswept, but through it all, I remain myself. When covered by the waters, I am; and the ebb but reveals me again.

Sometimes it is the other way around. A white person is set down in our midst, but the contrast is just as sharp for me. For instance, when I sit in the drafty basement that is The New World Cabaret with a white person, my color comes. We enter chatting about any little nothing that we have in common and are seated by the jazz waiters. In the abrupt way that jazz orchestras have, this one plunges into a number. It loses no time in circumlocutions, but gets right down to business. It constricts the thorax and splits the heart with its tempo and narcotic harmonies. This orchestra grows rambunctious, rears on its hind legs and attacks the tonal veil with primitive fury, rending it, clawing it until it breaks through the jungle beyond. I follow those heathen — follow them exultingly. I dance wildly inside myself; I yell within, I whoop; I shake my assegai[8] above my head, I hurl it true to the mark *yeeeeooww!* I am in the jungle and living in the jungle way. My face is painted red and yellow and my body is painted blue. My pulse is throbbing like a war drum. I want to slaughter something — give pain, give death to what, I do not know. But the piece ends. The men of the orchestra wipe their lips and rest their fingers. I creep back slowly to the veneer[9] we call civilization with the last tone and find the white friend sitting motionless in his seat, smoking calmly.

"Good music they have here," he remarks, drumming the table with his fingertips.

8

9

10

11

12

---

[6] **Hegira**: Mohammed's flight from Mecca to Medina in ad 622; hence, any trip or journey, especially one made to escape a dangerous or undesirable situation

[7] **Barnard**: the college in New York City from which Hurston graduated in 1928

[8] **assegai**: a slender spear or javelin with an iron tip, used in southern Africa

[9] **veneer**: a thick surface layer of find wood or costly material laid over a base of common material; any attractive but superficial appearance

My Notes

My Notes

13   Music. The great blobs of purple and red emotion have not touched him. He has only heard what I felt. He is far away and I see him dimly across the ocean and the continent that have fallen between us. He is so pale with his whiteness then I am *so* colored.

14   At certain times I have no race. I am *me*. When I set my hat at a certain angle and saunter down Seventh Avenue, Harlem City, feeling as snooty as the lions in front of the Forty-Second Street Library, for instance. So far as my feelings are concerned, Peggy Hopkins Joyce on the Boule Mich with her gorgeous raiment, stately carriage, knees knocking together in a most aristocratic manner, has nothing on me. The cosmic Zora emerges. I belong to no race nor time. I am the eternal feminine with its string of beads.

15   I have no separate feeling about being an American citizen and colored. I am merely a fragment of the great Soul that surges within the boundaries. My country, right or wrong.

16   Sometimes, I feel discriminated against, but it does not make me angry. It merely astonishes me. How can *any* deny themselves the pleasure of my company? It's beyond me.

17   But in the main, I feel like a brown bag of miscellany propped against a wall. Against a wall in company with other bags, white, red, and yellow. Pour out the contents, and there is discovered a jumble of small things priceless and worthless. A first-water[10] diamond, an empty spool, bits of broken glass, lengths of string, a key to a door long since crumbled away, a rusty knife blade, old shoes saved for a road that never was and never will be, a nail bent under the weight of things too heavy for any nail, a dried flower or two still a little fragrant. In your hand is a brown bag. On the ground before you is the jumble it held — so much like the jumble in the bags, could they be emptied, that all might be dumped in a single heap and the bags refilled without altering the content of any greatly. A bit of colored glass more or less would not matter. Perhaps that is how the Great Stuffer of Bags filled them in the first place — who knows?

GRAMMAR & USAGE
Notice the variety Hurston achieves in the sentences in this last paragraph. She uses simple, compound, compound-complex sentences, sentence fragments, inverted word order, commands, and questions. The variety shows a sophisticated mastery of words and sentence structure.

---

[10] **first-water**: of the best quality and purest luster

The Harlem Renaissance

Your teacher will share information with you on the Harlem Renaissance. Use a chart like the one below to keep track of the information you learn from your teacher's presentation.

What beliefs and goals did Hurston share with the Harlem Renaissance?	In what ways did Hurston follow her own path?

Quickwrite: After learning a little bit about the Harlem Renaissance, what questions do you have that you would like to explore further?

Use the KWHL chart on the next page to organize and explore your questions about the Harlem Renaissance. Use a variety of sources to gather information and prepare a brief presentation of your findings. Your questions may be related to politics, writers, music of the era, history, places, and social developments.

The Harlem Renaissance

	What I **K**now (activating prior knowledge)	What I **W**ant to Learn (research questions)	**H**ow I might learn (useful sources)	What I **L**earned
Politics and Beliefs				
Music				
Writers				

Working with a small group, craft a creative and informative presentation that demonstrates your research; you will present this to your classmates.

Hurston's Colorful Language

SUGGESTED LEARNING STRATEGIES: Previewing, Skimming/Scanning, Marking the Text, Think-Pair-Share, Oral Interpretation, Graphic Organizer, SIFT, Drafting, Close Reading

1. Zora Neale Hurston was a respected anthropologist. *Mules and Men* is a collection of folklore that Hurston compiled. One of the tales, "Why Women Always Take Advantage of Men," is performed in the teleplay *Zora Is My Name.* As you watch this production, take notes on the guiding questions below.

What does this folk tale seem to say about the relationships between men and women?	How are the props, the set, and the sound effects used as symbols?

2. Not only did Hurston collect folklore, she also wrote short stories. Preview one of Hurston's most famous short stories, "Sweat," by scanning Chunk 1 and underlining unfamiliar words. You will see that Hurston reproduces the actual speech of the characters.

3. Try to figure out the unfamiliar words you underlined by using the context. Next, work with a small group to formulate some "pronunciation rules" for figuring out how to say the words. Use the graphic organizer on the next page to guide your work. Some examples have been provided for you.

Hurston's Colorful Language

Characters Say	We Say
dat, wid	that, with ("th" is often replaced by "d")
skeer	scare (so "keer" must mean care)
ah	
fuh	

LITERARY TERMS

Diction is a writer's choice of words.

Dialect is the distinctive language, including the sounds, spelling, grammar, and diction, of a specific group or class of people.

WORD CONNECTIONS

Along with dialects, Africa has given us many musical words that we have incorporated into English. Among them are banjo, bongo, jazz, jive, marimba, and merengue.

1. Hurston is known for using different levels of diction, including dialect, in her writing. Review the information below. Then find examples of each level that Hurston uses in Chunk 1 of "Sweat." Mark the text by color-coding the examples.

High or formal diction usually contains language that creates an elevated tone. It is free of slang, idioms, colloquialisms, and contractions. It often contains polysyllabic words, sophisticated syntax, and elegant word choice.

Neutral diction uses ordinary language and vocabulary without elaborate words and may include contractions.

Informal or low diction is the language of everyday use. It is relaxed and conversational. It often includes common and simple words, idioms, slang, jargon, and contractions.

Dialect is a subgroup of a language with its own vocabulary and grammatical features. Writers often use regional dialects or dialects that reveal a person's economic or social class.

2. Your teacher will lead you in a guided reading of "Sweat." As the text is read, use the questions in the My Notes section of the text to guide your reading of each chunk. Annotate the chunk according to the directions given in the margin. Be prepared to use your annotations to support your ideas in a discussion.

3. After reading Chunk 3, look for similarities and differences among the porch talkers you saw in the video production of the folk tale that Hurston recorded called "Why Women Always Take Advantage of Men" and the men on the porch in "Sweat."

Porch Talkers

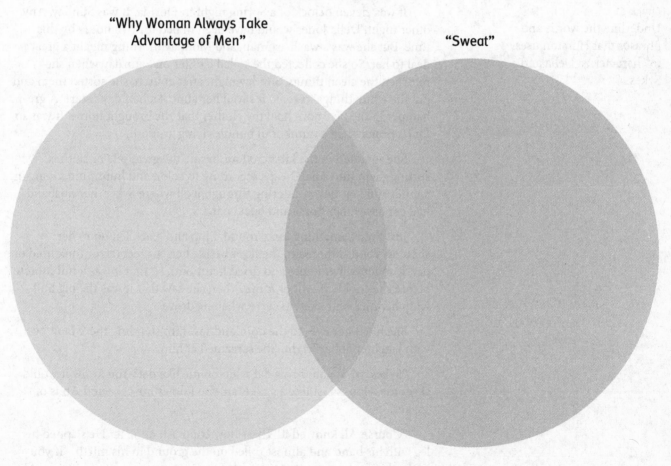

"Why Woman Always Take Advantage of Men"

"Sweat"

My Notes

Chunk 1
Underline the words and phrases that Hurston uses to characterize Delia and Sykes.

Chunk 2
Mark the words and phrases that indicate conflict(s) in the story.

Short Story

by Zora Neale Hurston

It was eleven o'clock of a Spring night in Florida. It was Sunday. Any other night, Delia Jones would have been in bed for two hours by this time. But she was a wash-woman, and Monday morning meant a great deal to her. So she collected the soiled clothes on Saturday when she returned the clean things. Sunday night after church, she sorted them and put the white things to soak. It saved her almost a half day's start. A great hamper in the bedroom held the clothes that she brought home. It was so much neater than a number of bundles lying around.

She squatted in the kitchen floor beside the great pile of clothes, sorting them into small heaps according to color, and humming a song in a mournful key, but wondering through it all where Sykes, her husband, had gone with her horse and buckboard.

Just then something long, round, limp and black fell upon her shoulders and slithered to the floor beside her. A great terror took hold of her. It softened her knees and dried her mouth so that it was a full minute before she could cry out or move. Then she saw that it was the big bull whip her husband liked to carry when he drove.

She lifted her eyes to the door and saw him standing there bent over with laughter at her fright. She screamed at him.

"Sykes, what you throw dat whip on me like dat? You know it would skeer me—looks just like a snake, an' you knows how skeered Ah is of snakes."

"Course Ah knowed it! That's how come Ah done it." He slapped his leg with his hand and almost rolled on the ground in his mirth. "If you such a big fool dat you got to have a fit over a earth worm or a string, Ah don't keer how bad Ah skeer you."

"You aint got no business doing it. Gawd knows it's a sin. Some day Ah'm gointuh drop dead from some of yo' foolishness. 'Nother thing, where you been wid mah rig? Ah feeds dat pony. He aint fuh you to be drivin' wid no bull whip."

"You sho is one aggravatin' nigger woman!" he declared and stepped into the room. She resumed her work and did not answer him at once. "Ah done tole you time and again to keep them white folks' clothes outa dis house."

He picked up the whip and glared down at her. Delia went on with her work. She went out into the yard and returned with a galvanized tub and set it on the washbench. She saw that Sykes had kicked all of the clothes together again, and now stood in her way truculently, his whole manner hoping, *praying*, for an argument. But she walked calmly around him and commenced to re-sort the things.

"Next time, Ah'm gointer kick 'em outdoors," he threatened as he struck a match along the leg of his corduroy breeches.

Delia never looked up from her work, and her thin, stooped shoulders sagged further.

"Ah aint for no fuss t'night, Sykes. Ah just come from taking sacrament at the church house."

He snorted scornfully. "Yeah, you just come from de church house on a Sunday night, but heah you is gone to work on them clothes. You ain't nothing but a hypocrite. One of them amen-corner Christians—sing, whoop, and shout, then come home and wash white folks clothes on the Sabbath."

He stepped roughly upon the whitest pile of things, kicking them helter-skelter as he crossed the room. His wife gave a little scream of dismay, and quickly gathered them together again.

"Sykes, you quit grindin' dirt into these clothes! How can Ah git through by Sat'day if Ah don't start on Sunday?"

"Ah don't keer if you never git through. Anyhow, Ah done promised Gawd and a couple of other men, Ah aint gointer have it in mah house. Don't gimme no lip neither, else Ah'll throw 'em out and put mah fist up side yo' head to boot."

Delia's habitual meekness seemed to slip from her shoulders like a blown scarf. She was on her feet; her poor little body, her bare knuckly hands bravely defying the strapping hulk before her.

"Looka heah, Sykes, you done gone too fur. Ah been married to you fur fifteen years, and Ah been takin' in washin' for fifteen years. Sweat, sweat, sweat! Work and sweat, cry and sweat, pray and sweat!"

"What's that got to do with me?" he asked brutally.

"What's it got to do with you, Sykes? Mah tub of suds is filled yo' belly with vittles more times than yo' hands is filled it. Mah sweat is done paid for this house and Ah reckon Ah kin keep on sweatin' in it."

WORD CONNECTIONS

Expect comes from the Latin prefix *ex-* meaning "out of" and the Latin verb *spectare* meaning "to look." *Spectator* and *spectacle* come from the same root.

© 2011 College Board. All rights reserved.

My Notes

She seized the iron skillet from the stove and struck a defensive pose, which act surprised him greatly, coming from her. It cowed him and he did not strike her as he usually did.

"Naw you won't," she panted, "that ole snaggle-toothed black woman you runnin' with aint comin' heah to pile up on *mah* sweat and blood. You aint paid for nothin' on this place, and Ah'm gointer stay right heah till Ah'm toted out foot foremost."

"Well, you better quit gittin' me riled up, else they'll be totin' you out sooner than you expect. Ah'm so tired of you Ah don't know whut to do. Gawd! how Ah hates skinny wimmen!"

A little awed by this new Delia, he sidled out of the door and slammed the back gate after him. He did not say where he had gone, but she knew too well. She knew very well that he would not return until nearly daybreak also. Her work over, she went on to bed but not to sleep at once. Things had come to a pretty pass!

She lay awake, gazing upon the debris that cluttered their matrimonial trail. Not an image left standing along the way. Anything like flowers had long ago been drowned in the salty stream that had been pressed from her heart. Her tears, her sweat, her blood. She had brought love to the union and he had brought a longing after the flesh. Two months after the wedding, he had given her the first brutal beating. She had the memory of his numerous trips to Orlando with all of his wages when he had returned to her penniless, even before the first year had passed. She was young and soft then, but now she thought of her knotty, muscled limbs, her harsh knuckly hands, and drew herself up into an unhappy little ball in the middle of the big feather bed. Too late now to hope for love, even if it were not Bertha it would be someone else. This case differed from the others only in that she was bolder than the others. Too late for everything except her little home. She had built it for her old days, and planted one by one the trees and flowers there. It was lovely to her, lovely.

Somehow, before sleep came, she found herself saying aloud: "Oh well, whatever goes over the Devil's back, is got to come under his belly. Sometime or ruther, Sykes, like everybody else, is gointer reap his sowing." After that she was able to build a spiritual earthworks against her husband. His shells could no longer reach her. *Amen.* She went to sleep and slept until he announced his presence in bed by kicking her feet and rudely snatching the cover away.

"Gimme some kivah heah, an' git yo' damn foots over on yo' own side! Ah oughter mash you in yo' mouf fuh drawing dat skillet on me."

Delia went clear to the rail without answering him. A triumphant indifference to all that he was or did.

The week was as full of work for Delia as all other weeks, and Saturday found her behind her little pony, collecting and delivering clothes.

It was a hot, hot day near the end of July. The village men on Joe Clarke's porch even chewed cane listlessly. They did not hurl the cane-knots as usual. They let them dribble over the edge of the porch. Even conversation had collapsed under the heat.

"Heah come Delia Jones," Jim Merchant said, as the shaggy pony came 'round the bend of the road toward them. The rusty buckboard was heaped with baskets of crisp, clean laundry.

"Yep," Joe Lindsay agreed. "Hot or col', rain or shine, jes ez reg'lar ez de weeks roll roun' Delia carries 'em an' fetches 'em on Sat'day."

"She better if she wanter eat," said Moss. "Sykes Jones aint wuth de shot an' powder hit would tek tuh kill 'em. Not to *huh* he aint. "

"He sho' aint," Walter Thomas chimed in. "It's too bad, too, cause she wuz a right pritty li'l trick when he got huh. Ah'd uh mah'ied huh mahseff if he hadnter beat me to it."

Delia nodded briefly at the men as she drove past.

"Too much knockin' will ruin *any* 'oman. He done beat huh 'nough tuh kill three women, let 'lone change they looks," said Elijah Moseley. "How Sykes kin stommuck dat big black greasy Mogul he's layin' roun' wid, gits me. Ah swear dat eight-rock couldn't kiss a sardine can Ah done throwed out de back do' 'way las' yeah."

"Aw, she's fat, thass how come. He's allus been crazy 'bout fat women," put in Merchant. "He'd a' been tied up wid one long time ago if he could a' found one tuh have him. Did Ah tell yuh 'bout him come sidlin' roun' *mah* wife—bringin' her a basket uh pee-cans outa his yard fuh a present? Yessir, mah wife! She tol' him tuh take 'em right straight back home, cause Delia works so hard ovah dat washtub she reckon everything on de place taste lak sweat an' soapsuds. Ah jus' wisht Ah'd a' caught 'im 'roun' dere! Ah'd a' made his hips ketch on fiah down dat shell road."

"Ah know he done it, too. Ah sees 'im grinnin' at every 'oman dat passes," Walter Thomas said. "But even so, he useter eat some mighty big hunks uh humble pie tuh git dat lil' 'oman he got. She wuz ez pritty ez a speckled pup! Dat wuz fifteen yeahs ago. He useter be so skeered uh losin' huh, she could make him do some parts of a husband's duty. Dey never wuz de same in de mind."

"There oughter be a law about him," said Lindsay. "He aint fit tuh carry guts tuh a bear."

© 2011 College Board. All rights reserved.

My Notes

Chunk 3
Underline the opinions of the men on the porch regarding Delia, Sykes, and Bertha.

Hurston's Colorful Language

Clarke spoke for the first time. "Taint no law on earth dat kin make a man be decent if it aint in 'im. There's plenty men dat takes a wife lak dey do a joint uh sugar-cane. It's round, juicy an' sweet when dey gits it. But dey squeeze an' grind, squeeze an' grind an' wring tell dey wring every drop uh pleasure dat's in 'em out. When dey's satisfied dat dey is wrung dry, dey treats 'em jes lak dey do a cane-chew. Dey throws 'em away. Dey knows whut dey is doin' while dey is at it, an' hates theirselves fuh it but they keeps on hangin' after huh tell she's empty. Den dey hates huh fuh bein' a cane-chew an' in de way."

"We oughter take Sykes an' dat stray 'oman uh his'n down in Lake Howell swamp an' lay on de rawhide till they cain't say 'Lawd a' mussy.' He allus wuz ... ovahbearin' ..., but since dat white 'oman from up north done teached 'im how to run a automobile, he done got too biggety to live—an' we oughter kill 'im," Old Man Anderson advised.

A grunt of approval went around the porch. But the heat was melting their civic virtue and Elijah Moseley began to bait Joe Clarke.

"Come on, Joe, git a melon outa dere an' slice it up for yo' customers. We'se all sufferin' wid de heat. De bear's done got *me*!"

"Thass right, Joe, a watermelon is jes' whut Ah needs tuh cure de eppizudicks," Walter Thomas joined forces with Moseley. "Come on dere, Joe. We all is steady customers an' you aint set us up in a long time. Ah chooses dat long, bowlegged Floridy favorite."

"A god, an' be dough. You all gimme twenty cents and slice way," Clarke retorted. "Ah needs a col' slice m'self. Heah, everybody chip in. Ah'll lend y'll mah meat knife."

The money was quickly subscribed and the huge melon brought forth. At that moment, Sykes and Bertha arrived. A determined silence fell on the porch and the melon was put away again.

Merchant snapped down the blade of his jackknife and moved toward the store door.

"Come on in, Joe, an' gimme a slab uh sow belly an' uh pound uh coffee—almost fuhgot 'twas Sat'day. Got to git on home." Most of the men left also.

Just then Delia drove past on her way home, as Sykes was ordering magnificently for Bertha. It pleased him for Delia to see.

"Git whutsoever yo' heart desires, Honey. Wait a minute, Joe. Give huh two bottles uh strawberry soda-water, uh quart uh parched ground-peas, an' a block uh chewin' gum."

With all this they left the store, with Sykes reminding Bertha that this was his town and she could have it if she wanted it.

The men returned soon after they left, and held their watermelon feast.

"Where did Sykes Jones git da 'oman from nohow?" Lindsay asked.

"Ovah Apopka. Guess dey musta been cleanin' out de town when she lef'. She don't look lak a thing but a hunk uh liver wid hair on it."

"Well, she sho' kin squall," Dave Carter contributed. "When she gits ready tuh laff, she jes' opens huh mouf an' latches it back tuh de las' notch. No ole grandpa alligator down in Lake Bell ain't got nothin' on huh."

Bertha had been in town three months now. Sykes was still paying her room rent at Della Lewis'—the only house in town that would have taken her in. Sykes took her frequently to Winter Park to "stomps." He still assured her that he was the swellest man in the state.

"Sho' you kin have dat lil' ole house soon's Ah kin git dat 'oman outa dere. Everything b'longs tuh me an' you sho' kin have it. Ah sho' 'bominates uh skinny 'oman. Lawdy, you sho' is got one portly shape on you! You kin git *anything* you wants. Dis is *mah* town an' you sho' kin have it."

Delia's work-worn knees crawled over the earth in Gethsemane and up the rocks of Calvary many, many times during these months. She avoided the villagers and meeting places in her efforts to be blind and deaf. But Bertha nullified this to a degree, by coming to Delia's house to call Sykes out to her at the gate.

Delia and Sykes fought all the time now with no peaceful interludes. They slept and ate in silence. Two or three times Delia had attempted a timid friendliness, but she was repulsed each time. It was plain that the breaches must remain agape.

* * *

The sun had burned July to August. The heat streamed down like a million hot arrows, smiting all things living upon the earth. Grass withered, leaves browned, snakes went blind in shedding and men and dogs went mad. Dog days!

Delia came home one day and found Sykes there before her. She wondered, but started to go on into the house without speaking, even though he was standing in the kitchen door and she must either stoop under his arm or ask him to move. He made no room for her. She noticed a soap box beside the steps, but paid no particular attention to it, knowing that he must have brought it there. As she was stooping to pass under his outstretched arm, he suddenly pushed her backward, laughingly.

"Look in de box dere Delia, Ah done brung yuh somethin'!"

My Notes

Chunk 4

LITERARY TERMS
Figurative language goes beyond literal meanings by using words or phrases to describe one thing in terms of another.

Hurston's Colorful Language

She nearly fell upon the box in her stumbling, and when she saw what it held, she all but fainted outright.

"Sykes! Sykes, mah Gawd! You take dat rattlesnake 'way from heah! You *gottuh*. Oh, Jesus, have mussy!"

"Ah aint gut tuh do nuthin' uh de kin'—fact is Ah aint got tuh do nothin' but die. Taint no use uh you puttin' on airs makin' out lak you skeered uh dat snake—he's gointer stay right heah tell he die. He wouldn't bite me cause Ah knows how tuh handle 'im. Nohow he wouldn't risk breakin' out his fangs 'gin *yo'* skinny laigs."

"Naw, now Sykes, don't keep dat thing 'roun' heah tuh skeer me tuh death. You knows Ah'm even feared uh earth worms. Thass de biggest snake Ah evah did see. Kill 'im Sykes, please."

"Doan ast me tuh do nothin' fuh yuh. Goin' roun' tryin' tuh be so damn astorperious. Naw, Ah aint gonna kill it. Ah think uh damn sight mo' uh him dan you! Dat's a nice snake an' anybody doan lak 'im kin jes' hit de grit."

The village soon heard that Sykes had the snake, and came to see and ask questions.

"How de hen-fire did you ketch dat six-foot rattler, Sykes?" Thomas asked.

"He's full uh frogs so he caint hardly move, thass how Ah eased up on 'im. But Ah'm a snake charmer an' knows how tuh handle 'em. Shux, dat aint nothin'. Ah could ketch one eve'y day if Ah so wanted tuh."

"Whut he needs is a heavy hick'ry club leaned real heavy on his head. Dat's de bes 'way tuh charm a rattlesnake."

"Naw, Walt, y'all jes' don't understand dese diamon' backs lak Ah do," said Sykes in a superior tone of voice.

The village agreed with Walter, but the snake stayed on. His box remained by the kitchen door with its screen wire covering. Two or three days later it had digested its meal of frogs and literally came to life. It rattled at every movement in the kitchen or the yard. One day as Delia came down the kitchen steps she saw his chalky-white fangs curved like scimitars hung in the wire meshes. This time she did not run away with averted eyes as usual. She stood for a long time in the doorway in a red fury that grew bloodier for every second that she regarded the creature that was her torment.

That night she broached the subject as soon as Sykes sat down to the table.

Chunk 5
Underline the words and phrases the characters use to describe each other.

"Sykes, Ah wants you tuh take dat snake 'way fum heah. You done starved me an' Ah put up widcher, you done beat me an Ah took dat, but you done kilt all mah insides bringin' dat varmint heah."

Sykes poured out a saucer full of coffee and drank it deliberately before he answered her.

"A whole lot Ah keer 'bout how you feels inside uh out. Dat snake aint goin' no damn wheah till Ah gits ready fuh 'im tuh go. So fur as beatin' is concerned, yuh aint took near all dat you gointer take ef yuh stay 'roun' *me*."

Delia pushed back her plate and got up from the table. "Ah hates you, Sykes," she said calmly. "Ah hates you tuh de same degree dat Ah useter love yuh. Ah done took an' took till mah belly is full up tuh mah neck. Dat's de reason Ah got mah letter fum de church an' moved mah membership tuh Woodbridge—so Ah don't haftuh take no sacrament wid yuh. Ah don't wantuh see yuh 'roun' me a-tall. Lay 'roun' wid dat 'oman all yuh wants tuh, but gwan 'way fum me an' mah house. Ah hates yuh lak uh suck-egg dog."

Sykes almost let the huge wad of corn bread and collard greens he was chewing fall out of his mouth in amazement. He had a hard time whipping himself up to the proper fury to try to answer Delia.

"Well, Ah'm glad you does hate me. Ah'm sho' tiahed uh you hangin' ontuh me. Ah don't want yuh. Look at yuh stringey ole neck! Yo' rawbony laigs an' arms is enough tuh cut uh man tuh death. You looks jes' lak de devvul's doll-baby tuh *me*. You cain't hate me no worse dan Ah hates you. Ah been hatin' *you* fuh years."

"Yo' ole black hide don't look lak nothin' tuh me, but uh passle uh wrinkled up rubber, wid yo' big ole yeahs flappin' on each side lak uh paih uh buzzard wings. Don't think Ah'm gointuh be run 'way fum mah house neither. Ah'm goin' tuh de white folks bout *you*, mah young man, de very nex' time you lay yo' han's on me. Mah cup is done run ovah." Delia said this with no signs of fear and Sykes departed from the house, threatening her, but made not the slightest move to carry out any of them.

That night he did not return at all, and the next day being Sunday, Delia was glad she did not have to quarrel before she hitched up her pony and drove the four miles to Woodbridge.

She stayed to the night service—"love feast"—which was very warm and full of spirit. In the emotional winds her domestic trials were borne far and wide so that she sang as she drove homeward,

Jurden water, black an' col'

Chills de body, not de soul

An' Ah wantah cross Jurden in uh calm time.

My Notes

Chunk 6
Underline the references to the snake.

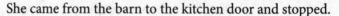

My Notes

She came from the barn to the kitchen door and stopped.

"Whut's de mattah, ol' satan, you aint kickin' up yo' racket?" She addressed the snake's box. Complete silence. She went on into the house with a new hope in its birth struggles. Perhaps her threat to go to the white folks had frightened Sykes! Perhaps he was sorry! Fifteen years of misery and suppression had brought Delia to the place where she would hope *anything* that looked towards a way over or through her wall of inhibitions.

She felt in the match safe behind the stove at once for a match. There was only one there.

"Dat [man] wouldn't fetch nothin' heah tuh save his rotten neck, but he kin run thew whut Ah brings quick enough. Now he done toted off nigh on tuh haff uh box uh matches. He done had dat 'oman heah in mah house, too."

Nobody but a woman could tell how she knew this even before she struck the match. But she did and it put her into a new fury.

Presently she brought in the tubs to put the white things to soak. This time she decided she need not bring the hamper out of the bedroom; she would go in there and do the sorting. She picked up the pot-bellied lamp and went in. The room was small and the hamper stood hard by the foot of the white iron bed. She could sit and reach through the bedposts—resting as she worked.

"Ah wantah cross Jurden in uh calm time." She was singing again. The mood of the "love feast" had returned. She threw back the lid of the basket almost gaily. Then, moved by both horror and terror, she sprang back toward the door. *There lay the snake in the basket!* He moved sluggishly at first, but even as she turned round and round, jumped up and down in an insanity of fear, he began to stir vigorously. She saw him pouring his awful beauty from the basket upon the bed, then she seized the lamp and ran as fast as she could to the kitchen. The wind from the open door blew out the light and the darkness added to her terror. She sped to the darkness of the yard, slamming the door after her before she thought to set down the lamp. She did not feel safe even on the ground, so she climbed up in the hay barn.

There for an hour or more she lay sprawled upon the hay a gibbering wreck.

Finally, she grew quiet, and after that, coherent thought. With this, stalked through her a cold, bloody rage. Hours of this. A period of introspection, a space of retrospection, then a mixture of both. Out of this an awful calm.

"Well, Ah done de bes' Ah could. If things aint right, Gawd knows taint mah fault."

She went to sleep—a twitchy sleep—and woke up to a faint gray sky. There was a loud hollow sound below. She peered out. Sykes was at the wood-pile, demolishing a wire-covered box.

He hurried to the kitchen door, but hung outside there some minutes before he entered, and stood some minutes more inside before he closed it after him.

The gray in the sky was spreading. Delia descended without fear now, and crouched beneath the low bedroom window. The drawn shade shut out the dawn, shut in the night. But the thin walls held back no sound.

"Dat ol' scratch is woke up now!" She mused at the tremendous whirr inside, which every woodsman knows, is one of the sound illusions. The rattler is a ventriloquist. His whirr sounds to the right, to the left, straight ahead, behind, close under foot—everywhere but where it is. Woe to him who guesses wrong unless he is prepared to hold up his end of the argument! Sometimes he strikes without rattling at all.

Inside, Sykes heard nothing until he knocked a pot lid off the stove while trying to reach the match safe in the dark. He had emptied his pockets at Bertha's.

The snake seemed to wake up under the stove and Sykes made a quick leap into the bedroom. In spite of the gin he had had, his head was clearing now.

"'Mah Gawd!" he chattered, "ef Ah could on'y strack uh light!"

The rattling ceased for a moment as he stood paralyzed. He waited. It seemed that the snake waited also.

"Oh, fuh de light! Ah thought he'd be too sick"—Sykes was muttering to himself when the whirr began again, closer, right underfoot this time. Long before this, Sykes' ability to think had been flattened down to primitive instinct and he leaped—onto the bed.

Outside Delia heard a cry that might have come from a maddened chimpanzee, a stricken gorilla. All the terror, all the horror, all the rage that man possibly could express, without a recognizable human sound.

My Notes

GRAMMAR & USAGE

Hurston uses sentence fragments to describe what Delia sees and hears. "All the terror, all the horror, all the rage...intermittent whirr of the reptile." These noun phrases focus on sounds and actions. Hurston continues to describe the scene with a series of participial phrases modifying nouns: "The shade torn violently down, a huge brown hand seizing the window...." Because participles are verb forms, these phrases emphasize the action of verbs and create a vivid scene.

My Notes

A tremendous stir inside there, another series of animal screams, the intermittent whirr of the reptile. The shade torn violently down from the window, letting in the red dawn, a huge brown hand seizing the window stick, great dull blows upon the wooden floor punctuating the gibberish of sound long after the rattle of the snake had abruptly subsided. All this Delia could see and hear from her place beneath the window, and it made her ill. She crept over to the four-o'clocks and stretched herself on the cool earth to recover.

She lay there. "Delia, Delia!" She could hear Sykes calling in a most despairing tone as one who expected no answer. The sun crept on up, and he called. Delia could not move—her legs were gone flabby. She never moved, he called, and the sun kept rising.

"Mah Gawd!" She heard him moan, "Mah Gawd fum Heben!" She heard him stumbling about and got up from her flower-bed. The sun was growing warm. As she approached the door she heard him call out hopefully, "Delia, is dat you Ah heah?"

She saw him on his hands and knees as soon as she reached the door. He crept an inch or two toward her—all that he was able, and she saw his horribly swollen neck and his one open eye shining with hope. A surge of pity too strong to support bore her away from that eye that must, could not, fail to see the tubs. He would see the lamp. Orlando with its doctors was too far. She could scarcely reach the Chinaberry tree, where she waited in the growing heat while inside she knew the cold river was creeping up and up to extinguish that eye which must know by now that she knew.

Discussion: Identify where the narration shifts from a third-person narrator to Delia's character. Analyze the impact of narration when the narrator's point of view shifts.

After you have finished reading "Sweat," look back through the text and find examples of foreshadowing for the story's ending. List them in the space below.

Hurston's upbringing and love of reading made her well-versed in the Bible, and Biblical allusions are a hallmark of her writing style. What are some of the Biblical allusions you noticed in "Why Women Always Take Advantage of Men" and "Sweat"? Use the chart below to identify and explain how the allusions create meaning in the text.

Biblical Allusions	Effect on the Text

4. At the beginning of the story, you discussed the whip as a symbol in the story. Discuss other symbols that you noticed in the story. Be sure to include details from the story for support.

Hurston's Colorful Language

LITERARY TERMS

Tone is the attitude a writer takes toward a subject.
Theme is the insight about life that is revealed in a work.

Once you have finished reading "Sweat," use SIFT to help you analyze the story. Focus on how the symbols, images, and figurative language Hurston uses in the story reveal her tone and a theme found in the story.

Stylistic Elements	How They Contribute to Tone/Theme
Symbols	
Images	
Figurative Language	

Writing Prompt: Using your teacher's model, write an analysis of Hurston's short story "Sweat" on separate paper. Choose a method of prewriting and then draft your analysis, weaving in quotes from the text as support.

Janie's Return Home

SUGGESTED LEARNING STRATEGIES: Word Map, Quickwrite, Visualizing, Think-Pair-Share, Oral Interpretation, Sketching, Graphic Organizer, Rereading

1. On separate paper, create a web using the words *horizons/dreams* as the central focus. On your web, write the connotations and denotations of those words. For example, one word associated with horizons would be *hopes.*

Horizons/ Dreams

Quickwrite: After completing your web, write a reflection about the imagery associated with these two words.

Janie's Return from a Long Journey

2. Read the first two paragraphs of Chapter 1 of *Their Eyes Were Watching God.* What distinctions do the first two paragraphs make between men and women?

3. What questions do these paragraphs raise for you?

WORD CONNECTIONS

Analogies may use geographical terms to compare relationships. For example, in continent : Africa :: state : Ohio, each set of words equals each other. Complete this analogy.

Ocean : island ::
desert : _____

a. tree
b. sand
c. oasis
d. dune

4. *Male students*: Interpret and analyze the first paragraph. Note your findings and be prepared to present them to the female students in your class.

   Female students: Interpret and analyze the second paragraph. Note your findings and be prepared to present them to the male students in your class.

LITERARY TERMS

Imagery is language that evokes a mental picture or physical sensation through vivid details that appeal to the senses.

The Porch Sitters

5. As Hurston describes the woman, where she has been, and the people who see her return, she uses evocative imagery. List several of the images and the senses they appeal to in the space below. How do these images impact the reader?

Image	Senses the Image Appeals To

6. How does the porch serve as a metaphor for judgment?

Reread the porch scene and look for any information "Mouth Almighty," or the porch sitters, reveals about the protagonist, Janie.

7. What story does Janie have to tell? Who is her audience?

SUGGESTED LEARNING STRATEGIES: **Marking the Text, Think-Pair-Share, Double-Entry Journal, Graphic Organizer , Close Reading, Rereading, Drafting, Sketching, Word Map**

My Notes

Poetry

ABOUT THE AUTHOR

Fascinated with jazz rhythms and the lyrics of blues music, Langston Hughes published his first book of poetry, *The Weary Blues,* in 1926. A major figure in the Harlem Renaissance, Hughes also wrote novels, short stories, plays, and nonfiction. His works captured and celebrated the colorful culture of black America.

Mother to Son

by Langston Hughes

Well, son, I'll tell you:
Life for me ain't been no crystal stair.
It's had tacks in it,
And splinters,
5   And boards all torn up,
And places with no carpet on the floor —
Bare.
But all the time
I'se been a-climbin' on
10   And reachin' landin's,
And turnin' corners,
And sometimes goin' in the dark
Where there ain't been no light.
So boy, don't you turn back.
15   Don't you set down on the steps
'Cause you finds it's kinder hard.
Don't you fall now —
For I'se still goin', honey,
I'se still climbin',
And life for me ain't been no crystal stair.

1. Identify the key *metaphor* in the poem "Mother to Son," and comment on its effectiveness.

WORD CONNECTIONS

A metaphor is a form of analogy, as is a simile. A metaphor is an implied analogy, while a simile is an explicit analogy.

2. How might the poem change if it were written from the son's point of view?

LITERARY TERMS
Point of view is the perspective from which a literary work is told.

Nanny's Life

3. Hurston organized *Their Eyes Were Watching God* as a frame novel, in which the first and last chapters form a frame for the story that Janie tells her friend Pheoby. Can you think of other stories, books, or films that use a frame structure?

4. Consider the following sentences from Chapter 2: "Janie saw her life like a great tree in leaf with things suffered, things enjoyed, things done and undone. Dawn and doom was in the branches." Why do you think Hurston chose to juxtapose opposing images as she presents the central simile?

5. As you continue reading Chapter 2, use your own double-entry journal (modeled below) to take notes on the *figurative language* Hurston uses.

Chapter 2: Exploring Figurative language

Figurative language from Chapter 2	Analysis, Commentary, Reflection...

6. Within the first two chapters of Hurston's novel, what images do you see repeated? What might these **motifs** represent?

ACADEMIC VOCABULARY

A **motif** is a recurrent theme, subject, character type, or image that becomes a unifying element in a text.

7. Sketch Janie's family tree.

8. Once you have finished reading Chapter 2, compare and contrast the voice of Nanny to the voice of Hughes's narrator in "Mother to Son." Create a graphic organizer on separate paper to record your thinking.

9. One of the hallmarks of Hurston's writing *style* is her use of narrative voice. List all the narrators you find in Chapter 2. As you continue to read *Their Eyes Were Watching God,* pay attention to the way Hurston skillfully shifts between different narrative voices.

10. You have seen how Hurston compares Janie's life to a tree and Nanny's life to a very different tree. On a separate sheet of paper, create a visual representation of your own life, using a tree as a *metaphor.* Under your visual representation, write an explanation of the tree metaphor you have created.

Nanny, Janie, and Logan

Chapters 3 and 4

Quickwrite: "There are years that ask questions and years that answer." Write a speculative response on what the upcoming year will hold for Janie. Will this year be the year that asks questions or one that answers them? Will this be the year that does both?

Your teacher will assign you to discussion groups. Discuss the questions that follow and take notes relating to the events in Chapters 3 and 4.

1. As Janie evaluates her marriage to Logan Killicks, Hurston presents the recurring image of the horizon (page 25): "The familiar people and things had failed her so she hung over the gate and looked up the road towards way off. She knew now that marriage did not make love. Janie's first dream was dead, so she became a woman." Discuss how Janie's frustration helps her growing self-awareness.

2. Nanny desires that Janie would have a life far different from her own and Leafy's. Discuss what Nanny desires for Janie and what actions Nanny takes to realize this desire. Read the text closely to identify examples of irony in Nanny's actions and the result of them.

3. What symbolic act does Janie perform when she leaves Logan? Examine the paragraph that begins, "The morning road air...." How does Hurston's word choice reveal her tone toward this development of the plot?

4. Reread the paragraph that begins, "Joe Starks was the name...." Who is the narrator? Why do you think Hurston choose to present Joe's introduction in this way? What is the impact of the shift in point of view from omniscient to Joe Starks's character?

5. Chapter 4 ends with Janie's leaving for Green Cove Springs with Joe Starks. Predict how Janie and Joe's relationship will develop after she runs out on Logan. Will her dream become truth? How do the *motifs* of the horizon and of the pear tree and bees factor into Janie's leaving?

Janie's New Life

Chapter 5

1. Read Chapter 5 and then write three questions for each of the following levels of questions:

- Literal (what the text says)
- Interpretive (what the text means)
- Universal (why it matters)

Literal	Interpretive	Universal
What does Joe Starks say when the audience requests that Janie speak?	Based on Joe Starks's statements about women, what can the reader infer?	How does society define male and female roles?

2. Share your questions with your classmates. With your class, choose three questions that best identify the central issues of Chapter 5. Write those questions below.

Chapter 6

As an anthropologist, Hurston collected stories, conversations, and other aspects of oral tradition that she then infused into her writing. As you read Chapter 6, watch for elements of humor such as tall tales/hyperbole, parody, and riddles.

3. In the space below, list examples for each element of humor, and describe its effect.

Example from the Chapter	Effect
Tall Tales/Hyperbole	
Parody	
Riddles	

Think about the characters, setting, and conflicts in Chapters 5 and 6. Then write analytical responses to the interpretive questions below.

4. Why does Joe pamper the mule he bought from Matt Bonner? What effect does his special treatment have on the mule? Do you see any parallels in his treatment of Janie?

5. Hurston often used Eatonville, her real-life childhood home, as a setting in her work. Describe Eatonville as it is presented in *Their Eyes Were Watching God*. What effect is the young town having on Joe, Janie, and their marriage?

6. "She had an inside and an outside now and suddenly she knew how not to mix them." When have you seen evidence of the two sides of Janie in Chapters 5 and 6? What is the reason for this disparity?

Writing Prompt: Using blues music as inspiration, craft a poetic reflection of "Janie's Blues" on separate paper.

The Two Sides of Janie

SUGGESTED LEARNING STRATEGIES: Close Reading, Marking the Text, Predicting, Shared Reading, Graphic Organizer

Chapters 7 and 8

1. After reading the first two paragraphs of Chapter 7, describe how the author's imagery expresses Janie's sense of her marriage.

2. As you read Chapters 7 and 8, use this graphic organizer to record characters' actions and emotional responses.

Important Plot Developments	Adjectives to Describe Janie's Emotional Response
Chapter 7:	
Chapter 8:	

Chapter 9

3. Use the chart above to create a two-sided mask with which you explore Janie's inner self in contrast to her outer self. The mask should include descriptive adjectives, relevant quotes, and symbolic representations of Janie's character.

The Two Sides of Janie

4. A close rereading of the second paragraph in Chapter 9, which begins "Janie starched and ironed her face..." will reveal several interesting stylistic choices that Hurston makes. Look carefully at these elements of style and take notes in the chart below about what you find.

Stylistic Element	Examples from Chapter 9	Effect on Tone
Diction		
Figurative Language		
Syntax		
Structure or Organization		
Point of View		

Writing Prompt: Choose one of these stylistic techniques and write about how it affects the tone of the paragraph or the chapter. Be sure to weave in a quote from the novel to illustrate your points.

Discussion Groups

SUGGESTED LEARNING STRATEGIES: Discussion Groups, Questioning the Text, Notetaking

You have approached the first half of *Their Eyes Were Watching God* in a variety of ways, such as shared reading, oral interpretation, and guided reading. For the second half of the novel, you will move to greater independence, reading on your own and participating in student-led discussion groups.

The remaining chapters of the novel can be divided into these broad chunks:

> Chapters 10 to 13 (Janie and Tea Cake in Eatonville);

> Chapters 14 to 19 (Janie and Tea Cake on the Muck).

You will read Chapter 20 with your class in the next activity.

1. For each chapter from 10–19, you will write literal, interpretive, and universal questions to help guide your group discussions. Use the following topics to help you create questions and guide your discussion of the novel:

   • Elements of Hurston's style (figurative language, diction, tone, imagery, syntax, structure) that impressed members of the group.

   • Janie's literal journey through a variety of settings as well as her figurative journey.

   • Hurston's recurring motifs, such as the pear tree and the horizon.

   • How Janie uses her voice or does not use her voice, as well as how her voice changes.

   • Hurston's approach to point of view and shift in narration/point of view.

   • How an author's style constructs and reflects a character's identity (one of the unit's essential questions).

   • Important themes of the novel.

2. At the first meeting of your discussion group, create a schedule for reading, making sure that your schedule reflects the timeline provided by your teacher. Make sure that each group member writes down the reading schedule in his or her calendar; it is imperative for each member of the group to maintain the reading schedule in order for discussions to be effective.

3. A notetaking guide is provided for you. You may copy this guide onto separate paper or modify it to fit your discussions; just be sure to take good notes during each discussion. These notes will help you understand the novel and prepare for writing an analytical essay.

Discussion Groups

You might use the following notetaking guide as a model for your notes, or create something similar to capture your discussions.

A. Complete before meeting with your discussion group.

Today's date:	Reading assignment:
Interpretive questions based on the reading assignment	Universal questions based on the reading assignment

B. Notes during the group's discussion.

Today's topics:

Topic 1:	Topic 2:
Notes:	Notes:

C. Individual reflection on today's group discussion.

The End of a Long Journey

1. As Chapter 20 is read aloud, use a double-entry journal like the model below to record and analyze the imagery and/or figurative language that surfaces in the text.

Passages from Chapter 20: Rich Imagery, Figurative Language	Interpretation, Analysis, Reflection

2. Revisit Chapter 1 and make connections between the images that surfaced initially in the novel and those that come at the end of the novel.

Chapter 1	Chapter 20	Analysis and Commentary

The Frame Story

Hurston chose to organize this novel by having Chapters 1 and 20 frame Janie's telling of her story to Pheoby. By the end of the novel, if you return to the first scene, you have a much clearer understanding of Janie's perception of her life and her "grand journey."

3. After rereading the first chapter, on separate paper write an interior monologue that captures the thoughts that may be going through Janie's mind as she walks past the porch sitters upon her return to Eatonville.

Thematic Statement

Now that you have read the novel and discussed it at length, think about the major themes presented in it.

4. Write a thematic statement in which you synthesize your understanding of the novel's literary elements and explain how they informed your interpretation of the author's purpose.

Critical Responses

Much has been written in response to *Their Eyes Were Watching God*. Henry Louis Gates says, "The curious aspect of the widespread critical attention being shown to Hurston's texts is that so many critics embracing such a diversity of theoretic approaches seem to find something new at which to marvel in her texts."

5. Read the assessments that follow and annotate them in the margins, comparing each one to your understanding of the themes of *Their Eyes Were Watching God*.

It is folklore fiction at its best, which we gratefully accept as an overdue replacement for so much faulty local color fiction about Negroes. But when will the Negro novelist of maturity, who knows how to tell a story convincingly—which is Miss Hurston's cradle gift, come to grips with motive fiction and social document fiction? Progressive southern fiction has already banished the legend of these entertaining pseudo-primitives whom the reading public still loves to laugh with, weep over and envy. Having gotten rid of condescension, let us now get over oversimplification!

(Alain Locke

Opportunity, June 1, 1938)

Critical Responses (continued)

In fact, when she [Janie] first talks with Pheoby, she speaks not of romance and adoration of Tea Cake but of experiences much wider than love or even Tea Cake as an individual: "Ah been a delegate to de big 'ssociation of life," she tells her; "Yessuh! De Grand Lodge, de big convention of livin' is just where Ah been dis year and a half y'all ain't seen me" (18). In contrast to some readers' focus on romance and Janie's relationship with Tea Cake, living—not just loving—is what Janie stresses in reviewing her own experience. Such a focus is also the omniscient narrator's. When in the book's final images, Janie pulls in her horizon "like a great fish-net," it is "life" (286)—including, but certainly not limited to love—that she finds in its meshes. When Janie does speak to Pheoby about love, it is not to depict her relationship with Tea Cake as perfect or necessarily even the sole love of her life but to describe love as many-faceted and ever-changing. Love, for a woman who is supremely confident and self-affirming, "ain't somethin' lak uh grindstone dat's de same thing everywhere and do the same thing tuh everything it touch. Love is lak de sea. It's uh movin' thing, but still and all, it takes its shape from de shore it meets, and it's different with every shore" (284). As Janie here suggests, she emerges from the novel as no conventional romantic heroine searching to duplicate her relationship with Tea Cake or turning away from life because of the futility of doing so but as an autonomous black woman who faces the future in a spirit of engagement and openness to the flux of experience, "the dawn and doom" she has learned make up love and life.

(Susan Edwards Meisenhelder, "Mink Skin or Coon Hide":
The Janus-faced Narrative of *Their Eyes Were Watching God*)

In a rich prose (which has, at the same time, a sort of nervous sensibility) she tells the tale of a girl who wanted things sweet with mah marriage, lak when you sit under a pear tree and think. Janie did not get sweetness when her Grandma married her to Mister Killicks with his sixty acres of West Florida land, and his sagging belly, and his toenails that looked like mules' foots; and

WORD CONNECTIONS

Omniscient is formed from two Latin words: *omnis* meaning "all" and *scientia* meaning "knowledge." *Omnipotent, omnibus,* and *omnivorous* use the prefix *omnis,* while *science* and *scientist* use the root.

GRAMMAR & USAGE

When you use direct quotations, you must identify the words quoted with quotation marks to avoid plagiarism. If you set apart an entire quote in a separate paragraph (as is done with the critical responses), you do not need to use beginning and ending quotation marks. If the quoted text includes a quotation within it, that quotation is set with double quotation marks.

If you use quoted text within a regular paragraph (not set apart on separate lines) that also includes a quotation, use the double quotation marks to identify the entire quoted passage and single quotation marks around the embedded quotation.

Critical Responses (continued)

she didn't get it when she ran off with Joe Starks and got to be the Mayor's wife, and sat on her own store porch. But when Tea Cake came along with his trampish clothes and his easy ways and his nice grin that made even a middle-aged woman like Janie sort of wishful the minute she sets eyes on him, he handed her the keys of the kingdom, and their life together (what there was of it) was rapture and fun and tenderness and understanding—the perfect relationship of man and woman, whether they be black or white.

(Sheila Hibben, *The New York Herald Tribune Weekly Book Review*, September 26, 1937)

The story of Janie's life down on the muck of Florida Glades, bean picking, hunting and the men shooting dice in the evening and how the hurricane came up and drove the animals and the Indians and finally the black people and the white people before it, and How Tea Cake, in Janie's eyes the 'son of Evening Son,' and incidentally the best crap shooter in the place, made Janie sing and glitter all over at last, is a little epic all by itself. Indeed, from first to last this is a well nigh perfect story—a little sententious at the start, but the rest is simple and beautiful and shining with humor.

(Lucille Tompkins, *The New York Times Book Review*, September 26, 1937)

6. On separate paper, craft three or four interpretive and universal questions about the four critical interpretations. You will then use these questions in a Socratic seminar with your peers.

Writing Prompt: Choose one of the critical reviews and defend, challenge, or qualify it, being sure to weave in quotes from the novel for support.

Oprah Winfrey Presents...

Filmmakers who adapt a novel face the challenge of conveying their interpretation of the major themes of the work. A close examination of the film adaptation of *Their Eyes Were Watching God* offers you the opportunity to critique a media production of Hurston's novel. You will watch the last approximately 28 minutes of the film, taking notes about what the filmmakers chose to add, to alter, and to delete, and the effects of these choices.

1. First, refresh your memory by scanning Chapter 14, when Janie and Tea Cake arrive on the muck, to the end of the novel. Make a list of the major elements and scenes found here that are essential to conveying the major themes of the novel.

2. What do you know about Oprah Winfrey, the producer of this film? List the accomplishments she would have on her résumé.

3. Using your list from question 1, what do you predict Oprah Winfrey will focus on in this film adaptation of *Their Eyes Were Watching God*?

4. As you watch the last part of the film, use the graphic organizer on the next page to take notes on what the filmmakers chose to add, alter, and delete. Most importantly, think about the effects of these choices.

Oprah Winfrey Presents...

Add	• What do film techniques add to the text? Consider visual images, camera angles and movement, framing, music, lighting, diegetic and nondiegetic sound, and so on. • What do the actors add to characterization? • Are any plotlines added?	**What is the effect of these additions?**
Alter	• What elements and scenes from the book are present but altered? In what ways? • Which scenes in the film present a mood that differs from the mood in the parallel scene from the novel? In what ways?	**What is the effect of these alterations?**
Delete	• What did the filmmakers leave out?	**What is the effect of these deletions?**

Revisiting and Revising Your Writing

5. Over the course of this unit, you have drafted several short pieces of writing. You have also studied Zora Neale Hurston's style extensively. Choose a piece of your own work and revise it, making deliberate stylistic choices. You might consider the following:

- Infuse figurative language.

- Consider whether the diction you use is consistent with your audience and purpose.

- Experiment with different kinds of diction.

- Focus on syntax by varying your sentence patterns and kinds of sentences.

- Change the structural or organizational pattern.

- Employ a different point of view or narrative voice.

6. In a writing group, share your revision, explain your stylistic choices, and get feedback on your work from your peers.

Writing an Analytical Essay

SUGGESTED LEARNING STRATEGIES: **Drafting, Self-Editing/
Peer Editing**

Assignment

Write an analytical essay in which you discuss how a key theme in *Their Eyes Were Watching God* by Zora Neale Hurston is expressed through her style and use of literary elements.

Steps

Planning

1. During your reading you have studied the literary elements and traced several aspects of style in *Their Eyes Were Watching God*.

2. Based on your class discussions and notes, identify a theme of the novel that you think is significant.

3. Examine the effect of Hurston's style and use of literary elements on the theme you have identified in her novel.

4. Create a thesis statement that captures your thinking. Then, use a prewriting strategy to explore ideas and create an organizational plan for your essay. Consider the order of your topics and the details and examples you can include to support each topic.

Drafting

5. Draft your essay. If you want, you might consult with your peers when necessary to restructure and organize ideas.

Revising

6. Read your essay carefully, looking closely at the stylistic choices you made in your initial draft. Revise your essay to reflect deliberate stylistic choices. Revise your essay to reflect an appropriate organizational structure and a clear analysis of how Hurston advances theme through style and literary elements.

7. Working in peer response groups, review the Scoring Guide criteria and solicit feedback to assist you with further revision.

8. Edit your essay, using available resources to prepare your work for publication. Make corrections in grammar, punctuation, and spelling.

....

↗**TECHNOLOGY TIP** Use word processing software to create your final draft. Format your essay attractively, use margins of at least one inch, and choose a font that is appropriate for academic writing.

SCORING GUIDE

Scoring Criteria	Exemplary	Proficient	Emerging
Ideas	A thorough and perceptive understanding of the novel and prompt creates an extraordinarily convincing text. The analysis demonstrates an exceptional insight on the effect of elements of style and/or literary elements on theme. Use of specific and well-chosen examples yields detailed support for the analysis.	A solid understanding of the novel and prompt creates a convincing text. The analysis demonstrates a general understanding of the effect of elements of style and/or literary elements on theme. Use of appropriate examples supports the position.	A superficial understanding of the novel and prompt creates an underdeveloped text. The essay attempts to analyze the effect of elements of style and/or literary elements on theme, but it may be simplistic or replaced by summary. Evidence to support the position may be weak or too few examples are used.
Organization	Organization is exceptional. Ideas move smoothly and comfortably with effective use of transitions enhancing the essay's coherence.	Organization is clear and easy to follow. Transitions are used to move between ideas.	The essay is difficult to follow. It may lack transitions and jump too rapidly between ideas.
Use of Language	Stylistic choices in language are exceptional. The writer successfully weaves textual evidence from the novel into his/her own prose and demonstrates strong control and mastery of standard writing conventions.	Stylistic choices in language are clear and appropriate. The writer weaves textual evidence from the novel into his/her own prose accurately. The writer demonstrates control of standard writing conventions. Though some errors may appear, they do not seriously impede readability.	Stylistic choices in language are less mature. At times, the writer attempts to incorporate textual evidence from the novel into his/her own prose yet may do so awkwardly or inaccurately. There are frequent errors in standard writing conventions that interfere with the meaning.
Evidence of the Writing Process	The essay demonstrates thoughtful planning, significant revision, and careful editing for grammar and conventions in preparing a publishable draft.	The essay demonstrates adequate planning, revision, and editing for grammar and conventions in preparing a publishable draft.	The essay lacks evidence of planning, revision, and/or editing for grammar and conventions. The draft is not ready for publication.

Writing an Analytical Essay

SCORING GUIDE

Scoring Criteria	Exemplary	Proficient	Emerging
Additional Criteria			

Comments:

Learning Focus:

Communicating Myself to Others

"Knowing others is intelligence; knowing yourself is true wisdom."
— Lao Tzu

One of the important goals of academic growth is to become more knowledgeable about what and how you learn, and how you use that knowledge to make future plans for academic study. As the end of school approaches, it is important for you to consider your goals for after high school and to create plans for achieving your goals. These goals will ultimately include the career of your choice and how you plan for that career. Effective self-presentation can be critical to attaining both career and personal goals.

You present yourself every day—in face-to-face situations as well as via media such as the Internet. You joke with others, you tell stories, you try to impress others. You also try to understand yourself: your talents, strengths, weaknesses, challenges, interests, skills. Understanding yourself and your motivation are essential to personal growth and to effective social, academic, and career interactions.

The ability to speak and communicate effectively is often listed by employers as a requirement for high-growth, high-performance jobs. Learning to communicate well and present yourself is a part of academic preparation. To succeed in self-presentation, you need to evaluate modes of communication, such as verbal, nonverbal, and written, and choose among them based on your communication purposes.

You can more effectively communicate yourself by focusing on your purpose, message, audience, context, and feedback from others. You are expected to present yourself in one-on-one situations, as well as in group situations. Learning good communication skills prepares you to be more comfortable and effective as a speaker, listener, and communicator.

My Communication Skills

1. Communication and self-expression are key elements in Zora Neale Hurston's *Their Eyes Were Watching God*. What are the ways that you communicate your voice and sense of self to others?

2. In this class, you have had a number of opportunities to communicate in various ways. Review the work in your portfolio to help you brainstorm a list of occasions and purposes for your communications. Categorize the ways in which you have communicated.

3. On separate paper, create a checklist for being a good communicator in the categories you have identified.

4. How has your understanding of this essential question changed: How do communication skills enhance self-expression?

Career Search

ACTIVITY 4.14

SUGGESTED LEARNING STRATEGIES: KWHL Chart, Discussion Groups, Graphic Organizer, Generating Questions, Role Playing, Notetaking

1. List two or three careers you think you might want to investigate.

2. Use KWHL to determine what you already know and what you need to know about these careers. Use the questions on the next page to help you investigate possible careers.

	What I **K**now (activating prior knowledge)	What I **W**ant to Learn (research questions)	**H**ow I might learn (useful sources)	What I **L**earned (Is this career for me?)
Career 1				
Career 2				
Career 3				

© 2011 College Board. All rights reserved.

Unit 4 • An American Journey 339

3. Some questions you may want to investigate include:
   - What are the characteristics of this career that interest you?
   - What specific skills and abilities are needed to succeed in this career?
   - What are the physical requirements, if any, of the career?
   - What are the opportunities for advancement?
   - What are the educational requirements for the career?
   - Where can a person acquire these qualifications?
   - Is this career continuing to expand or is it in decline?
   - How long does the average person stay in this career?

4. Write your goals for each step of the career pathway below and then add notes in response to the following questions:
   - How do you picture yourself in 10 years? Are you successful? Where are you living?
   - Is there any training or education that you will need in order to reach each step of your career pathway?
   - What skills do you already possess to help you achieve your goals?
   - What people do you know who will help you on your career pathway?

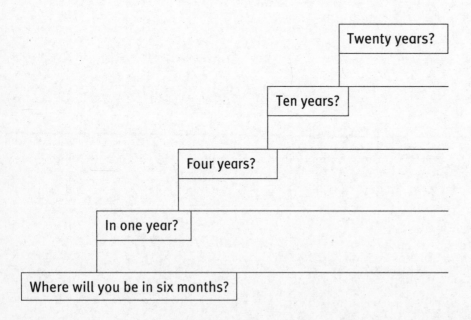

5. You will discuss how interviews are conducted. Use the space below to take notes.

6. Your teacher will pair you with another student. Your task will be to interview one another to gain information to introduce each other to small groups.

7. As you observe each introduction, take notes in the graphic organizer below about what you notice.

Verbal Communication	**Nonverbal Communication**
Includes words, pitch, tone, volume Other:	Includes movement, gestures, facial expressions, eye contact, spatial relations Other:

8. In Activity 4.13, you critiqued your own communication skills. You should now look for alignment between your communication strengths and weaknesses and the demands of the possible career you have chosen. What communication skills do you need to develop and how can you do this? On separate paper, list your goals for developing needed communication skills and an action plan for achieving them.

Creating a Résumé

ACADEMIC VOCABULARY

A **résumé** is a document that presents a person's skills, education, and work history and experience.

1. What is a **résumé**? What is it used for?

2. Advice for creating a successful résumé is plentiful. Locate three Web sites or other resources (such as career advice books) that provide directions or advice for writing a résumé. List the sources below.

3. Evaluate the sources and make a list of the most useful advice, using only what you have found to be valid sources. This advice will become a checklist for helping you edit your résumé. Write down at least six tips below.

4. You have considered how your communication strengths align with requirements of your chosen field. Now brainstorm your experiences that may have helped to prepare you for your chosen field. Think about skills and abilities; your accomplishments; your activities, including volunteer work; your education, including classes you have taken/are taking and books you have read, and so on. You may want to write this information on separate paper to help you prepare for creating your own résumé. Also look at sample résumés, either in books you can find in the local library or online, to evaluate the logic of their sequencing of information.

5. As you draft a résumé, consider these questions: What do I want to say about myself? What rhetoric can I use to "sell myself" to a prospective employer? One way to think about how to sell yourself is to develop a short summary about yourself that gives the highlights of your skills, experience, education, and personality. Try writing a short (2–3 sentences) summary in the space below. Be sure to use diction and tone that align with your purposes.

6. Many models are available to help you organize your résumé. Examine several résumé models, or templates, either through online resources or in career books. Choose a model and draft your résumé on separate paper or using a word processing program.

7. Revise your résumé, using your checklist, and then show your résumé to someone outside the classroom. Ask him or her to write a brief response to your work.

....

TECHNOLOGY TIP If you have appropriate equipment, you may want to create a video résumé. Remember to dress appropriately and present yourself in a professional manner.

Social Networking

Understanding Social Networking Web sites

Quickwrite: Draft a quickwrite about social networking Web sites. Some things to consider: What purpose do they serve? Who uses them? What can you find out about someone by looking at his or her page? What experiences have you had, good and bad, with sites like this?

1. Create and administer a survey about what impression your peers want to send when they customize their personal Web pages and what they do to convey that impression. Share your findings with the class.

2. Three articles dealing with social networking sites follow. As you read these articles, consider how the information and ideas in them affect your understanding of social networking sites. As you read, keep the following questions in mind:

   • What content is appropriate to put on a social networking site?

   • Who are some of the audiences who read these sites?

   • What are some of the standard features of a social networking page?

Narcissism on the Internet isn't risk-free

by Eric Gwinn

A new study argues that self-absorption in college students is at a new high.

"Young people born after 1982 are the most narcissistic generation in recent history," said Jean Twenge, a San Diego State University professor and lead author of the study of college students' attitudes about themselves.

That narcissism is helping to create a generation of Internet users who don't think twice about putting private details online for the world to see.

Blogs and social networking Web sites — such as MySpace and YouTube, where members write and post images and video about their lives and interests - are playing a big role.

"Current technology fuels the increase in narcissism," Twenge said in a statement. "By its very name, MySpace encourages attention-seeking, as does YouTube, whose slogan is 'Broadcast Yourself.'"

The authors of the study — which has tracked college students' attitudes about themselves yearly since 1982 — are not talking about pathological narcissistic personality disorder; just an attitude of "It's all about me."

"People our age really want to explore themselves and see how they compare to other people by posting up Web site profiles," says Patrick Fishbach, a student at Loyola University Chicago.

This generation is rapidly undergoing a bumpy transformation from being merely watchers of content to creators of content. They've learned the visual language of ads and TV shows but aren't remembering to target their messages.

"They're good at being an audience, but not at being the center of attention," says Nancy Baym, associate professor of communication studies at the University of Kansas. "They're thinking about, 'Who am I and how can I show myself to the world?' They're not thinking about parents, teachers, employers and all these other people who can see this."

Much like the cell phone talker who has loud private conversations in public, some users forget that their friends aren't the only ones who get the message.

"I have had friends who have written on their personal blogs about how much they hate their roommate," says Loyola student Dave Frantz, "and then act surprised when the roommate confronts them after having found the blog."

Social networks help young adults quickly keep tabs on friends. It's quicker to visit online profiles to see pictures and read short notes documenting last night's party than it is to talk about it over the phone. In the time it takes to have one phone conversation, you can flit among friends'

My Notes

WORD CONNECTIONS

Audience comes from the Latin verb *audire* meaning "to hear." From the same word come *audio, audition, audible*, and *audit*.

My Notes

profiles to read what they're doing and to leave notes of approval — and read notes they left for you on your profile.

"If you told someone, 'Call your 30 best friends today,' they wouldn't do it," says Kent Lindstrom, of the pioneering social networking site Friendster. "But they will use social networking to check in with 30 friends."

Besides thinking only their friends will see their posts, many social network users feel they're a small fish in an enormous pond, virtually invisible to anyone who might want to harm them.

"Some of them think, 'Who would be really that interested in my life? There are 6 million Sarahs out there. Who would pick me out of the pile?'" says Amanda Lenhart, who studies social networking for the Pew Internet & American Life Project. "It's about putting yourself out there for your friends."

"It's an obvious concept now, but it wasn't always," Lindstrom says. "It's similar to instant messaging or e-mail or search engines – there was a point where it didn't exist, and then when it came, you couldn't live without it."

Experts suggest all Internet users take a page from Apple and other large companies, and manage and protect their identities: Don't log into your profile at a public computer (you can leave behind your password for others to discover); let only people you know view your profile; and when you get an invite from someone you don't know, find out as much as you can about that person before accepting the invite.

"Having a blog or being part of a social network site doesn't increase risk," says David Finkelhor, a professor at the University of New Hampshire who has been tracking teens' online exposure to unwanted adult content. "Get filtering and blocking software, and be judicious about whom you talk to and the topics they raise."

"We should start thinking of ourselves as brands and control our message," Baym says. "That's what we're doing when we put ourselves out there. People don't have a sense of their identity as something they have property rights to."

Web of Risks

Students adore social-networking sites like Facebook, but indiscreet postings can mean really big trouble.

by Brad Stone with Robbie Brown

Cameron Walker learned the hard way that sharing information online can have unintended consequences. In 2005, the sophomore at Fisher College in Boston organized a student petition dedicated to getting a campus guard fired and posted it on the popular college social network Facebook.com. Walker wrote that the guard "loves to antagonize students ... and needs to be eliminated." It was a poor choice of words. Another student informed school officials, who logged on and interpreted the comments as threatening. Though Walker claimed he was trying only to expose the guard's demeanor, he was expelled. He's now enrolled at another college and admits he made a serious mistake. "I was a naive 21-year-old," he says.

Creating a page on a social-networking site is now a cherished form of self-expression at universities around the world. Students use ad-supported services like Facebook, MySpace, TagWorld and Bebo to make friends, plan their social lives and project their personalities. The most popular site among college students is Facebook, with more than 8 million members. A student's personal Facebook page is usually a revealing, dynamic chronicle of campus life—one clearly not meant for the eyes of parents, teachers or anyone else older than 25.

But adults are taking notice. Sites like Facebook are accessible to nearly anyone willing to spend the time to gain access: teachers, school administrators, even potential employers and the police. Such online services can create the illusion of privacy where none actually exists. Facebook, in particular, was designed to emphasize privacy and intimacy. Only other users at your school (with the same college e-mail domain name), and those in networks you join, can see your home page. But determined off-campus visitors can persuade a student or alumnus to help them access the student's page.

What happens when the identity you reveal to friends suddenly overwhelms the façade you present to grown-ups? The results can be awkward—or worse. Photos from drunken parties, recollections of sexual escapades, profanity or threats—all these indiscretions, posted online, have gotten students suspended or expelled, or harmed job prospects. In a couple of decades, a presidential candidate may be called on to answer for a college misadventure that he or she impetuously detailed in a blog entry.

Harvard student Marc Zuckerberg and a few classmates designed Facebook in 2003 to facilitate contact among students. After it launched in early 2004, the service spread like the flu in a freshman dorm, first at Harvard and then to all 2,100 four-year colleges. Last year the company opened its

My Notes

WORD CONNECTIONS

Illusion comes from the Latin verb *ludere* meaning "to play." Other words that come from the same word are *ludicrous, delude, allude, prelude, collusion.*

My Notes

digital doors to high schoolers. Early on, Zuckerberg left college and moved his fledgling enterprise to Silicon Valley, raising more than $35 million in venture capital. Facebook now has 100 employees and is supported by big advertisers like Apple and MasterCard.

Facebook's founders worried about privacy. That's why it isn't one big network but a series of connected smaller ones. "We decided early on that you get better information flow and more trust if you limit access to just those around you," says Zuckerberg. Besides restricting access to a student's classmates, Facebook offers extra privacy tools. Students can limit parts of their pages, such as photos, to specific people. Still, just 17 percent of customers ever change those privacy settings.

For many students, Facebook is not only an interactive diary and yearbook, but a pervasive way to stay in touch. Mitchell Perley, an Atlanta-born student at the University of Edinburgh in Scotland, is typical. On his page there's a photo with a friend at Disneyland, mentions of his membership in such Facebook groups as the Krispy Kreme Appreciation Society and listings of his favorite musicians and films. Perhaps most important, his page is linked to the pages of 99 friends at his college and 845 back home at various U.S. schools.

But not everyone's Facebook experiences have been positive. Brad Davis was a freshman at Emory in Atlanta in 2005 when he and friends commemorated a night of drinking by posting photos of themselves in their dorm, hoisting their libations. They created a Facebook group called the Dobbs 2nd Floor Alcoholics, named after their dorm. A dorm adviser saw the photos and reported the underage imbibers. The school ordered Davis and his friends to hang anti-drinking posters on their walls, and a citation went on their records.

The consequences for Jason Johnson were more serious. He was a student at the University of the Cumberlands, a Southern Baptist school in Williamsburg, Ky., when he created his own MySpace page. Visitors to his page could hear a favorite song, learn his birthday or find out he was gay. But Cumberlands' student handbook states that students must lead a "Christian life-style," which the school president explained included a ban on homosexuality. When school officials discovered Johnson's page, he was expelled. He hired a lawyer, who got the school to rescind the expulsion and let Johnson transfer with his academic record intact.

Students' indiscriminate postings may also get them into trouble when they're applying for a job or to graduate school. The postings could still be accessible online despite students' efforts to delete them. Even though companies are loath to admit it, researching candidates on social networks is becoming as easy and prevalent as entering their names into Google. Laurie Sybel, a director of career development at Vermont Technical College, had never looked at Facebook until she got a call from a big company about the internship application of a 19-year-old. The student was being rejected, Sybel recalls, because executives had viewed the student's Facebook page, which contained a photo of him holding a bottle of vodka. The company noted that the student was not only apparently breaking the law but demonstrating bad judgment by publishing the photo. In response, Vermont Technical, like other colleges, now integrates tips for social-network decorum into its career-guidance workshops.

Not all students want to temper their behavior. They point out that the Internet lets them express themselves and find like-minded souls. Still, adults aren't likely to stop prying any time soon. That means students who use Facebook and MySpace have a new burden. The Web may seem ephemeral, but what you casually post one night might just last a digital eternity. While social networking represents a powerful tool for today's students, they're advised to be prudent. Even if they have no plans to run for president someday.

GRAMMAR & USAGE

Notice that the writer does not choose to quote Sybel directly. Instead Sybel's words are summarized; the summary allows the writer to condense a large amount of information into a smaller space than direct quotations would take.

My Notes

My Notes

Article

Potential employers monitoring student social networking Web sites

by Matt McGowan

LUBBOCK, Texas — The next time a student learns he or she has been tagged in a photo from the last weekend's party on www.facebook.com or www.myspace.com, it may be in his or her best interest to take a look.

With more than 37,000 people on Facebook's Texas Tech University network and countless more on MySpace, students clearly are using social networking sites, but so are their future bosses.

According to a 2006 study conducted by CareerBuilder.com, 12 percent of hiring managers searched their applicants' social networking profiles before hiring them. Of those who checked job candidates' online network profiles, 63 percent did not hire an applicant based on what they had found on those sites.

CareerBuilder offers three tips when it comes to personal Web pages, said Theresa Chu, senior career adviser for the company: be careful, be prepared and be discreet.

Students can be careful by not posting anything on their own or their friends' sites that they would not want an employer to see, she said. They can be prepared by anticipating any questions employers might have after investigating their personal pages.

Discreetness, Chu said, comes through closely monitoring who has access to their online profiles and access to what applicants write on others' profiles.

"You can control what you put on your site, but you can't always control your friends," she said. "In terms of the comment function or being able to write on your wall on Facebook, you just want to make sure you're monitoring those comments. If you find that it's getting out of control, completely turn that function off."

Carol Albert, operations manager at the Eastridge Group, a multi-state group of staffing companies, said she has been in the hiring business for 16 years and routinely references applicants' profiles on social networks after an interview and before hiring them, especially for permanent or professional positions — positions college students often fill.

"For our permanent staff, our professional staff, it's worth a look," she said. "It's one of the tools, and it's becoming more and more useful now, because practically everybody has a MySpace page."

During 2005, in a study conducted by the National Association of Colleges and Employers, 11 percent of employers reported referencing an applicant's social networking site before hiring him or her, said Andrea Koncz, employment information manager for the association.

In a similar study conducted by the association in 2007, the number rose to 17 percent.

David Kraus, managing director of the Tech Career Service, said employers are turning to social networking sites more and more to take a closer look at job candidates, a trend that has and will continue to grow.

Because networking sites like Facebook and MySpace have become more popular in recent years, Kraus said, employers have caught wind and are utilizing their potential for background checks.

"Five years from now, or one year from now, who's to say there won't be something else that replaces that?" Kraus asked. "I don't know what it'll be, and it might take employers a few years to latch on to that, too."

When it comes to the content of social network profiles, Jay Killough, employer relations coordinator for the university's career service, said common sense and good judgment often are good indicators of where to draw the line between acceptable and scandalous. He recommends not post anything "your grandmother wouldn't approve of.". . .

My Notes

Social Networking

Building a Rubric to Evaluate Social Networking Pages

1. Work with your Embedded Assessment discussion group to create norms for appropriate self-presentation on a social networking page, based on what your group has learned about these sites and their potential audiences. Build consensus about what content should and should not appear on a page.

2. Next, collaborate to create a rubric for evaluating a page in terms of its appropriateness for audiences discussed in the articles. Choose three or more labels to define the levels. These will go across the top of the rubric.

3. With your group, list the standard features of a social networking page. Add these down the left side of the rubric.

4. Take a critical look at a page, considering visual appeal, and add descriptions for visual appeal to your rubric.

5. Fill in the rubric with short descriptions that clearly define criteria in each level for each feature.

6. As a group, create a social networking page for one of the characters in *Their Eyes Were Watching God*.

7. Use your rubric to evaluate a page. Revise your rubric if needed.

8. Use this rubric to guide the creation of your page that you will be sharing as part of Embedded Assessment 2. Your page can be a real page that you print to show your classmates or it can be a mock-up of a page.

Practicing for a Job Interview

SUGGESTED LEARNING STRATEGIES: Brainstorming, Discussion Groups, Notetaking, Role Playing, Generating Questions, Sharing and Responding, Graphic Organizer

An interview can be stressful for both the interviewer and the interviewee, but practicing can alleviate some of the anxiety. Your teacher will form you into groups to complete the following activities:

1. Study a sample résumé, and brainstorm questions that would help you learn more about the person who created the résumé. Take notes on separate paper. Evaluate the sequence of information in the résumé.

2. Now combine with another group for sharing and responding about the questions generated. Discuss what makes a good interview question, making a list of the qualities of good questions that you will use when you interview a classmate. Add the list to your notes.

3. In your original groups, revise your interview questions to reflect the guidelines your group agreed upon.

4. Now that you have practiced creating a résumé and have looked at a résumé from the viewpoint of an interviewer, how has your understanding of what a résumé is and what it can do been expanded?

5. Thinking from the perspective of another person is an important communication skill. Reread your interview questions from the point of view of an interviewee. How would you answer each question? Take notes to capture your thinking about how you would present yourself as you answer the questions.

6. Tone and diction are both important in an interview situation. Decide what tone you want to convey and how you might do that. What kind of diction would be appropriate in an interview situation?

Practicing for a Job Interview

You will role play a panel interview, using the questions your group generated. You should rotate roles, so that everyone gets a chance to interview and to be interviewed. You will use the fishbowl strategy so that students in the outer circle can provide feedback. When you are in the outer circle, you will observe one person involved in the role play. Take specific notes about all aspects of communication that you observe during the interview. Create a graphic organizer for notetaking; you might use the following format or develop one of your own.

I am observing: _____

Role (circle one): Interviewer   Interviewee

Verbal Responses I Heard	My Thoughts
Nonverbal Behaviors I Observed	My Thoughts

2. After the role play and feedback on your interview, take a moment to reflect on the experience. Think about what you have learned and how this learning will affect your work for Embedded Assessment 2. Write your answer in the space below.

3. Work with your group to set norms for the panel interview for Embedded Assessment 2 so that the experience will be a positive one for everyone involved. Make sure that everyone in the group has a copy of the norms.

Using Communication Skills to Present Myself

SUGGESTED LEARNING STRATEGIES: **Drafting, Self-Editing/
Peer Editing, Discussion Groups**

Assignment

Your assignment is to showcase the communication skills that you have developed in an interview with a panel of your peers in which you present your résumé and your media presentation about yourself.

Steps

1. Consider how you want to present yourself in the panel interview. For example, which of your strengths do you want to make sure the members of the panel notice? Create a plan for your self-presentation.

2. Create a résumé and revise it using the résumé checklist that your class generated.

3. Create a media presentation about yourself in the form of a social networking page and revise it based on the rubric your class agreed upon.

4. Within your Embedded Assessment group, assign roles for the interview panel process. In each round, the roles include interviewee, at least two interviewers, and at least two observers. Set a schedule for interviews within the deadlines set by your teacher.

5. Share your résumé and media presentation drafts with the members of your group who will be interviewing you.

6. When you receive the résumé(s) and media presentation(s) of the group member(s) you will be interviewing, work with your partner(s) to write interview questions.

7. Complete the interview process. After each interview, every group member should write a reflection about the roles they played: interviewer, interviewee, or observer.

SCORING GUIDE

Scoring Criteria	Exemplary	Proficient	Emerging
Résumé	The content and organization of the résumé thoroughly showcase the individual's strengths and skills. The tone and diction are positive and direct. The format follows standard résumé conventions. The overall impression of the résumé conveys a highly positive picture of the individual.	The content and organization of the résumé provide accurate details about the individual's background and experience. It demonstrates an understanding of standard résumé conventions. The overall impression of the résumé is adequate, but not highly persuasive about the individual.	The content and organization of the résumé are unclear or disorganized at times in a way that distracts from showcasing the individual. There are frequent errors in standard conventions. There is little or no evidence that the résumé has undergone revisions to sell the individual's details.
Media Presentation	The media presentation is engaging, well-organized, and effectively addresses the intended audience. Information is skillfully communicated.	The media presentation is interesting and accurately addresses the intended audience. Information is clearly communicated.	The media presentation is confusing at times and does little to address the intended audience. Information is difficult to follow.
Process	Throughout the entire process of planning and presenting, the group cooperates and works successfully to maintain purpose and to achieve goals.	Throughout the process of planning and presenting, the group cooperates and works together adequately.	Throughout the process of planning and presenting, the group's cooperation is lacking and impedes their ability to maintain a purpose or achieve goals.
Reflection	The reflective text perceptively and thoroughly analyzes each group member's participation and learning from the perspective of each role: interviewer, interviewee, and observer.	The reflective text clearly and adequately analyzes participation and learning from the perspective of each role: interviewer, interviewee, and observer.	The reflective text fails to sufficiently analyze participation and learning from the perspective of each role: interviewer, interviewee, and observer.

SCORING GUIDE

Scoring Criteria	Exemplary	Proficient	Emerging
Additional Criteria			

Comments:

Reflection

An important aspect of growing as a learner is to reflect on where you have been, what you have accomplished, what helped you to learn, and how you will apply your new knowledge in the future. Use the following questions to guide your thinking and to identify evidence of your learning. Use separate notebook paper.

Thinking about Concepts

1. Using specific examples from this unit, respond to the Essential Questions:

   • How can an author's style construct and reflect identity?

   • How do communication skills enhance self-expression?

2. Consider the new academic vocabulary from this unit (**Motif, Résumé**) as well as academic vocabulary from previous units and select 3–4 terms of which your understanding has grown. For each term, answer the following questions:

   • What was your understanding of the word prior to the unit?

   • How has your understanding of the word evolved throughout the unit?

   • How will you apply your understanding in the future?

Thinking about Connections

3. Review the activities and products (artifacts) you created. Choose those that most reflect your growth or increase in understanding.

4. For each artifact that you choose, record, respond, and reflect on your thinking and understanding, using the following questions as a guide:

   a. What skill/knowledge does this artifact reflect, and how did you learn this skill/knowledge?

   b. How did your understanding of the power of language expand through your engagement with this artifact?

   c. How will you apply this skill or knowledge in the future?

5. Create this reflection as Portfolio pages—one for each artifact you choose. Use the following model for your headings and commentary on questions.

Thinking About Thinking
Portfolio Entry

Concept:

Description of Artifact:

Commentary on Questions:

The Pursuit of
Happiness

Essential Questions

? What does it mean to
pursue happiness?

? How does a writer
represent research
through multiple texts?

Unit Overview

The pursuit of happiness is an integral part of
the American Dream and part of the foundation
of this country. Many people think that the
fulfillment of the American Dream centers on
financial success; however, riches are not the
path to happiness for everyone. In this unit, you
will examine how one person rejected wealth
in favor of a different pathway to happiness;
you will also look at how others have found
enlightenment in everyday experiences. Next,
you will research the American Dream and the
pursuit of happiness and articulate what that
dream means to you and your fellow Americans.

Unit 5

The Pursuit of Happiness

Contents

Goals

▶ To analyze and evaluate the structural and stylistic features of texts

▶ To compose a personal essay that employs stylistic techniques

▶ To synthesize research into a multi-genre research paper

ACADEMIC VOCABULARY

Coherence

Genre Conventions

Discourse

Texts not included in these materials.

Learning Focus:

The Search for Self

What does it mean to pursue happiness? Do we have a right to pursue happiness at all costs? In *Into the Wild,* the primary text you will study in the first half of the unit, Jon Krakauer explores this very idea, by investigating the life and death of a young man with an adventurous spirit, Chris McCandless.

Nonfiction texts such as *Into the Wild* can tell a compelling story as effectively as a fiction text. A good biographer uses all the literary elements associated with conveying ideas persuasively and retelling a story well to engage the reader.

Because biography is focused on telling the story of a real person whose experiences are deemed worthy of our attention, the biographer has the burden of making the life chronicled relevant to our own lives.

In this biography, using multiple genres to illuminate his subject, Krakauer investigates the circumstances surrounding the tragic fate of a young man with his heart set on discovering life and uncovering the true meaning of happiness. Working from extensive primary and secondary research, Krakauer presents a meditative account of the events leading up to McCandless's death, inviting the reader to evaluate McCandless's pursuit and at the same time to examine the biographer's perspective on events. Just like Krakauer, the reader cannot escape contemplating and evaluating his own beliefs and values associated with the pursuit of happiness as we follow Chris McCandless's story.

Independent Reading: In this unit, you will read texts that explore the pursuit of happiness and search for self. For independent reading, choose an autobiography, biography, memoir, or a collection of essays or short stories that explore this thematic concept.

Previewing the Unit

Essential Questions

What does it mean to pursue happiness?

How does a writer represent research through multiple texts?

Unit Overview and Learning Focus

Predict what you think this unit is about. Use the words or phrases that stood out to you when you read the Unit Overview and the Learning Focus.

Embedded Assessment

What knowledge must you have (what do you need to know) to succeed on the Embedded Assessment? What skills must you have (what must you be able to do to complete the Embedded Assessment successfully)?

Searching for Meaning

1. Review ideas of Transcendentalism and identify the core tenets of this literary movement or tradition.

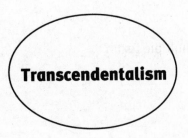

Transcendentalism

2. Work collaboratively with your peers to generate a working definition of Transcendentalism.

3. Read the passages on the next page and infer each author's perspective on the meaning and pursuit of happiness. Deductively apply the criteria of Transcendentalism to Tupac's poem and generate responses to these questions.

   • How does "In the Depths of Solitude" adhere to the core tenets of Transcendentalism?

   • What other contemporary literature aligns with the core tenets of Transcendentalism? Explain your choices.

from *Walden,* by Henry David Thoreau

…I went to the woods because I wished to live deliberately, to front only the essential facts of life, and see if I could not learn what it had to teach, and not, when I came to die discover that I had not lived. I did not wish to live what was not life, living is so dear; nor did I wish to practice resignation, unless it was quite necessary. I wanted to live deep and suck out all the marrow of life, to live sturdy and Spartanlike as to put to rout all that was not life…to drive life to a corner and reduce it to its lowest terms, and, if it proved to be mean, why then to get the whole and genuine meanness of it, and publish its meanness to the world; or if it were sublime, to know it by experience, and be able to give a true account of it in my next excursion.

from *Self-Reliance,* by Ralph Waldo Emerson

There is a time in every man's education when he arrives at the conviction that envy is ignorance; that imitation is suicide; that he must take himself for better, for worse, as his portion. …Trust thyself: Every heart vibrates to that iron string…. Great men have always done so and confided in themselves childlike to the genius of their age.

In the Depths of Solitude, by Tupac

I exist in the depths of solitude	
Pondering my true goal	
Trying to find peace of mind	
And still preserve my soul	
Constantly yearning to be accepted	5
And from all receive respect	
Never compromising but sometimes risky	
And that is my only regret	
A young heart with an old soul	
How can there be peace	10
How can I be in the depths of solitude	
When there are two inside of me	
This Duo within me causes	
The perfect opportunity	
To learn and live twice as fast	15
As those who accept simplicity	

WORD CONNECTIONS

Confide uses the Latin root *-fid-* meaning "to trust." This root is also found in *confidence*, *fidelity*, and *affadavit*.

My Credo

Quickwrite: What are some of the rules you learned in kindergarten? To what extent are those rules still applicable to your life today?

1. A **precept** is a rule, instruction, or principle that guides one's actions and/or moral behavior. Consider some of the precepts you have learned over the course of your life that guide your behavior and why they are significant to you. Write them in the graphic organizer below.

Precepts	Rationale, Significance, or Reflection

Credo from

All I Really Need to Know I Learned in Kindergarten

by Robert Fulghum

> **ABOUT THE AUTHOR**
> Robert Fulghum (b. 1937) grew up in Texas. He was a minister for many years before turning to writing, painting, and sculpting. He is the author of several best-selling books that primarily focus on thoughts about how to live a full and happy life. Fulghum has said, "The tragedy of modern man is not that he knows less and less about the meaning of his own life but that it bothers him less and less."

Each spring, for many years, I have set myself the task of writing a personal statement of belief: a Credo. When I was younger, the statement ran for many pages, trying to cover every base, with no loose ends. It sounded like a Supreme Court brief, as if words could resolve all conflicts about the meaning of existence.

The Credo has grown shorter in recent years—sometimes cynical, sometimes comical, sometimes bland—but I keep working at it. Recently I set out to get the statement of personal belief down to one page in simple terms, fully understanding the naïve idealism that implied…

I realized then that I already know most of what's necessary to live a meaningful life—that it isn't all that complicated. I know it. And have known it for a long, long time. Living it—well, that's another matter, yes? Here's my Credo:

All I really need to know about how to live and what to do and how to be I learned in kindergarten. Wisdom was not at the top of the graduate-school mountain, but there in the sand pile at Sunday school. These are the things I learned:

Share everything.

Play fair.

Don't hit people.

My Notes

How does the author's diction define the tone and advance the theme?

My Notes

How do Fulghum's syntax and punctuation convey tone and theme?

Put things back where you found them.

Clean up your own mess!

Don't take things that aren't yours.

Say you're sorry when you hurt somebody.

Wash your hands before you eat.

Flush.

Warm cookies and cold milk are good for you.

Live a balanced life—learn some and think some and draw and paint and sing and dance and play and work every day some.

Take a nap every afternoon.

When you go out into the world, watch out for traffic, hold hands, and stick together.

Be aware of wonder. Remember the little seed in the Styrofoam cup: The roots go down and the plant goes up and nobody really knows how or why, but we are all like that.

Goldfish and hamsters and white mice and even the little seed in the Styrofoam cup—they all die. So do we.

And then remember the Dick-and-Jane books and the first word you learned—the biggest word of all—LOOK.

…Think what a better world it would be if we all—the whole world—had cookies and milk about three o'clock every afternoon and then lay down with our blankies for a nap. Or if all governments had as a basic policy to always put things back where they found them and to clean up their own mess. And it is still true, no matter how old you are—when you go out into the world, it is best to hold hands and stick together.

GRAMMAR & USAGE

When Fulghum writes a series with a conjunction after every term, he is using **polysyndeton**: "Goldfish and hamsters and white mice and even the little seed…."

This rhetorical device puts emphasis on every item in the series—more so than if he had separated the items with commas and used a conjunction only before the final item.

Writing Prompt: Emulating Fulghum's style, on your own paper, draft a personal credo that asserts your precepts about the basic values that contribute to a meaningful life. Establish a specific tone, using diction, detail, and syntax. The credo might begin with your perception of life, identify where you learned important precepts, then identify those precepts, and finally offer a reflective closing remark.

Fulghum's credo is memorable and effective, not just because of the ideas, but because of his syntax.

"**Syntax** refers to the way words are arranged within sentences. How writers control and manipulate the sentence is a strong determiner of voice and imparts personality to the writing." Nancy Dean

Some of the elements of syntax are word order, sentence length, and punctuation. Punctuation can reinforce meaning, create a particular effect, and express the writer's voice. Look at the purpose of three punctuation marks:

- The dash marks a sudden change in thought or tone, sets off a brief summary, or sets off a parenthetical part of the sentence. A dash often conveys a casual tone.

- The colon directs reader attention to the words that follow. It is also used between independent clauses if the second summarizes or explains the first. A colon sets the expectation that important, closely related information will follow, giving emphasis to the words after the colon.

- The ellipsis usually represents words omitted from a quote or a pause.

2. Review Fulghum's text, and use the graphic organizer that follows to explore how sentence length and punctuation contribute to his tone or theme. Find specific examples of Fulghum's sentences that contain the element of syntax listed in the first column. Explain its function in the credo and how it advances the tone or theme of the text. In the last column, use the examples to guide a revision of a sentence in the draft of your credo.

3. After completing the graphic organizer, revise your draft to incorporate revisions of your syntax.

LITERARY TERMS

Syntax is the arrangement of words and the order of grammatical elements in a sentence. The way in which words, phrases, clauses, and sentences are put together contribute to conveying a writer's meaning.

WORD CONNECTIONS

When solving analogies, read the analogy as a sentence and try out each answer choice in the sentence to see which forms a correct relationship. For example, in the analogy ice : refrigerator :: battery : _____, answer choices may be case, flashlight, electric, or charger. What is the primary relationship? The refrigerator holds ice; which of the other words fits this relationship?

My Credo

Elements	Examples and Function of Fulghum's Syntax	Revision of Your Sentence
Simple Sentence		
Compound Sentence with Parallel Structure		
Dash		
Colon		
Ellipsis		

Just the Facts

SUGGESTED LEARNING STRATEGIES: Graphic Organizer, Notetaking, Discussion Groups, Brainstorming, Previewing, Close Reading

1. The cover of a book serves a crucial purpose: to entice readers to purchase or check out the book. Examine carefully the cover of *Into The Wild*. In the left column, record all the details you observe for each heading provided. In the right column, write why you think the cover designers made these specific choices and the effects of each choice.

Details You Observe	Effect of These Choices
Use of Color	
Photographic Image	
Key Words and Phrases	
Overall Effectiveness of the Cover Design	

2. List the facts stated on the front cover:

This information is presented in a fairly straightforward way. As you may know, different kinds of publications can present "the facts" quite differently, depending on the slant or particular angle on the story. Jon Krakauer's first piece of writing about Christopher McCandless was an article for *Outside* magazine. Krakauer wrote that article with a knowledge that his audience, the readers of *Outside,* would be interested in particular aspects of McCandless's story. For example, Krakauer writes about the terrain of the Alaskan wilderness and the supplies McCandless brought with him, understanding that his audience would be interested in this information.

3. Using just the facts you have read about Christopher McCandless, you will create a headline and lead for an article in a particular kind of publication. First, you will need to determine the target audience for the publication your teacher gives you and the strategies the publication uses to reach that target audience.

- Skim through the publication, examining the kinds of articles, the reading level, and especially the advertisements. Who seems to be the target audience? Consider such factors as age group, gender, level of education, ethnicity, and special interests.

- Organize your observations on a bubble cluster or other graphic organizer on a separate sheet of paper.

- Now look at the headlines of the articles. On your graphic organizer, make notes about the level of diction, the punctuation used, and any other features that you notice.

- Examine the lead, or first paragraph, of several of the articles. If you are going to imitate the style of this kind of publication, what will you need to do?

4. Using the notes you have taken and the few facts you know about Christopher McCandless, on separate paper write the headline and lead for an article in the kind of publication you have examined.

Looking at Structure

SUGGESTED LEARNING STRATEGIES: Think-Pair-Share, Marking the Text, Graphic Organizer

Biography

ABOUT THE AUTHOR
Jon Krakauer (b. 1954) started climbing mountains at age 8. He has chronicled his experiences in two best-selling books, *Into the Wild* and *Into Thin Air*. He wrote *Into Thin Air* after a failed expedition to climb Mt. Everest. The book earned him a nomination for the Pulitzer Prize.

From *Into the Wild*

by Jon Krakauer

My Notes

AUTHOR'S NOTE

1   In April 1992, a young man from a well-to-do East Coast family hitchhiked to Alaska and walked alone into the wilderness north of Mt. McKinley. Four months later his decomposed body was found by a party of moose hunters.

2   Shortly after the discovery of the corpse, I was asked by the editor of *Outside* magazine to report on the puzzling circumstances of the boy's death. His name turned out to be Christopher Johnson McCandless. He'd grown up, I learned, in an affluent suburb of Washington, D.C., where he'd excelled academically and had been an elite athlete.

3   Immediately after graduating, with honors, from Emory University in the summer of 1990, McCandless dropped out of sight. He changed his name, gave the entire balance of a twenty-four thousand-dollar savings account to charity, abandoned his car and most of his possessions, burned all the cash in his wallet. And then he invented a new life for himself, taking up residence at the ragged margin of our society, wandering across North America in search of raw, transcendent experience. His family had no idea where he was or what had become of him until his remains turned up in Alaska.

4   Working on a tight deadline, I wrote a nine-thousand-word-article, which ran in the January 1993 issue of the magazine, but my fascination with McCandless remained long after that issue of *Outside* was replaced on the newsstands by more current journalistic fare. I was haunted by the particulars of the boy's starvation and by vague, unsettling parallels between events in his life and those in my own. Unwilling to let McCandless go, I spent more than a year retracing the convoluted

path that led to his death in the Alaska taiga, chasing down details of his peregrinations with an interest that bordered on obsession. In trying to understand McCandless, I inevitably came to reflect on other, larger subjects as well: the grip wilderness has on the American imagination, the allure high-risk activities hold for young men of a certain mind, the complicated, highly charged bond that exists between fathers and sons. The result of this meandering inquiry is the book now before you.

5   I won't claim to be an impartial biographer. McCandless's strange tale struck a personal note that made a dispassionate rendering of the tragedy impossible. Through most of the book, I have tried – and largely succeeded, I think – to minimize my authorial presence. But let the reader be warned: I interrupt McCandless's story with fragments of a narrative drawn from my own youth. I do so in the hope that my experiences will throw some oblique light on the enigma of Chris McCandless.

6   He was an extremely intense young man and possessed a streak of stubborn idealism that did not mesh readily with modern existence. Long captivated by the writing of Leo Tolstoy, McCandless particularly admired how the great novelist had forsaken a life of wealth and privilege to wander among the destitute. In college McCandless began emulating Tolstoy's asceticism and moral rigor to a degree that first astonished, and then alarmed, those who were close to him. When the boy headed off into the Alaska bush, he entertained no illusions that he was trekking into a land of milk and honey; peril, adversity, and Tolstoyan renunciation were precisely what he was seeking. And that is what he found, in abundance.

7   For most of the sixteen-week ordeal, nevertheless, McCandless more than held his own. Indeed, were it not for one or two seemingly insignificant blunders, he would have walked out of the woods in August 1992 as anonymously as he had walked into them in April. Instead, his innocent mistakes turned out to be pivotal and irreversible, his name became the stuff of tabloid headlines, and his bewildered family was left clutching the shards of a fierce and painful love.

8   A surprising number of people have been affected by the story of Chris McCandless's life and death. In the weeks and months following the publication of the article in *Outside*, it generated more mail than any other article in the magazine's history. This correspondence, as one might expect, reflected sharply divergent points of view: some readers admired the boy immensely for his courage and noble ideals; others fulminated that he was a reckless idiot, a wacko, a narcissist who perished out of arrogance and stupidity—and was undeserving of the considerable media attention he received. My convictions should be apparent soon enough, but I will leave it to the reader to form his or her own opinion of Chris McCandless.

Jon Krakauer

Seattle

GRAMMAR & USAGE

Notice that Krakauer uses the adverbs *indeed* and *instead* as transitional words to open his sentences. As opening adverbs, they are followed by a comma. Here they help Krakauer emphasize his points. They can also be used to join two main clauses in a **compound sentence**, but they must be preceded by a semicolon and followed by a comma.

Meeting Christopher McCandless

SUGGESTED LEARNING STRATEGIES: **Close Reading, Graphic Organizer, Think-Pair-Share, Drafting**

Now that you have read a few chapters of *Into the Wild*, you have caught a glimpse of the enigmatic young man at the heart of the story. Although Krakauer is crafting a work of nonfiction, he employs many of the same techniques used in writing fiction. For example, he allows the reader to get to know Chris McCandless in the same ways that fiction authors use characterization. Write what you know of Christopher McCandless so far; you will add to the chart as you learn more.

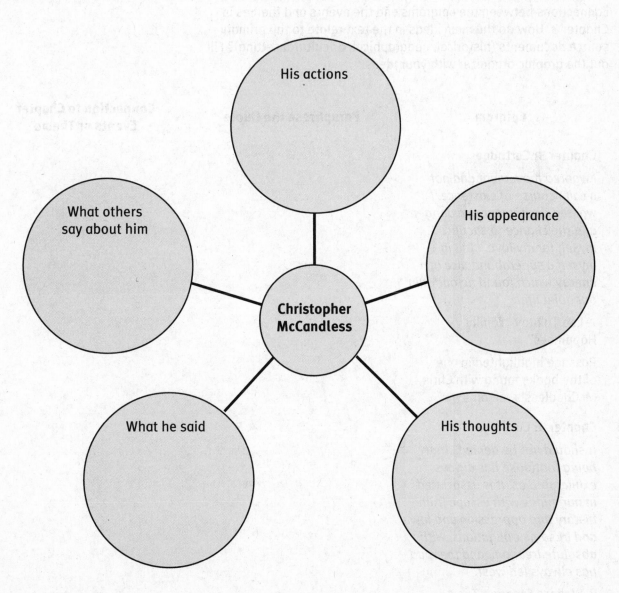

Literary Connections

1. Use an appropriate resource (such as a dictionary, thesaurus, glossary, literary handbook, or online resource) to define *epigram*.

2. Look at the epigrams that begin Chapter 3 below. Think about the connections between the epigrams and the events and themes in Chapter 3. How do the main ideas in the text relate to the primary source documents (historical, geographical, or cultural setting)? Fill out the graphic organizer with your ideas.

Epigram	Paraphrase the Quote	Connection to Chapter Events or Theme
Chapter 3: Carthage *I wanted movement and not a calm course of existence. I wanted excitement and danger and the chance to sacrifice myself for my love. I felt in myself a superabundance of energy which found no outlet in our quiet life.* —Leo Tolstoy "Family Happiness" Passage highlighted in one of the books found with Chris McCandless's remains		
Chapter 3: Carthage *It should not be denied...that being footloose has always exhilarated us. It is associated in our minds with escape from history and oppression and law and irksome obligations, with absolute freedom, and the road has always led west.* —Wallace Stegner, *The American West as Living Space*		

3. Read Chapters 4–7. Your teacher will assign you to a discussion group. Your group will take one of the chapters and analyze the connections between the chapter title, the epigram, and the chapter's events. Write an interpretive statement that sums up your analysis. Then identify and discuss the tenets of Transcendentalism that appear in the chapter. Record quotes that illuminate this philosophy.

Epigram/Chapter Title	Connections to Events/Theme	Interpretive Statement

Transcendentalism Quotes

4. What is the effect of Krakauer's use of epigrams from literary works in terms of conveying information and engaging the reader? What is the effect when the epigram is from McCandless's own writings?

5. Pair-share responses to the unit's Essential Question: What does it mean to pursue happiness?

Quickwrite: On separate paper, reflect on what the pursuit of happiness means to you. Use details in your description.

Shedding Light

One method Krakauer uses to reveal Christopher McCandless is by telling stories of people who are in some ways *foils* to McCandless. In Chapters 8 and 9, Krakauer introduces Gene Rosellini, John Mallon Waterman, Carl McCunn, Everett Ruess, and the Irish monks known as *papar*. Reread their stories and identify how these stories shed light on Chris McCandless.

Gene Rosellini	
John Mallon Waterman	
Carl McCunn	
Everett Ruess	
Irish monks known as *papar*	

What have you learned about Chris McCandless from these stories?

Many Ways of Showing

SUGGESTED LEARNING STRATEGIES: **Skimming/Scanning, Think-Pair-Share, Graphic Organizer, Quickwrite, Drafting, Brainstorming**

You have probably noticed that Krakauer uses many genres, or kinds of writing, to convey who Christopher McCandless was and how his life and death affected the people he encountered. For example, in Chapter 1, Krakauer uses a map, a postcard, an interview with Jim Gallien, and recreated dialogue based on that interview.

1. Review Chapters 2 through 13 and make a list of all the genres Krakauer uses.

Chapter	Genres Used	Purpose and Conventions of One Genre
1		
2		
3		
4		
5		
6		
7		
8		
9		
10		
11		
12		
13		

Many Ways of Showing

Quickwrite: Choose one of the genres Krakauer uses. Explore why Krakauer may have used that genre, and describe its effect.

Writing Prompt: Think about other material that Krakauer could have included in his book. Then choose two different genres and craft a piece of writing in each genre that could be included in *Into the Wild*. Identify where in the book each would fit. For example, you might write a poem from the point of view of Chris's yellow Datsun that would fit in Chapter 4, when the reader learns that McCandless abandoned his beloved car. You might also write a dialogue showing McCandless interacting with his coworkers and customers at McDonalds that would tie in with Chapter 5.

Bring an example of each of the genres you have chosen and add them to a class collection of genres.

SUGGESTED LEARNING STRATEGIES: **Skimming/Scanning, Graphic Organizer, Marking the Text, Quickwrite**

1. In Chapters 14 and 15, Krakauer answers those who would say that Christopher McCandless had a death wish by providing a compelling narrative of his own Alaskan adventure. Scan the two chapters and complete a Venn diagram to illustrate how McCandless and Krakauer are similar and different.

Quickwrite: Just as Krakauer tells the stories of other adventurers earlier, in Chapters 14 and 15 he tells his own story to shed some light on Christopher McCandless. Based on your understanding of their similarities and differences, what did you learn about McCandless from Krakauer's own story?

Writing Prompt: In some ways, both Jon Krakauer and Christopher McCandless could be called modern-day Transcendentalists. Review your notes on Transcendentalism. On separate paper, explain the ways these two men fit the description of the Transcendentalists.

A Personal Perspective

When Krakauer describes his own experiences in Chapters 14 and 15, he is actually writing a personal essay. You will be writing a personal essay for Embedded Assessment 1. Most personal essays are structured to include three parts:

Event or Incident: The author describes some incident or set of circumstances.

Response: The author describes his or her feelings and thoughts concerning the encounter. This is the initial response, without the benefit of reflection.

Reflection: The author reflects on the incident. This reflection usually occurs some time after the event or incident. In the reflection, the author will often transition from describing a situation *unique to him or her to a discussion more universal in nature.*

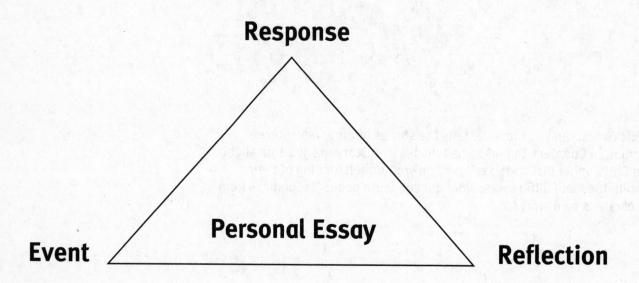

In Krakauer's account of climbing Devil's Thumb, he writes about a significant personal experience in which he learns about his own skills and inner strength. Although you might not have experienced anything as dramatic as a solo mountain climb, you have certainly had experiences that were significant to you. In preparation for Embedded Assessment 1, Writing a Personal Essay, on separate paper list significant experiences of your life and what you learned from each one.

The Pursuit of Happiness

In the *Declaration of Independence*, Thomas Jefferson stated, "We hold these truths to be self-evident, that all men are created equal, that they are endowed by their Creator with certain unalienable rights, that among these are Life, Liberty, and the pursuit of Happiness." It has a nice ring to it, but what does it mean, exactly? Our country is built on a claim that we all have the right to the "pursuit of happiness." *Happiness*, however, is an ambiguous term and means different things to different people.

1. Consult a book of famous quotations or find a Web site that lists famous quotations. Use "happiness" as your subject, and choose a couple of quotes that you find particularly insightful. You may add more quotations on your own paper.

Quotation	
Author	
What does it mean to you?	

Quotation	
Author	
What does it mean to you?	

2. As you read the quotations your classmates selected, locate one that seems to be in opposition to one you selected. Compose a dialogue between the speakers of the two quotations in which they discuss their contradictory views on happiness. Remember to follow the rules for writing dialogue:

- Indent to indicate a change in speaker.

- Put spoken words inside quotation marks.

- Use tag lines (he said, etc.) occasionally to help the reader follow the flow of the conversation.

3. Now that you have read, heard, and written about quotes on the pursuit of happiness, what new understanding do you have of the term?

4. Krakauer, in Chapter 16, reveals that Christopher McCandless's definition of happiness appears to have changed over time. Use the graphic organizer below to track the changes in his definition.

How would Chris have defined happiness?	
May 1992	**July 1992**

Evidence from the Text	

5. Why is the change in McCandless's attitude toward happiness particularly poignant?

At What Cost?

1. It is clear from the interviews Krakauer conducted with the people who encountered Christopher McCandless that he made a lasting impression on many of them. Create a concept map showing all the people McCandless met (and knew) and how his life and death influenced them. Be sure to provide evidence from the text, including page numbers.

2. Reread what Billie McCandless, Chris's mother, says at the end of the Epilogue. Do you think most of the people who knew Chris would agree? Explain.

Searching for the Author

SUGGESTED LEARNING STRATEGIES: Close Reading, Marking the Text, Skimming/Scanning, Graphic Organizer, Rereading

1. Reread the last paragraph of Chapter 18, this time using a highlighter to mark the text. First, highlight the most descriptive or vivid words Krakauer uses. In the margin, make notes about connotations that you associate with these words. Make notes about the effects of these carefully chosen words — what do you think Krakauer wants his readers to think or feel?

> **LITERARY TERMS**
> A word's **connotation** is the association and emotional overtones that go beyond the word's literal definition.

2. Next, look for *figurative language*. What is the effect of the comparison(s)? Again, what do you think Krakauer wants his reader to think or feel?

3. What word describes the tone in this last paragraph?

4. What would have been the readers' last impression if Krakauer had ended *Into the Wild* with Chapter 18?

5. Now skim the Epilogue. What is its lasting impression? How is it different from the last paragraph of Chapter 18?

Searching for the Author

Most biographies are written in chronological order, but Krakauer has organized *Into the Wild* differently. As you have been reading, you have been taking note of the major events (including dates) and the chapters in which Krakauer records them. Re-examine those notes to become aware of how the story of McCandless's life unfolds.

6. Choose three significant events in McCandless's life, identify where in the book Krakauer records the events, and think about why he chose to record the events at this point in the book, and reflect on the effect of his decision.

Event and Date	Chapter	Why Krakauer May Have Recorded the Event at This Point in the Book	Effect of Recording the Event at This Point in the Book

Early in this level, you learned that you can often find a particular slant in writing. In the Author's Note for *Into the Wild,* Jon Krakauer says, "I won't claim to be an impartial biographer." What does Jon Krakauer think about Christopher J. McCandless? Here are some important points to consider as you answer:

- Review the structure of the book, using the timeline you have created. Keep in mind that most biographies are written in chronological order. Why does Krakauer organize the story in a different way?

- Review the various genres Krakauer uses. What is the effect of this use?

- Consider the stories of other adventurers, including himself, that Krakauer includes. What point does he make by including these stories?

- Think about the interviews Krakauer conducts. What purpose do they serve?

- Scan the book for instances where it is clear to you what Krakauer's attitude toward Christopher McCandless is, and put a sticky note on those pages.

- Reflect on the closing chapters of *Into the Wild,* and think about situations in which the author used inductive or deductive reasoning. How did the author's conclusions affect meaning for the reader?

Writing Prompt: What, then, does Jon Krakauer think about Christopher J. McCandless? With careful consideration of all the factors listed, write a thoughtful response, using specific examples from the text to support your opinion.

Turning Life into Story

Before Reading

"I've managed to do a lot of things in my life I didn't think I was capable of and which many others didn't think me capable of either."

—Sandra Cisneros

Quickwrite: Write a response to the quote above, using examples from your own life or from your observation.

1. Sandra Cisneros calls her essay, "Straw into Gold: The Metamorphosis of the Everyday." This is an allusion to the fairy tale "Rumpelstiltskin." What is the connection between Cisneros's title and the action of the fairy tale?

During Reading

2. As you read "Straw into Gold: The Metamorphosis of the Everyday," highlight the things Cisneros turned out to be capable of doing, despite what anyone thought.

After Reading

3. Find and mark each reference Cisneros makes to turning straw into gold. Based on the prereading question about the title and your reading, how does Cisneros use this image to enhance the impact of her essay?

4. Go back to the list of significant experiences you created in Activity 5.10. Now that you have seen that even an act as simple as making tortillas can be significant, add to your list. Be sure your list includes anything you have managed to do, whether anyone (including you) thought you could or not.

5. Use the author's literary allusion as inspiration. Are there any images, comparisons, or allusions that you think you might use to tie your own essay together? If so, generate a list of possibilities to revisit or thread in later.

> ### LITERARY TERMS
> An **allusion** is a reference to someone or something that is known from history, literature, religion, politics, or some other branch of culture.

My Notes

Essay

> **ABOUT THE AUTHOR**
> Sandra Cisneros grew up in Chicago and now lives in San Antonio, Texas. She is a novelist, poet, short-story writer, and essayist. Her first book, *The House on Mango Street*, catapulted her to fame. In talking about her writing, Cisneros says she creates stories from things that have touched her deeply; "...in real life a story doesn't have shape, and it's the writer that gives it a beginning, a middle, and an end."

Straw into Gold:
The Metamorphosis of the Everyday

by Sandra Cisneros

When I was living in an artists' colony in the south of France, some fellow Latin Americans who taught at the university in Aix-en-Provence[1] invited me to share a home-cooked meal with them. I had been living abroad almost a year then on an NEA[2] grant, subsisting mainly on French bread and lentils while in France so that my money could last longer. So when the invitation to dinner arrived, I accepted without hesitation. Especially since they had promised Mexican food.

What I didn't realize when they made this invitation was that I was supposed to be involved in preparing this meal. I guess they assumed I knew how to cook Mexican food because I was Mexican. They wanted specifically tortillas, though I'd never made a tortilla in my life.

---

[1] **Aix-en-Provence (eks än prō väns')**: City in Southeastern France
[2] **NEA**: National Endowment for the Arts

It's true I had witnessed my mother rolling the little armies of dough into perfect circles, but my mother's family is from Guanajuato,[3] *provincials,*[4] country folk. They only know how to make flour tortillas. My father's family, on the other hand, is *chilango,*[5] from Mexico City. We ate corn tortillas but we didn't make them. Someone was sent to the corner tortilleria to buy some. I'd never seen anybody make corn tortillas. Ever.

Well, somehow my Latino hosts had gotten a hold of a packet of corn flour, and this is what they tossed my way with orders to produce tortillas. *Asi como sea.* Any ol' way, they said and went back to their cooking.

Why did I feel like the woman in the fairy tale who was locked in a room and ordered to spin straw into gold? I had the same sick feeling when I was required to write my critical essay for my MFA[6] exam — the only piece of noncreative writing necessary in order to get my graduate degree. How was I to start? There were rules involved here, unlike writing a poem or story, which I did intuitively. There was a step-by-step process needed and I had better know it. I felt as if making tortillas, or writing a critical paper for that matter, were tasks so impossible I wanted to break down into tears.

Somehow though, I managed to make those tortillas — crooked and burnt, but edible nonetheless. My hosts were absolutely ignorant when it came to Mexican food: they thought my tortillas were delicious. (I'm glad my mama wasn't there.) Thinking back and looking at that photograph documenting the three of us consuming those lopsided circles I am amazed. Just as I am amazed I could finish my MFA exam (lopsided and crooked, but finished all the same.) Didn't think I could do it. But I did.

I've managed to do a lot of things in my life I didn't think I was capable of and which many others didn't think me capable of either.

Especially because I am a woman, a Latina, an only daughter in a family of six men. My father would've liked to have seen me married long ago. In our culture, men and women don't leave their father's house except by way of marriage. I crossed my father's threshold with nothing carrying me but my own two feet. A woman whom no one came for and no one chased away.

To make matters worse, I had left before any of my six brothers had ventured away from home. I had broken a terrible taboo. Somehow, looking back at photos of myself as a child, I wonder if I was aware of having begun already my own quiet war.

GRAMMAR & USAGE

Notice that Cisneros uses a series without a conjunction before the last item: "I am a woman, a Latina, an only daughter...." This structure is called **asyndeton**. What is the effect of this rhetorical device?

My Notes

---

[3] **Guanajuato** (gwä nä hwä tō): state in central Mexico

[4] *provincials* (prō bēn sē ä läs): "country folk" (Spanish)

[5] *chilango* (chē län gō): "city folk" (Spanish)

[6] **MFA**: Master of Fine Arts

My Notes

I like to think that somehow my family, my Mexicanness, my poverty all had something to do with shaping me into a writer. I like to think my parents were preparing me all along for my life as an artist even though they didn't know it. From my father I inherited a love of wandering. He was born in Mexico City but as a young man he traveled into the U.S. vagabonding. He eventually was drafted and thus became a citizen. Some of the stories he has told about his first months in the U.S. with little or no English surface in my stories in *The House on Mango Street* as well as others I have in mind to write in the future. From him I inherited a sappy heart. (He still cries when he watches the Mexican soaps — especially if they deal with children who have forsaken their parents.)

My mother was born like me — in Chicago but of Mexican descent. It would be her tough, streetwise voice that would haunt all my stories and poems. An amazing woman who loves to draw and read books and can sing an opera. A smart cookie.

When I was a little girl we traveled to Mexico City so much I thought my grandparents' house on La Fortuna, Number 12, was home. It was the only constant in our nomadic ramblings from one Chicago flat to another. The house on Destiny Street, Number 12, in the colonia Tepeyac,[7] would be perhaps the only home I knew, and that nostalgia for a home would be a theme that would obsess me.

What would my teachers say if they knew I was a writer? Who would've guessed it? I wasn't a very bright student. I didn't much like school because we moved so much and I was always new and funny-looking. In my fifth-grade report card, I have nothing but an avalanche of C's and D's, but I don't remember being that stupid. I was good at art and I read plenty of library books and Kiki laughed at all my jokes. At home I was fine, but at school I never opened my mouth except when the teacher called on me, the first time I'd speak all day.

---

[7] **colonia Tepeyac (cô lō nēä tä pä yäc):** District of Mexico City

When I think how I see myself, it would have to be at age eleven. I know I'm thirty-two on the outside, but inside I'm eleven. I'm the girl in the picture with skinny arms and crumpled shirt and crooked hair. I didn't like school because all they saw was the outside me. School was lots of rules and sitting with your hands folded and being very afraid all the time. I liked looking out the window and thinking. I liked staring at the girl across the way writing her name over and over again in red ink. I wondered why the boy with the dirty collar in front of me didn't have a mama who took better care of him.

I think my mama and papa did the best they could to keep us warm and clean and never hungry. We had birthday and graduation parties and things like that, but there was another hunger that had to be fed. There was a hunger I didn't even have a name for. Was this when I began writing?

In 1966 we moved into a house, a real one, our first real home. This meant we didn't have to change schools and be the new kids on the block every couple of years. We could make friends and not be afraid we'd have to say good-bye to them and start all over. My brothers and the flock of boys they brought home would become important characters eventually for my stories — Louis and his cousins, Meme Ortiz and his dog with two names, one in English and one in Spanish.

My mother flourished in her own home. She took books out of the library and taught herself to garden, producing flowers so envied we had to put a lock on the gate to keep out the midnight flower thieves. My mother is still gardening to this day.

This was a period in my life, that slippery age when you are both child and woman and neither, I was to record in *The House on Mango Street*. I was still shy. I was a girl who couldn't come out of her shell.

How was I to know I would be recording and documenting the women who sat their sadness on an elbow and stared out the window? It would be the city streets of Chicago I would later record, but from a child's eyes.

I've done all kinds of things I didn't think I could do since then. I've gone to a prestigious university, studied with famous writers and taken away an MFA degree. I've taught poetry in the schools in Illinois and Texas. I've gotten an NEA grant and run away with it as far as my courage would take me. I've seen the bleached and bitter mountains of the Peloponnesus.[8] I've lived on a Greek island. I've been to Venice[9] twice. In Rapallo, I met Ilona once and forever and took her sad heart with me across the south of France and into Spain.

My Notes

GRAMMAR & USAGE

Cisneros lists her accomplishments with a series of verb phrases, all in the present perfect tense to indicate actions completed at some indefinite time in the past.

The auxiliary verb *have* is in the contraction (*I've*) and is understood in the phrases after the first: I've gone..., [I've] studied....

[8] **Peloponnesus (pel ə pə nē səs):** Peninsula forming the southeastern part of the Greek mainland
[9] **Venice (ven' is):** Seaport in northern Italy

Turning Life into Story

I've lived in Yugoslavia. I've been to the famous Nice[10] flower market behind the opera house. I've lived in a village in the pre-Alps[11] and witnessed the daily promenaders.

I've moved since Europe to the strange and wonderful country of Texas, land of Polaroid-blue skies and big bugs. I met a mayor with my last name. I met famous Chicana/o artists and writers and *politicos*.[12]

Texas is another chapter in my life. It brought with it the Dobie-Paisano Fellowship, a six-month residency on a 265-acre ranch. But most important Texas brought Mexico back to me.

Sitting at my favorite people-watching spot, the snaky Woolworth's counter across the street from the Alamo,[13] I can't think of anything else I'd rather be than a writer. I've traveled and lectured from Cape Cod to San Francisco, to Spain, Yugoslavia, Greece, Mexico, France, Italy, and finally today to Texas. Along the way there has been straw for the taking. With a little imagination, it can be spun into gold.

---

[10] **Nice (nēs):** seaport and resort in southeastern France

[11] **pre-Alps:** foothills to the Alps, a mountain range in south central Europe

[12] *politicos* **(pō lē tē cōs):** "politicians" (Spanish)

[13] **the Alamo (al' ə mō'):** mission in San Antonio, Texas, that was the scene of a famous battle between Texans and Mexican Stroops in 1836

A Snowball of Happiness

SUGGESTED LEARNING STRATEGIES: Close Reading, Read Aloud, Marking the Text, Revising, Quickwrite

Quickwrite: Reflect on a time when you misbehaved as a child and consider how you got caught. Describe the feelings and thoughts you experienced the moment your ill behavior was exposed and reflect on what you learned from the incident.

Essay

ABOUT THE AUTHOR
Annie Dillard is best known for her Pulitzer-Prize-winning work *Pilgrim at Tinker Creek*. In this chapter from her autobiography, *An American Childhood*, Dillard leads us running desperately through snow-filled backyards. Like all of Dillard's writing, this essay shows an unparalleled enthusiasm for life and skill at expressing it.

by Annie Dillard

Some boys taught me to play football. This was fine sport. You thought up a new strategy for every play and whispered it to the others. You went out for a pass, fooling everyone. Best, you got to throw yourself mightily at someone's running legs. Either you brought him down or you hit the ground flat on your chin, with your arms empty before you. It was all or nothing. If you hesitated in fear, you would miss and get hurt: you would take a hard fall while the kid got away, or you would get kicked in the face while the kid got away. But if you flung yourself wholeheartedly at the back of his knees—if you gathered and joined a body and soul and pointed them diving fearlessly—then you likely wouldn't get hurt, and you'd stop the ball. Your fate, and your team's score, depended on your concentration and courage. Nothing girls did could compare with it. 1

Boys welcomed me at baseball, too, for I had, through enthusiastic practice, what was weirdly known as a boy's arm. In winter, in the snow, there was neither baseball nor football, so the boys and I threw snowballs at passing cars. I got in trouble throwing snowballs, and have seldom been happier since. 2

A Snowball of Happiness

LITERARY TERMS
Details are the specific facts, observations, or incidents a writer uses to reveal elements of a story.

My Notes

3   On one weekday morning after Christmas, six inches of new snow had just fallen. We were standing up to our boot tops in snow on a front yard on trafficked Reynolds Street, waiting for cars. The cars traveled Reynolds Street slowly and evenly; they were targets all but wrapped in red ribbons, cream puffs. We couldn't miss.

4   I was seven; the boys were eight, nine, and ten. The oldest two Fahey boys were there—Mikey and Peter—polite blond boys who lived near me on Lloyd Street, and who already had four brothers and sisters. My parents approved Mikey and Peter Fahey. Chickie McBride was there, a tough kid, and Billy Paul and Mackie Kean too, from across Reynolds, where the boys grew up dark and furious, grew up skinny, knowing, and skilled. We had all drifted from our houses that morning looking for action, and had found it here on Reynolds Street.

5   It was cloudy but cold. The cars' tires laid behind them on the snowy street a complex trail of beige chunks like crenellated castle walls. I had stepped on some earlier; they squeaked. We could have wished for more traffic. When a car came, we all popped it one. In the intervals between cars we reverted to the natural solitude of children.

6   I started making an iceball—a perfect iceball, from perfectly white snow, perfectly spherical, and squeezed perfectly translucent so no snow remained all the way through. (The Fahey boys and I considered it unfair actually to throw an iceball at somebody, but it had been known to happen.)

7   I had just embarked on the iceball project when we heard tire chains come clanking from afar. A black Buick was moving toward us down the street. We all spread out, banged together some regular snowballs, took aim, and, when the Buick drew nigh, fired.

8   A soft snowball hit the driver's windshield right before the driver's face. It made a smashed star with a hump in the middle.

9   Often, of course, we hit our target, but this time, the only time in all of life, the car pulled over and stopped. Its wide black door opened; a man got out of it, running. He didn't even close the car door.

10   He ran after us, and we ran away from him, up the snowy Reynolds sidewalk. At the corner, I looked back; incredibly, he was still after us. He was in city clothes: a suit and tie, street shoes. Any normal adult would have quit, having sprung us into flight and made his point. This man was gaining on us. He was a thin man, all action. All of a sudden, we were running for our lives.

11   Wordless, we split up. We were on our turf; we could lose ourselves in the neighborhood backyards, everyone for himself. I paused and considered. Everyone had vanished except Mikey Fahey, who was just rounding the corner of a yellow brick house. Poor Mikey, I trailed him.

The driver of the Buick sensibly picked the two of us to follow. The man apparently had all day.

He chased Mikey and me around the yellow house and up a backyard path we knew by heart: under a low tree, up a bank, through a hedge, down some snowy steps, and across the grocery store's delivery driveway. We smashed through a gap in another hedge, entered a scruffy backyard and ran around its back porch and tight between houses to Edgerton Avenue; we ran across Edgerton to an alley and up our own sliding woodpile to the Halls' front yard; he kept coming. We ran up Lloyd Street and wound through mazy backyards toward the steep hilltop at Willard and Lang.

He chased us silently, block after block. He chased us silently over picket fences through thorny hedges, between houses, around garbage cans, and across streets. Every time I glanced back, choking for breath, I expected he would have quit. He must have been as breathless as we were. His jacket strained over his body. It was an immense discovery, pounding into my hot head with every sliding, joyous step, that this ordinary adult evidently knew what I thought only children who trained at football know: that you have to fling yourself at what you're doing, you have to point yourself, forget yourself, aim, dive.

Mikey and I had nowhere to go in our own neighborhood or out of it, but away from this man who was chasing us. He impelled us forward; we compelled him to follow our route. The air was cold; every breath tore my throat. We kept running, block after block; we kept improvising, backyard after backyard, running a frantic course and choosing it simultaneously, failing always to find small places or hard places to slow him down, and discovering always, exhilarated, dismayed, that only bare speed could save us—for he would never give up, this man—and we were losing speed.

He chased us through the backyard labyrinths of ten blocks before he caught us by our jackets. He caught us and we all stopped.

We three stood staggering, half blinded, coughing, in an obscure hilltop backyard: a man in his twenties, a boy, a girl. He had released our jackets, our pursuer, our captor, our hero: He knew we weren't going anywhere. We all played by the rules. Mikey and I unzipped our jackets. I pulled off my sopping mittens. Our tracks multiplied in the backyard's new snow. We had been breaking new snow all morning. We didn't look at each other. I was cherishing my excitement. The man's lower pants legs were wet; his cuffs were full of snow, and there was a prow of snow beneath them on his shoes and socks. Some trees bordered the little flat backyard, some messy winter trees. There was no one around: a clearing in a grove, and we the only players.

My Notes

12

13

14

15

16

A Snowball of Happiness

My Notes

WORD CONNECTIONS

Perfunctory comes from two Latin words: the prefix *per* meaning "through" and the root *fungi* meaning "perform." *Function* and *defunct* also use the same root.

17 It was a long time before he could speak. I had some difficulty at first recalling why we were there. My lips felt swollen; I couldn't see out of the sides of my eyes; I kept coughing.

18 "You stupid kids," he began perfunctorily.

19 We listened perfunctorily indeed, if we listened at all, for the chewing out was redundant, a mere formality, and beside the point. The point was that he had chased us passionately without giving up, and so he had caught us. Now he came down to earth. I wanted the glory to last forever.

20 But how could the glory have lasted forever? We could have run through every backyard in North America until we got to Panama. But when he trapped us at the lip of the Panama Canal, what precisely could he have done to prolong the drama of the chase and cap its glory? I brooded about this for the next few years. He could only have fried Mikey Fahey and me in boiling oil, say, or dismembered us piecemeal, or staked us to anthills. None of which I really wanted, and none of which any adult was likely to do, even in the spirit of fun. He could only chew us out there in the Panamanian jungle, after months or years of exalting pursuit. He could only begin, "You stupid kids," and continue in his ordinary Pittsburgh accent with his normal righteous anger and the usual common sense.

21 If in that snowy backyard the driver of the black Buick had cut off our heads, Mikey's and mine, I would have died happy, for nothing has required so much of me since as being chased all over Pittsburgh in the middle of winter—running terrified, exhausted—by this sainted skinny, furious redheaded man who wished to have a word with us. I don't know how he found his way back to his car.

Reflecting on Life Experiences

Personal essays are reflective in nature, which means that the author looks back on an experience that is significant in his or her life, describes the experience and how he or she felt at the time, and then reflects on the importance of that experience. "A View from Mount Ritter" is an example of a reflective personal essay written by a high school student.

Before Reading

Quickwrite: Describe a memorable experience with nature.

During Reading

Mark examples where the author tells how he felt.

Evaluate the introduction, organizational structure, and conclusion of the text. Are they effective? Explain.

After Reading

In the margin, identify which part of the essay is *description* of the significant experience. Identify where O'Connor uses words that appeal to the senses: sight, hearing, taste, touch, smell.

What other tools does O'Connor use to show, rather than tell, the event?

Draw a line to indicate where the author shifts from description of the experience to a *reflection* on the significance of it.

What tools does O'Connor use to enhance his reflection?

My Notes

Essay

A View From
Mount Ritter

Two weeks in the Sierras changed my attitude toward life
and what it takes to succeed.

by Joseph T. O'Connor

"I hate this," I thought. We were on our way to the top of Mount
Ritter in northeastern California. You would think everyone, near one of
the tallest ridges in the Sierra Nevadas, would be in high spirits. But on
this particular day the rain fell in torrents. Quarter-size hailstones pelted
our protective helmets as thunder echoed through the canyons.

It was the second week of my mountain expedition in California.
The first week there had not been a cloud in the sky, but on Tuesday of
week two, a dark cover crept in from the west, painting the sunlit, blue
sky black. The storm came in so fast we didn't even notice it until our
shadows suddenly disappeared.

"Here it comes," our guide warned. As if God himself had given
the order, the heavens opened, just a crack. Huge drops began falling
but abruptly stopped, as if to say, "You know what's coming, here's a
taste." As we began searching for shelter, a bolt of lightning ripped
open the blackish clouds overhead and in unison thunder cracked,
leaving everyone's ears ringing. We were in the midst of a huge July
thunderstorm. Ethan, our guide, had said that during the summer in the
high Sierras it might rain twice, but when it does, it's best not to be there.
Suddenly lightning struck a tree not 20 feet from where I was standing.

"Lightning positions!" Ethan yelled frantically. A little too frantically
for my taste. I thought he was used to this kind of thing. As scared as
I was, squatting in a giant puddle of water and hailstones, with forks
of lightning bouncing off the canyon walls around me, I couldn't help
chuckling to myself at the sight of Ethan's dinner-plate-sized eyeballs as
he panicked like an amateur. Soon after the lightning died down some,

we hiked to the shelter of nearby redwoods and put on rain gear. While we prayed for the rain to subside, I watched the stream we stood beside grow into a raging, white-water river. Another expeditioner, Mike, and I were under a full redwood donning our not-so-waterproof equipment when I realized we were standing on a small island.

"Mike! Let's go!" I yelled, my exclamation nearly drowned out by the roar of water surrounding us and another roll of thunder.

"I'm way ahead o' ya!" he screamed in his thick New York accent, and his goofy smile broke through the torrents. "Ya ready?"

"Yeah!" I yelled back, and jumped from our island into the knee-deep water. He followed as we slopped through the storm, losing our footing every few feet.

The unforgiving downpour lasted all day and into the night as we stumbled down the rocky cliffs seeking the driest place to set up camp. It was dusk before we found a small clearing in a pine forest, and began what was to be the worst night of my life. We constructed our tents in the dark, fumbling with the ropes with our frozen hands and finishing just as a stiffness like rigor mortis set in. We lay all night, shivering in our wet sleeping bags while rain poured down and a small stream made its way through our tent.

It's funny how these memories keep coming back to me as if it was just yesterday. All this happened last summer, after my junior year in high school. I had decided to attend a mountaineering program in the Sierras. Two weeks in the back country with no sign of civilization. It sounded exciting and slightly dangerous, and I've always been up for a good adventure. I found out on that trip that nature is underestimated. The experience was the most invigorating, fulfilling, stimulating two weeks of my life. For the first time since I could remember, my head was crystal clear. I felt born again, only 2 weeks old. On top of Mount Ritter, 13,000 feet above sea level, I was entranced at the sight of the orange-red sun as it peeked over the glistening peaks far off in the east. Cumulous clouds appeared transparent as they glowed bright red in the morning glory.

The wonder of all I'd experienced made me think seriously about what comes next. "Life after high school," I said to myself. "Uh-oh." What had I been doing for the last three years? I was so caught up in defying the advice of my parents and teachers to study and play by the rules that I hadn't considered the effects my actions would have on me.

"Youth is wholly experimental," Robert Louis Stevenson wrote. Sure, there will be mistakes, but there will also be successes. I was a confused kid. Everyone — my parents, teacher and coaches — offered suggestions, but I chose to ignore them. I had "potential," they told me. As a typical teen, I thought I could make it on my own.

GRAMMAR & USAGE

Complex sentences consist of at least one dependent, or subordinate, clause. O'Connor uses subordinate clauses as adverbs and adjectives.

While we prayed for the rain to subside (adverb clause modifying *watched*), I watched the stream *we stood beside* (adjective clause modifying *stream*) grow…

You can use adjectival and adverbial clauses to add information to a sentence or to combine sentences.

My Notes

WORD CONNECTIONS

Rebellion contains the Latin root *-bell-* from *bellum* meaning "war." *Rebel, antebellum*, and *rebellious* have the same root.

My Notes

_____

_____

_____

_____

_____

_____

I didn't want any help, and the more people tried to give it the more distant I grew.

I was the kid who thought he could be perfect at anything without any preparation.

I was lost in the daydream that I didn't need to study; I was going to play professional soccer. My game was good and I thought that practice, or getting good grades, for that matter, was unnecessary. Stubbornness and rebellion can be terrible things if they get out of control.

"To get back one's youth one has merely to repeat one's follies." A day before my awakening on that fateful July sunrise, I would have disagreed with this quotation from Oscar Wilde. But after recognizing the results of my own follies for the first time, I thoroughly agree.

This year, my final year in high school, I've at last cleared my head and buckled down. Judging by the past semester, I'm on the right track. My D average has U-turned into this report card's three B's and one A, landing me on my first Honor Roll. I intend to be on the Principal's List after this semester; then I hope to graduate and attend a community college in northern California, near the mountains, before transferring to a four-year school.

Thanks to that morning's conversion, I am a new person. Now, I know I'll have to work hard. The sun streaming over the eastern Sierras wiped out the dark clouds that blurred my vision. Jonathan Harker in Bram Stoker's "Dracula" must have felt exactly the same way when he wrote in his journal: "No man knows 'till he has suffered from the night how sweet and how dear to his heart and eye the morning can be."

Making Your Choice

SUGGESTED LEARNING STRATEGIES: Revisiting, Summarizing, Sharing and Responding, Think-Pair-Share, Adding, Deleting

Now that you have examined models of personal essays, it is time for you to make a decision about the subject of your own personal essay. Go back to Activity 5.10 and read the list of experiences that you have brainstormed. If any other experiences have occurred to you, add them to the list.

Now think carefully about the experiences you have listed. To produce the kind of reflection that is characteristic of a personal essay, you will probably need to avoid selecting an experience that happened in the recent past. It is difficult to reflect on an experience at first; usually, people need some distance from the event to see it clearly.

Second, it is important that you choose an experience that is significant — an experience that changed you in some way, an experience that taught you something important, or an experience that reveals something about your character. Look over your list and choose an experience that is significant to you and write briefly about it.

Summarize the Experience	How did you feel at the time of the experience?	Summarize Your Reflection on the Experience

If you find that you cannot fully complete any of the columns in the chart, you should consider choosing a different experience about which to write. Share your initial thinking with a partner. Ask your partner to highlight or underline a part of your writing that would benefit from more development. Use this as the basis for writing more about the experience, your reaction to it, and/or your reflection about it.

Writing a Personal Essay

SUGGESTED LEARNING STRATEGIES: **Brainstorming, Think-Pair-Share, Drafting, Group Discussions**

Assignment

Your assignment is to write a multi-paragraph reflective essay about a significant personal experience, being sure to describe the experience and your immediate response to it, as well as to reflect on the significance of the experience.

Steps

Planning

1. Throughout the unit you have encountered possible topics through various texts and personal responses. Consider those as a starting point to brainstorm potential topics for this task. Select two or three topics and use a think-pair-share to pick one appropriate for this assignment.

2. Use a prewriting strategy to generate content and explore ideas in regard to the personal experience, your immediate response to it, and your thoughts on the significance of the experience.

3. Create a rhetorical plan for the essay that considers your purpose, audience, and the organizational structure: event, response, and reflection.

Drafting

4. Draft your essay to incorporate your ideas within the organizational structure of a personal essay. Consider the following while writing:

   ▶ Description of the experience: begin with dialogue, action, a dramatic statement, or epigram.

   ▶ Sequence of ideas to show the development of feelings and thoughts as the event unfolds.

   ▶ Reflective commentary that reveals insight.

Revising

5. Share your draft in your writing group and use the scoring guide as a revision tool. Solicit feedback for revision in areas listed below and revise accordingly.

   ▶ Organizational Structure (e.g., event, response, reflection)

   ▶ Stylistic Elements (e.g., tone, detail, diction, syntax)

   ▶ Coherence of Ideas

6. Read your essay silently and mark the text to identify key words or phrases that capture the essence of your essay. Generate a list of potential titles that connect to marked ideas. Select one that would serve as a meaningful title.

Editing

7. Read your draft aloud and edit for grammar, punctuation, and spelling in preparation for publishing.

SCORING GUIDE

Scoring Criteria	Exemplary	Proficient	Emerging
Organization	The essay flows in a logical fashion; the reader can easily identify the description of the event and the author's reaction, as well as the reflection. The essay is unified effectively and provides a feeling of satisfaction in the end.	The essay is organized in such a way that the reader can identify the description of the event and the author's reaction, as well as the reflection.	The essay lacks organization, in that the reader may not be able to identify the description of the event, the author's reaction, and the reflection.
Description of Experience	The description has an intriguing lead that engages the reader in the text. The essay draws the reader into the experience by using details that appeal to the senses.	The essay clearly describes the experience.	The essay may describe the experience, but the description may be sketchy.
Description of Author's Feelings	The essay presents an explicit description of how the author felt at the time of the experience, using carefully chosen words to convey those emotions.	The essay clearly describes how the author felt at the time of the experience.	The essay may describe how the author felt at the time of the experience, but the description may be on the surface level.
Reflection	The reflection shows a mature and insightful understanding of the significance of the experience to the author.	The reflection reveals the significance of the experience to the author.	The reflection may be irrelevant or may show little understanding of the significance of the experience to the author.
Additional Criteria			

Comments:

Learning Focus:

Creative Research

Over the course of your middle or high school experience, you have probably written a research paper or know someone who has. What comes to mind when you think of writing a research paper? Maybe an assigned topic, the tediousness of creating note cards, an outline, strict structure, formal language appropriate to the English Language Arts discourse—language used in a particular context or subject. In this half of the unit, you will use the research skills (i.e., collecting, recording, and synthesizing information) of a traditional research paper; however, you will present ideas creatively with a great deal of freedom via a multi-genre research project.

A multi-genre research project differs from a traditional research paper because the subject necessitates that the writer know and understand the information well enough to assume multiple points of view and present ideas from a variety of angles on the topic. According to Sirpa Grierson, a professional writer, a reader "approaches multi-genre literature as if it were an exotic fruit—peeling back the layers of the text slowly, taking the time to savor everything as part of the experience of learning together." The multi-genre research project positions the writer to showcase a range of writing styles, craft, and genre conventions to convey a clear and knowledgeable perspective on an issue, topic, movement, or person of particular interest to the writer.

Consider your study of Krakauer's *Into the Wild* as a multi-genre text, which reveals research, both primary and secondary, in order to immerse the reader in understanding a series of events that lead to the tragic fate of a young man. Krakauer's commitment to cull the right information in order to convey his point of view and to help the reader discover the truth about his subject, Chris McCandless, is apparent in the presentation of ideas and research in his text. Think about the kind of research that Krakauer conducted in order to write *Into the Wild*. How does he represent research through a cohesive series of pieces in a variety of genres to convey meaning to the readers?

You will have an opportunity to conduct research on a topic or person of your choice and creatively present your findings in a multi-genre research project.

SUGGESTED LEARNING STRATEGIES: Notetaking, Think-Pair-Share

Before Reading

Create a working definition of a multi-genre research project.

During Reading

Read the sample multi-genre research project (MGR) from the perspective of a writer—what do you notice about the style and craft of the MGR? As you read, follow your teacher's instructions to annotate the text with your insights and observations.

Think about how this graphic organizer could help organize a multi-genre research project such as the one you are about to read.

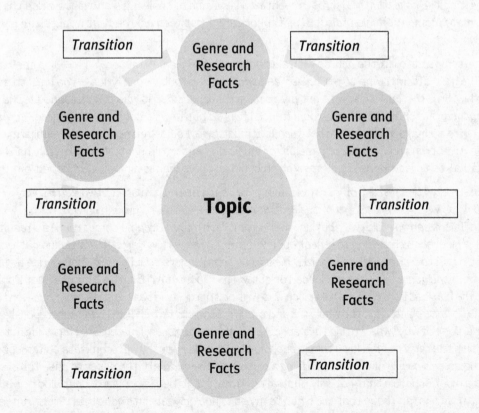

Student Sample, Multi-Genre Research Project

Dear Reader,

When first introduced to the Multi-Genre Research assignment, without hesitation, I selected the most prominent American musician ever to take the stage—Louis Armstrong. Armstrong's commitment to accomplishing his dreams is unsurpassed as he epitomizes what can happen when talent is given an opportunity to obtain success. So I thought, no problem—I get to talk about a cultural icon, his relevance to the music industry, and his rise to fame despite adversity—this is going to be easy as counting from one to three. Then, Mrs. Spencer walked us through the "steps of the assignment," and let me tell you, there were far more than three simple steps.

The journey to create a multi-genre research paper is no small undertaking. It begins with inquiry about a topic of personal interest. Upon discussion with peers, I realized that what I know and need to know to accomplish this task will "actually require" a significant amount of research. Thus leads to the next step, a personal favorite, not—research! Research leads to more questions—great. Once you have the information—how do you present it with a creative edge that shares passion, insight, and wonder? Seems easy, but it was quite the challenge. No great work of art was ever pulled off without a plan, right? Writing the collection of genres presented a labyrinth of challenges and discoveries that led to the ultimate moment of this project-a metaphorical link between genres that would blend my collection of work.

Initially, I attempted to link the genres with significant events from Armstong's life—too easy and predictable. The next attempt was to string genres together by popular song lyrics—too hard to get the ideas to flow. Frustrated with how to get my point across, I decided it was time to consult "the boss," Mrs. Spencer. After an enlightening conference I figured out how to connect the genres—create original song lyrics to make a connection between two musicians, Louis and me. The major similarity between Louis Armstrong and me, is our passion for music and entertainment. Now, the really hard part, finding a way to thread ideas from research on Louis and myself into a musical composition.

Louis Armstrong did not start off rich and famous; he began at the bottom and worked his way up as I plan to do as well. This is the crux of the American Dream—success through hard work and determination. Talent can go a long way, but unwavering ambition makes dreams come true. As a result, I came up with a nineteen-verse song to reflect our love for music as well as depict the arduous pathway to the limelight. I had to pick a widely recognized melody so that readers could sing my song lyrics as they transitioned from one genre to the next. Hence, I selected the rap from Will Smith's "Parents Just Don't Understand." The hardest part of the whole piece was writing to a certain beat and rhyme. If one word did not fit into the correct place, then the whole line and even verse would be off. Also, I had to incorporate the idea and purpose of why I was writing the paper. As for my genre pieces, I made sure that they acted as "breaks" within the rap itself by doing things such as placing a diary entry with complete sentences and paragraphs after a couple of verses, or adding a picture to the middle of the paper to ease the eyes. I also included a mock schedule that not only illustrated Armstrong's rise in popularity, but also served as a rest point from the rap. I hope that the lyrics to my song not only educate you about Armstrong's American dream, but provide insight into my dream as well.

Sincerely,
Jhoanne Mecija

Contents

The Fresh Prince of Jazz and Myself

The generation of American folk music dates back to as long as one can remember, and since then, has developed and grown into countless different types of music. Throughout the years, there have been hundreds of individuals who have greatly influenced the way music is looked upon; one of those includes the amazing and all time favorite jazz musician Louis Armstrong. He never lost his passion for music as he looked up to his idol Joe "King" Oliver. Louis Armstrong worked from the very bottom and worked to the top to fulfill his American Dream, making him one of the greatest influences in music and role models to young musicians like myself. As for my journey in fulfilling my American Dream in the meantime, I continue to walk, and during it, I break into song…

(To the tune of Fresh Prince of Bel-Air Introduction)
Now this is a story all about how
My life's compared to the Armstrong in renown
And I'd like to take a minute, yeah that'll do
To tell you how Louis achieved his dream and how I will too.

From Louisiana, born and raised
On the edge is where he spent most of his days
Sellin' stuff, runnin', workin' all hard
Playin' his first cornet in the yard.

When I was that age, I was up to some good
Started playing piano in my neighborhood
I got in one little lesson and my mom felt proud
She said, "You're going to keep playing it and be singing aloud."

I whistled a few tunes, the ones I would hear,
While piano books said "Beginner" to practice for a year.
If anything I could've said, "I quit; no more!"
But I thought, "No, forget it, this—I can't ignore."

While cleaning out my room, tired and astray
I found a diary entry written on some random day
Findin' out, discoverin', coverin', all cool,
Wonderin' if this thing actually came from school, it said:

Dear Diary,

Today was such a tiring day! I woke up to the sharp bites of the cold and absolutely did not want to get out of bed. I prepared for the upcoming day and the new assignments, the quizzes, and new challenges that needed to be taken on.

In first period, choir, my classmates and I listened to the lectures of our teacher, Mr. Hoshi. He ranted on about how he has been doing his job for the upcoming choir show and that we need to do ours, which is actually totally true, but apparently the message just doesn't seem to get out to all the choir students. Some of the songs that Advanced Girls learned for the holiday show included "Polar Express," "O Holy Night," "I Love Christmas," and "The Prayer." Being of those people who enjoy music, singing these songs and learning the different styles, beats, and rhythms of them really expanded my music library. Yes, Hoshi might fuss about how some of us don't know the words to the songs or the choreography to them, but what he says is true. As singers of this program, we should come prepared and learn our parts and words. Even though I have been turned down two times for this show's solo auditions, I continue to learn. I *can* be bitter, but I choose not to and to just accept it. I learn from these attempts and they only help me become stronger, especially with the guidance of a teacher like Mr. Hoshi. I can for sure say that I have never had a teacher like him before.

Anyway, the day went on, and I can't quite say it got better. I had an APUSH quiz, then after school I had to run 20 suicides on the basketball courts for conditioning because my coach is determined to win and make it to playoffs, which I think is possible. At practice, I had major pain from my calves down. All of this conditioning and running has not been good for them lately. After the hard practice, the drive home was soothing and partly relaxing as I listened to one of my CDs play songs that I sing along to. When I arrived home, dinner was the first thing on my mind because after that, I knew I had a pile of homework waiting for me.

As of right now, I'm just taking my homework one at a time. I've got some music on to cool me down, to help relax and take my stress away. Sometimes it's like a factor in escaping the troubles of life. I've heard it said that while doing a task that the left side of the brain takes control of, such as homework, the right side of the brain could be enriched at the same time with music in the background. I don't know if this is true, but I like to think it is just so it gives the mindset that it helps both sides of the brain. Although at times, I have to face turning off my music because I get so caught up with music that it serves as a distraction. Hopefully it won't be a long night tonight.

Your one and only,

Jhoanne Mecija

When the journey began, it started off real well,

Started making progress and began to excel,

But no—I can't forget how I started it all

With the touch of a piano and then it's easy to recall:

And so it Begins

The touch of a piano and sound of a note,
Started it all
As its results weren't remote.

Days that were spent watching and waiting
No longer existed,
Instead spent learning and contemplating.

A burst of sound fills the air,
Wishing, wondering, willing,
Sending smiles of joy and happiness everywhere.

The sound of music and its enticement,
So luring and yet so comforting,
Serves as an outlet to calm excitement.

Singing came along
As the journey continued,
And with it came the words to a song.

And so it began,
A legend, this star waiting to shine,
Carving her way for a better life plan.

So it remained to be
That her goal in life
Was to live where music held life's key.

For the King of Trumpets, named and crowned,

Becoming famous wasn't always sweet and sound

Stressin' out, messin', depressin' at times

Tensin' some muscles over some crimes

In a couple of days, all returns to good

Hard work and determination as it should

Louis got a lot of money and had more to grow

He said, "I never tried to prove nothing, just wanted to give a good show."

(Louis Armstrong)

He longed for a debut and when he found one

The papers said "Starring" and his name was bright as the sun

If anything he could say that this ad was rare

But he thought, "No, I like it. It's time to prepare!"

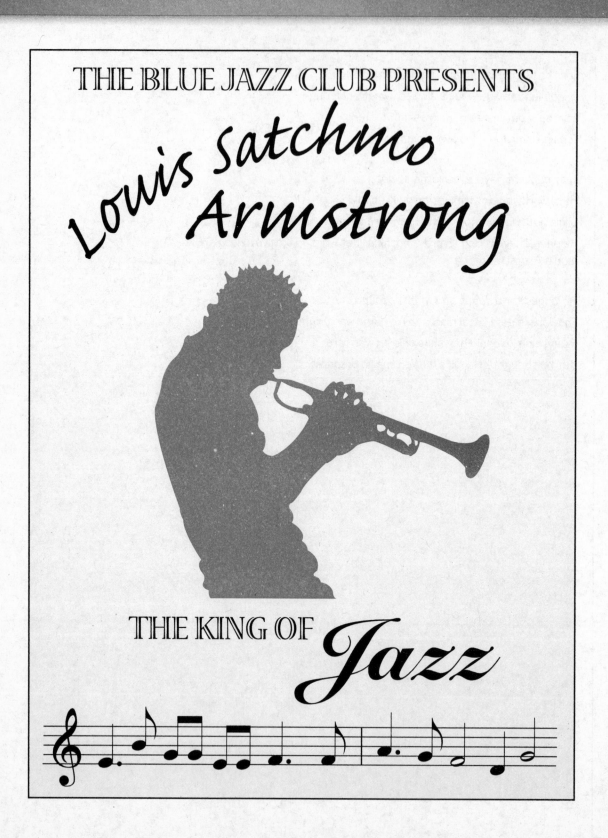

As Louis Armstrong's dream grew and gained

Popularity expanded—he entertained.

Growin' up, showin', playin' it cool

Hittin' some notes outside of school

When a couple of guys, come up with ideas

Started making articles about this player

He got in one good paper and the crowd was pleased

He said, "I have never felt so honored and joyful at ease."

The Blues Newspaper

A Great American Figure

IT WAS ON AUGUST 4, 1901 when a great musician had been born into this world. Louis Armstrong, Satchmo, the king of jazz folk music, has left his mark in the American history of music. He serves as an influence to all and inspiration to musicians across the country.

Armstrong was not merely a trumpet player, but took on other roles such as a singer, cornet player, and bandleader. This multitalented man became one of America's favorite people because of his popular music and style. Mostly known for his style of swing, he then developed this into the form of R&B, rhythm-and-blues. His passion and hard work has come a long way.

As a child growing up, Armstrong was not privileged like most other kids. He had to deal with racism, a lack of education, and living with poverty. Along with other jazz musicians that came from New Orleans, Louisiana, Louis Armstrong had to work to become as successful as he came to be. He was sent to a reform school at the age of twelve, where he began his musical journey as he learned to play the cornet. Along with that, he sold papers and coal and unloaded boats for money. Joe "King" Oliver, Louis Armstrong's role model, provided him his first real instrument, the cornet, which began his whole career.

Over time, Armstrong became more popular, joining bands from Chicago and making new hits. Of his famous groups included the Hot Five and Hot Seven. Individually, he created the famous songs "What a Wonderful World," "Hello Dolly," and "Mack the Knife." Producer Joe Glaser has even had his bands play for movies including *Pennies from Heaven,* a 1936 classic film. During his lifetime, Armstrong was published twice in his two biographies, *Satchmo: A Musical Autobiography* and *Swing That Music.*

In his last few years on earth, he suffered from heart trouble. He is proof to show that hard work, passion, and dedication pay off. Armstrong, a great musician and heart warming person, passed on July 6, 1971 at New York, New York. Even after his death, his music still lives on in every jazz lover's heart.

He received a fan mail and when it came here,

The envelope read "For Louis and his Wonderful Year"

If anything he could say he just didn't have enough time

But he thought, "No, forget it. This doesn't cost a dime!"

Hi Wonderful Fan,

   Glad to hear from ya! I love it when I hear that I have made someone's day or taken their troubles off of their minds. Let me tell you that. Now how could I not reply to such a sweet letter like yours? I am very flattered! And don't you worry about taking my time away because every spare minute I have I take out my laptop and type away. Brotha, I have one thing to say and it's that I, Louis Armstrong, am a sucker when it comes to writing!

   I really appreciate your support man! That show at the Blue Jazz Club was one of my favorite shows and I'm glad you enjoyed my music. I'll be on tour for who knows how long, and would sure love to keep in touch! If you'd like, you could come to another concert of mine and see me and Armstrong's Hot Five! The next show will be at <u>Waldorf Astoria</u>'s <u>Empire Room</u> at the big ol' apple itself—New York.

   Have you read any of my books? You should, they would be a great opportunity for you to learn a little more about me. On my part, I would like to learn more about you by reading what you have to say about your self. I am a man of my word, born and raised in Louisiana and you're darn right I'm going to reply with all my might and love to ya! My manager Joe Glaser does so much for me. He says he sends his love and gratitude too. Speak to you soon, buddy. It's time for me to perform!

Anxiously waiting for your reply,

Louis Armstrong

In a couple of days—fans just couldn't wait

So he started making plans on occupied dates

He squeezed in one little plan but he needed more in between

So he said, "I need a little schedule to help me keep clean"

Date	Time	Activity or Event
December 14, 1936	6:30 PM – 8:30 PM	Performance at the Blue Jazz Club
December 15, 1936	8:00 AM – 10:00 AM, 11:00 AM – 1:30 PM	Filming of "Pennies from Heaven"
December 17, 1936	6:00 PM	Flight to Chicago, then back home
December 18, 1936	10:00 AM – 12:45 PM, 2:00 PM – 4:30 PM	Filming of "Pennies from Heaven"
December 20, 1936	6:00 PM – 8:00 PM	Performance at Pixy Star Club
December 23, 1936	9:00 AM – 9:45 AM	Radio Recording
December 24, 1936	8:00 PM – 10:00 PM	Concert at Northern Pole Hotel
December 27, 1936	9:00 AM – 11:45 PM, 1:00 PM – 4:00 PM	Filming of "Pennies from Heaven"
January 1, 1937	2:00 PM	Flight to Miami and back

When the time was near, the crowd began to cheer

The performance was over, no need to shed a tear

If anything people were amazed to see him play,

Especially before he turned old and hair turned grey.

People wanted to know his personality

His style and his life, and his mentality

Look to his right and there's a person there!

Standing with a mic. and questions in the air.

Interviewer:	It is a great pleasure to be speaking to the king of Jazz himself—Louis Armstrong. How are you tonight?
Armstrong:	Well I am doing mighty fine; let me tell you that, Mama.
Interviewer:	Now, Mr. Armstrong, we the public has seen so much of you and has heard your music all across the streets of New York, Chicago, and Louisiana. How do you feel when you know that you have accomplished all of this?
Armstrong:	It's fantastic! To know that I can share my talents and ambitions to everyone in the world just puts a huge smile on my face.
Interviewer:	How did you get this far in your career? Was growing up just a piece of cake?
Armstrong:	Oh, no. Growing up was hard. I had to work my way up here. I lived in poverty and had to work countless jobs for money. That is until my idol found me.
Interviewer:	Oh? And who was your idol as a child?
Armstrong:	The one and only Joe "King" Oliver. The best trumpet player out there, let me tell you. He took his time to mentor me, a fine favor that I feel like I could never pay back with actions. As he moved to bigger dreams, I took his spot on the Kid Ory's band—where my passion and devotion developed strongly.
Interviewer:	Now, growing up your fame gradually increased. How did you feel about touring places and leaving home?
Armstrong:	Well, you know leaving home isn't always as dandy as it sounds. Touring, I must say, kept me awake, kept me alive. These different places only add to my experiences as a musician, but I always went on back home; never forgot my roots.
Interviewer:	What do you hope to achieve within the next few years?
Armstrong:	It's always nice to become even bigger from where I am today. I'd like to reach number one on those song charts. I'd like to even be played often on every radio station, but only *God* knows when all white men will come to their senses and end this racial feud that we face. The sound of my music on the radio lifts me to a place where I have never been before; it is like a Heaven for all musicians. I am just as proud as my momma would be when I hear my songs for the public.
Interviewer:	You are just heartwarming. Aside from all your business work and music accomplishments, how is your personal life going? Any "special someone" in your life?
Armstrong:	To tell you the truth, there has been one special gal in my life, but she's gone away. The name was Lil, my previous piano player. As time went on, I don't know what happened really, but it just didn't work out in the end.
Interviewer:	I'm sorry, sir.
Armstrong:	Oh, please. Don't give me your sympathy.

Interviewer:	What other areas do you excel in?
Armstrong:	If by excel you mean shine and lead, then other than that golden instrument that I rule, I also lead bands, sing, film stars, and sometimes even crack a joke here and there.
Interviewer:	My, my. We have a legendary man standing right in front of me! Mr. Armstrong, I would like to thank you with all my will for your time! You are a wonderful, talented, and gifted man. Don't let anyone take that away from you!
Armstrong:	Why thank you. I enjoy doing what I do and it is for people like you. My pleasure.

Louis Armstrong, the king and I,

Both have our music and dreams up high.

Though we have our own ways to execute

They will always be there to reach and shoot.

Cypress, California, born and raised

On the playground is where I spent most of my days

Chillin out, maxin', relaxin', all cool

Shootin' some B-ball out side of school

When a couple of songs, they were on my fav.'s list

Started playing loudly amongst the midst

I sang in one part of the song and I didn't care

Because people can look, judge, or do anything else especially stare

I walk up to the piano 'round seven or eight

Then I yelled to the fans "Hey, how you doin'?"

Look at my kingdom I was finally there

To sit on my throne as the Queen millionaire.

Louis Armstrong sought to entertain, enlighten, and bring enjoyment to those who loved music as much as he did. Armstrong accomplished his dreams through hard work and perseverance fueled by his desire to entertain others. His life's work defines the essence of the American Dream, a dream rooted in desire that can only come to pass when it is met with dedication to an art and an attentive commitment to excellence.

Reflective Endnotes

Genre #1: My Diary Entry

The reason for this genre is to show how music plays a part in my life, how I view and use it in everyday life. I write about a few influences and advice that have stuck with me or have stuck out to me throughout my life. I think that this is important in mentioning so that the audience can see my view in music and how I would interpret listening to music and being involved with it. With this shown and given, the audience can then make the connection that the paper's central topic is about music and how Louis Armstrong and I have our similarities and differences. I started this as the first genre to allow readers to get a feel of how I think.

Genre #2: Poem

This genre is supposed to be a poem about how I discovered my first interests for the piano and singing. It marks the beginning of my journey to my American Dream. This poem is about the irresistible spark of interest that I had when I was a child, and how soon those interests became my talents. I was influenced by my brother, who I would listen to play the piano after a lesson, and my by my dad, who would sing songs on the karaoke machine and dedicate them to my mother. It is important for readers to know where my roots came from.

Genre #3: Louis Armstrong Ad

This genre is an ad for Louis Armstrong to promote a concert or performance by him. It is supposed to give off a message to the public that Louis is becoming more famous and is in popular demand. The grey-scale coloring enhances the ad to makes it look more authentic and more appropriate for that time. Plain and simple is a way to get a message across, and this ad was definitely plain and simple. The "King of Jazz" will now be known to the public.

Genre #4: Newspaper Article

The Newspaper Article provides a brief history of Louis Armstrong, his development and achievements during his lifetime. This goes to show that Armstrong is in fact a great influence to music and society. This genre gives plenty of information to understand that he was an important role model and one of the greatest influences in today's music. I created this genre as a sort of tribute to Armstrong, not only to show the growth of his achievements, but to share the wealth of my knowledge of Armstrong and his success.

Genre #5: Reply to a fan letter

I think that this piece of genre is important because it displays the way Louis Armstrong handled business. I used an example that I found online; it was a letter of acceptance to a publisher for his book. The letter that Armstrong wrote showed exactly how his personality was—funny, joyful, and happy to do business. I tried myself to capture this tone of voice in my Armstrong letter to a fan. It is important to see how Armstrong handled the business part of his job, and it is amazing that he still handled it with such a bright attitude and a thankful tone.

Genre #6: Schedule

This charted schedule lists the places that Armstrong had to go to in order to complete some of his tasks. Its main idea is to display how busy Armstrong was beginning to get. Day after day he had work to do and places to fly out to. With such a busy schedule, it is shown just how popular Armstrong was and his growth as a musician. The chart was meant to be easy to read and attain information from so that it would be easy to understand his popular demand by the people.

Genre #7: Interview

The interview is one of the more important genres. This piece tells Armstrong's own opinion, history, and life stories given by him. Not only does it display his personality and jolly attitude, but also his hard work to get where he was at that day. I saved it for last to tie everything together. It was quite interesting, and at the same time a somewhat challenge, to pretend like I was Armstrong through the information that I researched. I did not want to lower his image, so I tried to make him seem as bright as possible with all the accurate facts that I have retrieved. This interview is important because it gives so much detail in a way that suits Armstrong when he speaks and tells his life story.

Annotated Bibliography

"Armstrong, Louis." <u>Collier's Encyclopedia</u>. 1989 ed.

In the encyclopedia was a short article on Louis Armstrong. I used this as a reference for more information, and just looked back at it when comparing information and also gaining information. Because the article was fairly short, this source was not one of the more important ones compared to the others.

Biographies–Louis Armstrong. 2000. Jazz at Lincoln Center. 8 Dec. 2005. <http://www.pbs.org/jazz/biography/artist_id_armstrong_louis.htm>.

This website provided Louis Armstrong's life story—from his birth, successes, and death. The page focuses on jazz influences and leaders, so it is like their "specialty" to be writing about a man like Louis Armstrong. There are also links that you can click on to listen to some of his songs that were recorded in the 1920's. I used some of the valuable information given on this site in some of my genres.

Jon Krakauer. <u>Into Thin Air</u>. United States: Villard Books, 1997.

This book was used as an example for my own multigenre paper. Jon Krakauer writes about his amazing, once in a lifetime experience on the one and only Mount Everest using different pieces of work, or genres, to help support his text and knowledge. After reading and understanding how he incorporated each genre piece into the writing itself, I learned to grasp the concept of adding my own genres into another piece of my work. This book sets as a perfect example for the multigenre paper.

Louis Armstrong. 6 Dec. 2005. <<u>http://www.redhotjazz.com/louie.html</u>>.

This website that I found helped with the information that I needed. This website, unlike some of the others, provides a long history of Louis' upcoming stardom and road to becoming famous. It also provided links to other key words if I didn't know what that word was. This was a valuable website and came quite in handy. It also lists the groups that Armstrong were in and which movies he was filmed in.

Louis Armstrong – Acceptance Letter. DIALOGUS. 4 Dec. 2005. <<u>http://www.dialogus2.org/enARMS/enARMS-acceptance.html</u>>.

This was a great example to my genre "Letter to the Fan." It's an actual letter that Louis Armstrong wrote to a publisher accepting her proposal. This shows how he handled business. It was quite entertaining to see how he wrote in letters. I tried using the same jolly and joking tone when writing the letter to a fan.

Louis Armstrong Quotes. FortuneCity. 8 Dec. 2005.
<http://tinpan.fortunecity.com /riff/ 11/quotes.html>.

This website contained quotes from musicians all over the world. Of these quotes were one of Louis Armstrong's. I used the one that said "I never tried to prove nothing, just wanted to give a good show." I thought that this quote just showed who Armstrong was, what kind of person he was. He was not only being humble and modest, but enjoying what he does. It fit perfectly into one of the song's beats, so I just had to add it in with my paper.

Louis Armstrong – Wikipedia, the free encyclopedia. 8 Jan. 2006, Wikimedia. 4 Dec. 2005. <http://en.wikipedia.org/wiki/Louis_Armstrong#Personality>.

Wikimedia's website about Louis Armstrong offers numerous subjects about him, such as his early life, early career, music, and his legacy. I was most attracted to the section about his personality. This allowed me to really get to know who Louis was as an individual and what he thought about society and his interests. This was important and useful for me to gain that one-on-one connection in my writing. In my "Letter to the Fan" genre, I copied Louis Armstrong's real signature that this website provided to make the letter seem more authentic and real.

The Official Site of the Louis Armstrong House & Archives. 2002. Louis Armstrong House & Archives. 29 Nov. 2005. <http://www.satchmo.net/bio/>.

This was another website that provided short information about Louis Armstrong and his achievements during his life. There are bullets that mark his achievements and a short paragraph about his past. This website became useful and important for quick and straight forward, needed information.

Portfolio in Black & White. Nuts and Bults Interactive. 1 Dec. 2005.
<http://discosantigos.com/Portfolio/1959_LouisArmstrong.html>.

I used the picture from this website for the ad genre that I made. I thought that it was a great picture that portrayed his happiness and love for his instrument. This photo makes Louis look like the happiest man on earth, and I chose this picture to use because it gave off a good feeling towards the ad that I made.

After Reading

After discussing how Krakauer's text, *Into the Wild,* meets the criteria of a multi-genre research project, refine your response to the unit's essential question: How does a writer represent research through multiple texts?

How has your encounter with the sample multi-genre research project contributed to your understanding of using this approach to study a subject of interest to you?

My Notes

Biographical Sketch

Sparky

by Earl Nightingale

For Sparky, school was all but impossible. He failed every subject in the eighth grade. He flunked physics in high school, getting a grade of zero. Sparky also flunked Latin, algebra, and English. He didn't do much better in sports. Although he did manage to make the school's golf team, he promptly lost the only important match of the season. There was a consolation match; he lost that, too.

Throughout his youth Sparky was awkward socially. He was not actually disliked by the other students; no one cared that much. He was astonished if a classmate ever said hello to him outside of school hours. There's no way to tell how he might have done at dating. Sparky never once asked a girl to go out in high school. He was too afraid of being turned down.

Sparky was a loser. He, his classmates…everyone knew it. So he rolled with it. Sparky had made up his mind early in life that if things were meant to work out, they would. Otherwise he would content himself with what appeared to be his inevitable mediocrity.

However, one thing was important to Sparky—drawing. He was proud of his artwork. Of course, no one else appreciated it. In his senior year of high school, he submitted some cartoons to the editors of the yearbook. The cartoons were turned down. Despite the particular rejection, Sparky was so convinced of his ability that he decided to become a professional artist.

After completing high school, he wrote a letter to Walt Disney Studios. He was told to send some samples of his artwork, and the subject for a cartoon was suggested. Sparky drew the proposed cartoon. He spent a great deal of time on it and on all the other drawings he submitted.

Finally, the reply came from Disney Studios. He had been rejected once again. Another loss for the loser.

So Sparky decided to write his own autobiography in cartoons. He described his childhood self—a little boy loser and chronic underachiever. The cartoon character would soon become famous worldwide. For Sparky, the boy who had such lack of success in school and whose work was rejected again and again was Charles Schulz. He created the "Peanuts" comic strip and the little cartoon character whose kite would never fly and who never succeeded in kicking a football, Charlie Brown.

A multi-genre research project consists of creative pieces—poetry, artwork, letters, diary entries, interviews, conversations, newspaper articles, scripts, speeches, email, obituaries, etc.—imaginative writing based on fact. The multi-genre research project begins with interest in the subject. Coherence in a multi-genre research project is developed along the way as the writer collects information, interprets it, and considers appropriate genre to creatively represent ideas. Use the graphic organizer below to record information as you conduct research.

> **LITERARY TERMS**
> Coherence is the quality of unity or logical connection among ideas. It is achieved by the clear and orderly presentation of ideas in a paragraph or essay.

Topic: Charles M. Schulz

MLA Format: "Sparky" by Earl Nightingale

Nightingale, Earl. Earl Nightingale's Greatest Discovery (PMA Book Series). New York: Dodd, Mead, 1987.

Melding Fact, Interpretation, and Imagination

Research Question:

How did Charles Schulz overcome obstacles to achieve his American Dream?

Research Facts:	Reflection:	Possible Genres:	Purpose/Rationale:
Record pertinent information from the source and include page numbers. Be sure to use quotation marks if it is a direct quote.	Question and comment on the facts presented. Imagine the people, the situation, the events surrounding the researched facts.	Consider possible genres to convey the facts and a creative response to the question posed or to comments. What is the best format for this information?	Note ideas for content to include within the genre.

Melding Facts, Interpretation, and Imagination

Topic: Charles M. Schulz

MLA Format:

"Charles M. Schulz." <u>Encyclopedia of World Biography.</u> 2010.
Advameg, Inc. 20 November 2008. <http://www.notablebiographies.
com/Ro-Sc/Schulz-Charles-M.html>

Melding Fact, Interpretation, and Imagination

Research Question:

How did Charles Schulz overcome obstacles to achieve his American Dream?

Research Facts:	Reflection:	Possible Genres:	Purpose/Rationale:
Record pertinent information from the source and include page numbers. Be sure to use quotation marks if it is a direct quote.	Question and comment on the facts presented. Imagine the people, the situation, the events surrounding the researched facts.	Consider possible genres to convey the facts and a creative response to the question posed or to comments. What is the best format for this information?	Note ideas for content to include within the genre.

CHARLES M. SCHULZ

From Notable Biographies

Born: November 26, 1922
Minneapolis, Minnesota
Died: February 12, 2000
Santa Rosa, California

AMERICAN CARTOONIST

Cartoonist and creator of *Peanuts*, Charles M. Schulz was the winner of two Reuben, two Peabody, and five Emmy awards and a member of the Cartoonist Hall of Fame.

Early life

Charles Monroe Schulz was born in Minneapolis, Minnesota, on November 26, 1922, the son of Carl and Dena Halverson Schulz. His father was a barber. Charles loved to read the comics section of the newspaper with his father and was given the nickname "Sparky" after Sparkplug, the horse in the *Barney Google* comic strip. He began to draw pictures of his favorite cartoon characters at age six. At school in St. Paul, Minnesota, he was bright and allowed to skip two grades, which made him often the smallest in his class. Noting his interest in drawing, his mother encouraged him to take a correspondence course (in which lessons and exercises are mailed to students and then returned when completed) from Art Instruction, Inc., in Minneapolis after he graduated from high school.

During World War II (1939–45; a war fought between the Axis: Italy, Japan, and Germany—and the Allies: France, England, the Soviet Union, and the United States), Schulz was drafted into the army and sent to Europe, rising to the rank of sergeant. After the war he returned to Minnesota as a young man with strong Christian beliefs. For a while he worked part-time for a Catholic magazine and taught for Art Instruction, Inc. Some of his work appeared in the *Saturday Evening Post*, and eventually he created a cartoon entitled *Li'l Folks* for the *St. Paul Pioneer Press*.

Creates "Peanuts"

In 1950 the United Feature Syndicate of New York decided to publish Schulz's new comic strip, which he had wanted to call Li'l Folks but which was named Peanuts by the company. In 1950 the cartoon began appearing in seven newspapers with the characters Charlie Brown, Shermy, Patty, and Snoopy. Within a year the strip appeared in thirty-five papers, and by 1956 it was in over a hundred. The Peanuts cartoons were centered on the simple and touching figures of a boy, Charlie Brown, and his dog, Snoopy and their family and school friends. Adults were never seen, only hinted at, and the action involved ordinary, everyday happenings.

My Notes

GRAMMAR & USAGE

One way writers vary sentence beginnings is with the use of participial phrases. Notice that the writer uses the participial phrase "noting his interest in drawing" to describe Schulz's mother. Be sure an introductory participial phrase is followed by the noun it modifies; otherwise it becomes a *dangling modifier*.

Melding Facts, Interpretation, and Imagination

Charlie Brown had a round head with half-circles for ears and nose, dots for eyes, and a line for a mouth. Things always seemed to go wrong for him, and he was often puzzled by the problems that life and his peers dealt out to him: the crabbiness of Lucy; the unanswerable questions of Linus, a young intellectual with a security blanket; the self-absorption of Schroeder the musician; the teasing of his schoolmates; and the behavior of Snoopy, the floppy-eared dog with the wild imagination, who sees himself as a fighter pilot trying to shoot down the Red Baron (based on a famous German pilot during World War I) when he is not running a "Beagle Scout" troop consisting of the bird, Woodstock, and his friends.

Charlie Brown's inability to cope with the constant disappointments in life, the failure and renewal of trust (such as Lucy's tricking him every time he tries to kick the football), and his touching efforts to accept what happens as deserved were traits shared to a lesser degree by the other characters. Even crabby Lucy cannot interest Schroeder or understand baseball; Linus is puzzled by life's mysteries and the refusal of the "Great Pumpkin" to show up on Halloween. The odd elements and defects of humanity in general were reflected by Schulz's gentle humor, which made the cartoon appealing to the public.

Schulz insisted that he was not trying to send any moral and religious messages in Peanuts. However, even to the casual reader Peanuts offered lessons to be learned. Schulz employed everyday humor to make a point, but usually it was the intellectual comment that carried the charge, even if it was only "Good Grief!" Grief was the human condition, but it was good when it taught us something about ourselves and was lightened by laughter.

Huge success

As the strip became more popular, new characters were added, including Sally, Charlie Brown's sister; Rerun, Lucy's brother; Peppermint Patty; Marcie; Franklin; José Peterson; Pigpen; Snoopy's brother Spike; and the bird, Woodstock. Schulz received the Reuben award from the National Cartoonists Society in 1955 and 1964.

By this time Schulz was famous across the world. Peanuts appeared in over twenty-three hundred newspapers. The cartoon branched out into television, and in 1965 the classic special A Charlie Brown Christmas won Peabody and Emmy awards. Many more television specials and Emmys were to follow. An off-Broadway stage production, You're a Good Man, Charlie Brown, was created in 1967 and ran for four years (it was also revived in 1999). Many volumes of Schulz's work were published in at least nineteen languages, and the success of Peanuts inspired clothes, stationery, toys, games, and other merchandise. Schulz also wrote a book, Why, Charlie Brown, Why? (which became a CBS television special) to help children understand the subject of cancer (his mother had died of cancer in 1943).

Besides the previously mentioned awards, Schulz received the Yale Humor Award, 1956; School Bell Award, National Education Association, 1960; and honorary degrees from Anderson College, 1963, and St. Mary's College of California, 1969. A "Charles M. Schulz Award" honoring comic artists was created by the United Feature Syndicate in 1980.

Later years

The year 1990 marked the fortieth anniversary of Peanuts. An exhibit at the Louvre, in Paris, France, called "Snoopy in Fashion," featured three hundred Snoopy dolls dressed in fashions created by more than fifteen world-famous designers. It later traveled to the United States. Also in 1990, the Smithsonian Institution featured an exhibit titled, "This Is Your Childhood, Charlie Brown … Children in American Culture, 1945–1970." By the late 1990s Peanuts ran in over two thousand newspapers throughout the world every day.

Schulz was diagnosed with cancer in November 1999 after the disease was discovered during an unrelated operation. He announced in December 1999 that he would retire in the year 2000, the day after the final Peanuts strip. Schulz died on February 12, 2000, one day before his farewell strip was to be in newspapers. Schulz was twice married, to Joyce Halverson in 1949 (divorced 1972) and to Jean Clyde in 1973. He had five children by his first marriage.

In March 2000 the Board of Supervisors of Sonoma County, California, passed a resolution to rename Sonoma County Airport after Schulz. In June 2000 plans were announced for bronze sculptures of eleven Peanuts characters to be placed on the St. Paul riverfront. That same month President Bill Clinton (1946–) signed a bill giving Schulz the Congressional Gold Medal. In 2002 an exhibition entitled "Speak Softly and Carry a Beagle: The Art of Charles Schulz" was held at the Norman Rockwell Museum in Stockbridge, Massachusetts. Also in 2002, it was announced that the proposed Charles M. Schulz Museum and Research Center in Santa Rosa, California, would be completed in August 2003.

My Notes

WORD CONNECTIONS

Diagnose contains the Greek root *-gno-* meaning "know." This root is also the basis for *agnostic*. Coming through Latin, the root appears in *recognize* and *cognitive*.

Melding Facts, Interpretation, and Imagination

Use this organizer to record notes and plans based on a third piece of research.

Topic: Charles M. Schulz

MLA Format:

Melding Fact, Interpretation, and Imagination

Research Question:

How did Charles Schulz overcome obstacles to achieve his American Dream?

Research Facts:	Reflection:	Possible Genres:	Purpose/Rationale:
Record pertinent information from the source and include page numbers. Be sure to use quotation marks if it is a direct quote.	*Question and comment on the facts presented. Imagine the people, the situation, the events surrounding the researched facts.*	*Consider possible genres to convey the facts and a creative response to the question posed or to comments. What is the best format for this information?*	*Note ideas for content to include within the genre.*

Use a resource that explains how to document sources using the MLA format and record an example, properly citing each of the genres listed below.

Recording Resources

Book:

Journal:

Internet:

Interview:

Magazine:

Video:

Others:

After you have shared resources, consider which ones you will use in conjunction with the ones studied as a whole class, and create an Annotated Bibliography that documents and annotates each source in alphabetical order.

Meeting in the Middle

Working from the class-generated thesis, collaborate to compose the body of genres that will make up your group MGR.

Planning: Take notes, share prewriting strategies, and consult additional resources as you consider these guiding questions in your planning.

- Represent ideas: What is important about this information in relation to the thesis?

- Genre conventions: What are the essential features and format specific to this genre?

- Purpose and audience: What is the purpose of the text, and who is the target audience?

- Use of language: What stylistic techniques address the purpose and audience?

ACADEMIC VOCABULARY

Genre conventions are the essential features and format that characterize a specific genre.

Drafting: Each group member will select one of the six different genres from your group brainstorm and individually generate a draft incorporating your planning.

To guide revision, use this peer response form to respond to genres shared within your writing groups.

Peer Conference

Writer:	Peer Responders:		
Focus area requested by the writer:	**What works well** (e.g., ideas, genre conventions, stylistic technique, etc.)	**Questioning:** I am confused/want to know more about... As a reader, I'm getting lost...	**Suggestions:** Here's what I think might help...Have you tried this strategy...

Thematic Threads to Create Flow

Define Coherence:

Make a prediction about the role of coherence in a multi-genre research project:

Review the student example of a multi-genre research project. How did the author link one genre to the next and sequence the ideas presented?

With the class, brainstorm a list of possible ways to link genres and provide transitions for the reader in a multi-genre research project.

LITERARY TERMS

A **motif** is a recurrent image, symbol, theme, character type, subject, or narrative detail that becomes a unifying element in an artistic work.

In groups, review the list above, and circle three that could work for your multi-genre research project. Now, discuss how each of the three would create a thematic or symbolic connection as well as how to thread it throughout the paper as a **motif** to clarify and unify meaning for the reader.

As you discuss your three options in your group, use the following focus questions as talking points for planning to use each symbolic link.

- How does the option work to advance our thesis?
- How does the option convey meaning to the reader about the topic/theme?
- How does the option connect the research and ideas to one of the following: topic, event, person, place, etc.?
- How does the option sequence our ideas to make our assertion and research clear to our readers?

Use the Creating Coherence chart below to organize your discussion points about how one genre connects to the next. Plot your ideas on the chart. Evaluate the effectiveness of your metaphor and revise accordingly.

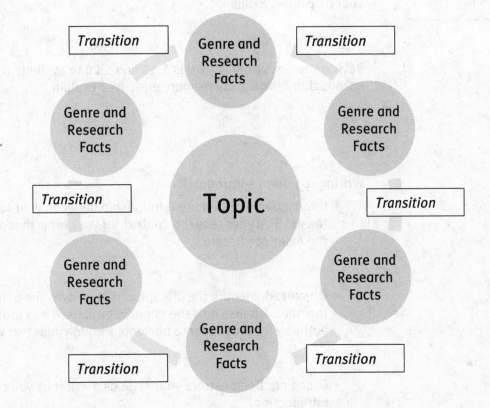

Discuss possibilities for visually representing the thematic strand, and sketch initial ideas. After considering all options, create a symbolic visual to convey meaning to potential readers for your thematic strand and collection of genres.

Introducing and Concluding the Multi-Genre Research Project

SUGGESTED LEARNING STRATEGIES: Sharing and Responding, Drafting, Think-Pair-Share, Free Writing

ACADEMIC VOCABULARY

Discourse is the verbal or written expression of thoughts and ideas.

Discourse is language and speech, especially the type of language used in a particular context or subject. Often in writing or speech we use language that is specific to a particular audience, purpose, context, and genre. Recall a time in which you changed or altered your discourse. Explain.

Review the texts from Activities 5.19 and 5.20 to evaluate their introductions. Which one is more effective? Explain.

Writing to Inform — Introduction

• Informative: Explain the relationship between your topic and thesis. Give your reader a context for your topic that addresses the American Dream.

• Organized: Identify the metaphor that weaves the genres together. Discuss how the paper is organized and provide a pathway for the reader to navigate through your text with ease.

• Engaging: Demonstrate your style as a writer as you craft your introduction.

Writing to Reflect — Conclusion

• Say: What have I said about the topic?

• Mean: What does this mean in relation to the American Dream?

• Matter: What is the larger significance of the topic and meaning to life in general?

Reflection

• Is my conclusion inductive or deductive? Explain.

Creative Packaging

SUGGESTED LEARNING STRATEGIES: Discussion Groups, Sketching, Sharing and Responding

Use the table below to organize your presentation of your multi-genre research project. You may also use this chart as a planning guide.

Section of MGR	Criteria	Ideas for Development
Cover Page	• Original Title • Symbolic Visuals • Heading (Name, Date, Period)	
Table of Contents	The table of contents provides an overview of sections in order of appearance in the paper. Be sure to include the following on your table of contents: introduction, genre collection, conclusion, reflective end notes, and annotated bibliography.	
Dear Reader Letter: (Introduction)	This opening letter provides some background information about your topic to your audience. It also introduces your thesis and how you wove together the collection of genres so the reader knows how to navigate through your paper.	
Collection of Genres	The body consists of a collection of genres created to help your reader understand your subject and thesis. This is where the multi-genre aspect of the paper is displayed via a minimum of six different genres threaded together with a metaphor or motif.	
Conclusion	What have you learned about the topic from this research project? What did you learn about the process from working on this project?	
Reflective End Notes	What genres did you include in your writing and why? Assemble your Reflective Endnotes so that the genres appear in sequential order and contain the following information: • Genre Number, Title, and Genre • Rationale: Explain why this particular genre was selected. • Reflection: How are the facts presented in the creative interpretation?	
Annotated Bibliography	Provide your list of research sources and a brief explanation of how you used that research in your project. Consult the *MLA Handbook* or style manual preferred by your teacher or an online writing lab for instructions on format.	

Carousel Wheel Reflection

What did you observe that worked well in other MGR papers that you would like to add to your own? Explain.

Reflection on the Multi-Genre Research Process

What did you learn from the research process from this group project?

How will you use that information to be successful when you create a multi-genre research project individually?

Care Enough to Really Search

SUGGESTED LEARNING STRATEGIES: Brainstorming, Sorting, Think-Pair-Share, KWHL Chart

Embedded Assessment Assignment: Your assignment is to write a multi-genre research project on a person, event, movement, or topic of interest to you as it relates to the American Dream.

Brainstorm a list of potential topics.

Select one and explain why you want to inquire into this topic.

KWHL Chart

What do you already know about this person/subject?	What do you want to know/learn about this person/subject?	How will you gather data and information about this person/subject?	What are you learning about this person/subject as it unfolds?

Writing a Multi-Genre Research Project

SUGGESTED LEARNING STRATEGIES: **Quickwrite, Think-Pair-Share, Graphic Organizer, Discussion Groups, Drafting**

Assignment

Your assignment is to write a multi-genre research project on a person, event, movement, or topic of interest to you as it relates to the American Dream.

Steps

Planning

1. Choose a prewriting strategy to generate ideas that provide a focus for your topic (person, event, movement, concept, etc.) as it relates to the American Dream. Quickwrite an exploration of your thinking on the topic and identify areas that require further insight—this quickwrite could be used to focus your research.

2. Think-pair-share your findings to help you consider your ideas, narrow your focus, and generate a research question. Next, draft a working thesis that answers your focus question and that can be used as a guiding factor to guide your research and multi-genre research project.

3. Conduct research (7-8 primary and secondary sources) to explore all aspects of your thesis. Use the notetaking guide from Activity 5.20 to help collect information and plan your ideas. Use resources to assist with documenting your sources correctly in an annotated bibliography.

4. Consider which ideas from your research you will include in your paper, and choose an appropriate genre to creatively express the connection between your research and your interpretation. Remember, you will need a minimum of six different genres in your collection.

5. Reflect on research and ideas and brainstorm a list of creative ways to connect the genres via a metaphor or motif (e.g., chapters, seasons, time, movie script, song lyrics, recipes, months of the year, colors in a rainbow, cartoons, visual art images, statistics, expository text, sports rules, etc.). Select an appropriate metaphor and consider how it connects to your thesis, research, genres, and ideas.

6. Assemble your writing pieces in a coherent order using the transitions (e.g., metaphor or motif) you select to guide your reader from one genre to the next.

Writing a Multi-Genre Research Project

Revising

7. Meet regularly in writing groups to share your drafts and solicit feedback to revise your drafts for the following:

   ▶ Coherence and clarity of ideas presented within the genre

   ▶ Seamless integration of research

   ▶ Appropriate genres to express ideas

   ▶ Appropriate use of conventions

   You might want to use the Peer Conference sheet from Activity 5.21 to help focus the feedback from your peers.

8. Use the chart in Activity 5.24 to organize your multi-genre research project. Do not forget to include a thematic link for the entire paper in the form of a metaphor or motif that moves the reader from one genre to the next

Editing

9. Reread your revised draft silently to make final edits (e.g., grammar, punctuation, spelling) in preparation for publishing a technically sound document.

10. Compose a title for your piece by generating a list of possible titles stemming from ideas, topics, or lines from the text. Review and rank your list. Select the title that is most engaging and captures the essence of your text.

⬀TECHNOLOGY TIP Depending on the genres you have selected for the group multi-genre research project, you may want to use products such as graphics programs, digital cameras, and so on to create parts of your project. You may want to create a multimedia presentation for the final product.

SCORING GUIDE

Scoring Criteria	Exemplary	Proficient	Emerging
Ideas	Multi-genre research project provides an extensive, well-researched response to the essential question. It includes substantial support for the ideas presented about the subject as it relates to the American Dream.	Multi-genre research project responds appropriately to the essential question. It provides adequate support for the ideas presented about the subject as it relates to the American Dream.	Multi-genre research project does not thoroughly address all aspects of the essential question, and/or provides inadequate support for the ideas presented about the subject as it relates to the American Dream.
Organization	The multi-genre paper is well-written and consists of: • Cover page: gripping title and symbolic visual that enhance ideas in the paper • Introduction: engages the reader in the topic providing a sophisticated context for the reader • Body: skillfully uses complex genres that seamlessly integrate in-depth research and ideas in support of the thesis • Transitions: uses a sophisticated metaphor to move the reader with ease from one genre to the next • Conclusion: provides in depth reflection that brings closure to the paper • Thorough annotated bibliography.	The multi-genre paper consists of: • Cover page: appropriate title with a relevant visual • Introduction: introduces the topic, contains a thesis, and sets the context • Body: uses six different genres that incorporate research and ideas in support of the thesis • Transitions: uses a metaphor to move the reader from one genre to the next • Conclusion: reflects and brings closure to the paper • Complete annotated bibliography.	The multi-genre paper may or may not consist of: • Incomplete cover page • Limited introduction that does not appropriately introduce the topic, contains an unclear thesis, and/or does not adequately explain to the reader how to proceed through the paper • Body that uses fewer than six different genres and/or does not incorporate research and ideas in support of the thesis • Transitions do not adequately move the reader from one genre to the next • Conclusion does not provide sufficient reflection and/or bring closure to the paper • Limited or missing annotated bibliography.

SCORING GUIDE

Scoring Criteria	Exemplary	Proficient	Emerging
Writing Process	Writing shows extensive evidence of thoughtful planning, significant revision, and careful editing for: • Coherence / clarity of ideas • Seamless integration of research • Genres that enhance ideas • Solid command of grammar, punctuation, and conventions.	Writing shows evidence of planning, revision, and editing for: • Coherence / clarity of ideas • Seamless integration of research • Appropriate genres to express ideas • Appropriate use of conventions.	Writing shows minimal evidence of planning and/or effective revision or editing. • Ideas are unclear • Very little integration of research • Genres used are not appropriate to express ideas • Extensive errors in grammar, punctuation, and conventions.
Additional Criteria			

Comments:

Reflection

An important aspect of growing as a learner is to reflect on where you have been, what you have accomplished, what helped you to learn, and how you will apply your new knowledge in the future. Use the following questions to guide your thinking and to identify evidence of your learning. Use separate notebook paper.

Thinking about Concepts

1. Using specific examples from this unit, respond to the Essential Questions:

   • What does it mean to pursue happiness?

   • How does a writer represent research through multiple texts?

2. Consider the new academic vocabulary from this unit (**Coherence, Genre Conventions, Discourse**) as well as academic vocabulary from previous units and select 3–4 terms of which your understanding has grown. For each term, answer the following questions:

   • What was your understanding of the word prior to the unit?

   • How has your understanding of the word evolved throughout the unit?

   • How will you apply your understanding in the future?

Thinking about Connections

3. Review the activities and products (artifacts) you created. Choose those that most reflect your growth or increase in understanding.

4. For each artifact that you choose, record, respond, and reflect on your thinking and understanding, using the following questions as a guide:

   a. What skill/knowledge does this artifact reflect, and how did you learn this skill/knowledge?

   b. How did your understanding of the power of language expand through your engagement with this artifact?

   c. How will you apply this skill or knowledge in the future?

5. Create this reflection as Portfolio pages—one for each artifact you choose. Use the following model for your headings and commentary on questions.

> ## Thinking About Thinking
> ### Portfolio Entry
>
> Concept:
>
> Description of Artifact:
>
> Commentary on Questions:

Grammar Handbook

Part 1: Using Pronouns Clearly

Because a pronoun REFERS BACK to a noun or TAKES THE PLACE OF that noun, you have to use the correct pronoun so that your reader clearly understands which noun your pronoun is referring to. Therefore, pronouns should:

1. Agree in number

If the pronoun takes the place of a singular noun, you have to use a singular pronoun.

> If a student parks a car on campus, he or she has to buy a parking sticker.
> (**NOT:** If a student parks a car on campus, they have to buy a parking sticker.)

Remember: the words everybody, anybody, anyone, each, neither, nobody, someone, a person, etc. are singular and take singular pronouns.

> Everybody ought to do his or her best. (NOT: their best)
> Neither of the girls brought her umbrella. (NOT: their umbrellas)

NOTE: Many people find the construction "his or her" wordy, so if it is possible to use a plural noun as your antecedent so that you can use "they" as your pronoun, it may be wise to do so. If you do use a singular noun and the context makes the gender clear, then it is permissible to use just "his" or "her" rather than "his or her."

2. Agree in person

If you are writing in the "first person" (I), don't confuse your reader by switching to the "second person" (you) or "third person" (he, she, they, it, etc.). Similarly, if you are using the "second person," don't switch to "first" or "third."

> When a person comes to class, he or she should have his or her homework ready.
> (**NOT:** When a person comes to class, you should have your homework ready.)

3. Refer clearly to a specific noun.

Don't be vague or ambiguous.

> **NOT:** Although the motorcycle hit the tree, it was not damaged. (Is "it" the motorcycle or the tree?)
> **NOT:** I don't think they should show violence on TV. (Who are "they"?)
> **NOT:** Vacation is coming soon, which is nice. (What is nice, the vacation or the fact that it is coming soon?)
> **NOT:** George worked in a national forest last summer. This may be his life's work. (What word does "this" refer to?)
> **NOT:** If you put this sheet in your notebook, you can refer to it. (What does "it" refer to, the sheet or your notebook?)

Pronoun Case

Pronoun case is really a very simple matter. There are three cases.

- Subjective case: pronouns used as subject.
- Objective case: pronouns used as objects of verbs or prepositions.
- Possessive case: pronouns which express ownership.

Pronouns as Subjects	Pronouns as Objects	Pronouns that show Possession
I	me	my (mine)
you	you	your (yours)
he, she, it	him, her, it	his, her (hers), it (its)
we	us	our (ours)
they	them	their (theirs)
who	whom	whose

The pronouns **this, that, these, those**, and **which** do not change form.

Some problems of case:

1. **In compound structures, where there are two pronouns or a noun and a pronoun, drop the other noun for a moment. Then you can see which case you want.**

    Not: Bob and me travel a good deal.
    (Would you say, "me travel"?)
    Not: He gave the flowers to Jane and I.
    (Would you say, "he gave the flowers to I"?)
    Not: Us men like the coach.
    (Would you say, "us like the coach"?)

2. **In comparisons. Comparisons usually follow than or as:**

    He is taller than I (am tall).
    This helps you as much as (it helps) me.
    She is as noisy as I (am).

Comparisons are really shorthand sentences which usually omit words, such as those in the parentheses in the sentences above. If you complete the comparison in your head, you can choose the correct case for the pronoun.

    Not: He is taller than me.
    (Would you say, "than me am tall"?)

3. **In formal and semiformal writing:**

Use the subjective form after a form of the verb to be.

    Formal: It is I.
    Informal: It is me.

Use whom in the objective case.

    Formal: To whom am I talking?
    Informal: Who am I talking to?

Part 2: Appositives

An appositive is a noun or pronoun — often with modifiers — set beside another noun or pronoun to explain or identify it. Here are some examples of appositives (the noun or pronoun will be in blue, the **appositive will be in boldface**).

> Your friend **Bill** is in trouble.
>
> My brother's car, **a sporty red convertible with bucket seats**, is the envy of my friends.
>
> The chief surgeon, **an expert in organ-transplant procedures**, took her nephew on a hospital tour.

An appositive phrase usually follows the word it explains or identifies, but it may also precede it.

> **A bold innovator**, Wassily Kadinsky is known for his colorful abstract paintings.
>
> **The first state to ratify the U. S. Constitution**, Delaware is rich in history.
>
> **A beautiful collie**, Skip was my favorite dog.

Punctuation of Appositives

In some cases, the noun being explained is too general without the appositive; the information is essential to the meaning of the sentence. When this is the case, do not place commas around the appositive; just leave it alone. If the sentence would be clear and complete without the appositive, then commas are necessary; place one before and one after the appositive. Here are some examples.

> The popular US president **John Kennedy** was known for his eloquent and inspirational speeches.

Here we do not put commas around the appositive, because it is essential information. Without the appositive, the sentence would be, "The popular US president was known for his eloquent and inspirational speeches." We wouldn't know which president was being referred to.

> John Kennedy, **the popular US president**, was known for his eloquent and inspirational speeches.

Here we put commas around the appositive because it is not essential information. Without the appositive, the sentence would be, "John Kennedy was known for his eloquent and inspirational speeches." We still know who the subject of the sentence is without the appositive.

Part 3: What is the Difference Between Adjectives and Adverbs?

The Basic Rules: Adjectives

Adjectives modify nouns. To modify means to change in some way. For example:

- "I ate a meal." *Meal* is a noun. We don't know what kind of meal; all we know is that someone ate a meal.
- "I ate an enormous lunch." *Lunch* is a noun, and *enormous* is an adjective that modifies it. It tells us what kind of meal the person ate.

Adjectives usually answer one of a few different questions: "What kind?" or "Which?" or "How many?" For example:

- "The *tall* girl is riding a *new* bike." *Tall* tells us which girl we're talking about. *New* tells us what kind of bike we're talking about.
- "The *tough* professor gave us the *final* exam." *Tough* tells us what kind of professor we're talking about. *Final* tells us which exam we're talking about.
- "*Fifteen* students passed the midterm exam; *twelve* students passed the final exam." *Fifteen* and *twelve* both tell us how many students; *midterm* and *final* both tell us which exam.

So, generally speaking, adjectives answer the following questions: Which? What kind of? How many?

The Basic Rules: Adverbs

Adverbs modify verbs, adjectives, and other adverbs. (You can recognize adverbs easily because many of them are formed by adding *-ly* to an adjective, though that is not always the case.) The most common question that adverbs answer is **how**.

Let's look at verbs first.

- "She sang *beautifully*." *Beautifully* is an adverb that modifies *sang*. It tells us **how** she sang.
- "The cellist played *carelessly*." *Carelessly* is an adverb that modifies *played*. It tells us **how** the cellist played.

Adverbs also modify adjectives and other adverbs.

- "That woman is *extremely* nice." *Nice* is an adjective that modifies the noun *woman*. *Extremely* is an adverb that modifies *nice*; it tells us **how** nice she is. **How** nice is she? She's extremely nice.
- "It was a *terribly* hot afternoon." *Hot* is an adjective that modifies the noun *afternoon*. *Terribly* is an adverb that modifies the adjective *hot*. **How** hot is it? Terribly hot.

So, generally speaking, adverbs answer the question **how**. (They can also answer the questions **when**, **where**, and **why**.)

Part 4: Verbals

Gerunds

A gerund is a verbal that ends in *-ing* and functions as a noun. The term *verbal* indicates that a gerund, like the other two kinds of verbals, is based on a verb and therefore expresses action or a state of being. However, since a gerund functions as a noun, it occupies some positions in a sentence that a noun ordinarily would, for example: subject, direct object, subject complement, and object of preposition.

Gerund as subject:

- Traveling might satisfy your desire for new experiences. (**Traveling** is the gerund.)
- The study abroad program might satisfy your desire for new experiences. (The gerund has been removed.)

Gerund as direct object:

- They do not appreciate my singing. (The gerund is **singing**.)
- They do not appreciate my assistance. (The gerund has been removed)

Gerund as subject complement:

- My cat's favorite activity is sleeping. (The gerund is **sleeping**.)
- My cat's favorite food is salmon. (The gerund has been removed.)

Gerund as object of preposition:

- The police arrested him for speeding. (The gerund is **speeding**.)
- The police arrested him for criminal activity. (The gerund has been removed.)

A Gerund Phrase is a group of words consisting of a gerund and the modifier(s) and/or (pro)noun(s) or noun phrase(s) that function as the direct object(s), indirect object(s), or complement(s) of the action or state expressed in the gerund, such as:

The gerund phrase functions as the subject of the sentence.

Finding **a needle** <u>in a haystack</u> would be easier than what we're trying to do.

Finding (gerund) **a needle** (direct object of action expressed in gerund) <u>in a haystack</u> (prepositional phrase as adverb)

The gerund phrase functions as the direct object of the verb *appreciate*.

I hope that you appreciate **my** offering you *this opportunity*.

my (possessive pronoun adjective form, modifying the gerund)
offering (gerund)
you (indirect object of action expressed in gerund)
this opportunity (direct object of action expressed in gerund)

The gerund phrase functions as the subject complement.

Ned's favorite tactic has been **lying to** his constituents.

lying to (gerund)
his constituents (direct object of action expressed in gerund)

The gerund phrase functions as the object of the preposition *for*.

You might get in trouble for **faking** an illness *to avoid work*.

faking (gerund)
an illness (direct object of action expressed in gerund)
to avoid work (infinitive phrase as adverb)

The gerund phrase functions as the subject of the sentence.

Being the boss made Jeff feel uneasy.

Being (gerund)
the boss (subject complement for Jeff, via state of being expressed in gerund)

Punctuation
A gerund virtually never requires any punctuation with it.

Points to remember:
1. A gerund is a verbal ending in -ing that is used as a noun.
2. A gerund phrase consists of a gerund plus modifier(s), object(s), and/or complement(s).
3. Gerunds and gerund phrases virtually never require punctuation.

Participles
A participle is a verbal that is used as an adjective and most often ends in *-ing* or *-ed*. The term *verbal* indicates that a participle, like the other two kinds of verbals, is based on a verb and therefore expresses action or a state of being. However, since they function as adjectives, participles modify nouns or pronouns. There are two types of participles: present participles and past participles. Present participles end in *-ing*. Past participles end in *-ed*, *-en*, *-d*, *-t*, or *-n*, as in the words *asked*, *eaten*, *saved*, *dealt*, and *seen*.

- The *crying* baby had a wet diaper.
- *Shaken*, he walked away from the *wrecked* car.
- The *burning* log fell off the fire.
- *Smiling*, she hugged the *panting* dog.

A participial phrase is a group of words consisting of a participle and the modifier(s) and/or (pro)noun(s) or noun phrase(s) that function as the direct object(s), indirect object(s), or complement(s) of the action or state expressed in the participle, such as:

Example: Removing his coat, Jack rushed to the river.

The participial phrase functions as an adjective modifying *Jack*.

Removing (participle)
his coat (direct object of action expressed in participle)

> **Example:** Delores noticed her cousin **walking** along the shoreline.

The participial phrase functions as an adjective modifying *cousin*.
walking (participle)
along the shoreline (prepositional phrase as adverb)

> **Example:** Children **introduced to** music early develop strong intellectual skills.

The participial phrase functions as an adjective modifying *children*.
introduced (to) (participle)
music (direct object of action expressed in participle)
early (adverb)

> **Example: Having been** a gymnast, Lynn knew the importance of exercise.

The participial phrase functions as an adjective modifying *Lynn*.
Having been (participle)
a gymnast (subject complement for Lynn, via state of being expressed in participle)

Placement: In order to prevent confusion, a participial phrase must be placed as close to the noun it modifies as possible, and the noun must be clearly stated.

- *Carrying a heavy pile of books,* his foot caught on a step.
- *Carrying a heavy pile of books,* he caught his foot on a step.

In the first sentence there is no clear indication of who or what is performing the action expressed in the participle carrying. Certainly foot can't be logically understood to function in this way. This situation is an example of a **dangling modifier** error since the modifier (the participial phrase) is not modifying any specific noun in the sentence and is thus left "dangling." Since a person must be doing the carrying for the sentence to make sense, a noun or pronoun that refers to a person must be in the place immediately after the participial phrase, as in the second sentence.

Punctuation: When a participial phrase begins a sentence, a comma should be placed after the phrase.

- *Arriving at the store,* I found that it was closed.
- *Washing and polishing the car,* Frank developed sore muscles.

If the participle or participial phrase comes in the middle of a sentence, it should be set off with commas only if the information is not essential to the meaning of the sentence.

- Sid, *watching an old movie,* drifted in and out of sleep.
- The church, *destroyed by a fire,* was never rebuilt.

Note that if the participial phrase is essential to the meaning of the sentence, no commas should be used:

- The student *earning the highest grade point average* will receive a special award.
- The guy *wearing the chicken costume* is my cousin.

If a participial phrase comes at the end of a sentence, a comma usually precedes the phrase if it modifies an earlier word in the sentence but not if the phrase directly follows the word it modifies.

- The local residents often saw Ken wandering through the streets.
  (The phrase modifies *Ken*, not *residents*.)
- Tom nervously watched the woman, alarmed by her silence.
  (The phrase modifies *Tom*, not *woman*.)

Points to remember

1. A participle is a verbal ending in *-ing* (present) or *-ed*, *-en*, *-d*, *-t*, or *-n* (past) that functions as an adjective, modifying a noun or pronoun.

2. A participial phrase consists of a participle plus modifier(s), object(s), and/or complement(s).

3. Participles and participial phrases must be placed as close to the nouns or pronouns they modify as possible, and those nouns or pronouns must be clearly stated.

4. A participial phrase is set off with commas when it:
   (a) comes at the beginning of a sentence
   (b) interrupts a sentence as a nonessential element
   (c) comes at the end of a sentence and is separated from the word it modifies.

Infinitives

An infinitive is a verbal consisting of the word *to* plus a verb (in its simplest "stem" form) and functioning as a noun, adjective, or adverb. The term *verbal* indicates that an infinitive, like the other two kinds of verbals, is based on a verb and therefore expresses action or a state of being. However, the infinitive may function as a subject, direct object, subject complement, adjective, or adverb in a sentence. Although an infinitive is easy to locate because of the *to* + verb form, deciding what function it has in a sentence can sometimes be confusing.

- *To wait* seemed foolish when decisive action was required. (subject)
- Everyone wanted *to go*. (direct object)
- His ambition is *to fly*. (subject complement)
- He lacked the strength *to resist*. (adjective)
- We must study *to learn*. (adverb)

Be sure not to confuse an infinitive—a verbal consisting of *to* plus a verb—with a prepositional phrase beginning with *to*, which consists of *to* plus a noun or pronoun and any modifiers.

- **Infinitives:** to fly, to draw, to become, to enter, to stand, to catch, to belong
- **Prepositional Phrases:** to him, to the committee, to my house, to the mountains, to us, to this address

An Infinitive Phrase is a group of words consisting of an infinitive and the modifier(s) and/or (pro)noun(s) or noun phrase(s) that function as the actor(s), direct object(s), indirect object(s), or complement(s) of the action or state expressed in the infinitive, such as:

We intended **to leave** <u>early</u>.

The infinitive phrase functions as the direct object of the verb *intended*.

to leave (infinitive)
<u>early</u> (adverb)

I have a paper **to write** <u>before class</u>.

The infinitive phrase functions as an adjective modifying *paper*.

to write (infinitive)
<u>before class</u> (prepositional phrase as adverb)

Phil agreed **to give** <u>me</u> *a ride*.

The infinitive phrase functions as the direct object of the verb *agreed*.

to give (infinitive)
<u>me</u> (indirect object of action expressed in infinitive)
a ride (direct object of action expressed in infinitive)

They asked <u>**me**</u> to bring *some food*.

The infinitive phrase functions as the direct object of the verb *asked*.

<u>**me**</u> (actor or "subject" of infinitive phrase)
to bring (infinitive)
some food (direct object of action expressed in infinitive)

Everyone wanted **Carol** to be <u>**the captain**</u> *of the team*.

The infinitive phrase functions as the direct object of the verb *wanted*.

Carol (actor or "subject" of infinitive phrase)
to be (infinitive)
<u>**the captain**</u> (subject complement for Carol, via state of being expressed in infinitive)
of the team (prepositional phrase as adjective)

Actors: In these last two examples the actor of the infinitive phrase could be roughly characterized as the "subject" of the action or state expressed in the infinitive. It is somewhat misleading to use the word *subject*, however, since an infinitive phrase is not a full clause with a subject and a finite verb. Also notice that when it is a pronoun, the actor appears in the objective case (*me*, not *I*, in the fourth example). Certain verbs, when they take an infinitive direct object, require an actor for the infinitive phrase; others can't have an actor. Still other verbs can go either way, as the charts below illustrate.

Verbs that take infinitive objects without actors:			
agree	begin	continue	decide
fail	hesitate	hope	intend
learn	neglect	offer	plan
prefer	pretend	promise	refuse
remember	start	try	

Examples:

- Most students *plan* to study.
- We *began* to learn.
- They *offered* to pay.
- They *neglected* to pay.
- She *promised* to return.

In all of these examples no actor can come between the italicized main (finite) verb and the infinitive direct-object phrase.

Verbs that take infinitive objects with actors:			
advise	allow	convince	remind
encourage	force	hire	teach
instruct	invite	permit	tell
implore	incite	appoint	order

Examples:

- He *reminded* me to buy milk.
- Their fathers *advise* them to study.
- She *forced* the defendant to admit the truth.
- You've *convinced* the director of the program to change her position.
- I *invite* you to consider the evidence.

In all of these examples an actor is required after the italicized main (finite) verb and before the infinitive direct-object phrase.

Verbs that use either pattern:				
ask	expect	(would) like	want	need

Examples:

- I *asked* to see the records.
- I *asked* him to show me the records.
- Trent *expected* his group to win.
- Trent *expected* to win.
- Brenda *likes* to drive fast.
- Brenda *likes* her friend to drive fast.

In all of these examples the italicized main verb can take an infinitive object with or without an actor.

Punctuation: If the infinitive is used as an adverb and is the beginning phrase in a sentence, it should be set off with a comma; otherwise, no punctuation is needed for an infinitive phrase.

- To buy a basket of flowers, John had to spend his last dollar.
- To improve your writing, you must consider your purpose and audience.

Points to remember:

1. An infinitive is a verbal consisting of the word *to* plus a verb; it may be used as a noun, adjective, or adverb.
2. An infinitive phrase consists of an infinitive plus modifier(s), object(s), complement(s), and/or actor(s).
3. An infinitive phrase requires a comma only if it is used as an adverb at the beginning of a sentence.

Split infinitives

Split infinitives occur when additional words are included between *to* and the verb in an infinitive. Many readers find a single adverb splitting the infinitive to be acceptable, but this practice should be avoided in formal writing.

Examples:

- I like *to* on a nice day *walk* in the woods. (unacceptable)
  On a nice day, I like *to walk* in the woods. (revised)
- I needed *to* quickly *gather* my personal possessions. (acceptable in informal contexts)
  I needed *to gather* my personal possessions quickly. (revised for formal contexts)

Part 5: Prepositions for Time, Place, and Introducing Objects

One point in time

On is used with days:

- I will see you **on** Monday.
- The week begins **on** Sunday.

At is used with noon, night, midnight, and with the time of day:

- My plane leaves **at** noon.
- The movie starts **at** 6 p.m.

In is used with other parts of the day, with months, with years, with seasons:

- He likes to read **in** the afternoon.
- The days are long **in** August.
- The book was published **in** 1999.
- The flowers will bloom **in** spring.

Extended time

To express extended time, English uses the following prepositions: **since, for, by, from–to, from–until, during, (with)in**

- She has been gone **since** yesterday. *(She left yesterday and has not returned.)*
- I'm going to Paris **for** two weeks. *(I will spend two weeks there.)*
- The movie showed **from** August **to** October. *(Beginning in August and ending in October.)*
- The decorations were up **from** spring **until** fall. *(Beginning in spring and ending in fall.)*
- I watch TV **during** the evening. *(For some period of time in the evening.)*
- We must finish the project **within** a year. *(No longer than a year.)*

Place

To express notions of place, English uses the following prepositions: to talk about the point itself: **in**, to express something contained: **inside**, to talk about the surface: **on**, to talk about a general vicinity, **at**.

- There is a wasp **in** the room.
- Put the present **inside** the box.
- I left your keys **on** the table.
- She was waiting **at** the corner.

To introduce objects of verbs

English uses the following prepositions to introduce objects of the following verbs.

At: glance, laugh, look, rejoice, smile, stare
- She took a quick glance **at** her reflection.
  (*exception with* **mirror**: She took a quick glance **in** the mirror.)
- You didn't laugh **at** his joke.
- I'm looking **at** the computer monitor.
- We rejoiced **at** his safe rescue.
- That pretty girl smiled **at** you.
- Stop staring **at** me.

Of: approve, consist, smell
- I don't approve **of** his speech.
- My contribution to the article consists **of** many pages.
- He came home smelling **of** garlic.

Of (or about): dream, think
- I dream **of** finishing college in four years.
- Can you think **of** a number between one and ten?
- I am thinking **about** this problem.

For: call, hope, look, wait, watch, wish
- Did someone call **for** a taxi?
- He hopes **for** a raise in salary next year.
- I'm looking **for** my keys.
- We'll wait **for** her here.
- You go buy the tickets and I'll watch **for** the train.
- If you wish **for** an "A" in this class, you must work hard.

Part 6: Identifying Independent and Dependent Clauses

When you want to use commas and semicolons in sentences and when you are concerned about whether a sentence is or is not a fragment, a good way to start is to be able to recognize dependent and independent clauses. The definitions offered here will help you with this.

Independent Clause

An independent clause is a group of words that contains a subject and verb and expresses a complete thought. An independent clause is a sentence.

> Jim studied in the Sweet Shop for his chemistry quiz.

Dependent Clause

A dependent clause is a group of words that contains a subject and verb but does not express a complete thought. A dependent clause cannot be a sentence. Often a dependent clause is marked by a **dependent marker word**.

> When Jim studied in the Sweet Shop for his chemistry quiz . . . (What happened when he studied? The thought is incomplete.)

Dependent Marker Word

A dependent marker word is a word added to the beginning of an independent clause that makes it into a dependent clause.

> When Jim studied in the Sweet Shop for his chemistry quiz, it was very noisy.

Some common dependent markers are: **after, although, as, as if, because, before, even if, even though, if, in order to, since, though, unless, until, whatever, when, whenever, whether,** and **while.**

Connecting Dependent and Independent Clauses

There are two types of words that can be used as connectors at the beginning of an independent clause: coordinating conjunctions and independent marker words.

1. Coordinating Conjunction

The seven coordinating conjunctions used as connecting words at the beginning of an independent clause are **and, but, for, or, nor, so,** and **yet.** When the second independent clause in a sentence begins with a coordinating conjunction, a comma is needed before the coordinating conjunction:

Jim studied in the Sweet Shop for his chemistry quiz, **but** it was hard to concentrate because of the noise.

2. Independent Marker Word

An independent marker word is a connecting word used at the beginning of an independent clause. These words can always begin a sentence that can stand alone. When the second independent clause in a sentence has an independent marker word, a semicolon is needed before the independent marker word.

Jim studied in the Sweet Shop for his chemistry quiz; **however**, it was hard to concentrate because of the noise.

Some common independent markers are: **also, consequently, furthermore, however, moreover, nevertheless,** and **therefore**.

Some Common Errors to Avoid

Comma Splices

A comma splice is the use of a comma between two independent clauses. You can usually fix the error by changing the comma to a period and therefore making the two clauses into two separate sentences, by changing the comma to a semicolon, or by making one clause dependent by inserting a dependent marker word in front of it.

Incorrect: I like this class, it is very interesting.

Correct: I like this class. It is very interesting.
- (or) I like this class; it is very interesting.
- (or) I like this class, and it is very interesting.
- (or) I like this class because it is very interesting.
- (or) Because it is very interesting, I like this class.

Fused Sentences

Fused sentences happen when there are two independent clauses not separated by any form of punctuation. This error is also known as a run-on sentence. The error can sometimes be corrected by adding a period, semicolon, or colon to separate the two sentences.

Incorrect: My professor is intelligent I've learned a lot from her.

Correct: My professor is intelligent. I've learned a lot from her.
- (or) My professor is intelligent; I've learned a lot from her.
- (or) My professor is intelligent, and I've learned a lot from her.
- (or) My professor is intelligent; moreover, I've learned a lot from her.

Sentence Fragments

Sentence fragments happen by treating a dependent clause or other incomplete thought as a complete sentence. You can usually fix this error by combining it with another sentence to make a complete thought or by removing the dependent marker.

Incorrect: Because I forgot the exam was today.

Correct: Because I forgot the exam was today, I didn't study.
- (or) I forgot the exam was today.

Part 7: Parallel Structure

Parallel structure means using the same pattern of words to show that two or more ideas have the same level of importance. This can happen at the word, phrase, or clause level. The usual way to join parallel structures is with the use of coordinating **conjunctions** such as "and" or "or."

Words and Phrases

With the -ing form (gerund) of words:

> **Parallel:** Mary likes hiking, swimming, and bicycling.

With infinitive phrases:

> **Parallel:** Mary likes **to hike**, **to swim**, and **to ride** a bicycle.
> OR
> Mary likes to **hike**, **swim**, and **ride** a bicycle.

(Note: You can use "to" before all the verbs in a sentence or only before the first one.)

Do not mix forms.

Example 1

> **Not Parallel:**
> Mary likes hiking, swimming, and **to ride** a bicycle.

> **Parallel:**
> Mary likes hiking, swimming, and riding a bicycle.

Example 2

> **Not Parallel:**
> The production manager was asked to write his report quickly, accurate **ly**, and **in a detailed manner**.

> **Parallel:**
> The production manager was asked to write his report quickly, accurately, and thoroughly.

Example 3

> **Not Parallel:**
> The teacher said that he was a poor student because he wait**ed** until the last minute to study for the exam, complet**ed** his lab problems in a careless manner, and **his motivation was** low.

> **Parallel:**
> The teacher said that he was a poor student because he wait**ed** until the last minute to study for the exam, complet**ed** his lab problems in a careless manner, and lack**ed** motivation.

Clauses

A parallel structure that begins with clauses must keep on with clauses. Changing to another pattern or changing the voice of the verb (from active to passive or vice versa) will break the parallelism.

Example 1

> **Not Parallel:**
> The coach told the players **that they should get** a lot of sleep, **that they should not eat** too much, and <u>to do</u> some warm-up exercises before the game.

> **Parallel:**
> The coach told the players **that they should get** a lot of sleep, **that they should not eat** too much, and **that they should do** some warm-up exercises before the game.

OR

Parallel:

The coach told the players that they should **get** a lot of sleep, not **eat** too much, and **do** some warm-up exercises before the game.

Example 2

Not Parallel:

The salesman expected **that he would present** his product at the meeting, **that there would be** time for him to show his slide presentation, and **that questions would be asked** by prospective buyers. (**passive**)

Parallel:

The salesman expected **that he would present** his product at the meeting, **that there would be** time for him to show his slide presentation, and **that prospective buyers would ask** him questions.

Lists After a Colon

Be sure to keep all the elements in a list in the same form.

Example 1

Not Parallel:

The dictionary can be used for these purposes: to find **word meanings, pronunciations, correct spellings,** and **looking up irregular verbs**.

Parallel:

The dictionary can be used for these purposes: to find **word meanings, pronunciations, correct spellings,** and **irregular verbs**.

Proofreading Strategies to Try:

- Skim your paper, pausing at the words "and" and "or." Check on each side of these words to see whether the items joined are parallel. If not, make them parallel.
- If you have several items in a list, put them in a column to see if they are parallel.
- Listen to the sound of the items in a list or the items being compared. Do you hear the same kinds of sounds? For example, is there a series of "-ing" words beginning each item? Or do your hear a rhythm being repeated? If something is breaking that rhythm or repetition of sound, check to see if it needs to be made parallel.

Part 8: Introduction and General Usage in Defining Clauses

Relative pronouns are **that, who, whom, whose, which, where, when,** and **why.** They are used to join clauses to make a complex sentence. Relative pronouns are used at the beginning of the subordinate clause which gives some specific information about the main clause.

This is the house *that* Jack built.
I don't know the day *when* Jane marries him.
The professor, *whom* I respect, was tenured.

In English, the choice of the relative pronoun depends on the type of clause it is used in. There are two types of clauses distinguished: *defining* (*restrictive*) relative clauses and *non-defining* (*non-restrictive*) relative clauses. In both types of clauses the relative pronoun can function as a subject, an object, or a possessive.

Relative Pronouns in Defining Clauses

Defining relative clauses (also known as *restrictive relative clauses*) provide some essential information that explains the main clause. The information is crucial for understanding the sentence correctly and cannot be omitted. Defining clauses are opened by a relative pronoun and **ARE NOT** separated by a comma from the main clause.

The table below sums up the use of relative pronouns in defining clauses:

Function in the sentence	Reference to				
	People	Things/concepts	Place	Time	Reason
Subject	who, that	which, that			
Object	(that, who, whom)	(which, that)	where	when	why
Possessive	whose	whose, of which			

Examples

Relative pronoun used as a subject:

> This is the house *that* had a great Christmas decoration.
> It took me a while to get used to people *who* eat popcorn during the movie.

Relative pronoun used as an object:

1. As can be seen from the table, referring to a person or thing, the relative pronoun **may be omitted** in the object position:

> This is the man (who / that) I wanted to speak to and whose name I'd forgotten.

> The library didn't have the book (which / that) I wanted.

> I didn't like the book (which / that) John gave me.

> This is the house *where* I lived *when* I first came to the US.

2. In American English, *whom* is not used very often. **Whom** is more formal than *who* and is very often omitted in **speech**:

> **Grammatically Correct:** The woman to *whom* you have just spoken is my teacher.

> **Common in Speech:** The woman (*who*) you have just spoken to is my teacher.

However, *whom* may not be omitted if preceded by a preposition:

> I have found you the tutor <u>for</u> *whom* you were looking.

Relative pronoun used as a possessive:

Whose is the only possessive relative pronoun in English. It can be used with both people and things:

> The family *whose* house burnt in the fire was immediately given a suite in a hotel.
> The book *whose* author is now being shown in the news has become a bestseller.

General remarks: That, Who, Which compared

The relative pronoun *that* can only be used in defining clauses. It can also be substituted for *who* (referring to persons) or *which* (referring to things). *That* is often used in speech; *who* and *which* are more common in written English.

> William Kellogg was the man *that* lived in the late 19th century and had some weird ideas about raising children. (spoken, less formal)

William Kellogg was the man *who* lived in the late 19th century and had some weird ideas about raising children. (written, more formal)

Although your computer may suggest to correct it, referring to things, *which* may be used in the defining clause to put additional emphasis on the explanation. Again, the sentence with *which* is more formal than the one with *that*: Note that since it is the defining clause, there is NO comma used preceding *which*:

The café *that* sells the best coffee in town has recently been closed. (less formal)
The café *which* sells the best coffee in town has recently been closed. (more formal)

Some special uses of relative pronouns in defining clauses

that / who
Referring to people, both *that* and *who* can be used. *That* may be used to refer to someone in general:

He is the kind of person *that/who* will never let you down.
I am looking for someone *that/who* could give me a ride to Chicago.

However, when a particular person is being spoken about, *who* is preferred:

The old lady *who* lives next door is a teacher.
The girl *who* wore a red dress attracted everybody's attention at the party.

that / which
There are several cases when *that* is more appropriate and is preferred to *which*.

After the pronouns *all, any(thing), every(thing), few, little, many, much, no(thing), none, some(thing)*:

The police usually ask for every detail *that* helps identify the missing person. (*that* used as the subject)
Marrying a congressman is *all* (that) she wants. (*that* used as the object)

After verbs that answer the question **WHAT?** For example, *say, suggest, state, declare, hope, think, write*, etc. In this case, the whole relative clause functions as the object of the main clause:

Some people *say* (that) success is one percent of talent and ninety-nine percent of hard work.
The chairman *stated* at the meeting (that) his company is part of a big-time entertainment industry.

After the noun modified by an adjective *in the superlative degree*:

This is the *funniest* story (that) I have ever read! (*that* used as the object)

After ordinal numbers, e.g., *first, second, etc.*:

The first draft (that) we submitted was really horrible. (*that* used as the object)

If the verb in the main clause is a form of *BE*:

This is a claim that has absolutely no reason in it. (*that* used as the subject)

Relative Pronouns in Non-Defining Clauses

Non-defining relative clauses (also known as non-restrictive, or parenthetical, clauses) provide some additional information which is not essential and may be omitted without affecting the contents of the sentence. All relative pronouns EXCEPT "that" can be used in non-defining clauses; however, the pronouns MAY NOT be omitted. Non-defining clauses ARE separated by commas.

The table below sums up the use of relative pronouns in non-defining clauses:

Function in the sentence	Reference to				
	People	Things/concepts	Place	Time	Reason
Subject	who	which			
Object	who, whom	which	where	when	why
Possessive	whose	whose, of which			

a. Relative pronoun used as a subject:

The writer, **who** lives in this luxurious mansion, has just published his second novel.

b. Relative pronoun used as an object:

The house at the end of the street, **which** my grandfather built, needs renovating.

c. Relative pronoun used as a possessive:

William Kellogg, **whose** name has become a famous breakfast foods brand-name, had some weird ideas about raising children.

Some Special Uses of Relative Pronouns in Non-Defining Clauses

a. which
If you are referring to the previous clause as a whole, use *which*:
My friend eventually decided to get divorced, **which** upset me a lot.

b. of whom, of which
Use *of whom* for persons and *of which* for things or concepts after numbers and words such as *most, many, some, both, none*:
I saw a lot of new people at the party, <u>some</u> **of whom** seemed familiar.
He was always coming up with new ideas, <u>most</u> **of which** were absolutely impracticable.

Part 9: Sentence Types and Punctuation Patterns

To punctuate a sentence, you can use and combine some of these patterns.

Pattern One: Simple Sentence
This pattern is an example of a simple sentence:

Independent clause [.]

Example: Doctors are concerned about the rising death rate from asthma.

Pattern Two: Compound Sentence
This pattern is an example of a compound sentence with a coordinating conjunction:

Independent clause [,] coordinating conjunction independent clause [.]

There are seven coordinating conjunctions: **and, but, for, or, nor, so, yet.**

Example: Doctors are concerned about the rising death rate from asthma, but they don't know the reasons for it.

Pattern Three: Compound Sentence

This pattern is an example of a compound sentence with a semicolon.

Independent clause [;] independent clause [.]

Example: Doctors are concerned about the rising death rate from asthma; they are unsure of its cause.

Pattern Four: Compound Sentence

This pattern is an example of a compound sentence with an independent marker.

Independent clause [;] independent marker [,] independent clause [.]

Examples of independent markers are the following: therefore, moreover, thus, consequently, however, also.

Example: Doctors are concerned about the rising death rate from asthma; therefore, they have called for more research into its causes.

Pattern Five: Complex Sentence

This pattern is an example of a complex sentence with a dependent marker.

Dependent marker dependent clause [,] Independent clause [.]

Examples of dependent markers are as follows: because, before, since, while, although, if, until, when, after, as, as if.

Example: *Because* doctors are concerned about the rising death rate from asthma, they have called for more research into its causes.

Pattern Six: Complex Sentence

This pattern is an example of a complex sentence with a dependent marker following the independent clause.

Independent clause dependent marker dependent clause [.]

Example: Doctors are concerned about the rising death rate from asthma because it is a common, treatable illness.

Pattern Seven

This pattern includes an independent clause with an embedded non-essential clause or phrase. A non-essential clause or phrase is one that can be removed without changing the meaning of the sentence or making it ungrammatical. In other words, the non-essential clause or phrase gives additional information, but the sentence can stand alone without it.

First part of an independent clause [,] non-essential clause or phrase, rest of the independent clause [.]

Example: Many doctors, including both pediatricians and family practice physicians, are concerned about the rising death rate from asthma.

Pattern Eight

This pattern includes an independent clause with an embedded essential clause or phrase. An essential clause or phrase is one that cannot be removed without changing the overall meaning of the sentence.

First part of an independent clause essential clause or phrase rest of the independent clause [.]

Example: Many doctors who are concerned about the rising death rate from asthma have called for more research into its causes.

Part 10: Making Subjects and Verbs Agree

1. When the subject of a sentence is composed of two or more nouns or pronouns connected by *and*, use a plural verb.

   She and **her friends** **are** at the fair.

2. When two or more singular nouns or pronouns are connected by *or* or *nor*, use a singular verb.

   The **book** or **the pen** **is** in the drawer.

3. When a compound subject contains both a singular and a plural noun or pronoun joined by *or* or *nor*, the verb should agree with the part of the subject that is nearer the verb.

   The **boy** or **his friends** **run** every day.
   His **friends** or **the boy** **runs** every day.

4. *Doesn't* is a contraction of *does not* and should be used only with a singular subject. *Don't* is a contraction of *do not* and should be used only with a plural subject. The exception to this rule appears in the case of the first person and second person pronouns *I* and *you*. With these pronouns, the contraction *don't* should be used. [Note that formal writing generally avoids the use of contractions.]

   He doesn't **like** it.
   They don't **like** it.

5. Do not be misled by a phrase that comes between the subject and the verb. The verb agrees with the subject, not with a noun or pronoun in the phrase.

   One of the boxes **is** open
   The **people** who listen to that music **are** few.
   The **team captain**, as well as his players, **is** anxious.
   The **book**, including all the chapters in the first section, **is** boring.
   The **woman** with all the dogs **walks** down my street.

6. The words *each*, *each one*, *either*, *neither*, *everyone*, *everybody*, *anybody*, *anyone*, *nobody*, *somebody*, *someone*, and *no one* are singular and require a singular verb.

   Each of these hot dogs **is** juicy.
   Everybody **knows** Mr. Jones.
   Either **is** correct.

7. Nouns such as *civics*, *mathematics*, *dollars*, *measles*, and *news* require singular verbs.

   The news **is** on at six.

   Note: The word **dollars** is a special case. When talking about an amount of money, it requires a singular verb, but when referring to the dollars themselves, a plural verb is required.

   Five dollars **is** a lot of money.
   Dollars **are** often used instead of rubles in Russia.

8. Nouns such as *scissors*, *tweezers*, *trousers*, and *shears* require plural verbs. (There are two parts to these things.)

   These scissors **are** dull.
   Those trousers **are** made of wool.

9. In sentences beginning with *there is* or *there are*, the subject follows the verb. Since *there* is not the subject, the verb agrees with what follows.

There **are** many questions.
There **is** a question.

10. Collective nouns are words that imply more than one person but that are considered singular and take a singular verb, such as: *group*, *team*, *committee*, *class*, and *family*.

   The team **runs** during practice.
   The committee **decides** how to proceed.
   The family **has** a long history.
   My family **has never been able to agree**.

   In some cases, a sentence may call for the use of a plural verb when using a collective noun.

   The crew **are preparing** to dock the ship.

   This sentence is referring to the individual efforts of each crew member.

11. Expressions such as *with*, *together with*, *including*, *accompanied by*, *in addition to*, or *as well* do not change the number of the subject. If the subject is singular, the verb is too.

   The President, accompanied by his wife, **is** traveling to India.
   All of the books, including yours, **are** in that box.

Sequence of Tenses

Simple Present: They walk.

Present Perfect: They have walked.

Simple Past: They walked.

Past Perfect: They had walked.

Future: They will walk.

Future Perfect: They will have walked.

Problems in sequencing tenses usually occur with the perfect tenses, all of which are formed by adding an auxiliary or auxiliaries to the past participle, the third principal part.

   ring, rang, rung
   walk, walked, walked

The most common auxiliaries are forms of "be," "can," "do," "may," "must," "ought," "shall," "will," "has," "have," "had," and they are the forms we shall use in this most basic discussion.

Present Perfect

The present perfect consists of a past participle (the third principal part) with "has" or "have." It designates action which began in the past but which continues into the present or the effect of which still continues.

   1. Betty taught for ten years. (simple past)
   2. Betty has taught for ten years. (present perfect)

The implication in (1) is that Betty has retired; in (2), that she is still teaching.

   1. John did his homework. He can go to the movies.
   2. If John has done his homework, he can go to the movies.

Infinitives, too, have perfect tense forms when combined with "have," and sometimes problems arise when infinitives are used with verbs such as "hope," "plan," "expect," and "intend," all of which usually point to the future (I wanted to go to the movie. Janet meant to see the doctor.) The perfect tense sets up a sequence by marking the action which began and usually was completed before the action in the main verb.

1. I am happy to have participated in this campaign!
2. John had hoped to have won the trophy.

Thus the action of the main verb points back in time; the action of the perfect infinitive has been completed.

The past perfect tense designates action in the past just as simple past does, but the action of the past perfect is action completed in the past before another action.

1. John raised vegetables and later sold them. (past)
2. John sold vegetables that he had raised. (past perfect)

The vegetables were raised before they were sold.

1. Renee washed the car when George arrived. (simple past)
2. Renee had washed the car when George arrived. (past perfect)

In (1), she waited until George arrived and then washed the car. In (2), she had already finished washing the car by the time he arrived.

In sentences expressing condition and result, the past perfect tense is used in the part that states the condition.

1. If I had done my exercises, I would have passed the test.
2. I think George would have been elected if he hadn't sounded so pompous.

Future Perfect Tense

The future perfect tense designates action that will have been completed at a specified time in the future.

1. Saturday I will finish my housework. (simple future)
2. By Saturday noon, I will have finished my housework. (future perfect)

Part 11: Using Active Versus Passive Voice

In a sentence using **active voice**, the subject of the sentence performs the action expressed in the verb.

The dog *bit* **the boy.**

The arrow points from the subject performing the action (the dog) to the individual being acted upon (the boy). This is an example of a sentence using the active voice.

Scientists *have conducted* **experiments** to test the hypothesis.

Sample active voice sentence with the subject performing the action described by the verb.

Watching a framed, mobile world through a car's windshield *reminds* me of watching a movie or TV.

The active voice sentence subject (watching a framed, mobile world) performs the action of reminding the speaker of something.

Each example above includes a sentence subject performing the action expressed by the verb.

Examples:

	Active	Passive
Simple Present	• The company ships the computers to many foreign countries.	• Computers are shipped to many foreign countries
Present Progressive	• The chef is preparing the food.	• The food is being prepared.
Simple Past	• The delivery man delivered the package yesterday.	• The package was delivered yesterday.
Past Progressive	• The producer was making an announcement.	• An announcement was being made.
Future	• Our representative will pick up the computer.	• The computer will be picked up.
Present Perfect	• Someone has made the arrangements for us.	• The arrangements have been made for us.
Past Perfect	• They had given us visas for three months.	• They had been given visas for three months.
Future Perfect	• By next month we will have finished this job.	• By next month this job will have been finished.

Part 12: Irregular Verbs: Overview and List

In English, regular verbs consist of three main parts: the root form (present), the (simple) past, and the past participle. Regular verbs have an *-ed* ending added to the root verb for both the simple past and past participle. Irregular verbs do not follow this pattern, and instead take on an alternative pattern.

The following is a partial list of irregular verbs found in English. Each listing consists of the present/root form of the verb, the (simple) past form of the verb, and the past participle form of the verb.

List of Irregular Verbs in English		
Present	Past	Past Participle
be	was, were	been
become	became	become
begin	began	begun
blow	blew	blown
break	broke	broken
bring	brought	brought
build	built	built
burst	burst	burst
buy	bought	bought
catch	caught	caught
choose	chose	chosen
come	came	come
cut	cut	cut

Present	Past	Past Participle
deal	dealt	dealt
do	did	done
drink	drank	drunk
drive	drove	driven
eat	ate	eaten
fall	fell	fallen
feed	fed	fed
feel	felt	felt
fight	fought	fought
find	found	found
fly	flew	flown
forbid	forbade	forbidden
forget	forgot	forgotten

Present	Past	Past Participle
forgive	forgave	forgiven
freeze	froze	frozen
get	got	gotten
give	gave	given
go	went	gone
grow	grew	grown
have	had	had
hear	heard	heard
hide	hid	hidden
hold	held	held
hurt	hurt	hurt
keep	kept	kept
know	knew	known
lay	laid	laid
lead	led	led
leave	left	left
let	let	let
lie	lay	lain
lose	lost	lost
make	made	made
meet	met	met
pay	paid	paid
quit	quit	quit
read	read	read
ride	rode	ridden
run	ran	run
say	said	said

Present	Past	Past Participle
see	saw	seen
seek	sought	sought
sell	sold	sold
send	sent	sent
shake	shook	sent
shine	shone	shone
sing	sang	sung
sit	sat	sat
sleep	slept	slept
speak	spoke	spoken
spend	spent	spent
spring	sprang	sprung
stand	stood	stood
steal	stole	stolen
swim	swam	swum
swing	swung	swung
take	took	taken
teach	taught	taught
tear	tore	torn
tell	told	told
think	thought	thought
throw	threw	thrown
understand	understood	understood
wake	woke (waked)	woken (waked)
wear	wore	worn
win	won	won
write	wrote	written

Commonly Confused Verbs

LIE versus LAY

Lie vs. Lay Usage		
Present	Past	Past Participle
lie, lying (to tell a falsehood)	I lied to my mother.	I have lied under oath.
lie, lying (to recline)	I lay on the bed because I was tired.	He has lain in the grass.
lay, laying (to put, place)	I laid the baby in her cradle.	We have laid the dishes on the table.

Example sentences:

After **laying** down his weapon, the soldier **lay** down to sleep.

Will you **lay** out my clothes while I **lie** down to rest?

SIT versus SET

Sit vs. Set Usage		
Present	Past	Past Participle
sit (to be seated or come to resting position)	I sat in my favorite chair.	You have sat there for three hours.
set (to put or place)	I set my glass on the table.	She has set her books on my desk again.

Example sentence:

Let's **set** the table before we **sit** down to rest.

RISE versus RAISE

Rise vs. Raise Usage		
Present	Past	Past Participle
rise (steady or customary upward movement)	The balloon rose into the air.	He has risen to a position of power.
raise (to cause to rise)	They raised their hands because they knew the answer.	I have raised the curtain many times.

Example sentence:

The boy **raised** the flag just before the sun **rose**.

Part 13: Capitalization and Punctuation

A Little Help with Capitals

If you have a question about whether a specific word should be capitalized that doesn't fit under one of these rules, try checking a dictionary to see if the word is capitalized there.

Use capital letters in the following ways:

The first words of a sentence

When he tells a joke, he sometimes forgets the punch line.

The pronoun "I"

The last time I visited Atlanta was several years ago.

Proper nouns (the names of specific people, places, organizations, and sometimes things)

Worrill Fabrication Company
Golden Gate Bridge
Supreme Court
Livingston, Missouri
Atlantic Ocean
Mothers Against Drunk Driving

Family relationships (when used as proper names)

I sent a thank-you note to Aunt Abigail, but not to my other aunts.
Here is a present I bought for Mother.
Did you buy a present for your mother?

The names of God, specific deities, religious figures, and holy books

God the Father
the Virgin Mary
the Bible
the Greek gods
Moses
Shiva
Buddha
Zeus

Exception: Do not capitalize the non-specific use of the word "god."

The word "polytheistic" means the worship of more than one god.

Titles preceding names, but not titles that follow names

She worked as the assistant to Mayor Hanolovi.
I was able to interview Miriam Moss, mayor of Littonville.

Directions that are names (North, South, East, and West when used as sections of the country, but not as compass directions)

The Patels have moved to the Southwest.
Jim's house is two miles north of Otterbein.

The days of the week, the months of the year, and holidays (but not the seasons used generally)

Halloween
October
Friday
winter
spring
fall

Exception: Seasons are capitalized when used in a title.

The Fall 1999 Semester

The names of countries, nationalities, and specific languages

Costa Rica
Spanish
French
English

The first word in a sentence that is a direct quote

Emerson once said, "A foolish consistency is the hobgoblin of little minds."

The major words in the titles of books, articles, and songs (but not short prepositions or the articles "the," "a," or "an," if they are not the first word of the title)

One of Jerry's favorite books is *The Catcher in the Rye*.

Members of national, political, racial, social, civic, and athletic groups

> Green Bay Packers
> African-Americans
> Democrats
> Friends of the Wilderness
> Chinese

Periods and events (but not century numbers)

> Victorian Era
> Great Depression
> Constitutional Convention
> sixteenth century

Trademarks

> Pepsi
> Honda
> IBM
> Microsoft Word

Words and abbreviations of specific names (but not names of things that came from specific things but are now general types)

> Freudian   UN
> NBC   french fries
> pasteurize   italics

Comma

Use a comma to join two independent clauses by a comma and a coordinating conjunction (*and, but, or, for, nor, so*).

> Road construction can be inconvenient, but it is necessary.
>
> The new house has a large fenced backyard, so I am sure our dog will enjoy it.

Use a comma after an introductory phrase, prepositional phrase, or dependent clause.

> To get a good grade, you must complete all your assignments.
>
> Because Dad caught the chicken pox, we canceled our vacation.
>
> After the wedding, the guests attended the reception.

Use a comma to separate elements in a series. Although there is no set rule that requires a comma before the last item in a series, it seems to be a general academic convention to include it. The examples below demonstrate this trend.

> On her vacation, Lisa visited Greece, Spain, and Italy.
>
> In their speeches, many of the candidates promised to help protect the environment, bring about world peace, and end world hunger.

Use a comma to separate nonessential elements from a sentence. More specifically, when a sentence includes information that is not crucial to the message or intent of the sentence, enclose it in or separate it by commas.

> John's truck, a red Chevrolet, needs new tires.
>
> When he realized he had overslept, Matt rushed to his car and hurried to work.

Use a comma between coordinate adjectives (adjectives that are equal and reversible).

> The irritable, fidgety crowd waited impatiently for the rally speeches to begin.

> The sturdy, compact suitcase made a perfect gift.

Use a comma after a transitional element (*however, therefore, nonetheless, also, otherwise, finally, instead, thus, of course, above all, for example, in other words, as a result, on the other hand, in conclusion, in addition*)

> For example, the Red Sox, Yankees, and Indians are popular baseball teams.

> If you really want to get a good grade this semester, however, you must complete all assignments, attend class, and study your notes.

Use a comma with quoted words.

> "Yes," she promised. Todd replied, saying, "I will be back this afternoon."

Use a comma in a date.

> October 25, 1999
> Monday, October 25, 1999
> 25 October 1999

Use a comma in a number.

> 15,000,000
> 1614 High Street

Use a comma in a personal title.

> Pam Smith, MD
> Mike Rose, Chief Financial Officer for Operations, reported the quarter's earnings.

Use a comma to separate a city name from the state.

> West Lafayette, Indiana
> Dallas, Texas

Avoid comma splices (two independent clauses joined only by a comma). Instead, separate the clauses with a period, with a comma followed by a coordinating conjunction, or with a semicolon.

Semicolon

Use a semicolon to join two independent clauses when the second clause restates the first or when the two clauses are of equal emphasis.

> Road construction in Dallas has hindered travel around town; streets have become covered with bulldozers, trucks, and cones.

Use a semicolon to join two independent clauses when the second clause begins with a conjunctive adverb (*however, therefore, moreover, furthermore, thus, meanwhile, nonetheless, otherwise*) or a transition (*in fact, for example, that is, for instance, in addition, in other words, on the other hand, even so*).

> Terrorism in the United States has become a recent concern; in fact, the concern for America's safety has led to an awareness of global terrorism.

Use a semicolon to join elements of a series when individual items of the series already include commas.

> Recent sites of the Olympic Games include Athens, Greece; Salt Lake City, Utah; Sydney, Australia; Nagano, Japan.

Colon

Use a colon to join two independent clauses when you wish to emphasize the second clause.

Road construction in Dallas has hindered travel around town: parts of Main, Fifth, and West Street are closed during the construction.

Use a colon after an independent clause when it is followed by a list, a quotation, an appositive, or other idea directly related to the independent clause.

Julie went to the store for some groceries: milk, bread, coffee, and cheese.

In his Gettysburg Address, Abraham Lincoln urges Americans to rededicate themselves to the unfinished work of the deceased soldiers: "It is for us the living rather to be dedicated here to the unfinished work which they who fought here have thus far so nobly advanced. It is rather for us to be here dedicated to the great task remaining before us — that from these honored dead we take increased devotion to that cause for which they gave the last full measure of devotion — that we here highly resolve that these dead shall not have died in vain, that this nation under God shall have a new birth of freedom, and that government of the people, by the people, for the people shall not perish from the earth."

I know the perfect job for her: a politician.

Use a colon at the end of a business letter greeting.

To Whom It May Concern:

Use a colon to separate the hour and minute(s) in a time notation.

12:00 p.m.

Use a colon to separate the chapter and verse in a Biblical reference.

Matthew 1:6

Parentheses

Parentheses are used to emphasize content. They place more emphasis on the enclosed content than commas. Use parentheses to set off nonessential material, such as dates, clarifying information, or sources, from a sentence.

Muhammed Ali (1942-present), arguably the greatest athlete of all time, claimed he would "float like a butterfly, sting like a bee."

Use parentheses to enclose numbered items in a sentence.

He asked everyone to bring (1) a folding tent, (2) food and water for two days, and (3) a sleeping bag.

Also use parentheses for literary citations embedded in text or to give the explanation of an acronym.

Research by Wegener and Petty (1994) supports...
The AMA (American Medical Association) recommends regular exercise.

Dash

Dashes are used to set off or emphasize the content enclosed within dashes or the content that follows a dash. Dashes place more emphasis on this content than parentheses.

Perhaps one reason why the term has been so problematic—so resistant to definition, and yet so transitory in those definitions—is because of its multitude of applications.

In terms of public legitimacy—that is, in terms of garnering support from state legislators, parents, donors, and university administrators—English departments are primarily places where advanced literacy is taught.

The U.S.S. *Constitution* became known as "Old Ironsides" during the War of 1812—during which the cannonballs fired from the British H.M.S. *Guerriere* merely bounced off the sides of the *Constitution*.

To some of you, my proposals may seem radical—even revolutionary.

Use a dash to set off an appositive phrase that already includes commas. An appositive is a word that adds explanatory or clarifying information to the noun that precedes it.

The cousins—Tina, Todd, and Sam—arrived at the party together.

Quotation Marks

Use quotation marks to enclose direct quotations. Note that commas and periods are placed inside the closing quotation mark, and colons and semicolons are placed outside. The placement of question and exclamation marks depends on the situation.

He asked, "When will you be arriving?" I answered, "Sometime after 6:30."

Use quotation marks to indicate the novel, ironic, or reserved use of a word.

History is stained with blood spilled in the name of "justice."

Use quotation marks around the titles of short poems, song titles, short stories, magazine or newspaper articles, essays, speeches, chapter titles, short films, and episodes of television or radio shows.

"Self-Reliance," by Ralph Waldo Emerson
"Just Like a Woman," by Bob Dylan
"The Smelly Car," an episode of Seinfeld

Do not use quotation marks in indirect or block quotations. Indirect quotations are not exact wordings but rather rephrasings or summaries of another person's words. In this case, it is not necessary to use quotation marks. However, indirect quotations still require proper citations, and you will be committing plagiarism if you fail to do so.

Mr. Johnson, a local farmer, reported last night that he saw an alien spaceship on his own property.

Italics

Underlining and Italics are often used interchangeably. Before word-processing programs were widely available, writers would underline certain words to indicate to publishers to italicize whatever was underlined. Although the general trend has been moving toward italicizing instead of underlining, you should remain consistent with your choice throughout your paper. To be safe, you could check with your teacher to find out which he/she prefers. Italicize the titles of magazines, books, newspapers, academic journals, films, television shows, long poems, plays of three or more acts, operas, musical albums, works of art, websites, and individual trains, planes, or ships.

Time
Romeo and Juliet by William Shakespeare
The Metamorphosis of Narcissus by Salvador Dali
Amazon.com
Titanic

Italicize foreign words.

Semper fi, the motto of the U.S. Marine Corps, means "always faithful."

Italicize a word or phrase to add emphasis.

The *truth* is of utmost concern!

Italicize a word when referring to that word.

The word *justice* is often misunderstood and therefore misused.

Hyphen

Two words brought together as a compound may be written separately, written as one word, or connected by hyphens. For example, three modern dictionaries all have the same listings for the following compounds:

> hair stylist
> hairsplitter
> hair-raiser

Another modern dictionary, however, lists *hairstylist*, not *hair stylist*. Compounding is obviously in a state of flux, and authorities do not always agree in all cases, but the uses of the hyphen offered here are generally agreed upon.

1. Use a hyphen to join two or more words serving as a single adjective before a noun:

   > a one-way street
   > chocolate-covered peanuts
   > well-known author

   However, when compound modifiers come after a noun, they are not hyphenated:

   > The peanuts were chocolate covered.
   > The author was well known.

2. Use a hyphen with compound numbers:

   > forty-six
   > sixty-three
   > Our much-loved teacher was sixty-three years old.

3. Use a hyphen to avoid confusion or an awkward combination of letters:

   > re-sign a petition (vs. resign from a job)
   > semi-independent (but semiconscious)
   > shell-like (but childlike)

4. Use a hyphen with the prefixes *ex-* (meaning former), *self-*, *all-*; with the suffix *-elect*; between a prefix and a capitalized word; and with figures or letters:

   > ex-husband
   > self-assured
   > mid-September
   > all-inclusive
   > mayor-elect
   > anti-American
   > T-shirt
   > pre-Civil War
   > mid-1980s

5. Use a hyphen to divide words at the end of a line if necessary, and make the break only between syllables:

   > pref-er-ence
   > sell-ing
   > in-di-vid-u-al-ist

6. For line breaks, divide already hyphenated words only at the hyphen:

   > mass-
   > produced

Apostrophe

The apostrophe has three uses:

- to form possessives of nouns
- to show the omission of letters
- to indicate certain plurals of lowercase letters

Forming Possessives of Nouns

To see if you need to make a possessive, turn the phrase around and make it an "of the..." phrase. For example:

the boy's hat = the hat of the boy
three days' journey = journey of three days

If the noun after "of" is a building, an object, or a piece of furniture, then **no** apostrophe is needed!

room of the hotel = hotel room
door of the car = car door
leg of the table = table leg

Once you've determined whether you need to make a possessive, follow these rules to create one.

- **add 's to the singular form of the word (even if it ends in -*s*):**

  the owner's car
  James's hat (James' hat is also acceptable. For plural, proper nouns that are possessive, use an apostrophe after the 's': "The Eggles' presentation was good." The Eggles are a husband and wife consultant team.)

- **add 's to the plural forms that do not end in -*s*:**

  the children's game
  the geese's honking

- **add ' to the end of plural nouns that end in -*s*:**

  houses' roofs
  three friends' letters

- **add 's to the end of compound words:**

  my brother-in-law's money

- **add 's to the last noun to show joint possession of an object:**

  Todd and Anne's apartment

Showing omission of letters

Apostrophes are used in contractions. A contraction is a word (or set of numbers) in which one or more letters (or numbers) have been omitted. The apostrophe shows this omission. Contractions are common in speaking and in informal writing. To use an apostrophe to create a contraction, place an apostrophe where the omitted letter(s) would go. Here are some examples:

don't = do not
I'm = I am
he'll = he will
who's = who is
could've= could have (NOT "could of"!)
'60 = 1960

Don't use apostrophes for possessive pronouns or for noun plurals.

Apostrophes should not be used with possessive pronouns because possessive pronouns already show possession — they don't need an apostrophe. *His, her, its, my, yours, ours* are all possessive pronouns. Here are some examples:

wrong: his' book
correct: his book

wrong: The group made it's decision.
correct: The group made its decision.

(Note: *Its* and *it's* are not the same thing. *It's* is a contraction for "it is" and *its* is a possessive pronoun meaning "belonging to it." It's raining out= it is raining out. A simple way to remember this rule is the fact that you don't use an apostrophe for the possessive *his* or *hers*, so don't do it with *its*!)

wrong: a friend of yours'
correct: a friend of yours

Proofreading for apostrophes

A good time to proofread is when you have finished writing the paper. Try the following strategies to proofread for apostrophes:

- If you tend to leave out apostrophes, check every word that ends in *-s* or *-es* to see if it needs an apostrophe.
- If you put in too many apostrophes, check every apostrophe to see if you can justify it with a rule for using apostrophes.

Ellipsis

An ellipsis (a row of three dots: ...) must be used whenever anything is omitted from within a quoted passage—word, phrase, line, or paragraph-- regardless of its source or use. It would, therefore, apply to all usage, including technical, non-technical, medical, journalistic, fiction, etc. The usual form is a "bare" ellipsis (just the three dots, preceded and followed by a space), although the MLA Handbook for Writers of Research Papers recommends that the writer enclose an ellipsis in brackets [...] when omitting part of an original quotation, to differentiate instances of deleted text from ellipses included in the original text. In all cases, the entire quoted passage, including ellipses, is preceded and followed by quotation marks and the source properly cited.

Two things to consider: 1) using ellipses is a form of "editing" the source material, so be certain that the final outcome does not change the original meaning or intent of the quoted passage; and 2) if quoted text ends up with more ellipses than words, consider paraphrasing rather than using direct quotes.

Brackets

Brackets are most often used to clarify the meaning of quoted material. If the context of your quote might be unclear, you may add a few words to provide clarity. Enclose the added material in brackets.

Added Material: The quarterback told the reporter, "It's quite simple. They [the other team] played a better game, scored more points, and that's why we lost."

Resources

SpringBoard Learning Strategies

READING STRATEGIES

STRATEGY	DEFINITION	PURPOSE
Close Reading	Accessing small chunks of text to read, reread, mark, and annotate key passages, word-for-word, sentence-by-sentence, and line-by-line	To develop comprehensive understanding by engaging in one or more focused readings of a text
Diffusing	Reading a passage, noting unfamiliar words, discovering meaning of unfamiliar words using context clues, dictionaries, and/or thesauruses, and replacing unfamiliar words with familiar ones	To facilitate a close reading of text, the use of resources, an understanding of synonyms, and increased comprehension of text
Double-Entry Journal	Creating a two-column journal (also called Dialectical Journal) with a student-selected passage in one column and the student's response in the second column (e.g., asking questions of the text, forming personal responses, interpreting the text, reflecting on the process of making meaning of the text)	To respond to a specific passage with comments, questions, or insights to foster active involvement with a text and to facilitate increased comprehension
Graphic Organizer	Using a visual representation for the organization of information	To facilitate increased comprehension and discussion
KWHL Chart	Setting up discussion with use of a graphic organizer. Allows students to activate prior knowledge by answering "What do I *know*?" sets a purpose by answering "What do I *want* to know?" helps preview a task by answering "*How* will I learn it?" and reflects on new knowledge by answering "What have I *learned*?"	To organize thinking, access prior knowledge, and reflect on learning to increase comprehension and engagement
Marking the Text	Selecting text by highlighting, underlining, and/or annotating for specific components, such as main idea, imagery, literary devices, and so on	To focus reading for specific purposes, such as author's craft, and to organize information from selections; to facilitate reexamination of a text
Metacognitive Markers	Responding to text with a system of cueing marks where students use a **?** for questions about the text; a **!** for reactions related to the text; and an ***** for comments about the text and underline to signal key ideas	To track responses to texts and use those responses as a point of departure for talking or writing about texts
Predicting	Making guesses about the text by using the title and pictures and/or thinking ahead about events which may occur based on evidence in the text	To help students become actively involved, interested, and mentally prepared to understand ideas
Previewing	Examining a text's structure, features, layout, and so on, prior to reading	To gain familiarity with the text, make connections to the text, and extend prior knowledge to set a purpose for reading
QHT	Expanding prior knowledge of vocabulary words by marking words with a Q, H, or T (Q signals words students do not know; H signals words students have heard and might be able to identify; T signals words students know well enough to teach to their peers.)	To allow students to build on their prior knowledge of words, to provide a forum for peer teaching and learning of new words, and to serve as a pre-reading exercise to aid in comprehension

STRATEGY	DEFINITION	PURPOSE
Questioning the Text*	Developing literal, interpretive, and universal questions about the text while reading a text	To engage more actively with texts, read with greater purpose and focus, and ultimately answer questions to gain greater insight into the text
Quickwrite	Responding to a text by writing for a short, specific amount of time about a designated topic or idea related to a text	To activate background knowledge, clarify issues, facilitate making connections, and allow for reflection
RAFT	Responding to and analyzing text by brainstorming various roles (e.g., self, characters from other texts), audiences (e.g., a different character, a real person), formats (e.g., letter, brochure, essay, travel guide), and topics; readers may choose one particular role, audience, format, and topic to create a new text	To initiate reader response; to facilitate an analysis of a text to gain focus prior to creating a new text
Rereading	Encountering the same text with more than one reading	To identify additional details; to clarify meaning and/or reinforce comprehension of texts
SIFT*	Analyzing a fictional text by examining stylistic elements, especially symbol, images, and figures of speech, in order to show how all work together to reveal tone and theme.	To focus and facilitate an analysis of a fictional text by examining the title and text for symbolism, identifying images and sensory details, analyzing figurative language and identifying how all these elements reveal tone and theme
Skimming/Scanning	Skimming by rapid or superficial reading of a text to form an overall impression or to obtain a general understanding of the material; scanning by focusing on key words, phrases, or specific details to provide speedy recognition of information	To quickly form an overall impression prior to an in-depth study of a text; to answer specific questions or quickly locate targeted information or detail in a text

*AP strategy

READING STRATEGIES (Continued)

STRATEGY	DEFINITION	PURPOSE
SMELL*	Analyzing a persuasive speech or essay by asking five essential questions: • **S**ender-receiver relationship—What is the sender-receiver relationship? Who are the images and language meant to attract? Describe the speaker of the text. • **M**essage—What is the message? Summarize the statement made in the text. • **E**motional Strategies—What is the desired effect? • **L**ogical Strategies—What logic is operating? How does it (or its absence) affect the message? Consider the logic of the images as well as the words. • **L**anguage—What does the language of the text describe? How does it affect the meaning and effectiveness of the writing? Consider the language of the images as well as the words.	To analyze a persuasive speech or essay by focusing on five essential questions
SOAPSTone*	Analyzing text by discussing and identifying *Speaker, Occasion, Audience, Purpose, Subject,* and *Tone*	To use an analytical process to understand the author's craft
Summarizing/ Paraphrasing	Restating in one's own words the main idea or essential information expressed in a text, whether it be narration, dialogue, or informational text	To facilitate comprehension and recall of a text
Think Aloud	Talking through a difficult passage or task by using a form of metacognition whereby the reader expresses how he/she has made sense of the text	To reflect on how readers make meaning of challenging texts
TP-CASTT*	Analyzing a poetic text by identifying and discussing *Title, Paraphrase, Connotation, Attitude, Shift, Theme,* and *Title* again	To use an analytical process to understand the author's craft
Visualizing	Forming a picture (mentally and/or literally) while reading a text	To increase reading comprehension and promote active engagement with text
Word Maps	Using a clearly defined graphic organizer such as concept circles or word webs to identify and reinforce word meanings	To provide a visual tool for identifying and remembering multiple aspects of words and word meanings

*AP strategy

WRITING STRATEGIES

STRATEGY	DEFINITION	PURPOSE
Adding	Making conscious choices to enhance a text by adding additional words, phrases, sentences, or ideas	To refine and clarify the writer's thoughts during revision and/or drafting
Brainstorming	Using a flexible but deliberate process of listing multiple ideas in a short period of time without excluding any idea from the preliminary list	To generate ideas, concepts, or key words that provide a focus and/or establish organization as part of the prewriting or revision process
Deleting	Providing clarity and cohesiveness for a text by eliminating words, phrases, sentences, or ideas	To refine and clarify the writer's thoughts during revision and/or drafting
Double-Entry Journal	Creating a two-column journal (also called Dialectical Journal) with a student-selected passage in one column and the student's response in the second column (e.g., asking questions of the text, forming personal responses, interpreting the text, reflecting on the process of making meaning of the text)	To assist in organizing key textual elements and responses noted during reading in order to generate textual support that can be incorporated into a piece of writing at a later time
Drafting	Composing a text in its initial form	To incorporate brainstormed or initial ideas into a written format
Free writing	Using a fluid brainstorming process to write without constraints in order to solidify and convey the writer's purpose	To refine and clarify the writer's thoughts, spark new ideas, and/or generate content during revision and/or drafting
Generating Questions	Clarifying and developing ideas by asking questions of the draft. May be part of self-editing or peer editing	To clarify and develop ideas in a draft. Used during drafting and as part of writer response
Graphic Organizer	Representing ideas and information visually (e.g., Venn diagrams, flowcharts, cluster maps)	To provide a visual system for organizing multiple ideas, details, and/or textual support to be included in a piece of writing
Looping	Focusing on one section of a text and generating new ideas from that section and then repeating the process with the newly generated segments	To refine and clarify the writer's thoughts, spark new ideas, and/or generate new content during revision and/or drafting
Mapping	Creating a graphic organizer that serves as a visual representation of the organizational plan for a written text	To generate ideas, concepts, or key words that provide a focus and/or establish organization during the prewriting, drafting, or revision process

WRITING STRATEGIES (Continued)

STRATEGY	DEFINITION	PURPOSE
Marking the Draft	Interacting with the draft version of a piece of writing by highlighting, underlining, color-coding, and annotating to indicate revision ideas.	To encourage focused, reflective thinking about revising drafts
Outlining	Using a system of numerals and letters in order to identify topics and supporting details and ensure an appropriate balance of ideas	To generate ideas, concepts, or key words that provide a focus and/or establish organization prior to writing an initial draft and/or during the revision process
Quickwrite	Writing for a short, specific amount of time about a designated topic related to a text	To generate multiple ideas in a quick fashion that could be turned into longer pieces of writing at a later time (May be considered as part of the drafting process)
RAFT	Generating and/or transforming a text by identifying and/or manipulating its component parts of *Role, Audience, Format,* and *Topic*	To consider the main elements of the writer's own work in order to generate a focus and purpose during the prewriting and drafting stages of the writing process
Rearranging	Selecting components of a text and moving them to another place within the text and/or modifying the order in which the author's ideas are presented	To refine and clarify the writer's thoughts during revision and/or drafting
Revisiting Prior Work	Looking through a collection of previously completed work to identify successes and challenges that may have been encountered with particular formats, conventions, style, word choice, and so on	To build on prior experience in preparation for a new piece of writing and/or to revise a previous piece of writing
Self Editing/Peer Editing	Working with a partner to examine a text closely in order to identify areas that might need to be corrected for grammar, punctuation, spelling	To provide a systematic process for editing a written text to ensure correctness of identified components such as conventions of standard English
Sharing and Responding	Communicating with another person or a small group of peers who respond to a piece of writing as focused readers (not necessarily as evaluators)	To make suggestions for improvement to the work of others and/or to receive appropriate and relevant feedback on the writer's own work, used during the drafting and revision process
Sketching	Drawing or sketching ideas or ordering of ideas. Includes storyboarding, visualizing	To generate and/or clarify ideas by visualizing them; may be part of prewriting
Substituting	Replacing original words or phrases in a text with new words or phrases that achieve the desired effect	To refine and clarify the writer's thoughts during revision and/or drafting
Transformation of Text	Providing opportunities for students to create new text from a studied text by changing the genre, vernacular, time period, culture, point of view, and so on	To highlight the elements of a genre, point of view and so on; to illustrate how elements of style work together
TWIST*	Arriving at a thesis statement that incorporates the following literary elements: tone, word choice (diction), imagery, style and theme	To craft an interpretive thesis in response to a prompt about a passage
Webbing	Developing a graphic organizer that consists of a series of circles connected with lines to indicate relationships among ideas	To generate ideas, concepts, or key words that provide a focus and/or establish organization prior to writing an initial draft and/or during the revision process

*AP strategy

SPEAKING AND LISTENING STRATEGIES

STRATEGY	DEFINITION	PURPOSE
Notetaking	Creating a record of information while listening to a speaker	To facilitate active listening; to record and organize ideas that assist in processing information
Oral Interpretation	Reading a text orally while providing the necessary inflection and emphasis that demonstrate an understanding of the meaning of the text	To share with an audience the reader's personal insight into a text through voice, fluency, tone, and purpose
Oral Reading	Reading aloud one's own text or the texts of others (e.g., echo reading, choral reading, paired readings).	To share one's own work or the work of others; build fluency and increase confidence in presenting to a group
Role Playing	Assuming the role or persona of a character	To develop the voice, emotions, and mannerisms of a character to facilitate improved comprehension of a text
Rehearsal	Encouraging multiple practices of a piece of text prior to a performance	To provide students with an opportunity to clarify the meaning of a text prior to a performance as they refine the use of dramatic conventions (e.g., gestures, vocal interpretations, facial expressions)

COLLABORATIVE STRATEGIES

STRATEGY	DEFINITION	PURPOSE
Think-Pair-Share	Considering and thinking about a topic or question and then writing what has been learned; pairing with a peer or a small group to share ideas; sharing ideas and discussion with a larger group	To construct meaning about a topic or question; to test thinking in relation to the ideas of others; to prepare for a discussion with a larger group
Discussion Groups	Engaging in an interactive, small group discussion, often with an assigned role; to consider a topic, text, question, and so on	To gain new understanding or insight of a text from multiple perspectives

Web Organizer

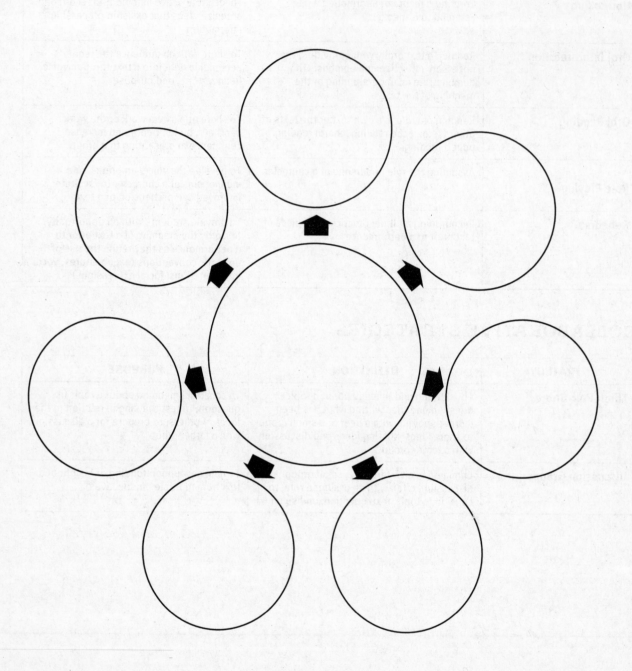

Glossary
Glosario

A

active-voice verbs: a verb form indicating that the subject performs the action
verbos en voz activa: forma verbal que indica que el sujeto realiza la acción

advertising techniques: specific methods used in print, graphics, or videos to persuade people to buy a product or use a service
técnicas publicitarias: métodos específicos usados en impresos, gráfica o videos para persuadir a las personas a comprar un producto o usar un servicio

alliteration: the repetition of initial consonant sounds in words that are close together
aliteración: repetición de sonidos consonánticos iniciales en palabras cercanas

allusion: a reference to a well-known person, event, or place from history, music, art, or another literary work
alusión: referencia a una persona, evento o lugar muy conocidos de la historia, música, arte u otra obra literaria

anaphora: the repetition of the same word or group of words at the beginnings of two or more clauses or lines
anáfora: repetición de la misma palabra o grupo de palabras al comienzo de una o más cláusulas o versos

anecdotal evidence: evidence based on personal accounts of incidents
evidencia anecdótica: evidencia basada en relatos personales de los hechos

annotated bibliography: a list of sources used in research along with comments about each source
bibliografía anotada: lista de fuentes utilizadas en la investigación, junto con comentarios acerca de cada fuente

antagonist: the character who opposes or struggles again the main character
antagonista: personaje que se opone o lucha contra el personaje principal

aphorism: a succinct statement expressing an opinion or general truth
aforismo: afirmación breve que expresa una opinión o verdad general

archetypes: universal symbols—images, characters, motifs, or patterns—that recur in myths, art and literature through the world
arquetipos: símbolos universales —imágenes, personajes, motivos o patrones— reiterativos en los mitos, el arte y la literatura alrededor del mundo

archival footage: film footage taken from another, previously recorded, source
cortometraje de archivo: fragmento de película tomada de otra fuente grabada previamente

argument: a form of writing that presents a particular opinion or idea and supports it with evidence
argumento: forma de redacción que presenta una opinión o idea particular y la apoya con evidencia

argumentation: the structure of an argument includes the *hook* (quotation, example, or idea that catches readers' attention), *claim* (the opinion or thesis statement), *support* (evidence in the form of facts, statistics, examples, anecdotes, or expert opinions), *concession* (the writer's admission that the other side of the argument has a valid point), *refutation* (a well-reasoned denial of an opponent's point, based on solid evidence), and *call to action* (an inspired request of readers)
argumentación: la estructura de una argumentación incluye el gancho (cita, ejemplo o idea que capta la atención del lector), afirmación (declaración de opinión o tesis), apoyo (evidencia en forma de hechos, estadísticas, ejemplos, anécdotas u opiniones de expertos), concesión (admisión por parte del escritor de que la otra parte del debate tiene un punto válido), refutación (negación bien razonada de una opinión del oponente, basada en evidencia sólida) y llamado a la acción (petición inspirada de lectores)

argument by analogy: a comparison of two similar situations, implying that the outcome of one will resemble the outcome of the other
argumento por analogía: comparación de dos situaciones semejantes, infiriendo que el resultado de será parecido al resultado de la otra

aside: a short speech spoken by an actor directly to the audience and unheard by other actors on stage
aparte: alocución breve dicha por un actor directamente al público y que no escuchan los demás actores que están en el escenario

assonance: the repetition of similar vowel sounds in accented syllables, followed by different consonant sounds, in words that are close together
asonancia: repetición de sonidos vocálicos similares en sílabas acentuadas, seguida de diferentes sonidos consonánticos, en palabras que están cercanas

audience: the intended readers, listeners, or viewers of specific types of written, spoken or visual texts
público: lectores objetivo, oyentes o espectadores de tipos específicos de textos escritos, hablados o visuales

audience analysis: determining the knowledge, beliefs, and needs of a target audience in order to reach them successfully
análisis del público: determinar los conocimientos, creencias y necesidades de una audiencia objetivo de modo de llegar a ella con éxito

author's purpose: the specific reason or reasons for the writing; what the author hopes to accomplish
propósito del autor: razón específica para escribir; lo que el autor espera lograr

B

balanced sentence: a sentence that presents ideas of equal weight in similar grammatical forms to emphasize the similarity or difference between the ideas
oración balanceada: oración que representa ideas de igual peso en formas gramaticales similares para enfatizar la semejanza o diferencia entre las ideas

bias: an inclination or mental leaning for or against something, which prevents impartial judgment
sesgo: inclinación o tendencia mental a favor o en contra de algo, lo que impide una opinión imparcial

blank verse: unrhymed verse
verso libre: verso que no tiene rima

blocking: in drama, how actors position themselves in relation to one another, the audience, and the objects on the stage
bloqueo: en drama, el modo en que los actores se sitúan entre sí, con el público y los objetos en el escenario

C

caricature: a visual or verbal representation in which characteristics or traits are exaggerated or distorted for emphasis
caricatura: representación visual o verbal en la que las características o rasgos se exageran o se distorsionan para dar énfasis

characterization: the methods a writer uses to develop characters
caracterización: métodos que usa un escritor para desarrollar personajes

characters: people, animals, or imaginary creatures that take part in the action of a story. A short story usually centers on a *main character*, but may also contain one or more *minor characters*, who are not as complex, but whose thoughts, words, or actions move the plot along. A character who is *dynamic* changes in response to the events of the narrative; a character who is *static* remains the same throughout the narrative. A *round* character is fully developed—he or she shows a variety of traits; a *flat* character is one-dimensional, usually showing only one trait.
personajes: personas, animales o criaturas imaginarias que participan en la acción de un cuento. Un cuento corto normalmente se centra en un *personaje principal*, pero puede también contener uno o más *personajes secundarios*, que no son tan complejos, pero cuyos pensamientos, palabras o acciones hacen avanzar la trama. Un personaje que es *dinámico* cambia según los eventos del relato; un personaje que es *estático* permanece igual a lo largo del relato. Un personaje *complejo* está completamente desarrollado: muestra una diversidad de rasgos; un personaje *simple* es unidimensional, mostrando normalmente sólo un rasgo.

chorus: in traditional or classic drama, a group of performers who speak as one and comment on the action of the play
coro: en el drama tradicional o clásico, grupo de actores que hablan al unísono y comentan la acción de la obra teatral

cinematic elements: the features of cinema—movies, film, video—that contribute to its form and structure: *angles* (the view from which the image is shot); *framing* (how a scene is structured); *lighting* (the type of lighting used to light a scene); and *mise en scène* (the composition, setting, or staging of an image, or a scene in a film); *sound* (the sound effects and music accompanying each scene)
elementos cinematográficos: las características del cine—películas, filmaciones, video—que contribuyen a darle forma y estructura: *angulación* (vista desde la cual se toma la imagen); *encuadre* (cómo se estructura una escena); *iluminación* (tipo de iluminación que se usa para una escena); y *montaje* (composición, ambiente o escenificación de una imagen o escena en una película); *sonido* (efectos sonoros y música que acompañan cada escena)

claim: a position statement (or thesis) that asserts an idea or makes an argument
afirmación: declaración de opinión (o tesis) que asevera una idea o establece un debate

cliché: an overused expression or idea
cliché: expresión o idea que se usa en exceso

climax: the point at which the action reaches its peak; the point of greatest interest or suspense in a story; the turning point at which the outcome of the conflict is decided
clímax: punto en el que la acción alcanza su punto culminante; punto de mayor interés en un cuento; punto de inflexión en el que se decide el resultado del conflicto

coherence: the quality of unity or logical connection among ideas; the clear and orderly presentation of ideas in a paragraph or essay
coherencia: calidad de unidad o relación lógica entre las ideas; presentación clara y ordenada de las ideas en un párrafo o ensayo

commentary: in an expository essay or paragraph, the explanation of the importance or relevance of supporting detail and the way the details support the larger analysis
comentario: ensayo o párrafo expositivo, explicación de la importancia o relevancia de los detalles de apoyo, y la manera en que los detalles apoyan el análisis principal

complex sentence: a sentence containing one independent clause and one or more subordinate clauses
oración compleja: oración que contiene una cláusula independiente y una o más cláusulas subordinadas

complications: the events in a plot that develop the conflict; the complications move the plot forward in its rising action
complicaciones: sucesos de una trama que desarrollan el conflicto; las complicaciones hacen avanzar la trama en su acción ascendente

compound sentence: a sentence containing two independent clauses
oración compuesta: oración que contiene dos cláusulas independientes

concession: an admission in an argument that the opposing side has valid points
concesión: admitir en un debate que el lado opositor tiene opiniones válidas

conflict: a struggle or problem in a story. An *internal conflict* occurs when a character struggles between opposing needs or desires or emotions within his or her own mind. An *external conflict* occurs when a character struggles against an outside force. This force may be another character, a societal expectation, or something in the physical world.

conflicto: lucha o problema en un cuento. Un *conflicto interno* ocurre cuando un personaje lucha entre necesidades o deseos o emociones que se contraponen dentro de su mente. Un *conflicto externo* ocurre cuando un personaje lucha contra una fuerza externa. Esta fuerza puede ser otro personaje, una expectativa social o algo del mundo físico.

connotation: the associations and emotional overtones attached to a word beyond its literal definition or denotation. A connotation may be positive, negative, or neutral.

connotación: asociaciones y alusiones emocionales unidas a una palabra más allá de su definición literal o denotación. Una connotación puede ser positiva, negativa o neutra.

consonance: the repetition of final consonant sounds in stressed syllables with different vowel sounds

consonancia: repetición de sonidos consonánticos finales en sílabas acentuadas con diferentes sonidos vocálicos

context: the circumstances or conditions in which something takes place

contexto: circunstancias o condiciones en las que algo ocurre

conventions: standard practices and forms

convenciones: prácticas y formas usuales

couplet: two consecutive lines of verse with end rhyme; a couplet usually expresses a complete unit of thought

copla: dos líneas de versos consecutivos con rima final; una copla normalmente expresa una unidad de pensamiento completa

credibility: the quality of being trusted or believed

credibilidad: calidad de ser confiable o creíble

critical lens: a particular identifiable perspective as in Reader Response Criticism, Cultural Criticism, etc., through which a text can be analyzed and interpreted

ojo crítico: punto de vista particular identificable como por ejemplo Teoría de la recepción, Crítica sociocultural, etc., por medio del que se puede analizar e interpretar un texto

cultural conflict: a struggle that occurs when people with different cultural expectations or attitudes interact

conflicto cultural: lucha que ocurre cuando interactúan personas con diferentes expectativas o actitudes culturales

culture: the shared set of arts, ideas, skills, institutions, customs, attitude, values and achievements that characterize a group of people, and that are passed on or taught to succeeding generations

cultura: conjunto de artes, ideas, destrezas, instituciones, costumbres, actitud, valores y logros compartidos que caracterizan a un grupo de personas, y que se transfieren o enseñan a las generaciones siguientes

cumulative (or loose) sentence: a sentence in which the main clause comes first, followed by subordinate structures or clauses

oración acumulativa (o frases sueltas): oración cuya cláusula principal viene primero, seguida de estructuras o cláusulas subordinadas

D

deductive reasoning: a process of using general information from which to draw a specific conclusion

razonamiento deductivo: proceso en que se usa información general para sacar una conclusión específica

denotation: the exact literal meaning of a word

denotación: significado literal exacto de una palabra

detail: a specific fact, observation, or incident; any of the small pieces or parts that make up something else

detalle: hecho, observación o incidente específico; cualquiera de las pequeñas piezas o partes que constituyen otra cosa

dialect: the distinctive language, including the sounds, spelling, grammar, and diction, of a specific group or class of people

dialecto: lenguaje distintivo, incluyendo sonidos, ortografía, gramática y dicción, de un grupo o clase específico de personas

dialogue: the words spoken by characters in a narrative or film

diálogo: palabras que dicen los personajes en un relato o película

diction: the writer's choice of words; a stylistic element that helps convey voice and tone

dicción: selección de palabras por parte del escritor; elemento estilístico que ayuda a transmitir voz y tono

diegetic sound: actual noises associated with the shooting of a scene, such as voices and background sounds

sonido diegético: sonidos reales asociados con la filmación de una escena, como por ejemplo voces y sonidos de fondo

discourse: the language or speech used in a particular context or subject

discurso: lenguaje o habla usada en un contexto o tema en particular

documentary or nonfiction film: a genre of filmmaking that provides a visual record of factual events, using photographs, video footage, and interviews

documental o película de no-ficción: género cinematográfico que realiza un registro visual de sucesos basados en hechos por medio del uso de fotografías, registro en videos y entrevistas

drama: a play written for stage, radio, film, or television, usually about a serious topic or situation

drama: obra teatral escrita para representar en un escenario, radio, cine o televisión, normalmente sobre un tema o situación seria

E

editorial: an article in a newspaper or magazine expressing the opinion of its editor or publisher

editorial: artículo de periódico o revista, que expresa la opinión de su editor

effect: the result or influence of using a specific literary or cinematic device

efecto: resultado o influencia de usar un recurso literario o cinematográfico específico

empirical evidence: evidence based on experiences and direct observation through research
evidencia empírica: evidencia basada en experiencias y en la observación directa por medio de la investigación

epigram: a short witty saying
epigrama: dicho corto e ingenioso

ethos: (ethical appeal) a rhetorical appeal that focuses on ethics, or the character or qualifications of the speaker
ethos: (recurso ético) recurso retórico centrado en la ética o en el carácter o capacidades del orador

evidence: the information that supports or proves an idea or claim; forms of evidence include facts, statistics (numerical facts), expert opinions, examples, and anecdotes; *see also*, anecdotal, empirical, and logical evidence
evidencia: información que apoya o prueba una idea o afirmación; formas de evidencia incluyen hechos, estadística (datos numéricos), opiniones de expertos, ejemplos y anécdotas; *ver también* evidencia anecdótica, empírica y lógica

exaggeration: representing something as larger, better, or worse than it really is
exageración: representar algo como más grande, mejor o peor que lo que realmente es

explicit theme: a theme that is clearly stated by the writer
tema explícito: tema que está claramente establecido por el escritor

exposition: events that give a reader background information needed to understand a story. During exposition, characters are introduced, the setting is described, and the conflict begins to unfold.
exposición: sucesos que dan al lector los antecedentes necesarios para comprender un cuento. Durante la exposición, se presentan los personajes, se describe el ambiente y se comienza a revelar el conflicto.

extended metaphor: a metaphor extended over several lines or throughout an entire poem
metáfora extendida: metáfora que se extiende por varios versos o a través de un poema completo

F

falling action: the events in a play, story, or novel that follow the climax, or moment of greatest suspense, and lead to the resolution
acción descendente: sucesos de una obra teatral, cuento o novela posteriores al clímax, o momento de mayor suspenso, y que conllevan a la resolución

fallacy: a false or misleading argument
falacia: argumento falso o engañoso

figurative language: imaginative language not meant to be taken literally; figurative language uses figures of speech
lenguaje figurativo: lenguaje imaginativo que no pretende ser tomado literalmente; el lenguaje figurativo usa figuras literarias

flashback: an interruption in the sequence of events to relate events that occurred in the past
flashback: interrupción en la secuencia de los sucesos para relatar sucesos ocurridos en el pasado

fixed form: a form of poetry in which the length and pattern are determined by established usage of tradition, such as a sonnet
forma fija: forma de poesía en la que la longitud y el patrón están determinados por el uso de la tradición, como un soneto

foil: a character whose actions or thoughts are juxtaposed against those of a major character in order to highlight key attributes of the major character
antagonista: personaje cuyas acciones o pensamientos se yuxtaponen a los de un personaje principal con el fin de destacar atributos clave del personaje principal

folk tale: a story without a known author that has been preserved through oral retellings
cuento folclórico: cuento sin autor conocido que se ha conservado por medio de relatos orales

footage: literally, a length of film; the expression is still used to refer to digital video clips
metraje: literalmente, la longitud de una película; la expresión aún se usa para referirse a video clips digitales

foreshadowing: the use of hints or clues in a narrative to suggest future action
presagio: uso de claves o pistas en un relato para sugerir una acción futura

free verse: poetry without a fixed pattern of meter and rhyme
verso libre: poesía que no sigue ningún patrón, ritmo o rima regular

G

genre: a kind or style of literature or art, each with its own specific characteristics. For example, poetry, short story, and novel are literary genres. Painting and sculpture are artistic genres.
género: tipo o estilo de literatura o arte, cada uno con sus propias características específicas. Por ejemplo, la poesía, el cuento corto y la novela son géneros literarios. La pintura y la escultura son géneros artísticos.

genre conventions: the essential features and format that characterize a specific genre
convenciones genéricas: características básicas y el formato que caracterizan un género específico

graphics: images or text used to provide information on screen
gráfica: imágenes o texto que se usa para dar información en pantalla

graphic novel: a book-length narrative, or story, in the form of a comic strip rather than words
novela gráfica: narrativa o cuento del largo de un libro, en forma de tira cómica más que palabras

H

hamartia: a tragic hero's fatal flaw; an ingrained character trait that causes a hero to make decisions that ultimately lead to his or her death or downfall
hamartia: error fatal de un héroe trágico; característica propia de un personaje que causa que un héroe tome decisiones que finalmente llevan a su muerte o caída

hero: the main character or protagonist of a play, with whom audiences become emotionally invested

héroe: personaje principal o protagonista de una obra teatral, con el que el público se involucra emocionalmente

hook: an interesting quotation, anecdote, or example at the beginning of a piece of writing that grabs readers' attention

gancho: cita, anécdota o ejemplo interesante al comienzo de un escrito, que capta la atención del lector

humor: the quality of being amusing

humor: calidad de ser divertido

hyperbole: exaggeration used to suggest strong emotion or create a comic effect

hipérbole: exageración que se usa para sugerir una emoción fuerte o crear un efecto cómico

I

iamb: a metrical foot that consists of an unstressed syllable followed by a stressed syllable

yambo: pie métrico que consta de una sílaba átona seguida de una sílaba acentuada

iambic pentameter: a rhythmic pattern of five feet (or units) of one unstressed syllable followed by a stressed syllable

pentámetro yámbico: patrón rítmico de cinco pies (o unidades) de una sílaba átona seguida de una sílaba acentuada

image: a word or phrase that appeals to one of more of the five senses and creates a picture

imagen: palabra o frase que apela a uno o más de los cinco sentido y crea un cuadro

imagery: the verbal expression of sensory experience; descriptive or figurative language used to create word pictures; imagery is created by details that appeal to one or more of the five senses

imaginería: lenguaje descriptivo o figurativo utilizado para crear imágenes verbales; la imaginería es creada por detalles que apelan a uno o más de los cinco sentidos

implied theme: a theme that is understood through the writer's diction, language construction, and use of literary devices

tema implícito: tema que se entiende a través de la dicción del escritor, construcción lingüística y uso de recursos literarios

inductive reasoning: a process of looking at individual facts to draw a general conclusion

razonamiento inductivo: proceso de observación de hechos individuales para sacar una conclusión general

interior monologue: a literary device in which a character's internal emotions and thoughts are presented

monólogo interior: recurso literario en el que se presentan las emociones internas y pensamientos de un personaje

irony: a literary device that exploits readers' expectations; irony occurs when what is expected turns out to be quite different from what actually happens. *Dramatic irony* is a form of irony in which the reader or audience knows more about the circumstances or future events in a story than the characters within it; *verbal irony* occurs when a speaker or narrator says one thing while meaning the opposite; *situational irony* occurs

when an event contradicts the expectations of the characters or the reader.

ironía: recurso literario que explota las expectativas de los lectores; la ironía ocurre cuando lo que se espera resulta ser bastante diferente de lo que realmente ocurre. La *ironía dramática* es una forma de ironía en la que el lector o la audiencia saben más acerca de las circunstancias o sucesos futuros de un cuento que los personajes del mismo; la *ironía verbal* ocurre cuando un orador o narrador dice una cosa queriendo decir lo contrario; la *ironía situacional* ocurre cuando un suceso contradice las expectativas de los personajes o del lector.

J

justice: the quality of being reasonable and fair in the administration of the law; the ideal of rightness or fairness

justicia: calidad de ser razonable e imparcial en la administración de la ley; ideal de rectitud o equidad

juxtaposition: the arrangement of two or more things for the purpose of comparison

yuxtaposición: ordenamiento de dos o más cosas con el objeto de compararlas

L

literary theory: attempts to establish principles for interpreting and evaluating literary texts

teoría literaria: intento de establecer principios para interpretar y evaluar textos literarios

logical evidence: evidence based on facts and a clear rationale

evidencia lógica: evidencia basada en hechos y una clara fundamentación

logos: (logical appeal) a rhetorical appeal that uses logic to appeal to the sense of reason

logos: (apelación lógica) apelación retórica que usa la lógica para apelar al sentido de la razón

M

metacognition: the ability to know and be aware of one's own thought processes; self-reflection

metacognición: capacidad de conocer y estar consciente de los propios procesos del pensamiento; introspección

metaphor: a comparison between two unlike things in which one thing is spoken of as if it were another; for example, the moon was a crisp white cracker

metáfora: comparación entre dos cosas diferentes en la que se habla de una cosa como si fuera otra; por ejemplo, la luna era una galletita blanca crujiente

meter: a pattern of stressed and unstressed syllables in poetry

métrica: patrón de sílabas acentuadas y átonas en poesía

monologue: a dramatic speech delivered by a single character in a play

monólogo: discurso dramático que hace un solo personaje en una obra teatral

montage: a composite picture that is created by bringing together a number of images and arranging them to create a connected whole

montaje: cuadro compuesto que se crea al reunir un número de imágenes y que al organizarlas se crea un todo relacionado

mood: the atmosphere or general feeling in a literary work
carácter: atmósfera o sentimiento general en una obra literaria

motif: a recurrent image, symbol, theme, character type, subject, or narrative detail that becomes a unifying element in an artistic work.
motivo: imagen, símbolo, tema, tipo de personaje, tema o detalle narrativo recurrente que se convierte en un elemento unificador en una obra artística.

myth: a traditional story that explains the actions of gods or heroes or the origins of the elements of nature
mito: cuento tradicional que explica las acciones de dioses o héroes, o los orígenes de los elementos de la naturaleza

N

narration: the act of telling a story
narración: acto de contar un cuento

non-diegetic sound: voice-overs and commentary, sounds that do not come from the action on screen.
sonido no diegético: voces y comentarios superpuestos, sonidos que no provienen de la acción en pantalla.

O

objective: based on factual information
objetivo: basado en información de hechos

objectivity: the representation of facts or ideas without injecting personal feelings or biases
objetividad: representación de los hechos o ideas sin agregar sentimientos o prejuicios personales

ode: a lyric poem expressing feelings or thoughts of a speaker, often celebrating a person, event, or a thing
oda: poema lírico que expresa sentimientos o pensamientos de un orador, que frecuentemente celebra a una persona, suceso o cosa

onomatopoeia: words whose sound suggest their meaning
onomatopeya: palabras cuyo sonido sugiere su significado

oral tradition: the passing down of stories, tales, proverbs, and other culturally important stories and ideas through oral retellings
tradición oral: traspaso de historias, cuentos, proverbios y otras historias de importancia cultural por medio de relatos orales

oxymoron: words that appear to contradict each other; e.g., cold fire
oxímoron: palabras que parecen contradecirse mutuamente; por ejemplo, fuego frío

P

parallel structure (parallelism): refers to a grammatical or structural similarity between sentences or parts of a sentence, so that elements of equal importance are equally developed and similarly phrased for emphasis
estructura paralela (paralelismo): se refiere a una similitud gramatical o estructural entre oraciones o partes de una

oración, de modo que los elementos de igual importancia se desarrollen por igual y se expresen de manera similar para dar énfasis

paraphrase: to briefly restate ideas from another source in one's own words
parafrasear: volver a presentar las ideas de otra fuente en nuestras propias palabras

parody: a literary or artistic work that imitates the characteristic style of an author or a work for comic effect or ridicule
parodia: obra literaria o artística que imita el estilo característico de un autor o una obra para dar un efecto cómico o ridículo

passive-voice verbs: verb form in which the subject receives the action; the passive voice consists of a form of the verb be plus a past participle of the verb
verbos en voz pasiva: forma verbal en la que el sujeto recibe la acción; la voz pasiva se forma con el verbo ser más el participio pasado de un verbo

pathos: (emotional appeal) a rhetorical appeal to readers' or listeners' senses or emotions
pathos: (apelación emocional) apelación retórica a los sentidos o emociones de los lectores u oyentes

periodic sentence: a sentence that makes sense only when the end of the sentence is reached; that is, when the main clause comes last
oración periódica: oración que tiene sentido sólo cuando se llega al final de la oración; es decir, cuando la cláusula principal viene al final

persona: the voice assumed by a writer to express ideas or beliefs that may not be his or her own
personaje: voz que asume un escritor para expresar ideas o creencias que pueden no ser las propias

personification: a figure of speech that gives human qualities to an animal, object, or idea
personificación: figura literaria que da características humanas a un animal, objeto o idea

persuasive argument: an argument that convinces readers to accept or believe a writer's perspective on a topic
argumento persuasivo: argumento que convence a los lectores a aceptar o creer en la perspectiva de un escritor acerca de un tema

perspective: a way of looking at the world or a mental concept about things or events, one that judges relationships within or among things or events
perspectiva: manera de visualizar el mundo o concepto mental de las cosas o sucesos, que juzga las relaciones dentro o entre cosas o sucesos

photo essay: a collection of photographic images that reveal the author's perspective on the subject
ensayo fotográfico: recolección de imágenes fotográficas que revelan la perspectiva del autor acerca del tema

plagiarism: the unattributed use of another writer's words or ideas
plagio: usar como propias las palabras o ideas de otro escritor

plot: the sequence of related events that make up a story or novel
trama: secuencia de sucesos relacionados que conforman un cuento o novela

poetic structure: the organization of words, lines, and images as well as ideas
estructura poética: organización de las palabras, versos e imágenes, así como también de las ideas

point of view: the perspective from which a narrative is told; i.e., first person, third person limited, third person omniscient
punto de vista: perspectiva desde la cual se cuenta un relato; es decir, primera persona, tercera persona limitada, tercera persona omnisciente

precept: a rule, instruction, or principle that guides somebody's actions and/or moral behavior
precepto: regla, instrucción o principio que guía las acciones y/o conducta moral de alguien

primary footage: film footage shot by the filmmaker for the text at hand
metraje principal: filmación hecha por el cineasta para el texto que tiene a mano

primary source: an original document containing firsthand information about a subject
fuente primaria: documento original que contiene información de primera mano acerca de un tema

prologue: the introduction or preface to a literary work
prólogo: introducción o prefacio de una obra literaria

prose: ordinary written or spoken language using sentences and paragraphs, without deliberate or regular meter or rhyme; not poetry or song
prosa: forma común del lenguaje escrito o hablado, usando oraciones y párrafos, sin métrica o rima deliberada o regular; ni poesía ni canción

protagonist: the central character in a work of literature, the one who is involved in the main conflict in the plot
protagonista: personaje central de una obra literaria, el que participa en el conflicto principal de la trama

Q

quatrain: a four-line stanza in a poem
cuarteta: en un poema, estrofa de cuatro versos

R

reasoning: the thinking or logic used to make a claim in an argument
razonamiento: pensamiento o lógica que se usa para hacer una afirmación en un argumento

refrain: a regularly repeated line or group of lines in a poem or song, usually at the end of a stanza
estribillo: verso o grupo de versos que se repiten con regularidad en un poema o canción, normalmente al final de una estrofa

refutation: the reasoning used to disprove an opposing point
refutación: razonamiento que se usa para rechazar una opinión contraria

reliability: the extent to which a source provides good quality and trustworthy information
confiabilidad: grado en el que una fuente da información confiable y de buena calidad

repetition: the use of any element of language—a sound, a word, a phrase, a line, or a stanza—more than once
repetición: uso de cualquier elemento del lenguaje—un sonido, una palabra, una frase, un verso o una estrofa—más de una vez

resolution (denouement): the end of a play, story, or novel in which the main conflict is finally resolved
resolución (desenlace): final de una obra teatral, cuento o novela, en el que el conflicto principal finalmente se resuelve

résumé: a document that outlines a person's skills, education, and work history
currículum vitae: documento que resume las destrezas, educación y experiencia laboral de una persona

rhetoric: the art of using words to persuade in writing or speaking
retórica: arte de usar las palabras para persuadir por escrito o de manera hablada

rhetorical appeals: the use of emotional, ethical, and logical arguments to persuade in writing or speaking
recursos retóricos: uso de argumentos emocionales, éticos y lógicos para persuadir por escrito o de manera hablada

rhetorical context: the subject, purpose, audience, occasion, or situation in which writing occurs
contexto retórico: sujeto, propósito, audiencia, ocasión o situación en que ocurre el escrito

rhetorical devices: specific techniques used in writing or speaking to create a literary effect or enhance effectiveness
dispositivos retóricos: técnicas específicas que se usan al escribir o al hablar para crear un efecto literario o mejorar la efectividad

rhetorical question: a question that is asked for effect or one for which the answer is obvious
pregunta retórica: pregunta hecha para producir un efecto o cuya respuesta es obvia

rhyme: the repetition of sounds at the ends of words
rima: repetición de sonidos al final de las palabras

rhyme scheme: a consistent pattern of rhyme throughout a poem
esquema de la rima: patrón consistente de una rima a lo largo de un poema

rhythm: the pattern of stressed and unstressed syllables in spoken or written language, especially in poetry
ritmo: patrón de sílabas acentuadas y no acentuadas en lenguaje hablado o escrito, especialmente en poesía

rising action: the movement of a plot toward a climax or moment of greatest excitement; the rising action is fueled by the characters' responses to the conflict
acción ascendente: movimiento de una trama hacia el clímax o momento de mayor emoción; la acción ascendente es impulsada por las reacciones de los personajes ante el conflicto

S

satire: a manner of writing that mixes a critical attitude with wit and humor in an effort to improve mankind and human institutions
sátira: manera de escribir que mezcla una actitud crítica con ingenio y humor en un esfuerzo por mejorar a la humanidad y las instituciones humanas

scenario: an outline, a brief account, a script, or a synopsis of a proposed series of events
escenario: bosquejo, relato breve, libreto o sinopsis de una serie de sucesos propuestos

secondary source: discussion about or commentary on a primary source; the key feature of a secondary source is that it offers an interpretation of information gathered from primary sources
fuente secundaria: discusión o comentario acerca de una fuente primaria; la característica clave de una fuente secundaria es que ofrece una interpretación de la información recopilada en las fuentes primarias

sensory details: details that appeal to or evoke one or more of the five senses--sight, sound, smell, taste, touch
detalles sensoriales: detalles que apelan o evocan uno o más de los cinco sentidos: vista, oído, gusto, olfato, tacto

sensory images: images that appeal to the reader's senses—sight, sound, smell, taste, touch
imágenes sensoriales: imágenes que apelan a los sentidos del lector: vista, oído, olfato, gusto, tacto

setting: the time and place in which a story happens
ambiente: tiempo y lugar en el que ocurre un relato

simile: a comparison of two or more unlike things using the words *like or as*; for example, the moon was as white as milk
símil: comparación entre dos o más cosas diferentes usando las palabras *como o tan*; por ejemplo, la luna estaba tan blanca como la leche

slanters: rhetorical devices used to present the subject in a biased way.
soslayo: recursos retóricos para presentar el tema de modo sesgado.

slogan: a short, catchy phrase used for advertising by a business, club, or political party
eslogan: frase corta y tendenciosa que usa como publicidad para un negocio, club o partido político

social commentary: an expression of an opinion with the goal of promoting change by appealing to a sense of justice
comentario social: expresión de una opinión con el objeto de promover el cambio al apelar a un sentido de justicia

soliloquy: a long speech delivered by an actor alone on the stage
soliloquio: discurso largo realizado por un actor sobre el escenario

sonnet: a fourteen-line lyric poem, usually written in iambic pentameter and following a strict pattern of rhyme
soneto: poema lírico de catorce versos, normalmente escrito en un pentámetro yámbico y que sigue un patrón de rima estricto

speaker: the imaginary voice or persona of the writer or author
orador: voz o persona imaginaria del escritor o autor

stakeholder: a person motivated or affected by a course of action
participante: persona motivada o afectada por el curso de una acción

stanza: a group of lines, usually similar in length and pattern, that form a unit within a poem
estrofa: grupo de versos, normalmente similares en longitud y patrón, que forman una unidad dentro de un poema

stereotype: an oversimplified, generalized conception, opinion, and/or image about particular groups of people.
estereotipo: concepto generalizado, opinión y/o imagen demasiado simplificada acerca de grupos específicos de personas.

structure: the way a literary work is organized; the arrangement of the parts in a literary work
estructura: manera en que la obra literaria está organizada; disposición de las partes en una obra literaria

style: the distinctive way a writer uses language, characterized by elements of diction, syntax, imagery, etc.
estilo: manera distintiva en que un escritor usa el lenguaje, caracterizada por elementos de dicción, sintaxis, lenguaje figurado, etc.

subculture: a smaller subsection of a culture; for example, within the culture of a high school may be many subcultures
subcultura: subsección más pequeña de una cultura; por ejemplo, dentro de la cultura de una escuela secundaria puede haber muchas subculturas

subjectivity: based on one's personal point of view, opinion, or values
subjetividad: en base en nuestro punto de vista, opinión o valores personales

subtext: the underlying or implicit meaning in dialogue or the implied relationship between characters in a book, movie, play or film. The subtext of a work is not explicitly stated.
subtexto: significado subyacente o implícito en el diálogo o la relación implícita entre los personajes de un libro, película, u obra teatral. El subtexto de una obra no se establece de manera explícita.

survey: a method of collecting data from a group of people; it can be written, such as a print or online questionnaire, or oral, such as an in-person interview
encuesta: método para recolectar datos de un grupo de personas; puede ser escrita, como un impreso o cuestionario en línea, u oral, como en una entrevista personal

symbol: anything (object, animal, event, person, or place) that represents itself but also stands for something else on a figurative level
símbolo: cualquier cosa (objeto, animal, evento, persona o lugar) que se representa a sí misma, pero también representa otra cosa a nivel figurativo

symbolic: serving as a symbol; involving the use of symbols or symbolism
simbólico: que sirve como símbolo; que implica el uso de

símbolos o simbolismo

syntax: the arrangement of words and the order of grammatical elements in a sentence; the way in which words are put together to make meaningful elements, such as phrases, clauses, and sentences

sintaxis: disposición de las palabras y orden de los elementos gramaticales en una oración; manera en que las palabras se juntan para formar elementos significativos, como frases, cláusulas y oraciones

synthesis: the act of combining ideas from different sources to create, express, or support a new idea

síntesis: acto de combinar ideas de diferentes fuentes para crear, expresar o apoyar una nueva idea

T

target audience: the intended group for which a work is designed to appeal or reach

público objetivo: grupo al que se pretende apelar o llegar con una obra

thematic statement: an interpretive statement articulating the central meaning or message of a text

oración temática: afirmación interpretativa que articula el significado o mensaje central de un texto

theatrical elements: elements employed by dramatists and directors to tell a story on stage. Elements include *costumes* (the clothing worn by actors to express their characters), *makeup* (cosmetics used to change actors' appearances and express their characters), *props* (objects used to help set the scene, advance a plot and make a story realistic), *set* (the place where the action takes place, as suggested by objects, such as furniture, placed on a stage), *acting choices* (gestures, movements, staging, and vocal techniques actors use to convey their characters and tell a story).

elementos teatrales: elementos que utilizan los dramaturgos y directores para contar una historia en el escenario. Los elementos incluyen *vestuario* (ropa que usan los actores para expresar sus personajes), *maquillaje* (cosméticos que se usan para cambiar la apariencia de los actores y expresar sus personajes), *elementos* (objetos que se usan para ayudar a montar la escena, avanzar la trama y crear una historia realista), *plató* (lugar donde tiene lugar la acción, según lo sugieren los objetos, como muebles, colocados sobre un escenario), *opciones de actuación* (gestos, movimientos, representación y técnicas vocales que se usan para transmitir sus personajes y narrar una historia).

theme: a writer's central idea or main message about life; *see also*, explicit theme, implied theme

tema: idea central o mensaje principal acerca de la vida de un escritor; *véase también*, tema explícito, tema implícito

thesis: the main idea or point of an essay or article; in an argumentative essay the thesis is the writer's position on an issue

tesis: idea o punto principal de un ensayo o artículo; en un ensayo argumentativo, la tesis es la opinión del autor acerca de un tema

topic sentence: a sentence that states the main idea of a paragraph; in an essay, it also makes a point that supports the thesis statement

oración principal: oración que establece la idea principal de un párrafo; en un ensayo, también establece una proposición que apoya el enunciado de la tesis

tone: a writer's or speaker's attitude toward a subject

tono: actitud de un escritor u orador acerca de un tema

tragedy: a dramatic play that tells the story of a character, usually of a noble birth, who meets an untimely and unhappy death or downfall, often because of a specific character flaw or twist of fate

tragedia: obra teatral dramática que cuenta la historia de un personaje, normalmente de origen noble, que encuentra una muerte o caída imprevista o infeliz, con frecuencia debido a un defecto específico del personaje o una vuelta del destino

tragic hero: an archetypal hero based on the Greek concept of tragedy; the tragic hero has a flaw that makes him vulnerable to downfall or death

héroe trágico: héroe arquetípico basado en el concepto griego de la tragedia; el héroe trágico tiene un defecto que lo hace vulnerable a la caída o a la muerte

U

understatement: the representation of something as smaller or less significant than it really is; the opposite of exaggeration or hyperbole

subestimación: representación de algo como más pequeño o menos importante de lo que realmente es; lo opuesto a la exageración o hipérbole

V

valid: believable or truthful

válido: creíble o verídico

validity: the quality of truth or accuracy in a source

validez: calidad de verdad o precisión en una fuente

vignette: a picture or visual or a brief descriptive literary piece

viñeta: ilustración o representación visual o pieza literaria descriptiva breve

vocal delivery: the way words are expressed on stage, through volume, pitch, rate or speed of speech, pauses, pronunciation, and articulation

presentación vocal: manera en que se expresan las palabras en el escenario, por medio del volumen, tono, rapidez o velocidad del discurso, pausas, pronunciación y articulación

voice: the way a writer or speaker uses words and tone to express ideas as well as his or her personas

voz: manera en que el escritor u orador usa las palabras y el tono para expresar ideas, así como también su personaje

Index of Skills

Literary Skills

Allusion, 228, 309, 391
Analogy, 26, 197, 315
    alternative word meanings, 135
    antonyms, 253
    expressed using letters, 223
    rhetorical, 134
    geographical terms, 311
    as sentence, 369
    synonyms, 253
Anaphora, 263
Annotated bibliography, 425–426
Anticipation guide, 6
Antithesis, 29
Aphorism, 23, 228
Argument
    by analogy, 227, 228
    persuasive, 83
    structure, 77
Audience, 111
Bias, 124
Biographical sketch, 8
Biography, 362, 367
Call to action, 77
Caricature, 174
Character analysis, 246–247
Characterization, 257–258, 262,
    274, 298, 375, 378
    in film, 249–250
Claim, 77
Coherence, 429
Communication, 337
Compare/contrast, 11, 65, 254, 297,
    381
Concession, 77,119, 183
Conflict, 254, 298
Connotation, 11, 12, 311, 387
Deductive reasoning, 117
Denotation, 11
Details, 398
Dialect, 286, 296
Diction, 35, 147, 168, 170, 183, 367
    formal, 147, 296
    high, 296
    informal, 296
    in interview, 353
    low, 296
    neutral, 296
Discourse, 440

Drama games, 244–245
Dysphemisms, 134
Epigram, 376
Ethos, 224
Euphemisms, 134
Evidence, 115, 151
Extended metaphor, 227
Fallacies, 100, 156–157
Figurative language, 303, 316, 387
Film, 288
    analysis of, 331–332
    characters in, 249–250
Foils, 238, 248, 378
Foreshadowing, 309
Frame story, 327
Genre conventions, 436
Hook, 77
Hyperbole, 174
Humor
    analysis of, 172–173
    elements of, 321
Image, defined, 8
Imagery, 312, 323
Inductive reasoning, 117
Innuendo, 134
Invective, 175
Irony, 174, 260, 319
Literary elements, 286
Literary movements
    Harlem Renaissance, 293
    Puritans, 14
    Revolutionaries, 15
    Transcendentalists, 16, 364, 377
Logos, 224
Metaphor, 227, 228, 256, 313, 315
Motif, 317, 438
Multi-genre research project, 409–
    426
Notetaking guide, 326
Oral tradition, 286
Parallelism, 228
Parody, 168, 175, 188, 193
Pathos, 224
Personal essay, structure of, 382
Personification, 53
Plot, 275
Point of view, 315
Precept, 366
Reasoning, 115

    deductive, 117
    inductive, 117
Refutation, 77, 119
    methods of, 122
Repetition, 227, 228
Research, 13, 429
    primary sources, 7, 13, 17
    secondary sources, 7, 13
Résumé, 342–343
Rhetoric, 29, 107, 134, 145, 156,
    157, 158, 182, 212, 224, 226, 228,
    232, 343
Rhetorical devices, 212, 224, 226,
    228, 368, 393
Rhetorical question, 107, 228
Ridicule, 174
Sarcasm, 174
Satire, 168, 169–171, 172
    characteristics, 174–175
    writing, 187
Secondary audience, 111
Simile, 228, 316
Social commentary, 238, 265
Style, 309
Stylistic elements, 286, 310, 324
Support, for claim, 77
Survey, 78–80, 102
Syntax, 168, 178, 222, 369
Synthesis, 12
Target audience, 111
Theme, 275, 310, 367
Tone, 34, 68, 90, 168, 176, 183, 310,
    353, 367
Wit, 174

Reading Skills

Anticipation guide, 6
Context clues, 255
Editorial, 140
Independent reading, 4, 100, 212,
    286, 362
Inferring meaning, 64, 67
Levels of questions, 320
Notetaking guide, 326
Questioning the text, 320, 322, 325
RAFT, 195
Research
    primary sources, 4, 7, 13
    secondary sources, 4, 7

Vocabulary Skills

Index of Authors and Titles

Text Credits:

"Ellis Island" by Joseph Bruchac from *The Remembered Earth*, 1979, Red Earth Press. Used by permission.

David Ignatow, "Europe and America" from *Against the Evidence: Selected Poems 1934–1994* copyright © 1993 by David Ignatow and reprinted by permission of Wesleyan University Press.

"Shine, Perishing Republic," copyright 1934 by Robinson Jeffers and renewed 1962 by Donnan Jeffers and Garth Jeffers, from *Selected Poetry of Robinson Jeffers* by Robinson Jeffers. Used by permission of Random House, Inc.

"I, Too, Sing America" from *The Collected Poems of Langston Hughes* by Langston Hughes, edited by Arnold Rampersad with David Roessel, Associate Editor, copyright © 1994 by the Estate of Langston Hughes. Used by permission of Alfred A. Knopf, a division of Random House, Inc.

"Indian Singing in Twentieth Century America" from *Indian Singing* by Gail Tremblay, 1998. Reprinted by permission of Calyx Books.

"next to of course god america i" from *Complete Poems: 1904–1962* by E. E. Cummings, edited by George J. Firmage. Copyright 1926, 1954, © 1991 by the Trustees for the E. E. Cummings Trust. Copyright © 1985 by George James Firmage. Used by permission of Liveright Publishing Corporation.

Excerpt from "They Live the Dream" from *The American Dream* by Dan Rather. Copyright © 2001 by Dan Rather. Reproduced by permission of HarperCollins Publishers.

"Lifelong Dreamer—Vietnam Boat Person" by Mary-Beth McLaughlin from *The Toledo Blade,* January 29, 1991. Reproduced with permission.

"Money" from *The Gods of Winter* by Dana Gioia. Copyright © 1991 by Dana Gioia. Reprinted with the permission of Graywolf Press, Saint Paul, MInnesota, www.graywolfpress.org

From *A Raisin in the Sun* by Lorraine Hansberry, copyright © 1958 by Robert Nemiroff, as an unpublished work. Copyright © 1959, 1966, 1984 by Robert Nemiroff. Copyright renewed 1986, 1987 by Robert Nemiroff. Used by permission of Random House, Inc.

"Harlan Man" words and music by Steve Earle. Copyright © 1999 Primary Wave Earle, WB Music Corporation and South Nashville Music. All rights for Primary Wave Earle and South Nashville Music administered by Wixen Music Publishing. All Rights Reserved. Used by permission of Hal Leonard Corporation and Alfred Publishing Company, Inc.

"The Mountain" words and music by Steve Earle. Copyright © 1999 Primary Wave Earle, WB Music Corporation and South Nashville Music. All rights for Primary Wave Earle and South Nashville Music administered by Wixen Music Publishing. All Rights Reserved. Used by permission of Hal Leonard Corporation and Alfred Publishing Company, Inc.

"Who Burns for the Perfection of Paper," from *City of Coughing and Dead Radiators* by Martin Espada. Copyright © 1993 by Martin Espada. Used by permission of W. W. Norton & Company, Inc.

"Roberto Acuna Talks About Farm Workers" from *Working* by Studs Terkel. Copyright 1997 Studs Terkel. Reprinted by permission of Donadio & Olson, Inc.

Excerpt from *Nickel and Dimed: On (Not) Getting By in America* by Barbara Ehrenreich. Copyright © 2001 by Barbara Ehrenreich. Reprinted by arrangement with Henry Holt and Company, LLC.

"The Right to Fail" from *The Lunacy Boom* by William Zinsser. Copyright © 1969, 1970 by William K. Zinsser. Reproduced by permission of the author.

"Oh my! The future of news" by Jeremy Wagstaff. Copyright © Loose Wire Pte Ltd. Used by permission of Jeremy Wagstaff, a writer and technology columnist; jeremywagstaff.com.

From "A Day in the Life of the Media: Intro" from *2006 State of the News Media* by The Project for Excellence in Journalism. Reproduced by permission of the Pew Research Center's Project for Excellence in Journalism.

"How the Rise of the Daily Me Threatens Democracy" by Cass Sunstein as appeared in the *Financial Times,* Jan. 11, 2008. Reprinted by permission of Cass Sunstein.

"The Newspaper Is Dying—Hooray for Democracy" by Andrew Potter as appeared in *Maclean's Magazine*, April 7, 2008. Used by permission of the author.

"Facebook Photos Sting Minnesota High School Students," *The Associated Press,* January 11, 2008. Used with permission of The Associated Press copyright © 2009. All rights reserved.

"Federal Way schools restrict Gore film 'Inconvenient Truth' called too controversial" by Robert McClure and Lisa Stiffler in *Seattle Post-Intelligencer,* January 11, 2007. Copyright © 2007 The Hearst Corporation. Used by permission.

"Abolish high school football!" by Raymond A. Schroth. Used by permission of the author.

"Facing consequences at Eden Prairie High" from the *Minneapolis/St. Paul Star Tribune,* January 10, 2008. Reprinted with permission of the Star Tribune, Minneapolis, MN.

"Time to raise the bar in high schools" by Jack O'Connell from *Ventura County Star,* June 13, 2004. Used by permission.

"New Michigan Graduation Requirements Shortchange Many Students," by Nick Thomas from *Online NewsHour Extra* (posted Sept. 14, 2006). © 2006 MacNeil-Lehrer Productions. Reprinted with permission.

"Why I Hate Cell Phones" by Sara Reihani as appeared in *The Campanile,* May 5, 2008. Used by permission.

"An Inside Look at Editorial Cartoons" by Bill Brennen, *The Grand Island Independent,* March 27, 2001. Courtesy of The Grand Island Independent.

"Let's Hear it For the Cheerleaders" by David Bouchier, from *The New York Times,* August 2, 1998. Copyright © 1998 The New York Times. All rights reserved. Used by permission and protected by the Copyright Laws of the United States. The print, copying, redistribution, or retransmission of the Material without express written permission is prohibited. http://www.nytimes.com

"How to Poison the Earth" by Linnea Saukko from *Student Writers at Work and in the Company of Other Writers.* Copyright © 1984 by Bedford/St. Martin's and used with permission of the publisher.

"Gambling in Schools" by Howard Mohr from *Mirth of a Nation: The Best Contemporary Humor* compiled by Michael J. Rosen, Harper Paperbacks, 2000. Used by permission.

"Maintaining the Crime Supply" from *The Snarling Citizen* by Barbara Ehrenreich. Copyright © 1995 by Barbara Ehrenreich. Reprinted by permission of Farrar, Straus and Giroux, LLC.

"In Depth, but Shallowly" from *Bad Habits: A 100% Fact Free Book* by Dave Barry, humorist. Used by permission.

"Girl Moved to Tears by Of Mice and Men Cliffs Notes" from *The Onion,* August 18, 2008. Copyright © 2009, by Onion, Inc. Reprinted with permission of The Onion. http://www.theonion.com